Soviet Economic Management under Khrushchev

The *Sovnarkhoz* reform of 1957 was designed by Khrushchev to improve efficiency in the Soviet economic system by decentralizing economic decision making from all-Union branch ministries in Moscow to the governments of the individual republics and regional economic councils. Based on extensive original research, including unpublished archival material, this book examines the reform, discussing the motivations for it, which included Khrushchev's attempt to strengthen his own power base. The book explores how the process of reform was implemented, especially its impact on the republics, and analyzes why the reform, which was reversed in 1959, failed. Overall, the book reveals a great deal about the workings, and the shortcomings, of the Soviet economic system at its height.

Nataliya Kibita is an Honorary Research Fellow and seminar tutor in the Faculty of Law, Business and Social Sciences at the University of Glasgow. She is also a teaching fellow at the University of Edinburgh, UK.

BASEES/Routledge Series on Russian and East European Studies

Series editor:

Richard Sakwa, *Department of Politics and International Relations, University of Kent*

Editorial Committee:

Roy Allison, *St Antony's College, Oxford*
Birgit Beumers, *Department of Russian, University of Bristol*
Richard Connolly, *Centre for Russian and East European Studies, University of Birmingham*
Terry Cox, *Department of Central and East European Studies, University of Glasgow*
Peter Duncan, *School of Slavonic and East European Studies, University College London*
Zoe Knox, *School of Historical Studies, University of Leicester*
Rosalind Marsh, *Department of European Studies and Modern Languages, University of Bath*
David Moon, *Department of History, University of York*
Hilary Pilkington, *Department of Sociology, University of Manchester*
Graham Timmins, *Department of Politics, University of Birmingham*
Stephen White, *Department of Politics, University of Glasgow*

Founding Editorial Committee Member:

George Blazyca, *Centre for Contemporary European Studies, University of Paisley*

This series is published on behalf of BASEES (the British Association for Slavonic and East European Studies). The series comprises original, high-quality, research-level work by both new and established scholars on all aspects of Russian, Soviet, post-Soviet and East European studies in humanities and social science subjects.

1. **Ukraine's Foreign and Security Policy, 1991–2000**
   Roman Wolczuk

2. **Political Parties in the Russian Regions**
   Derek S. Hutcheson

3. **Local Communities and Post-Communist Transformation**
   Edited by Simon Smith

4. **Repression and Resistance in Communist Europe**
   J.C. Sharman

5. **Political Elites and the New Russia**
   Anton Steen

6. **Dostoevsky and the Idea of Russianness**
   Sarah Hudspith

7. **Performing Russia**
   Folk revival and Russian identity
   Laura J. Olson

8. **Russian Transformations**
   Edited by Leo McCann

9. **Soviet Music and Society under Lenin and Stalin**
   The baton and sickle
   Edited by Neil Edmunds

10. **State Building in Ukraine**
    The Ukrainian parliament, 1990–2003
    Sarah Whitmore

11. **Defending Human Rights in Russia**
    Sergei Kovalyov, dissident and Human Rights Commissioner, 1969–2003
    Emma Gilligan

12. **Small-Town Russia**
    Postcommunist livelihoods and identities: a Portrait of the intelligentsia in Achit, Bednodemyanovsk and Zubtsov, 1999–2000
    Anne White

13. **Russian Society and the Orthodox Church**
    Religion in Russia after communism
    Zoe Knox

14. **Russian Literary Culture in the Camera Age**
    The word as image
    Stephen Hutchings

15. **Between Stalin and Hitler**
    Class war and race war on the Dvina, 1940–46
    Geoffrey Swain

16. **Literature in Post-Communist Russia and Eastern Europe**
    The Russian, Czech and Slovak fiction of the changes 1988–98
    Rajendra A. Chitnis

17. **The Legacy of Soviet Dissent**
    Dissidents, democratisation and radical nationalism in Russia
    Robert Horvath

18. **Russian and Soviet Film Adaptations of Literature, 1900–2001**
    Screening the word
    Edited by Stephen Hutchings and Anat Vernitski

19. **Russia as a Great Power**
    Dimensions of security under Putin
    Edited by Jakob Hedenskog, Vilhelm Konnander, Bertil Nygren, Ingmar Oldberg and Christer Pursiainen

20. **Katyn and the Soviet Massacre of 1940**
    Truth, justice and memory
    George Sanford

21. **Conscience, Dissent and Reform in Soviet Russia**
    Philip Boobbyer

22. **The Limits of Russian Democratisation**
Emergency powers and states of emergency
Alexander N. Domrin

23. **The Dilemmas of Destalinisation**
A social and cultural history of reform in the Khrushchev era
Edited by Polly Jones

24. **News Media and Power in Russia**
Olessia Koltsova

25. **Post-Soviet Civil Society**
Democratization in Russia and the Baltic states
Anders Uhlin

26. **The Collapse of Communist Power in Poland**
Jacqueline Hayden

27. **Television, Democracy and Elections in Russia**
Sarah Oates

28. **Russian Constitutionalism**
Historical and contemporary development
Andrey N. Medushevsky

29. **Late Stalinist Russia**
Society between reconstruction and reinvention
Edited by Juliane Fürst

30. **The Transformation of Urban Space in Post-Soviet Russia**
Konstantin Axenov, Isolde Brade and Evgenij Bondarchuk

31. **Western Intellectuals and the Soviet Union, 1920–40**
From Red Square to the Left Bank
Ludmila Stern

32. **The Germans of the Soviet Union**
Irina Mukhina

33. **Re-constructing the Post-Soviet Industrial Region**
The Donbas in transition
Edited by Adam Swain

34. **Chechnya – Russia's 'War on Terror'**
John Russell

35. **The New Right in the New Europe**
Czech transformation and right-wing politics, 1989–2006
Seán Hanley

36. **Democracy and Myth in Russia and Eastern Europe**
Edited by Alexander Wöll and Harald Wydra

37. **Energy Dependency, Politics and Corruption in the Former Soviet Union**
Russia's power, oligarchs' profits and Ukraine's missing energy policy, 1995–2006
Margarita M. Balmaceda

38. **Peopling the Russian Periphery**
Borderland colonization in Eurasian history
Edited by Nicholas B Breyfogle, Abby Schrader and Willard Sunderland

39. **Russian Legal Culture Before and After Communism**
Criminal justice, politics and the public sphere
Frances Nethercott

40. **Political and Social Thought in Post-Communist Russia**
Axel Kaehne

41. **The Demise of the Soviet Communist Party**
Atsushi Ogushi

42. **Russian Policy towards China and Japan**
The El'tsin and Putin periods
Natasha Kuhrt

43. **Soviet Karelia**
Politics, planning and terror in Stalin's Russia, 1920–1939
Nick Baron

44. **Reinventing Poland**
Economic and political transformation and evolving national identity
Edited by Martin Myant and Terry Cox

45. **The Russian Revolution in Retreat, 1920–24**
Soviet workers and the new communist elite
Simon Pirani

46. **Democratisation and Gender in Contemporary Russia**
Suvi Salmenniemi

47. **Narrating Post/Communism**
Colonial discourse and Europe's borderline civilization
Nataša Kovačević

48. **Globalization and the State in Central and Eastern Europe**
The politics of foreign direct investment
Jan Drahokoupil

49. **Local Politics and Democratisation in Russia**
Cameron Ross

50. **The Emancipation of the Serfs in Russia**
Peace arbitrators and the development of civil society
Roxanne Easley

51. **Federalism and Local Politics in Russia**
Edited by Cameron Ross and Adrian Campbell

52. **Transitional Justice in Eastern Europe and the former Soviet Union**
Reckoning with the communist past
Edited by Lavinia Stan

53. **The Post-Soviet Russian Media**
Conflicting signals
Edited by Birgit Beumers, Stephen Hutchings and Natalia Rulyova

54. **Minority Rights in Central and Eastern Europe**
Edited by Bernd Rechel

55. **Television and Culture in Putin's Russia**
Remote control
Stephen Hutchings and Natalia Rulyova

56. **The Making of Modern Lithuania**
    Tomas Balkelis

57. **Soviet State and Society Under Nikita Khrushchev**
    Melanie Ilic and Jeremy Smith

58. **Communism, Nationalism and Ethnicity in Poland, 1944–1950**
    Michael Fleming

59. **Democratic Elections in Poland, 1991–2007**
    Frances Millard

60. **Critical Theory in Russia and the West**
    Alastair Renfrew and Galin Tihanov

61. **Promoting Democracy and Human Rights in Russia**
    European organization and Russia's socialization
    Sinikukka Saari

62. **The Myth of the Russian Intelligentsia**
    Old intellectuals in the new Russia
    Inna Kochetkova

63. **Russia's Federal Relations**
    Putin's reforms and management of the regions
    Elena A. Chebankova

64. **Constitutional Bargaining in Russia, 1990–93**
    Institutions and uncertainty
    Edward Morgan-Jones

65. **Building Big Business in Russia**
    The impact of informal corporate governance practices
    Yuko Adachi

66. **Russia and Islam**
    State, society and radicalism
    Roland Dannreuther and Luke March

67. **Celebrity and Glamour in Contemporary Russia**
    Shocking chic
    Edited by Helena Goscilo and Vlad Strukov

68. **The Socialist Alternative to Bolshevik Russia**
    The Socialist Revolutionary Party, 1917–1939
    Elizabeth White

69. **Learning to Labour in Post-Soviet Russia**
    Vocational youth in transition
    Charles Walker

70. **Television and Presidential Power in Putin's Russia**
    Tina Burrett

71. **Political Theory and Community Building in Post-Soviet Russia**
    Edited by Oleg Kharkhordin and Risto Alapuro

72. **Disease, Health Care and Government in Late Imperial Russia**
    Life and death on the Volga, 1823–1914
    Charlotte E. Henze

73. **Khrushchev in the Kremlin**
    Policy and government in the Soviet Union, 1953–1964
    Edited by Melanie Ilic and Jeremy Smith

74. Citizens in the Making in Post-Soviet States
Olena Nikolayenko

75. The Decline of Regionalism in Putin's Russia
Boundary issues
J. Paul Goode

76. The Communist Youth League and the Transformation of the Soviet Union, 1917–1932
Matthias Neumann

77. Putin's United Russia Party
S.P. Roberts

78. The European Union and its Eastern Neighbours
Towards a more ambitious partnership?
Elena Korosteleva

79. Russia's Identity in International Relations
Images, perceptions, misperceptions
Edited by Ray Taras

80. Putin as Celebrity and Cultural Icon
Edited by Helena Goscilo

81. Russia – Democracy Versus Modernization
A dilemma for Russia and for the world
Edited by Vladislav Inozemtsev and Piotr Dutkiewicz

82. Putin's Preventative Counter-Revolution
Post-Soviet authoritarianism and the spectre of velvet revolution
Robert Horvath

83. The Baltic States from the Soviet Union to the European Union
Identity, discourse and power in the post-communist transition of Estonia, Latvia and Lithuania
Richard Mole

84. The EU–Russia Borderland
New contexts for regional cooperation
Edited by Heikki Eskelinen, Ilkka Liikanen and James W. Scott

85. The Economic Sources of Social Order Development in Post-Socialist Eastern Europe
Richard Connolly

86. East European Diasporas, Migration and Cosmopolitanism
Edited by Ulrike Ziemer and Sean P. Roberts

87. Civil Society in Putin's Russia
Elena Chebankova

88. Post-Communist Poland – Contested Pasts and Future Identities
Ewa Ochman

89. Soviet Economic Management under Khrushchev
The *Sovnarkhoz* reform
Nataliya Kibita

90. Soviet Consumer Culture in the Brezhnev Era
Natalya Chernyshova

91. The Transition to Democracy in Hungary
Árpád Göncz and the post-communist Hungarian presidency
Dae Soon Kim

Soviet Economic Management under Khrushchev
The *Sovnarkhoz* reform

Nataliya Kibita

LONDON AND NEW YORK

First published 2013
by Routledge
2 Park Square, Milton Park, Abingdon, Oxfordshire OX14 4RN

Simultaneously published in the USA and Canada
by Routledge
711 Third Avenue, New York, NY 10017

*Routledge is an imprint of the Taylor and Francis Group,
an informa business*

First issued in paperback 2015

© 2013 Nataliya Kibita

The right of Nataliya Kibita to be identified as author
of this work has been asserted by her in accordance
with the Copyright, Designs and Patent Act 1988.

All rights reserved. No part of this book may be reprinted or
reproduced or utilised in any form or by any electronic,
mechanical, or other means, now known or hereafter invented,
including photocopying and recording, or in any information
storage or retrieval system, without permission in writing
from the publishers.

Trademark notice: Product or corporate names may be
trademarks or registered trademarks, and are used only
for identification and explanation without intent to infringe.

British Library Cataloguing in Publication Data
A catalogue record for this book is available from the British Library.

Library of Congress Cataloging in Publication Data
Kibita, Nataliya.
  Soviet economic management under Khrushchev : the Sovnarkhoz
reform / Nataliya Kibita.
    pages ; cm. – (BASEES/Routledge series on Russian and East
European Studies ; 89)
  1. Decentralization in management – Soviet Union. 2. Decentralization in
management – Ukraine. 3. Regional economics – Soviet Union. 4. Central
planning – Soviet Union. 5. Central planning – Ukraine. 6. Soviet
Union – Economic policy – 1956–1958. 7. Ukraine – Economic policy.
8. Administrative economic councils – Soviet Union. 9. Administrative
economic councils – Ukraine. I. Title. II. Series: BASEES/Routledge
Series on Russian and East European Studies ; 89.
  HC336.K495 2013
  330.947'0852–dc23   2012047420

ISBN 978-0-415-60568-7 (hbk)
ISBN 978-1-138-18295-0 (pbk)
ISBN 978-0-203-50319-5 (ebk)

Typeset in Times New Roman
by Cenveo Publisher Services

To Adam and for Aglaya

Contents

List of tables	xv
Foreword	xvi
Preface	xviii
Acknowledgements	xx
List of abbreviations	xxi

Introduction   1

PART I
The search for a more efficient economic administration   9

1   1953–1956: exploring the horizons for administrative reorganization   11

2   XX CPSU congress – December 1956 CC CPSU Plenum: the height of expectations   23

3   The *Sovnarkhoz* reform   35

PART II
Decentralization of decision making: hopes and disillusionment   43

4   Setting new elements   45

5   First disillusionment: plan for 1958   55

6   Republican budgetary rights   63

7   Decentralizing the supply system: losing control over resources   67

8   Gosplan of Ukraine: setting its authority in the republic   79

PART III
Recentralizing economic administration 89

9 The turning point 91
10 November 1962 CC CPSU Plenum: giving up on the reform? 107
11 Recentralization in Ukraine 115

Epilogue 124
Conclusions 129
Notes 141
Bibliography 178
Index 194

Tables

4.1	Economic administrative regions of Ukraine, 1957	46
4.2	Chairmen of the Ukrainian *sovnarkhozy*, 1957	47
4.3	Information on the staff of the Ukrainian *sovnarkhozy* on 18 June 1957	49
5.1	Some 1958 plan indices presented by Ukraine and rejected by USSR Gosplan	59
5.2	Planned domestic supply and export of some consumer goods, 1957	59
6.1	Proposals of shares of *rayon* and *oblast'* profits to be left for the local budgets, 1958	66
11.1	Ukrainian *sovnarkhozy* after 1963 merging	116
11.2	Number of professional staff (without servicing staff and security)	119
C.1	Annual growth rate and value added of Ukrainian industry, 1957–1965	137

Foreword

In his epic biography, William Taubman referred to Khrushchev's 'daring but bumbling attempt to reform communism'. Khrushchev was certainly a reformer, but were his efforts 'bumbling' or was their failure down to something more structural in the Soviet state? Khrushchev's other biographer, William Tompson, wrote in an article comparing Khrushchev and Gorbachev that 'to speak of the *apparat's* opposition to reform in both the Khrushchev and Gorbachev periods is clearly a simplification of its position, but it is not an unjustified oversimplification'. Resistance to Khrushchev's reforms on the part of those affected by them is the key to understanding why Khrushchev's reforms appeared so 'bumbling'. At a meeting with Fidel Castro in May 1963, some eighteen months before his removal from office, Khrushchev declared: 'you'd think as First Secretary I could change anything in this country – like hell I can! No matter what changes I propose and carry out, everything stays the same'.

Arguably Khrushchev's most radical reform, certainly as far as the economy was concerned, was the decision in 1957 to take economic power away from the Moscow-based economic ministries, which had held sway under Stalin, and decentralize power to a series of regional 'councils of the national economy', *sovety narodnogo khozyaistva* or *sovnarkhozy*. As Nataliya Kibita shows, this was very much Khrushchev's idea, a reform arising from earlier initiatives towards strengthening the powers of the republics taken in the years between Stalin's death in 1953 and Khrushchev's denunciation of him in 1956. So, when in 1963 these councils were brought under the control of a country-wide USSR Council of the National Economy, Khrushchev's reform seemed to have been stood on its head, and the old centralized economic administration recreated in a new guise.

By taking Ukraine as the focus of her study, Kibita is able to move away from a top-down discussion of what the reform was meant to be and provide the reader with a bottom-up vision of the *Sovnarkhoz* reform's implementation at republican level. What she explores in this detailed analysis of the implementation and evolution of the reform is the inter-relationship between the various layers of the administration responsible for restructuring resource allocation, the process of constant negotiation and renegotiation of powers between councils and ministries, and the slow but sure resurgence of forces pushing for recentralization. When the reform was first implemented, the Moscow Party Secretary commented to a colleague: 'What shall we do? They're appointing people we have never heard of to these councils'. And, true enough, many of the turf wars about how to enact the reform involved bitter disputes over the deployment of personnel. However, behind the issue of personnel was the broader issue of where would power lie: was planning to be based 'below', where those responsible knew what was happening to the economy, or was it to be based 'above', where those responsible knew what ought to be happening?

Kibita shows clearly that the resurgence of centralizing tendencies can be traced back to 1959, and that the vanguard institution in this process was GOSPLAN. At first its moves were strongly resisted, but gradually its view prevailed: that the interests of the country as a whole were paramount, and that the rights the reform had given to republican administrations were just manifestations of 'localism'. Yet this was a slow and contested process, for resistance was not overcome until November 1962 when the principle of recentralization was finally conceded and the moves began to establish an All-Union *Sovnarkhoz* in March 1963. The *Sovnarkhoz* reform was quietly abandoned as soon as Khrushchev was overthrown in October 1964.

Kibita's study of the *Sovnarkhoz* reform gives us a unique insight into the frustrations of being a reformer in the Soviet administration, frustrations shared by Khrushchev. As she notes in the conclusion: 'the central *apparat* proved more rigid than Khrushchev expected and stayed true to its values ... [making] a remarkable demonstration of its power to protect its own interests'. Kibita concludes that the *Sovnarkhoz* reform began well with a dramatic increase in production, and that after 1959 'each recentralization impulse exacerbated the [subsequent] slow down in growth'. The logic is clear; the origins of the economic sclerosis of the Brezhnev years can be found in GOSPLAN's resurgence during its struggle against Khrushchev's *sovnarkhozy*. Kibita makes this clear in the Brezhnev era joke which opens her study: at the annual parade on the anniversary of the October Revolution, Brezhnev is curious to know who the four young men in black suits are who bring up the rear of the parade; he is informed that they are 'the boys from GOSPLAN' who despite their modest appearance have 'huge destructive power'. GOSPLAN, destroyer of the Soviet Union – no truer word was spoken in jest.

Geoffrey Swain
Alec Nove Chair in Russian and
East European Studies, University of Glasgow.

Preface

'Ideology tends to fade over time when it runs counter to the behavioral sources of individual wealth maximizing, as recent events in Eastern Europe attest'.[1] Douglass North wrote this in 1990. The Soviet Union had not disintegrated yet, but the Eastern bloc had, and the ideas of the market economy penetrated the post-communist countries of Eastern Europe. In the Soviet Union, Mikhail Gorbachev was still struggling with the results of *perestroika* and its impact on the Soviet system.

In 1985, Gorbachev launched *perestroika*, which was supposed to introduce elements of the market economy into the Soviet system and give the Soviet economy a jump-start. He carried on with the communist ideology, and did not question the integrity of the Soviet state. In the new institutional system, decision making was decentralized. He fully, and inevitably, relied on the Party and the state machine to enforce decentralization and guarantee the enforcement of contracts. Still, control over resources was lost.

There are plenty of theories on why and how the Soviet Union disintegrated and more theories will appear as our knowledge of various aspects of the Soviet system expands.

The purpose of this book is not to give another account of the collapse of the Soviet Union, but rather to contribute to the understanding of those fragile links within the Soviet system that determined its weakness. This book is about the first failed attempt to formally decentralize economic decision making in the Soviet Union 34 years prior to *perestroika*, the *Sovnarkhoz* reform. The book discusses the application of the *Sovnarkhoz* reform in the second largest Union republic, Ukraine, and the relations between the centre (Moscow) and the periphery (Ukrainian SSR).

Despite its rigid political structure and centrally administered planned economy, the Soviet system exhibited quite a few features of a huge corporation. The success and efficiency of both depended highly on the balance between the central political and economic control and decentralized decision making and resource management; on the expedient communication of relevant and up-to-date information from the bottom of production to the decision makers; and on the incentive structure that should induce all participants to make decisions for common benefit.

The book explores an attempt of the Soviet leadership to find the golden mean between central policy making and peripheral policy implementation. The similar attempt made by Gorbachev led to the disintegration of the Soviet Union. In the 1950s and early 1960s, however, the devotion of the republican leaders to the Soviet system was not questioned. The economic opportunities that opened up with the reform did not expand to the point where the republican leaders questioned their belief in the advantages of the planned economy over the market economy. Thus, the *Sovnarkhoz* reform did not have drastic consequences for the integrity of the Soviet federation. Nonetheless, the reform revealed that decentralized decision making led to the loss of control over resources by the centre and did not make the centre any better informed on the economy. The republic-level authorities, on whom the CC CPSU relied to protect the all-Union interests in the republics, were as responsive to the incentives of wealth- or power-maximizing as those whom they were supposed to control, the regional economic councils and enterprises. Political defection was a matter of time.

The *Sovnarkhoz* reform was a rather positive page in Ukraine's Soviet history. It was the only relatively long period when the Ukrainian leadership was in a strong position and was strongly motivated to enhance the republican rights and protect republican interests.

Note

1 Douglass C. North, *Institutions, Institutional Change and Economic Performance*, Cambridge: Cambridge University Press, 2007, p. 132, note 2.

Acknowledgements

This book is a result of a long process of reworking and rethinking my PhD thesis which I submitted to the University of Geneva in 2008. After the defence, my thesis advisor Wladimir Berelowitch encouraged me to write a book and so after a short break I 're-plunged' into the subject. I am very grateful to him for the encouragement to write a book and his belief in my ability to do so.

To the best of my skills, I have tried to address all outstanding issues that were brought up at the defence as well as at the conferences and seminars where I was given a chance to present my work. I give my thanks to Donald Filtzer, Jeremy Smith, Valerii Vasil'ev, Peter Duncan, Stephen White, Terry Cox and all those commenters who expressed their opinion on my findings at my presentations. Thanks also to the Department of Central and East European Studies at the University of Glasgow for providing me with a supportive academic environment, and to Sarah Lennon for editing my manuscript.

The book, I believe, has considerably improved as a result of the penetrating and judicious comments of Geoffrey Swain. I am greatly indebted to him for sharing his ideas with me and for his patient availability at the final stage of writing, as well as for contributing the foreword.

I could not have finished working on this book without the dedicated support of my family. My deep gratitude and appreciation goes to my husband, whose endurance was tested during our lengthy discussion of the Soviet economic system and whose comments and arguments were of great value to me in clarifying my thoughts; and to my mother for her immeasurable help during the last year of working on the book which, coincidentally, happened to be the first year of life of our daughter.

Abbreviations

CC CPSU	Central Committee of the Communist Party of the Soviet Union
CC CPUk	Central Committee of the Communist Party of Ukraine
CM	Council of Ministers
CMUk	Council of Ministers of Ukraine
FYP	Five Year Plan
Glavk	Line production administration of a ministry
Glavkhimsbyt	Main department for sales of chemical production
Glavkomplekt(y)	Main department(s) for sales of equipment and installations
Glavmetallosbyt	Main department for sales of metal production
Glavsbyt(y)	Main administration(s) for sales
Glavsnabsbyt(y)	Main department(s) for supplies and sales
GlUMPP	Main administration(s) for inter-republican deliveries
Gorkom(y)	City (or town) Committee of the Communist Party
Gosbank	State Bank
Gosekonomkomissiya	USSR CM State Commission for current operational planning
Gosekonomsovet	USSR CM State Scientific and Economic Council
Goskontrol'	Party-State control
Gosplan	State Planning Committee (Commission)
Gosstroi	USSR CM State Committee for Construction
Ispolkom(y)	Executive committee(s)
Kolkhoz	Collective farm
Kolkhoznik(i)	Collective farm member(s)
Kraikom(y)	Territorial committee(s) of the Communist Party
Obkom(y)	Regional committee(s) of the Communist Party
Oblast'(i)	Province(s)
Oblispolkom(y)	Regional executive committee(s)
Oblstatupravlenie	*Oblast'* statistical agency

xxii *Abbreviations*

Prombank	Industrial Bank
Raikom(y)	District committee(s) of the Communist Party
Rayon	District
Sbyt(y)	Sales organ(s)
Sel'khozbank	Agricultural Bank
Snab(y)	Supply organ(s)
Snabsbyt(y)	Supply and sales organ(s)
Sovkhozy	State farms
Sovnarkhoz(y)	Council(s) of the national economy
Soyuzglavmetal	USSR Gosplan State committee for metallurgy
Torgbank	Commercial Bank
TsK KPSS	*Tsentral'nyi Komitet Kommunisticheskoi Partii Sovetskogo Soyuza* (Central Committee of the Communist Party of the Soviet Union)
TsSU	Central Statistical Agency
Ukrglavmetallosnabsbyt	Ukrainian main administration for supplies and sales of metal production
Ukrglavsnabsbyt(y)	Ukrainian main administration(s) for supplies and sales
Ukrsovnarkhoz	Ukrainian Republican Council of the national economy
Ukrstatupravlenie	Ukrainian statistical agency
VSNKh	Supreme Council of the National Economy
VTsSPS	All-Union Central Council of Trade Unions

Archives

GARF	State Archive of the Russian Federation (*Gosudarstvennyi Arkhiv Rossiiskoi Federatsii*), Moscow
RGAE	Russian State Economic Archive
RGANI	Russian State Archive of Recent History (*Rossiiskii Gosudarstvennyi Arkhiv Noveishei Istorii*), Moscow
RGASPI	Russian State Archive of Social and Political History (*Rossiiskii Gosudarstvennyi Arkhiv Sotsial'no-Politicheskoi Istorii*), Moscow
TsDAVOU	Official abbreviation for the Central State Archive of the Highest Organs of Government and Administration of Ukraine (*Tsentral'nyi derzhavnyi arkhiv vyshchykh organiv vlady ta upravlinnya Ukrainy*), Kiev
TsDAGOU	Official abbreviation for the Central State Archive of Public Organizations of Ukraine (*Tsentral'nyi derzhavnyi arkhiv hromads'kykh ob'iednan' Ukrainy*), Kiev

Introduction

At the demonstration dedicated to the celebration of the October revolution, the forces of the Moscow garrison marched. Then the army demonstrated its military might: missiles, tanks, self-propelled artillery. Four young men in classic black suits with cases in their hands brought up the rear of the military parade. Brezhnev asks Andropov [the Chairman of the KGB]: 'Are these your people?' 'No', responds Andropov. Then he asks Shchelokov [the USSR Minister of Interior]: 'Are those your guys in civilian clothing?' 'No', responds Shchelokov. 'No!? Then who are these people!?' Kosygin bends over to Brezhnev and says: 'Those are my boys, from Gosplan! They look modest, but they have huge destructive power'.

(Anecdote from the Brezhnev era)

The mid-1950s in the Soviet Union was a time of great change. For better or worse, the system was changing, and changing fast. Stalin died in March 1953, and a few months later Lavrentii Beria was arrested. The Virgin Land campaign and the dismantling of the Gulag came soon after, followed by massive re-housing to newly built apartment blocks (*khrushchoby*), new magazines (*Neva, Nash sovremennik, Koster* for children), new theatres (*Sovremennik, Kremlevskii*), the legalization of abortion, the replacement of steam engines with diesel locomotives, the restoration of relations between the Soviet Union and Yugoslavia, and so on. The dynamics of the change accelerated after the XX CPSU Congress and Nikita Khrushchev's secret speech, releasing its energy through further rehabilitation, turmoil in Poland and Hungary, 'thaw' in culture, contacts with the capitalist West, the festivals of Italian and Finnish cinema, art exhibitions from different countries, the International Youth festival, and even the production of vacuum cleaners, refrigerators, cars, and new fashions in clothing and furniture. Life sizzled. Members of the CC CPSU Presidium gathered for meetings and actually *discussed* problems, while the CPSU First Secretary Nikita Sergeevich Khrushchev travelled a lot, both within the country and abroad.

From their dead leader, the first post-Stalin leadership inherited a set of problems in domestic and foreign affairs that required a new approach and new solutions. One of the most urgent problems was to improve the life of the Soviet people. To a large extent, the legitimacy of the new leadership and its prestige depended on how efficient it would be in improving the life of common people. From letters, the leadership knew that people were infuriated with the huge gap between the salaries and bonuses received by 'the rich', the intelligentsia and the Party and government *apparat*, and the pay of the common workers; and with injustice in the distribution of housing and with the lack of food products and consumer goods.[1] Russian historian Galina Ivanova interprets these complaints:

> At first sight, the opinions and wishes expressed in the majority of these letters look like the typical demands of the lumpen proletariat. However, with more careful examination of their motives, they denounce the millionaires, the dacha owners 'behind their green fences', and it is clear that a determined social protest movement was emerging as people demanded simple social justice.[2]

So, fear of social unrest forced both the Chairman of the Soviet government Georgii Malenkov and the leader of the Communist Party Nikita Khrushchev 'at the first convenient occasion to demonstrate at least in words their care' for the wellbeing of the people.[3] This acknowledgment of social problems translated into increased expenditure on social programs. In the years that followed, among other things, the government increased salaries and pensions, and the benefits paid to single mothers and families with many children. The state also fully covered the cost of education and health care. Khrushchev intended the state to take care of the old and the young, and to provide everyone with individual housing.[4] After the death of Stalin, as the list of social programs grew, the expenses of the state drastically increased. The state of course tried to economize, first of all on its *apparat*; however, it became imperative to improve the economy.

After Stalin's death, the economy grew steadily, showing an average annual growth rate of 9.6 per cent for industry and 6.7 per cent for GNP.[5] The economic situation, however, was far from satisfactory. The balance between heavy and light industries remained in favour of the former. Shortages of food products and consumer goods persisted. Technological progress was slow and labour productivity was low. The cost of production was increasing whilst its quality was decreasing.

At the beginning of the 1950s, the Soviet leadership could not yet know that the Soviet economy had already reached its peak. In about ten years all sources of growth would deteriorate and the exceptional growth of the capital stock would decline; capital accumulation would begin to run into diminishing returns and total factor productivity growth would go negative. Investment decisions would turn out to be erroneous and the institutional system inherited from Stalin would be incapable of boosting and sustaining the technological progress so necessary to move the economy from 'extensive development' to 'intensive development'.[6] At the beginning of the 1950s, the problems seemed obvious and the new leadership believed it understood their nature and how to resolve them. With utmost enthusiasm and confidence, the Chairman of the Soviet government G. Malenkov and the CPSU First Secretary N. Khrushchev launched their policies aimed at leading the country to prosperity.

Economic policies of the first half of the 1950s varied in nature, ranging from those that were based on elements of economic reasoning, such as some that were selectively applied in agriculture,[7] to relatively useless reorganizations of the industrial ministries in the centre. The conservative approach, based on identifying economic problems with poor organization of the administrative *apparat*, nonetheless prevailed. The search for a more efficient administrative system started soon after Stalin's death with the traditional reshuffling of the ministries in the centre. Yet, as previously, this reshuffling brought no positive results, and by 1954 the new leadership was ready to take an unprecedented step and invited the republics to participate in the management of industry in their territories. The policy of enhancing republican economic rights was no longer a heresy, absurd, or seditious, and for the years to come, it was pursued by the centre in parallel to enhancing the economic flexibility of the central ministerial *apparat* and the USSR State Bank (*Gosbank*).

After three years of fighting red tape and over-centralized decision making, First Secretary of the Central Committee of the Communist Party of the Soviet Union (CC CPSU) N.S. Khrushchev, by now the most active, certainly most well-known, policy-maker in the CC CPSU Presidium, saw no other alternative to improving economic administration than to abolish the industrial and construction ministries altogether and distribute their functions between the republican and regional managers, reducing the size of the central *apparat*. In January 1957, he presented to his Presidium colleagues a project that argued for the benefits of switching the functions of the central *apparat* from active involvement with the so-called operational management of industry to active branch policy making. Operational decision making should be transferred to the local authorities.

On the basis of Khrushchev's note, six months later, the managerial functions of the industrial and construction ministries were transferred to the 105 newly-created councils of the national economy (*sovety narodnogo khozyaistva*, or *sovnarkhozy*) that took full responsibility for production and construction, republic Planning Committees (Gosplans), now in charge of managing republican economies, and USSR Gosplan, the central planning agency that assumed the administrative functions of those ministries that could not and should not be transferred below central level. The *Sovnarkhoz* reform started. The reform rhetoric emphasized great urgency and the importance of developing complex regional economies, contrasting the inefficiency of the ministries with the competence of the *sovnarkhozy*. Economic growth was expected as the *sovnarkhozy* would increase inter-branch cooperation and specialization and reveal the production capacities that had been jealously concealed from the planners and the Party by the ministries now abolished.

As the reform progressed, the economic problems that the reform was designed to eliminate did not disappear and new problems in centre-republican economic relations appeared. The central *apparat* and the leadership responded with the recentralization of control over resources and the curtailment of the reform. Less than a year after Khrushchev was ousted from power, the *Sovnarkhoz* system was dismantled. Industry and construction were again administered through the branch ministries, central but also republican.

The general opinion about the *Sovnarkhoz* reform in historical literature is that it was a failure.[8] Khrushchev had political and economic motives for moving management directly to the economic administrative regions, but 'the aims of the reform were utopian: to catch up within a few years [to] the world's developed countries' per capita production, and to draw large groups of society into administrative work'.[9] The reform generated a system that was not more efficient than that of the ministries, and according to some scholars, for example Tompson, it created one that was even worse.[10] The *sovnarkhozy* failed to deliver in economic terms and, although economic successes at the beginning of the reform were beyond dispute, the reform brought few, if any, lasting benefits.[11]

The reform transformed ministerial departmentalism into regional *mestnichestvo* or localism. Ubiquitously pursued by the peripheral managers, the tendency towards *mestnichestvo* had a negative effect on the economy. Supply uncertainties intensified and the problem of resource management through hoarding of production exacerbated.[12] To secure deliveries, explained Filtzer, 'the managers often by-passed official supply channels and engaged in direct barter with one another, swapping, for example, surplus steel for machinery or building materials'.[13] At the same time, Kaser credited localism for eliminating local disproportions and agreed with Conyngham and Dyker that *mestnichestvo* was largely a result of the supply problems.[14]

Localism had a strong effect on branch development and technological progress too. The reform did not abolish the branch principle of administering industry, but neither did it ensure the development of branches. It did not provide coordination between the enterprises of the same branch that were dispersed all over the territory, and it did not make any provision for solving common problems for each branch.[15] Regional economies were losing branch-level specialization and technological progress was slowed down.[16] Nove argued that, compared to the ministerial system, the *Sovnarkhoz* system was more vulnerable to errors in investment plans and the dissipation of resources, *raspylenie sredstv*.[17] Bahry observed that the *sovnarkhozy* siphoned financial resources 'away from centrally defined priorities', and Conyngham noted that the *sovnarkhozy* continued the tradition of plan deception and simulation, and *shturmovshchina*, or storming, in production.[18]

When Moscow started curtailing the reform, Nove and Swearer concluded that the policy of recentralization was the centre's reaction to the economic consequences of localism developed by the *sovnarkhozy*. Mieczkowski noticed that recentralization did not eliminate *mestnichestvo*. Moreover, the new regionalization held after the November 1962 CC CPSU Plenum reduced the number of the *sovnarkhozy*, which only exacerbated localism, since the newly merged economic regions were much larger and had more production capacity.[19] Hough described the reform as chaotic. Filtzer observed that supply problems led to 'bureaucratic anarchy'. Grossman compared the problems of this period to those in 1936–1937 and noted that in a rapidly expanding Soviet economy the burden of planning, checking for plan fulfilment and collecting data increased.[20]

An important aspect of the reform which has been addressed in the literature, but which lies beyond the scope of this book, is the role of the Party in the reform. Originally, Khrushchev expected Party functionaries to be active in economic decision making and control, and to suppress the tendency towards localism. In all functions, however, the Party was far from successful. According to Conyngham, the operational role of the Party in economic decision making did not increase, although in planning, argued Hough, the involvement of the regional committees of the Communist Party (*obkomy*) and the republican central committees was increased, or at least their role was no less important 'than it had been during the ministerial period'. Armstrong claimed that Party secretaries interfered occasionally in industrial decision making. Rigby argued that in general the reform enlarged the powers of Party officialdom at the republican and regional level and therewith the importance of Party lines of control and communication.[21] In performing its controlling function, the Party undoubtedly failed, since localism 'began to infect the party apparatus', and, as Hough observed, the local Party functionaries had major difficulties in maintaining their authority over those they were required to supervise, the ex-ministerial administrators who now came to run regional economies.[22]

The group of scholars that emphasized the positive aspects of the *Sovnarkhoz* system is much smaller. The most unusual interpretation of the reform was given by David Granick in his 1962 article. He analysed the influence of industrial technological advancement, 'the accumulation of capital resources, the creation of a skilled managerial group, and the changes in the characteristics of the labor force', on the economic administration and came to the conclusion that the reform was 'an administrative innovation' that had shown 'some movement toward the market economy model'.[23] A similar argument was also advanced in the memoirs of Aleksandr Lyashko, a member of the CC CPUk Presidium in 1965, who asserted that through the *Sovnarkhoz* system, the economic administration would have fully developed and prepared the Soviet economy for transition to the market economy much better than the way it was done during Gorbachev's *perestroika*.[24]

Howard Swearer, also writing in 1962, concluded that the reform 'marked a drastic break with past organizational principles', but was only partially successful.[25] To Z. Frank and J. Waelbroeck, 'the *Sovnarkhoz* system simplified and unified the transmission lines between Moscow and enterprises. ... The reform had undoubtedly helped to mitigate the risk of dangerous inconsistency which the extension of central planning to all economic life entailed'.[26] Yu. Vedeneev, too, considered that for the regions the reform entailed positive aspects as it enhanced the possibilities for inter-branch cooperation inside the regions, provided balanced supplies inside the regions and conditions for grouping enterprises into associations, *ob''edineniya*.[27] A group of Russian scholars in 1993 argued for the principle advantages of territorial administration over branch administration in the Soviet Union and insisted that, for all its shortcomings and failures, the

Sovnarkhoz reform could not be blamed for the slowdown in technological development, since the highest numbers of new types and models of machinery, equipment and other instruments were created in the period from 1961 to 1965.[28]

Several observations can be made about the existing literature on the *Sovnarkhoz* reform. First, most scholars have offered a centrist interpretation of the reform, the few exceptions being those who studied the reform directly in one republic. For example, Borys Lewytzkyj, Vasil'ev and Koropeckyj studied the Ukrainian case. They analysed the flaws and benefits of the *Sovnarkhoz* system from the standpoint of Moscow. Second, existing analysis is built around two groups of actors, the centre (the central leadership and the central governmental *apparat*) and the economic regions (regional Party functionaries and *sovnarkhozy*), and finds *mestnichestvo* pursued by the *sovnarkhozy* to be a fundamental failure of the reform. The republic-level authorities in this analysis of the reform are generally non-existent, they are voiceless and their position is unknown. Third, although some authors pointed to the failure of the reform to address systemic problems and set new stimuli and 'improved conditions for truly effective work by economic actors',[29] to align 'the lower echelons' objectives' with 'the objectives at the top' and ensure that complete information was provided to the centre,[30] they too do not explain why the reform failed to address systemic problems.

The present book addresses these issues. It interprets the reform from the perspective of a republic, examines the place and role of the republican authorities in the *Sovnarkhoz* system and, based on an analysis of the policies of central and republican planners and the relations between them, offers an interpretation of the reasons for the reform's failures. The book also examines the pre-reform period in Ukraine, an even more understudied page of Ukrainian history than the *Sovnarkhoz* reform, when the Ukrainian administrative *apparat* fully emerged and the Ukrainian leadership developed high aspirations for economic autonomy.

The application of the *Sovnarkhoz* reform in Ukraine was in some respects similar to that in other republics. The similarity between Ukraine and the other republics was in the managerial and administrative response of the republic-level and regional managers to new opportunities the reform offered and the tendency towards *mestnichestvo* (localism), where managers all over the country at all levels, including USSR Gosplan, pursued their own interests. Unlike in other republics, the Central Committee of the Communist Party of Ukraine (CC CPUk) was sometimes in a position to push for decisions that did not quite correspond to the general policy. Two major instances are discussed in the book: first, the increase in the number of economic regions in Ukraine from 11 to 14 in 1960 when USSR Gosplan moved forward with the recentralization policy and was preparing to merge economic regions; second, constraining, or effectively debarring, the newly established Ukrainian Republican *Sovnarkhoz*, or *Ukrsovnarkhoz*, from active participation in economic administration. The ability of the Ukrainian authorities to deviate from central policies favouring republic interests was certainly due to the exceptional status and economic weight of Ukraine. At the same time, of crucial importance here was Khrushchev's personal warm feelings about Ukraine and his patronage of the Ukrainians. One of the results of special relations between Khrushchev and Ukraine was an increased number of Ukrainians in top positions in the CC CPSU, the Ministry of Defence, and other all-Union agencies.[31] Another result was the transfer of Crimea from Russia to the Ukrainian SSR.

To a large extent, the *Sovnarkhoz* reform was not a surprise to the Ukrainian republic authorities. By the end of 1956, after almost four years of reorganizing the ministries, Ukrainians saw no other alternative way to improve economic administration than to devolve a share of the authority of central ministries to their republican counterparts and correlate the decision-making authority with responsibility for the implementation of decisions. Thereby Khrushchev's January 1957 decentralization corresponded to, or maybe was even inspired by, the vision of the Ukrainian authorities of the economic administration, even though the decentralization was partial and did not reflect the full scale of the necessary, certainly from Ukraine's perspective, enhancement of their economic rights. Ukraine's republican authorities were nonetheless taken by surprise by the structure of the economic administration and the very idea of regional economic councils. They did not consider it reasonable to devolve operational decision-making authority over production and construction all the way down to the economic regions, bypassing the level of the republican capitals.

The reform sought to boost economic growth all over the country by bringing economic administration closer to production. Peripheral managers were instructed to develop their economies, to maximize the use of local inputs and cut out irrational long-distance cross-hauls. Inter-republican economic relations along branch lines would be orchestrated by USSR Gosplan. Republic-level authorities, and Gosplans in particular, had two major tasks: a) to ensure that the republics met their production targets and fulfilled their inter-republic supply obligations to customers from other republics; and b) to control and suppress manifestations of *mestnichestvo*.

This seemingly simple scenario in practice required each participating party to fulfil contradictory tasks and demanded that managers and planners act against their incentives. The *sovnarkhozy* were effectively motivated to protect local interests, yet they were obliged to pursue all-Union interests as well. USSR Gosplan had incentives to retain centralized control over the economy, yet it was compelled to devolve economic authority. The role and position of Gosplan of Ukraine, now *de facto* the main economic authority in the republic, was particularly ambiguous, whereas its intended role was ambitious.

The intention of Gosplan of Ukraine and of the Ukrainian leadership was to centralize control over the republican economy in Kiev. However, unlike the *sovnarkhozy* and USSR Gosplan, Gosplan of Ukraine did not directly control production or inputs of non-Ukrainian origin, so it was dependent on the resources of either the *sovnarkhozy* or the central planners. The formal authority of Gosplan of Ukraine, which appeared to be limited without sufficient and effective economic or administrative levers to influence the *sovnarkhozy*, was determined not in Kiev, but in Moscow. Gosplan of Ukraine was accountable to Moscow for the economic performance of the republic and the fulfilment by the republic of its supply obligations to non-Ukrainian customers and for suppressing regional *mestnichestvo*, whereas, to ensure inter-republican deliveries, Gosplan of Ukraine was dependent on the *sovnarkhozy*.

As the reform progressed, the tension between Gosplan of Ukraine and USSR Gosplan increased. By the end of the reform, Kiev had not only issued proposals and criticized separate decisions or actions of the central *apparat*, but had also challenged those elements of the system that it considered to be most damaging to the integrity of the Soviet economy. Responsibility for the republic's economy, together with the experience and confidence they had accumulated, allowed the economic and political authorities of Ukraine to take positions that differed from those of the central leadership and pursue policies that did not fully correlate with the central line. This had a major impact on the interpretation of the republic's initiatives in Moscow, as well as Moscow's initiatives in Kiev, and consequently on the evolution of the reform.

The implementation of the recentralization policy launched by USSR Gosplan in 1959 was successfully delayed by officials in Kiev. Recentralization caught up with the republic only after the November 1962 CC CPSU Plenum. The policy of recentralization and then the abandonment of the *Sovnarkhoz* system was the response of the central *apparat* to the growing ambitions of the republican authorities, as well as to the fact that a significant amount of information and resources escaped Moscow's control. *Mestnichestvo*, now pursued and perceived by the Ukrainian authorities as a logical economic response to the system, had potentially political implications, from Moscow's perspective.

The reform failed the moment Khrushchev entrusted the central ex-ministerial bureaucracy and planners to implement the reform and relied on the regional authorities to prioritize the interests of the entire country over local interests without setting systemic incentives or constraining mechanisms. By placing USSR Gosplan in charge of orchestrating the reform, setting the necessary administrative mechanisms and defining the rules, roles, functions and responsibilities for each participating party, Khrushchev effectively lost control over its application. As a result, the central leadership and USSR Gosplan did not always promote the same policy. Very often, the decisions and policies of the central leadership were not fulfilled or translated into specific procedures and the central leadership followed the 'general line' of USSR Gosplan.

Nonetheless, the years of the reform saw a great outburst of managerial activity in the republics, the proof of which was an increasing number of *tolkachi*. It allowed the Ukrainian SSR to complete the formation of its administrative system and it revealed the power of regional groups formed around common economic interests. After the *Sovnarkhoz* reform, a return to the previous highly centralized ministerial system of administering the economy was impossible.

Part I
The search for a more efficient economic administration

1   1953–1956
Exploring the horizons for administrative reorganization

The March 1953 amalgamation of ministries and the subsequent enhancement of ministerial rights affected the economic bureaucracy. The arrest of Beria a few months later, at first glance, appeared not to. Yet it was the 2–7 July 1953 CC CPSU Plenum that triggered two major interconnected tendencies that started the gradual devolution of the central ministries' decision-making authority to the republic ministries and led to the *Sovnarkhoz* reform in 1957. The first tendency was the consolidation of Khrushchev's personal position in the CC CPSU Presidium and the increased involvement of the Communist Party in state affairs. The second was the revived activity of the republican authorities and their growing involvement in the management of their economies. In combination with the failed reorganizations of the ministerial system, these two tendencies contributed to Khrushchev's decision to abolish the ministries and transfer their authority to the regional economic councils.

March 1953: reshuffling the ministries

Immediately after Stalin's death on 5 March 1953, the Soviet leadership started the reorganization of the ministerial system. In spring 1953, Khrushchev did not yet occupy the dominant position in the CC CPSU Presidium. In the list of members of the CC CPSU Presidium he was listed fifth, after G. Malenkov, L. Beria, V. Molotov and K. Voroshilov, which indicated his importance.[1] The reorganization took place on a massive scale and involved ministries and various departments in the capital as well as in the republics. The official purpose of the reorganization was the traditional one, to increase the efficiency of the administrations concerned.[2] The approach applied was no less traditional, that of amalgamation.[3] On 5 March, the day of Stalin's death, 15 ministries were amalgamated into five; ten days later, another 25 ministries were amalgamated into nine.[4] With the last merger, the rights of the ministers were enhanced and their responsibilities were extended.[5]

The extension of the managerial flexibility of the ministers was supposed to translate into economic growth. Yet no economic breakthroughs occurred, and a year later the ministries were split back. The spring 1953 reorganization proved to be nothing more than another organizational reshuffle. Nonetheless, the rights granted to the ministers were not revoked, which in the end left the ministries administratively stronger than before Stalin's death.

Mirroring the March reorganization in Moscow, the republics implemented the analogous amalgamations. In Ukraine, after the merging of the ministries and republican organizations, the total number of the economic agencies was reduced from 66 to 32.[6] The rights of the republic ministers remained, however, unchanged and the status of the enlarged republican administration remained Union-Republic.

Beria's arrest and criticism of the ministries in Ukraine

It is unlikely that the industrial ministers expected the arrest of Beria at the CC CPSU Presidium meeting on 26 June 1953 to have an impact on the stability of the system. There were no reasons for such an assumption. Beria was accused of withdrawing the *apparat* of MVD from Party control, of distorting nationality policy in Western Ukraine, Lithuania and Latvia, and other sins in foreign and domestic policies.[7] Beria was even accused of intentionally slowing down solutions to agricultural problems and problems of supplying the urban population with agricultural products.[8] But he was not held responsible for the March amalgamation of the ministries[9] or any failures in the work of industrial ministries.

Yet in their discussions of the crimes of Beria at the plenums of *obkomy* and town committees of the Communist Party (*gorkomy*), Ukrainian communists found it relevant to talk about shortcomings in the work of the all-Union ministries in the republic. At the plenum of the Dnepropetrovsk *gorkom*, the speakers criticized the USSR Ministry of the Metallurgical Industry[10] for not financing and supplying equipment to the Dzerzhinskii metallurgical plant. N.M. Fomenko, the director of the plant, also complained that

> in our *oblast'*, we mine the ore, but we [the plant] do not have ore. In our *oblast'*, we produce coke, but we have no coke. The plant needs six thousand tonnes of coke every day, but now we do not have a gram.[11]

At the plenum of the Zhdanov *gorkom*, it was stated that the agglomerate factory in Kerch was supplying the metallurgical mill *Azovstal'* with agglomerate of bad quality. I.F.(T.) Tevosyan[12] had been informed but his ministry had not taken any action.[13] The Party organization of the Yasinovat machine-building plant complained that the Ministry of Coal Mining had delayed the commissioning of the plant. An electrician at the Slavyansk acid-proof plant criticized the Minister of Construction Materials Industry P.A. Yudin for not talking to the workers when he visited the plant: 'there are considerable shortcomings in the work of the plant and the workers could have helped to analyse the reasons for this'.[14] The Ministry of Power Plants and Electronic Industry did not provide the necessary assistance for launching new production and left a lot of technical questions unsolved, causing the plant to systematically disrupt the plan.[15]

Nothing in the criticism of the ministries implicated Beria. The problems that were described at the regional plenums characterized the system and were not new. Moreover, if criticism of the relations between the industrial ministries and Party organizations was expected, by analogy, to echo the criticism heard in Moscow regarding relations (or rather the lack of them) between the Party and the MVD, no such remarks were made either.[16] None of the speakers claimed that the Party should get involved with industrial administration. Instead, they implied that they understood their own economic problems better than the ministries in Moscow. The CC CPUk Plenum (29–30 July 1953), in its turn, did not develop any issues beyond the agenda set in Moscow and focused on discussing the need to consolidate Party control over the MVD organs in Ukraine,[17] to continue the fight against Ukrainian and Jewish bourgeois nationalists that had been disorganized by Beria's assistants P.Ya. Meshik and S. Mil'shtein in the Western regions, and to consolidate the work of Party organizations in industry and particularly in agriculture.[18] Later the same year, during the discussions of Malenkov's speech at the Fifth session of the USSR Supreme Soviet, Ukrainians got another opportunity to criticize the ministries. Information on these discussions was submitted to Moscow as well.[19]

So, if these complaints about the work of the ministries were heard only in the provinces, and were irrelevant to the Beria affair, why did the CC CPUk secretary A.I. Kirichenko report to Khrushchev about these discussions? Was it Party discipline that made Kirichenko report this criticism of the all-Union ministries? Or was it his personal initiative? It was probably both. Kirichenko did follow Party discipline, but he must have also realized that he had information that had potential value for Khrushchev in the power game between the Party and the governmental *apparat*. After all, Kirichenko participated in the CC CPSU Plenum and heard Khrushchev's indignation about Beria's views on the Party, assigning a secondary role to it in state affairs and limiting its activity to personnel and propaganda.[20] The mistakes of the all-Union ministries in the republics could justify the necessity to increase the involvement of the Party with the industrial administration. They could equally justify the necessity to transfer some authority from the central administrative *apparat* to the republics. In the latter case, the examples of poor management on the part of the all-Union ministries from Ukraine and other republics could be of use to a special commission that had been created some time before August 1953 to work on enhancing republican rights.

Khrushchev: setting a republican vector

Indeed, although the republican vector in the central leadership's economic policy was outlined in 1954, the preparation work started soon after Stalin died. It is difficult to say whether the idea of enhancing economic rights of the republican governments was prompted by the republics or whether Khrushchev came to it independently – according to Khrushchev himself he had thought and even shared his ideas about the devolution of economic decision making with Malenkov about ten years earlier[21] – but in August 1953, at the meeting of the specially formed commission, Khrushchev explained that 'some sort of decentralization' was necessary. Remaining rather vague about the specifics, he nonetheless outlined certain points and made it clear that he believed that local cadres were capable of performing certain functions of the central *apparat*. After all, people who were sitting in the all-Union ministries in Moscow did come from the periphery.

To start with, Khrushchev insisted that the republics should organize and be responsible for the supplies of food products and consumer goods to the population, that they should 'show some initiative'. 'Why should the Union minister provide salt and matches to the population of Kobelyaki, which is 100–120 kilometres from Poltava?' asked Khrushchev. If there are no matches or salt in Kobelyaki, then the CC CPUk has the right to complain to the CC CPSU. 'Is this right? [This is] nonsense. There is no canned food in Kobelyaki. Why should I, sitting here in Moscow, be responsible for your Kobelyaki[?]'.[22]

Khrushchev was against the practice of fixing centralized prices on agricultural production and distributing all agricultural production, without exception:

> We sell watermelons in Kherson and Irkutsk for the same price. We sell cabbage in October and in March for the same price. ... Is this correct? Or let us take Uzbekistan [for example]. Fruits in Moscow and Uzbekistan cost the same; this is also wrong.[23]

Meat, milk, potatoes, wheat, rye, corn and cucumbers were produced locally and Khrushchev saw no need to distribute them in Moscow. Furthermore, continued Khrushchev, 'when we divide them between the republics "incorrectly", the republics reproach us':

> Potato is grown in Byelorussia, but they [Byelorussians] cannot distribute it. For the deficit of potato in Byelorussian stores, we are responsible. This is a folly. ... We should say, dear leaders of the republics, develop your economy, trade, if you please, and be responsible to the Union government. So now you are responsible for the interruptions [of food supplies].[24]

Of course, Khrushchev allowed that the production in which the republics specialized, such as sugar in Ukraine or cotton and fruits in Uzbekistan, could not be distributed by local authorities. Thus some cities and regions should be supplied centrally, such as Moscow, Leningrad, Donbas and Ural. Canned food should be distributed by the centre for the army and for export, and by the local authorities for local consumption.[25] He further argued that administration of the machine-building and instrument-making industries, military industry, aviation industry, construction of automobiles and tractors, or chemical industry should remain centralized. However, he argued that railways, commerce, coal, metallurgy and certainly construction should be administered by the republics and that all light industry factories should be subordinated to the republic Councils of Ministers. Finally, though the army ought to be centralized, in economic administration centralization 'is our weakness' that causes incredible bureaucracy.[26] Partial decentralization of decision making in industry and agriculture, according to Khrushchev, would not only improve economic administration, but would increase the responsibility of the republics for the fulfilment of the plans and allow the central *apparat* to better control the fulfilment of production plans. 'Now we [the centre] are adopting the plan and the republic controls us, whereas in the future we will control [the republic]',[27] reasoned Khrushchev.

Thereby, in 1953, the central leadership started to explore the idea of devolution of the economic administration from central to republic *apparat*. It remained focused, nonetheless, on enhancing managerial rights of the ministers in Moscow and the by now traditional strategy of merging administrative units and reducing the size of the *apparat*.

Reorganizing the ministries

After Beria's arrest, the Chairman of the Soviet government G. Malenkov proposed slowing down the growth of heavy industry and channelling the freed investments into housing construction, public health care, trade, light industry and agriculture.[28] Starting on 1 July, the taxes for peasants were reduced,[29] and after the revision of tax policy, responsibility for the development of agriculture was transferred from the state *apparat* to the Party.[30]

In his August 1953 speech devoted to the forthcoming September 1953 CC CPSU Plenum, the First Party Secretary Khrushchev tackled the agricultural problem with zeal. He approved the already implemented tax policy and new stimulus policies, such as the annulment of the debts of collective farms (*kolkhozy*) and collective farm members (*kolkhozniki*), the reduction in the volume of state deliveries and the increase in state procurement prices. At the same time, with utmost disdain, Khrushchev attacked the agricultural bureaucracy. 'We have 308 thousand agricultural specialists of all qualifications. 18.5 thousand work in the *kolkhozy*, 50 thousand work in the MTS [Machine Tractor Stations]. Where are the rest?'[31] So, the staff of the USSR Ministry of Agriculture, and of all administrations and institutes that ran this branch of the economy, had to be cut and red tape had to be fought.

> They are sitting there [in the USSR Ministry of Agriculture] and they do their calculations, and the minister counts each calf in each area. They even foresee whether it will be a bull or a cow. (Laughter.) Everything is in the plan. But this is bureaucratic rapture with one's own bureaucratic procedure (*kantselyariya*), but life goes on quite differently.[32]

Khrushchev's message was quite clear: there were too many people in the administration who, above all, were not quite competent in what they were doing. They would be more useful in the fields.

In January 1954, the CC CPSU issued a resolution ordering staff cuts in the Soviet and Party organizations and the enhancement of the economic rights of the local authorities.[33] 'During the discussion of this resolution in the regions, more than a thousand suggestions were made on the improvement of economic administration in the *raiony, oblasti* and republics'.[34] The turn of the governmental *apparat* came later that year when the CC CPSU (Khrushchev) and the USSR Council of Ministers (CM) (Malenkov) issued at least three resolutions aiming to improve the ministerial system.[35]

As with the Party and Soviet organizations, the June 1954 resolution ordered staff cuts and the merging of offices. The purpose of the staff cuts was twofold: to reduce red tape, and to increase the educated labour force in industry. Officially, by 1954, for every seven workers and functionaries employed in the economy one worked in the *apparat*. Sending at least 450 thousand people from the administrative offices to factories and plants and thereby saving more than 5 billion roubles annually seemed like a reasonable idea.[36]

The August 1954 resolution on *Gosbank* restored its authority over production.[37] *Gosbank* was instructed to increase administrative control, and control over the financial and economic activities of enterprises: over the fulfilment of production plans, plans for commodity circulation and accumulations; over the reduction of production costs; over the payment discipline of enterprises. It was also instructed to increase control over material stocks accumulated by enterprises.[38]

The October 1954 resolution dealt directly with the ministries. The resolution focused on three issues: red tape, the inflated administrative *apparat* and excessive centralization. To fight the excessive centralization that was 'still present' in just 'some branches', the ministers were instructed to examine the prospects for transferring enterprises and organizations from the jurisdiction of Union-Republic ministries in Moscow to the republic ministries.[39] In 1954, 200 main administrations (*glavki*) and departments and 147 trusts directly subordinated to them were abolished.[40] For years to come, the ministerial *apparat* would find itself under pressure of staff cuts, increasing fiscal control of *Gosbank* and under the growing insistence on the part of the central leadership to transfer enterprises to republican management. Yet the ministries would also enjoy the enhancement of their managerial authority.

Transferring industry to the republics

The process of transferring industry under republican jurisdiction started at the beginning of 1954 by creating republic ministries for the most important republican industries that had been until now administered by the all-Union ministries. In Ukraine, following Khrushchev's suggestion from August 1953, two ministries appeared: the Union-Republic Ministry of Ferrous Metallurgy on 8 February 1954 and the Ministry of Coal Mining on 19 April.[41] Also, following Khrushchev's advice, these ministries were not located in Kiev but where their industries were concentrated: in Dnepropetrovsk for ferrous metallurgy and in Stalino for coal mining.[42] Soon, however, it became clear that republican ministries would remain highly dependent on the central offices in their decision making.[43] So, as the two ministries were being created, the Council of Ministers of Ukraine (CMUk) drafted an extended proposal arguing in favour of enhancing the economic rights and responsibilities of the Ukrainian government, ministers and directors of enterprises. The Ukrainian government based this on seven resolutions issued in 1953–1954 that enhanced the decision-making authority of the all-Union ministers.[44]

Ukraine had a number of issues on the agenda. First of all, the republic needed to establish an appropriate administrative system. It needed more industrial and non-industrial ministries that would assume administration of all enterprises, the main administrations or *glavki*, and organizations and trusts. Situations where a number of enterprises belonged to a branch for which there existed a Ukrainian ministry (of Union-Republic status) yet remained under the control of Moscow complicated the management of the entire branch, causing production waste and ineffective use of inputs and production capacities. Such was the situation, for example, in the Ministry of Construction Materials Industry where, out of 306 enterprises located in Ukraine, 71 remained under direct control of the Moscow office; or in the Ministry of Consumer Goods where, out of 350 enterprises, 19 were run by the central *apparat*. The republic also requested that funds which were assigned to the republic be managed by its supply organizations (*snaby*) and sales organizations (*sbyty*) independently from the central *sbyty*. This principle had to be applied with regard to the future *sbyty* (for ferrous metallurgy, construction materials and electricity), as well as to those that had been already functioning in Ukraine (the Ukrainian offices of *Glavkhimsbyt* (sales of chemical production) and *Glavbumsbyt* (sales of paper)).[45] To crown its administrative system, the republic hoped to obtain republican offices of *Gosbank*, Industrial Bank (*Prombank*), Agricultural Bank (*Sel'khozbank*) and Commercial Bank (*Torgbank*) that 'would allow the CMUk to exert financial control over the fulfilment of production plans by enterprises';[46] and to change the status of the Statistical Agency of Ukraine from all-Union to Union-Republic, which would allow the CMUk to influence its work and request specific data.[47]

Second, Ukraine expected to be involved in planning. Considering the forthcoming transfer of industry to republican control, the centre should no longer draft detailed plans. Central planners should set only main aggregate targets for the republic and let the republican government reformulate them for the industrial branches of the economy. The same logic was applied with regard to funds: the centre should assign funds for material inputs (materials and equipment) to the republic in total, including the needs of republican and Union-Republic ministries, without specifying what the funds should be spent on. 'At present, funded production is allocated to the central offices of the Union-Republic ministries and administrations which decide where to spend the funds'. Such procedures reduced the opportunities of using the funds in the most efficient way.[48]

Third, Ukraine hoped for more rights and flexibility in financial matters, credit policy and especially pricing. The Ukrainian government wanted to have the right to move credits for capital investment, salaries and grants (*stipendii*) between the republican and local budgets, to issue short-term loans to enterprises to cover deficits related to seasonal work, and to reduce the prices of old and unmarketable goods, both commercial and industrial.[49]

Ukraine asked for the republican ministries to be allowed to fix the prices of new products, equipment and spare parts for internal industrial consumption and for production manufactured from industrial waste, in cases where such prices had not already been fixed by the USSR Ministries or the USSR CM. Ukrainian ministries would then eliminate delays in sales caused by the absence of prices. For consumer goods, the ministers, in accordance with Gosplan of Ukraine, the Ukrainian Ministry of Commerce and the Ukrainian Ministry of Finance, should be permitted to fix temporary, wholesale and retail prices of new products, which would be valid for up to one year.[50]

The Ukrainian government expected to enhance the economic rights of enterprise directors as well. They would show better results, Kiev argued, if a) they could cooperate with enterprises regardless of their ministry affiliation; b) they were allowed to employ their free production capacities by accepting orders from other enterprises and using productive inputs supplied by their clients; c) they could spend their above-plan accumulations (up to 100 thousand roubles) on developing new production and on experimentation; and d) they were free to redistribute quarterly wages funds based on actual needs.[51] Whether progressive in its thinking or not, in making this proposal the Ukrainian government sounded confident in its understanding of economic problems and its willingness to assume substantially more economic authority and responsibility than they had. The Ukrainian government claimed to be competent enough to run republican industry more efficiently than the central ministerial *apparat*, and it argued that the chosen policy of transferring enterprises to republican control would have limited, if any, economic effect if the rights of the republican managers remained half-hearted and the central ministerial *apparat* did not release its iron grip over supplies and finances.

Ukraine was not the only republic that lobbied for the enhancement of its decision-making flexibility. By the first months of 1955, other Union republics drafted similar proposals. To study these republican proposals, the central government – now under the chairmanship of Nikolai Bulganin, who replaced Malenkov in this post at the January 1955 CC CPSU Plenum[52] – formed a commission chaired by Aleksei Kosygin. It included representatives from the RSFSR, Byelorussia, Kazakhstan, Georgia, Uzbekistan and Ukraine.[53]

The Kosygin commission worked on two sets of proposals: enhancing the rights of the republican governments and enhancing the rights of the republican ministers. The proposals approved by the Kosygin commission were presented to the Presidium and generally included, although with some limitations, in the USSR CM resolution of 4 May 1955 'On changes in the procedures for state planning and financing the economy of the Union republics'. In 76 paragraphs dealing with the republican governments and 36 paragraphs concerning the republican ministers, the central leadership set new margins for the republics' decision-making authority in planning, capital construction, budget, labour and salaries, agriculture and other areas.[54]

For example, from this point forward USSR Gosplan had to fix aggregate plan targets for gross output (*valovaya produktsiya*) and commercial production for enterprises under republican jurisdiction. The republican governments would 'divide' the plan targets between enterprises and distribute all production manufactured by the republican enterprises. The centre would distribute only that part of production that did not remain within the republic that produced it. The same principle would be applied for planning capital construction: republics would receive aggregate targets for labour, investment and material funds, fuel and equipment.[55] Furthermore, budgetary expenditures, the distribution of income and expenses between the republican and *oblasti* budgets, would no longer be specified by the centre. The income received above that planned would be left to the republican government to finance housing and communal construction. To reduce the shortages, the central leadership agreed to Ukraine's suggestion and left the republics between 25 and 50 per cent of the above-plan production of food, consumer goods, agricultural machinery, appliances and fertilizers, and, of particular importance for the new housing program, construction materials manufactured by enterprises of all jurisdictions (cement, paints, window glass, radiators, fillings, ceramic and decorative tiles, bath tubs, gas pipes, roofing iron, timber and so on).[56]

The 1955 May resolution did not meet all the demands of the Union republics. Credit, supply and pricing policy remained entirely under the control of the central *apparat*.[57] In the areas where republican rights were enhanced,[58] the republics did not become fully independent either: on most issues, the republic had either to inform the all-Union relevant administration of its decision or to consult a central agency before making the decision. So, as Moscow finally agreed to create Ukrainian branches of *Gosbank, Prombank, Sel'khozbank* and *Torgbank*, Ukraine's decision making on financial matters did not increase.[59] Decisions on current financial issues, as well as the planning of credits for the coal mining and ferrous metallurgy industries, which were now partially under republican management, remained centralized.[60]

Transferring construction industry to Ukraine

At the beginning of 1955, Ukrainians tried to extend their managerial authority beyond the coal mining and ferrous metallurgy industries and addressed the central leadership with the suggestion of transferring to republican control all brickworks, lime plants and enterprises of granite mining and processing that were located in the territory of Ukraine, along with all associated trusts and physical capital. The suggestion was made in the context of Khrushchev's new massive housing campaign[61] and aimed to improve the housing situation in the republic.[62] The transfer of all brickworks, lime plants and enterprises of granite mining and processing to the republic, argued Kirichenko, would allow the republic to optimize production costs and increase output. These enterprises were dispersed among various ministries. The ministries did not cooperate or fully use the production capacities of their construction enterprises. They assigned understated plan targets to them, which in the end were not even met.[63] For example, of all brickworks situated in Ukraine, only 150 belonged to the Ukrainian Ministry of Construction Materials Industry, the other 650 were run by various ministries and departments. The latter, however, produced only 58 per cent of the republic's bricks.[64] The Ukrainian leadership claimed that the republic would run these enterprises more efficiently and referred to the example of 82 enterprises that increased output twofold after they had been transferred to the Ukrainian Ministry of Construction Materials Industry.[65] In February 1955, the central leadership supported the idea of the Ukrainian leadership and agreed, with some reservations, to transfer brickworks and lime plants to republican control.[66] Central investments in housing construction in Ukraine for 1955, however, were reduced.[67]

Ukraine enjoyed much less support in April 1955 when, despite the clear indication of the Kosygin commission that the centre would not grant full control over any industry to any republic, it nonetheless asked for authority over all construction organizations of the USSR Ministries of Construction, Construction Materials Industry, Machine-Building and Instrument-Making, Chemical Industry, Consumer Goods, Food Products, Meat and Milk Products, Procurement (*zagotovok*) and some others, with up to 3 billion roubles of total volume of construction work. Control over this group of enterprises would have permitted Ukraine to improve the administration of industrial construction by cutting administrative staff and merging small organizations into larger ones.[68] In the centre, this argument, although popular at the time, was not found weighty enough. So when in 1956 some republican construction ministries were created,[69] they did not obtain full control over all republican construction enterprises.[70]

Conclusion

The policy aimed at improving economic administration and fighting corruption and red tape in the ministerial *apparat* was economically motivated. Since 1951, labour productivity had grown more slowly than real wages. From 1951 to 1955, labour productivity in industry increased by 33 per cent, whereas real wages increased by 37 per cent.[71] In 1955, N. Bulganin blamed the ministries for failing to make use of machinery and equipment which could increase labour productivity. The mines of the Ministry of Coal Mining Industry, for example, had 24 combines in 1940 and 1,600 in 1954; the number of electric locomotives increased by a factor of six. Yet productivity in 1954 was only slightly higher than in 1940. Between one-third and one-quarter of coal mining combines and other machinery stayed idle. In metallurgy, idle time of open-hearth furnaces constituted 14 per cent in 1954 and idle time of certain rolling mills was 20–30 per cent of nominal working time. During the first half of 1955, all ministries and departments had uninstalled equipment worth about 13 billion roubles, including above-norm stocks of equipment worth 5.5 billion roubles.[72] Ministries inflated salaries. Instead of adjusting the salary rate to the production norms achieved, production norms were adjusted to the salary rate.[73] The inflated ministerial *apparat* slowed down the decision-making process, causing financial losses. In 1954, the Ministry of Fishing Industry spent more than it earned by selling fish, resulting in losses of 392 million roubles to the state.[74]

So, considering the absence of any evidence that the republics would administer enterprises less competently, transferring management of enterprises from central to peripheral control was an option worth trying. In the years 1954–1955, more than 11,000 enterprises were transferred to the jurisdiction of the republics. In the country as a whole, the share of republican or local enterprises increased from 33 per cent in 1950 to 47 per cent in 1955.[75] In Ukraine, the numbers were higher. The share of planned republican and local industry increased from 35 per cent in 1950 to 67 per cent in 1955.[76]

At the same time, it is important to distinguish between the transfer of enterprises from central to peripheral control and the enhancement of economic rights and decision-making authority, or, to be more specific, the power of republican ministers and governments. From Bulganin's and Khrushchev's perspective in 1954–1955, the transfer of enterprises to the republics did not necessarily mean that the republican decision-making authority should be enhanced. Rather, on the contrary, once liberated from the burden of making operational decisions, the central managers would become more efficient in general branch administration and policy making. This logic explains the further enhancement of the authority of the all-Union ministers during 1955[77] and the modest, from the republics' perspective, enhancement of republican decision-making authority, as well as the refusal of the central leadership to devolve control over even a share of material or financial resources from the centre to the republican governments or to tie the all-Union ministers to an obligation to consult the republican governments about planning issues.[78] From the republics' perspective, the transfer of enterprises from central to republic ministries would have been unnecessary had the central *apparat* been efficient. Since it was not, its powers should be devolved.

By the July 1955 Plenum, the central leadership was working on the idea of developing complex economic regions.[79] At the meeting of the Party organization of plant No 23 in August 1955, Khrushchev explained a new policy:

> We have a huge amount of cross-hauls. Why? Because it is necessary to regionalize complex development of the economy. Our country is huge, comrades: from Omsk we transport [potatoes] to Vladivostok, which is six thousand kilometres away. This potato, comrades, is more expensive than the pineapples. It is cheaper to import the pineapples from India by sea, than to bring this potato. It is necessary to work on this problem, to study it.[80]

A year later, Khrushchev spoke about supplying the inputs for certain economic regions, such as Ural or Donbas, and suggested creating 'interministerial supply offices'.[81]

Regionalization of economic administration made particular sense in the case of the RSFSR. Due to its scale, switching enterprises from the all-Union to republican jurisdiction would not bring administration any closer to production. By December 1955, the Presidium received the results of a joint commission of specialists from the USSR CM State Commission for current operational planning (*Gosekonomkomissiya*) and the USSR Gosplan which analysed 68 enterprises of machine-building and repairing in the regions of Transbaïkalie and the Far East. The commission discovered that the ministries under-loaded their enterprises, although the equipment needs for agricultural machinery and installations in these regions were not met; that the all-Union ministries manufactured similar equipment and machinery to one another and that their enterprises had failed to specialize; and that enterprises cooperated only if they belonged to the same ministry. Ministerial departmentalism created superfluous transportation and inflated production costs.[82] The commission advised the USSR CM to create repair workshops for common use and to organize the production of the necessary materials and equipment on the spot in order to avoid costly railway transportation.[83] The Chairman of USSR *Gosekonomkomissiya* M.Z. Saburov and the Chairman of USSR Gosplan N.K. Baibakov went even further and suggested creating a department of *Gosekonomkomissiya* in Khabarovsk which would plan for the region. The commission effectively confirmed what was already known, that 'the entire state is divided vertically, but horizontally, there was no coordination'.[84]

2 XX CPSU congress – December 1956 CC CPSU Plenum
The height of expectations

The Twentieth CPSU Congress (14–25 February) and the December 1956 CC CPSU Plenum gave a huge impulse to Ukraine's expectations as to the prospects for centre–republic economic relations and the enhancement of republican economic authority. At the XX Congress, Khrushchev evaluated the work of the republic ministries positively: 'administration of enterprises became more specific and efficient'.[1] In its report to the Congress on 24 February 1956, the CC CPSU emphasized the need to extend the rights of the republican ministers to the everyday operational management of enterprises, which would promote initiative, reinforce the republics and consolidate friendship between the peoples of the country.[2] The Sixth Five Year Plan (FYP) directives that had been approved at the Congress included, for the first time, 'a separate section devoted to republican and regional development. In earlier years such documents had concentrated instead on the development of various economic branches, with less emphasis on the regional dimension'.[3]

Inspired by the rhetoric of the XX Congress, Ukrainian ministers drafted numerous proposals on the reorganization of economic administration and the devolution of economic authority from the centre to the republic: decentralization should spread beyond the central agenda and embrace such areas as economic and financial control, economic research, statistics, and even international relations and foreign trade. In these areas, the authority of the republics should be either partly or considerably extended.

New areas for decentralization

Thus, *control organizations* should be fully subordinated to the Ukrainian government; they would then be more efficient and more useful. According to Deputy Minister of Commerce A. Romanov, the performance of Gosplan of Ukraine, the Ministry of State Control (Ministry of *Goskontrol'*), the Ministry of Finance, the Ministry of Commerce, and some other agencies was unsatisfactory because there was no single system or common procedure. The central *apparat* failed to clearly determine their functions and, as a result, they did similar work, focusing on secondary economic events and interpreting random episodes as typical.[4] At the same time, the Ministry of *Goskontrol'* had no authority and provided very little help to the Ukrainian government in solving economic problems: 'This Ministry does not have any serious rights and is responsible for nothing. There is no organ in our country more irresponsible than the Ministry of *Goskontrol'*", claimed Romanov. So,

> Under present conditions, the further existence of the Ministry of *Goskontrol'* with its curtailed rights and bureaucratic control methods is practically pointless. The *apparat* of *Goskontrol'* numbers 205 people. The average monthly salary of one employee is 1,600 roubles. The *apparat* is expensive, and the return is not even modest.[5]

The control–inspection department for Ukraine of the USSR Ministry of Finance was wasting money too: it had about 600 people on its staff, but half of their working time was spent on making the same audit as the Ministry of *Goskontrol'*.[6]

Romanov suggested abolishing the Ministry of *Goskontrol'* and the control–inspection department for Ukraine of the USSR Ministry of Finance, and creating instead a State Control–Economic Committee preferably headed by a vice-chairman of the CM. This committee would a) search for unused production capacities and manpower, and financial reserves in the industrial branches; and b) undertake its own research on economic problems in industry, agriculture, commerce, transport, etc.[7] In tune with Romanov, the Ukrainian Minister of Finance N. Shchetinin developed the argument about the purpose of the control–inspection department for Ukraine of the USSR Ministry of Finance: 'The control *apparat* that is functioning in the territory of the republic ... acts on the instructions of the USSR Ministry of Finance that ignores republican interests'.[8] So instead of reporting violations to the republican authorities, they reported them directly to Moscow, leaving the next auditors to discover the same violations. Since the USSR Ministry of Finance had no influence on correcting the violations, the control–inspection department would be more useful under republican jurisdiction, argued Shchetinin. It could also extend its functions to studying the causes of material losses.[9]

This criticism of the control organizations by Ukrainian ministers certainly fitted into the context of the XX Congress and Khrushchev's general dissatisfaction with the performance of the Ministry of *Goskontrol'*, although Khrushchev did not advocate the idea of decentralizing the control organizations.[10] Yet, at the same time, the specific criticism of the Ukrainian Ministry of *Goskontrol'* could have been a response to the results of the audit held by the latter in autumn 1955 when it established that the 12 Ukrainian ministries and agencies and the Ukrainian office of *Gosbank* had developed the same negative practices as their Moscow counterparts. Namely, they inflated the administrative staff and the wage funds, and, even more alarming to the centre, some of the audited ministries ignored the instructions of the central *apparat*.[11] The Ukrainian Minister of *Goskontrol'* K.S. Karavaev admitted in his report that the all-Union ministries shared responsibility with the Ukrainian ministries for the problems that had been uncovered, since they did not establish mechanisms that would 'favour the reinforcement of state discipline' and thereby facilitated violations.[12] Nonetheless, his conclusions undermined the campaign of the Ukrainian authorities to enhance the economic rights of the republic. Romanov could not deny the violations that were uncovered, but he could question the competence of the Ministry of *Goskontrol'*.

Ukrainian ministers also sought to develop *economic research* in the republic. According to the Ukrainian Minister of Commerce G. Sakhnovskii, economic science lagged behind because economic research was dispersed among numerous ministries and departments. More importantly, Ukrainian scientific organizations and even Gosplan or the Ministry of Finance were denied full access to statistical data. At the same time, the Ministry of Finance was doing very little to actually finance the economy, focusing, instead, on searching for sources of revenue; the Ukrainian office of *Gosbank* failed to signal any serious problems, and the Ukrainian Ministry of Commerce failed to work out a clear policy on price formation. Prices were fixed by the regional executive committees (*oblispolkomy*), republican governments, the USSR Ministry of Commerce and the USSR CM, as well as by local producers. As a result, price diversity was large, particularly for items of local and cooperative industry.[13] The industrial ministries, even when they discovered reserves, did not reveal them and there was no reason to expect that in the immediate future they would. Gosplan of Ukraine did not study or criticize the ministries, and nobody criticized Gosplan. Echoing Romanov, Sakhnovskii blamed the Ministry of *Goskontrol'* and the control–inspection department for Ukraine of the USSR Ministry of Finance for the unfortunate results of economic work in the country and in the republic, and proposed concentrating economic work in the Ukrainian Ministry of Finance. The Ministry of Finance was to receive all materials, from demographic to economic statistics, and instead of controlling accounting indices, it would control the fulfilment of economic indices.[14] (The enthusiasm of G. Sakhnovskii for reorganizing economic and control work in the republic must have originated from his expectation of replacing M. Shchetinin as the Minister of Finance of Ukraine. Shchetinin would become Sakhnovskii's First Deputy. The nomination did not happen and Sakhnovskii and Shchetinin remained in their posts.[15])

By 5 March, a specially formed commission that included Sakhnovskii, Shchetinin, the Chairman of Gosplan of Ukraine A. Baranovskii and the General Administrator (*upravlyayushchii*) of the Ukrainian office of *Gosbank* G. Kovalenko, finished a proposal based on Sakhnovskii's note. The commission agreed with Sakhnovskii's analysis and his idea of transferring the functions of financial audit and control over enterprises to the Ukrainian Ministry of Finance, and suggested that the USSR CM establish a single system of price-formation and create a pricing administration that would compose common methodological instructions for setting prices and monitor that prices, once fixed, were correct.[16] The commission suggested that research on the Ukrainian economy be transferred from Moscow to Kiev, and that the Ukrainian Ministry of Agriculture, the Ukrainian Ministry of Commerce and the Ukrainian Ministry of Finance should each create scientific-research institutes. For Gosplan of Ukraine, the commission advised creating a department for perspective planning that would analyse the economic development of the republic and a pricing department that would draft proposals on prices for industrial production and consumer goods for central government. Furthermore, all Ukrainian ministries and departments should restructure and form departments that would analyse the development of their branches.[17] To make future research available to the public, the commission proposed publishing a new magazine on the Ukrainian economy which would highlight such concerns as 'issues of practical (*konkretnoi*) economics', analyse financial and economic activity of certain enterprises, and publish reference material of importance to economic agents.[18]

The participation, or rather non-participation, of the republics in commercial relations with other countries was brought up by Kirichenko with the Presidium during the work of the XX Congress. He objected to the existing procedure whereby the privilege of visits to foreign exhibitions and fairs was monopolized by the central *apparat*. From the point of view of the republics, these trips were pointless because information on the newest achievements in engineering and production that was obtained abroad never reached the republics and consequently the production sites.[19] During the first half of 1956, 487 specialists were scheduled to visit various foreign exhibitions and fairs. Yet none of them was sent by a republican CM, observed Kirichenko. Only one republican minister was invited to join the delegates: a specialist from the RSFSR Ministry of Local Industry. Clearly, there was no place for directors of enterprises.[20]

Sakhnovskii went much further when, after witnessing a free exchange of opinions at the XI session of the UN Economic conference in Geneva in 1956, he suggested 'reviewing the existing practice of foreign trade and decentralizing, to some extent, the procedures for purchasing merchandise abroad'.[21] He proposed allowing not only the republic ministries, but also cooperative unions, cities, industrial trusts and specialized trade organizations, to buy goods abroad:

> It is a fact that when the USSR Ministry of Foreign Trade is buying on the foreign market, it inevitably organizes contractors because of the large volumes of its purchases. For example, last year the Ministry of Foreign Trade purchased one million tonnes of sugar. Such a volume could sometimes not even be provided by a single state, let alone a single company. Whether the Ministry wanted it or not, it was forced to deal with a number of suppliers who, under the circumstances, imposed conditions that aggravated the transaction: prices, delivery conditions, quality, etc. Many West European countries continue to refuse to sell us certain products or grant export licences, explaining that the products are of strategic significance.[22]

In the case of an embargo on selling strategic products to the countries of Eastern Europe and especially to the USSR, said Sakhnovskii, there was still a chance that those products would be sold to a town's municipal trust. He also hoped that by striking small unrelated deals, it would be possible to get credits.[23]

'Sources for the development of such foreign trade operations could be such things as goods manufactured above the plan, above-plan revenues from local budgets, and the income of cooperative organizations',[24] continued Sakhnovskii. The Ministry of Foreign Trade would, of course, establish procedures and volume limits and 'possibly' issue permits to buy or sell.[25] Sakhnovskii's idea was supported by the CC CPUk and Kirichenko and was submitted as 'certain propositions on the foreign trade of the USSR' to the CC CPSU.[26]

Did Sakhnovskii or Kirichenko count on a revolution in the administration of foreign trade? Regardless of Moscow's reaction, the very fact that Sakhnovskii and Kirichenko thought that it was worth trying to de-monopolize foreign trade is a remarkable testimony to the effect that the XX Congress had on the Ukrainian leadership and their perception of the potential for centre–republic economic relations.

At the beginning of April, a Ukrainian commission chaired by the CMUk Vice-Chairman V. Valuev (the same commission that drafted Ukrainian proposals on the extension of republican rights at the beginning of 1955) submitted a general proposal on the enhancement of republic's economic rights. In expectation of the unleashing of republican sovereign rights,[27] the Valuev commission repeated a number of Ukraine's requests from previous years, namely: to change the status of the Statistical Agency of Ukraine from all-Union to Union-Republic; to create republican supply offices for the Ukrainian Ministry of Ferrous Metallurgy and Ministry of Coal Mining; to allow the Ukrainian office of *Gosbank* to issue loans based on the decisions of the republican CM to cover temporary cash shortages of enterprises; to establish a reserve fund for the CM of Ukraine of 5–7 per cent of the budget (in previous years, Ukraine claimed 3 per cent)[28]; to allow the republic to set the wholesale and retail prices for the produce of republican, local and cooperative industries; to leave all above-plan production manufactured by all enterprises located in the territory of the republic within the republic; and to allow the republic to redistribute the accumulations intended for capital repair among enterprises. New requests were made in the areas of planning, construction work, budget and credit, taxes, labour, salary and cost prices, agriculture and state purchases. For example, the Valuev commission asked that the CMUk be allowed to fix plan targets for labour, personnel and wages funds, for reducing the prime cost of industrial production and for costs of construction works for republican and Union-Republic ministries; to allow the republican government, in accordance with the USSR Ministry of Finance, to fix the level and sources of payments to the all-Union budget; to issue credits for technological innovation and retail trade; to set the turnover tax on consumer goods produced by the republican and local industry which had not yet been priced by central government; and to set the level of investment in construction works.[29]

The complex approach of the Ukrainian authorities to the reorganization of economic administration was in sharp contrast to the general perception of republican policy that was dominant among the central *apparat* and the CC CPSU Presidium. While the Ukrainian authorities explored opportunities for reorganizing the economic administration and pushed at the limits of devolving administrative authority, the Presidium insisted on continuing to limit this reorganization process to transferring enterprises to republican management. This became clear when in spring 1956 the central leadership initiated the reorganization of 13 all-Union ministries (State Purchases, State farms (*sovkhozy*), Commerce, Meat and Milk Industry, Fishing Industry, Food Industry, Textile Industry, Light Industry, for Inland Navigation, of the Construction Materials Industry, Paper and Wood Processing Industries, for Automobile Transport and Road Construction, and Public Health).[30]

Reorganization of 13 ministries

By the end of May 1956, the Presidium had agreed on a) merging the Ministry of Light Industry along with the Ministry of Textile Industry into the Ministry of Light Industry; b) the abolition of the USSR Ministry of Justice;[31] c) the reorganization of the USSR Ministry of State Purchases into the Union-Republic Ministry for Grain Production; d) abolition of the Union-Republic Ministry for Automobile Transport and Road Construction and creation of the main administration for road construction; and e) abolition of the USSR Ministry for Inland Navigation and the creation of a republic ministry for the RSFSR and administrations for those republics that needed them. The remaining eight ministries had to be reorganized.[32] Judging by the remarks of the Ukrainian government, the rules for the forthcoming transfer of enterprises to republican control remained unchanged. Union-Republic ministries in Moscow, merged or reorganized, would retain general administration over a number of enterprises, set plan targets, control the fulfilment of the plan, supplies and investment, and develop general technological policy, as well as measures to be taken to implement the latest scientific and technological innovations in production.[33] Such an organization of the economic administration would not change anything in the existing order and would not improve the day-to-day management of enterprises, concluded Kiev. It would be reasonable, instead, to a) transfer all enterprises, research institutes, experimental enterprises, workhouses, laboratories and project organizations of the ministries concerned to republican control; and b) transfer the administration of supplies and financing of capital investment to the republic ministries.[34] The functions of the central ministerial offices should be limited to developing general policy for the branches, perspective planning, implementing advanced experience, import–export relations and coordination of the work of the project organizations on standard and special projects.[35]

The ideas of the Ukrainian leadership had not been taken into consideration and decision-making authority remained mainly with the central *apparat*, which, judging by the results of the audit held by the Ministry of *Goskontrol'* in Ukraine in 1954–1955, was rather understandable, since Ukrainian ministers clearly demonstrated the same tendency to ignore the instructions of higher authorities as their counterparts from the central *apparat*. Nonetheless, some progress had been made as the leadership increased the involvement of the republican governments in planning. Thus, based on the Directives for the Sixth FYP adopted at the XX Congress, the republics had to draft the 1957 plan for industries of republican and Union-Republic status and give proposals for the development of industries of all-Union jurisdiction located in their territories.[36]

Planning failures and the December 1956 CC CPSU Plenum

The reorganization of 13 ministries in spring and summer 1956 did not promise any reorganization of USSR Gosplan or *Gosekonomkomissiya*. Moreover, as the central ministries were 'losing' enterprises to their republican counterparts, planners held a tight grip over the plans.[37] Dissatisfaction with the performance of the central planners started to build up after Khrushchev's August 1956 visits to the Urals, Siberia, Kazakhstan and Ukrainian Donbas. After the trip to the Urals, Siberia and Kazakhstan, Khrushchev concluded that USSR Gosplan and *Gosekonomkomissiya* were failing to fulfil plans and implement central resolutions. So the Presidium immediately instructed N. Bulganin, M. Pervukhin, G. Malenkov and L. Brezhnev 'to examine the problem of increasing the responsibility of the USSR Gosplan and *Gosekonomkomissiya* for the implementation of Party and government directives and of approved plan targets'.[38] After his visit to Donbas, at the Presidium meeting held on 24 August, Khrushchev blamed Gosplan and *Gosekonomkomissiya* for the muddle in the construction of mines. However, later, in the resolution issued after this meeting, the Presidium did not hold the planners responsible for improving the situation,[39] nor was any criticism heard of the investment control figures for 1957 proposed by Saburov and Baibakov at the 31 August Presidium meeting. Quite on the contrary, the Presidium in general approved the proposed numbers, and instructed both of them to consider the remarks expressed during the Presidium meeting and to continue working on and composing 'a feasible plan'.[40]

In the autumn, the Presidium was less tolerant. By the end of November 1956 it was recognized that the FYP and the plan for 1957 had to be reviewed 'in order to reduce public tension'.[41] The financing of housing construction had to be increased and the 'material well-being of workers' ought to be improved. The USSR CM was instructed to decide which industrial branches would take investment cuts.[42] Corrections to the Directives for the FYP as well as the plan for 1957 were on the agenda of the CC CPSU Plenum scheduled for 20–24 December.[43]

At the Presidium meeting one week prior to the Plenum, Khrushchev could not conceal his frustration about the draft plan for 1957: 'The indices appeared to be without foundation. All these numbers are abstract. This is a failure in planning. Investments are being withdrawn from circulation. ... Such planning is wrong'.[44] Saburov and Baibakov were again instructed to review the drafts of both the five-year and the annual plans, which they did. Two days before the Plenum started, both plans were approved.[45] However, the efforts of Gosplan and *Gosekonomkomissiya* did not change the scenario of the Plenum, where *Gosekonomkomissiya* was given the role of scapegoat for the planning failures.[46]

The agenda of the December 1956 CC CPSU Plenum included discussion of how to improve economic administration by increasing the number of economic and cultural matters under republican jurisdiction; revision of the budgetary rights of the republics; changes to the planning system and the system of financing the economy; further enhancement of the rights of the all-Union ministers; increasing the competence of the USSR Gosplan, the USSR CM State Committee for New Technologies, USSR CM State Committee for Construction (*Gosstroi*) and the State Committee for Labour and Wages.[47] In his report, Bulganin called for the vigorous eradication of shortcomings in planning that were slowing down the implementation of economic programs initiated by the Party and reminded the audience that excessive centralization in the economic administration was stifling the initiative of local managers.[48]

> Despite the favourable conditions created for more efficient perspective and current planning [the split of USSR Gosplan in 1955 into two organizations: Gosplan for perspective planning and *Gosekonomkomissiya* for current planning], a drastic improvement in the work of our central planning organizations has not occurred. This is particularly the case with *Gosekonomkomissiya* about which we may say that very often it simply goes with the stream.[49]

Both USSR Gosplan and *Gosekonomkomissiya* studied industrial branches or the economy of the country in a general and superficial way and had tenuous relations with localities, large enterprises and scientific institutes. Functionaries of both organizations did not visit production sites and were not aware of the true situation in the regions.[50] Yet, since for the day-to-day functioning of the economy current planning was more important than perspective planning, Bulganin criticized *Gosekonomkomissiya* most, and he did not forget to mention Saburov's personal responsibility for these problems. From 25 December, Saburov was no longer the Chairman of *Gosekonomkomissiya*, although he kept his position as the First Vice-Chairman of the USSR CM. His place was given to Vice-Chairman of the USSR CM Pervukhin.[51] The style and work methods of the USSR Gosplan were criticized as well, but Baibakov retained his post until May 1957.[52]

The Ukrainian leadership knew that planners would be criticized and came to the Plenum well prepared. In their assessment of the work of the central planners that they prepared for Kirichenko, the Ukrainian planners emphasized three points. First, when composing the plan for 1957, *Gosekonomkomissiya* ignored republican proposals and relied on the opinion of a narrow circle of specialists from the central *apparat*. The second issue originated from the first and was about miscalculations in the plan that resulted from ignoring production capacities and the discrepancy between the production targets on the one hand and material and financial inputs on the other.[53] The third problem was that the republican authorities were not informed of the results of the audits held by USSR Gosplan and *Gosekonomkomissiya*. 'Yet it is obvious that these organs [local Party and Soviet bodies] could do a lot to correct shortcomings uncovered in the fulfilment of plans.'[54]

As the Vice-Chairman of Gosplan of Ukraine A. Baranovskii spelled out the problems of the Ukrainian planners for Kirichenko, he pointed to the fact that the plans of both Gosplan and *Gosekonomkomissiya* did not reflect a number of the Party's or government's decisions and instructions, which complicated the implementation of central instructions and plan fulfilment.[55] And of course, Baranovskii did justice to the role of the CC CPSU in correcting planning mistakes, although he did emphasize that those mistakes would have not been made had the republican draft plans been considered. Gosplan of Ukraine did not suggest any reorganization of the planning organizations. To improve the perspective and current plans, central planners were to rely on the republics to estimate their production capacities and investment and supply needs.

The criticism of the planning organizations at the December 1956 Plenum did not change the general policy of reorganizing the economic administration that was announced at the XX Congress. The economic rights of the republics had to be increased, along with the authority of the all-Union ministers and the role of the all-Union committees and commissions in promoting technological innovations and regulating construction and labour policy. At the same time, the leadership counted on closer cooperation between the central *apparat* and the republican governments, so the list of matters with which the republican governments should be involved had to be expanded. It did not, however, include financing, credit and supplies.[56]

By the December 1956 Plenum, the position of Khrushchev in the Presidium had been considerably consolidated, not least due to the replacement of Malenkov with Bulganin. Khrushchev promoted the Party's role in the management of the economy; he pushed for the reorganization of the ministerial system and supported the transfer of enterprises to the management of local authorities and the enhancement of republican economic rights. Still, to Khrushchev, not to mention the central *apparat* or his Presidium colleagues, who fully realized that the over-centralized economic administration was choking in red tape and slowed down economic growth, the policy of enhancing republican economic rights remained secondary to enhancing the decision-making authority of the central *apparat*. This determined the non-systemic character of the policy of enhancing republican economic rights when, despite their increased responsibility for the performance of the enterprises transferred to them, the republic-level authorities remained highly dependent on the central *apparat*.

In the centre, the transfer of enterprises to the republics took place against the background of rivalry between the Party and governmental *apparat*.[57] In Ukraine, however, the conflict of interests between the Party and the government was not on the same scale, particularly on the issue of enhancing republican economic rights where the interests of the CC CPUk and the Ukrainian ministerial bureaucracy were more aligned. Two reasons explain such lack of conflict in Ukraine. First of all, the Ukrainian ministerial bureaucracy was not as powerful as the central *apparat* or the CC CPUk. Second, the transfer of enterprises to republican control and the project of further extending republican economic authority meant an increase in power not just for the republican governmental *apparat* but for

32 *Search for efficient economic administration*

the CC CPUk as well. Thus, while Ukraine certainly supported Khrushchev's intention to promote the Party's dominance in economic matters, it concentrated its efforts on reducing the republic's dependence on the central ministries.

Ukraine's response to the December 1956 CC CPSU Plenum

Following what had become a tradition, the Ukrainian ministries responded to the rhetoric of the December 1956 Plenum by drafting detailed proposals on how to improve economic administration or, more specifically, on the absolute need to decentralize the economic administration. By now, however, the tone of the proposals had become more impatient and the criticism of the existing system more categorical. Thus, the Ukrainian Minister for Site Construction of the Coal Mining Industry G. Krasnikovskii, for example, insisted that the Ukrainian ministries should enjoy the same power as the all-Union ministries, whose authority was largely enhanced by 15 governmental resolutions and decrees issued in the period between April 1953 and September 1956.[58] The ex-USSR Minister of Coal Mining Industry and now the Ukrainian Minister of Coal Mining A. Zasyad'ko drafted an elaborate proposal where he argued for the enhancement of the decision-making authority of his ministry in a full range of areas, but he also openly described the existing planning procedure as unconstitutional.[59] Ukraine should participate in composing the plan, insisted Zasyad'ko.

> *Gosekonomkomissiya* inserts the indices of the economic plan for the *Minugleprom* [the Ministry of Coal Mining] of Ukraine into the economic plan for the Ukrainian SSR automatically. They are based on the plan indices fixed by the USSR Ministry of Coal Mining. Neither Gosplan [of Ukraine] nor the CM of Ukraine participates in this process. Such a planning process is wrong in essence, as well as wrong according to the Constitution, because economic plan indices for the republican coal mining industry form the basis for planning the state budget of the Ukrainian SSR, which is approved by the Supreme Soviet of the UkSSR.[60]

While being responsible for the performance of the branch, the CMUk is deprived of any opportunity to solve important problems in the coal mining industry, Zasyad'ko stated. With respect to financing industry, Zasyad'ko pointed out that although major industrial branches were transferred to republican control and republican offices of *Gosbank* and *Prombank* had been organized, financial problems could only be solved in the centre. Each time the republic Ministry of Coal Mining needed a credit, it had to address the CMUk, which would then forward the request to the *Gosbank* or *Prombank* in Moscow. In order to fully and expeditiously finance such industries as coal mining and metallurgy, the Ukrainian offices of these banks should obtain the necessary rights and resources to issue credits.[61] He added, 'It is also necessary to transfer some financial resources from the USSR CM to the CMUk, in order to allow the latter to render emergency financial help to its ministries and organizations'.[62]

Although Zasyad'ko essentially repeated the proposals of the Valuev commission from early 1955 and some of the later requests of other Ukrainian ministers, his style was clearly more rigid and the wording more direct. The tone of the documents could be certainly explained by his character. According to Sergei Khrushchev, Zasyad'ko had a reputation for independent thinking even during Stalinist times.[63] And yet, it is interesting how Zasyad'ko arrived in Ukraine. From 1947 Zasyad'ko was in Moscow. He occupied several ministerial chairs. He was the Minister of Coal Mining of the Western regions of the USSR (until 1948) and then the USSR Minister of the Coal Mining Industry (1948–1955). In March 1955, he became the Deputy Minister of Coal Mining.[64] At the beginning of August 1956, when planning his trip to Donbas, Khrushchev suggested that Zasyad'ko, whom Khrushchev had known since the Second World War,[65] should be sent to Ukraine: 'About Zasyad'ko: they say he stopped drinking. Then let us make him a minister in Ukraine'.[66] On 8 August, A.F. Zasyad'ko replaced A.S. Kuz'mich as the Ukrainian Minister of Coal Mining.[67] Was there any particular reason for this replacement? Or did Khrushchev just want to have someone loyal to him in the Ukrainian Ministry, someone who might provide the necessary information and support? If this was the case, it would explain the wording chosen by Zasyad'ko and the fact that in 1957 he was moved back to Moscow, to USSR Gosplan, to chair the department of coal mining industry.[68]

The proposal of the Ukrainian Minister of Construction N. Gorbas' was about the supply system and responsibility for decisions. The system could be improved only if it was decentralized down to the level of republican capitals. Gorbas' explained that the moment that plans were legislated, they stopped existing for anybody. There was no systematic control over plan realization. Suppliers were not held responsible for fulfilling deliveries. Unauthorized modifications or cancellations of the orders by the suppliers were commonplace. Quarter delivery plans were not coordinated with the transportation plans of the ministries-suppliers and nobody was responsible for this.[69] The supply system became obsolete and generated excessive documentation, which had a direct effect on the *apparat*. The *apparat* for the *sbyty* in Moscow became bloated, whereas in the periphery, it lost its efficiency. The number of intermediary delivery offices swelled and yet almost everything was still distributed in Moscow.[70]

To overcome administrative centralization and the lack of control over transactions, Gorbas' proposed decentralizing the system for issuing orders for materials to consumers (factories and mines, etc.) and creating new procedures for establishing direct relations between suppliers and consumers.[71] Only the planning and transportation of materials should remain under centralized control. *Sbyty* in the *oblasti* should draft detailed demands for the entire region. This would save on transportation costs.[72] In the conclusion of his proposal, Gorbas' proposed organizing a Ukrainian Ministry for Material and Technical Supplies.[73] This Ministry would concentrate on supplying the republican economy and improving control over the realization of supply plans and the utilization of material resources. Having the right to temporarily suspend deliveries to those consumers who accumulated stock above the permitted norms and redirect them to those consumers whose stock was below the norms, this Ministry could minimize the overstocking of materials and increase return on inputs. The Ministry could also speed up certain deliveries without involving the Soviet and Party organs. *Snaby* and *sbyty* could be merged.[74]

To a different extent, the problems outlined by the Ukrainian ministers after the December 1956 Plenum would be addressed by the *Sovnarkhoz* reform, but not solved. After the XX Congress, the December 1956 Plenum further boosted the expectation of the Ukrainian republican authorities that their economic authority would be extended. For them, there was no other alternative for reorganizing economic administration than to devolve the authority of the central ministries down to republican level and to correlate authority for decision making with responsibility for decision fulfilment at all administrative levels. So Khrushchev's general idea about decentralizing economic administration and decision making that he presented to his Presidium colleagues in January 1957 fully corresponded to the vision of the Ukrainian ministers on the necessary scale of decentralization. However, it did not correspond to the organizational form that the reform proposed. Khrushchev's decentralization was designed to go all the way down to the economic regions; Kiev would not monopolize authority over republican production and construction. This was not what the emerging ministerial bureaucracy of Ukraine expected.

3 The *Sovnarkhoz* reform

Khrushchev's note on reorganization of industry and construction[1]

One month after the December 1956 CC CPSU Plenum, on 28 January 1957, Khrushchev presented the Presidium with a note on the reorganization of the administration of industry and construction in which he suggested abolishing the branch ministries. According to Yurii Aksyutin, Khrushchev had raised the idea earlier in summer 1956, after it was recognized that the territorial administration of construction provided by *Glavmosstroi* in Moscow, and by identical construction organizations in Leningrad and Kiev, was cost effective. So, as the press criticized ministerial departmentalism, Khrushchev shared his views and intentions with his colleagues.

> And immediately ran across 'incomprehension'. Thus, the Vice-Chairman of the USSR CM I.T. Tevosyan called this intention [Khrushchev's idea to abolish the ministries] 'a mistake' and the next day, to confirm these words, he sent Nikita Khrushchev a note in which he explained his arguments against the proposed reorganization: it would lead to disconnection between branches of the economy and do damage to common technological policy. And how did Khrushchev respond? When he recognized that Tevosyan was against his ideas, Khrushchev insisted that Tevosyan was sent as ambassador to Japan.[2]

At the December 1956 Plenum, although the ministries had been criticized, Khrushchev did not come forward with his reorganization. Even at the meeting of the heads of the CC CPSU departments held before the Plenum, on 11 December 1956, when speaking about administration of construction, Khrushchev reassured his audience that no changes would be introduced here: maybe in some regions, construction could be managed by the territorial organizations, but in general, the branch principle was going to be maintained.[3] At the Plenum, 'the resistance to his intention in the CC CPSU Presidium on the part of Molotov, Malenkov, Kaganovich, Pervukhin and even Saburov was so strong that the CC CPSU First Secretary had to retreat' and agree to the idea of planning for economic regions and the transfer of the function of current planning to *Gosekonomkomissiya*.⁴

Yet just a month later, Khrushchev overturned the decisions of the December 1956 Plenum and insisted on realizing his project. In the introductory paragraph of his note, Khrushchev admitted that it was correct in principle to transfer enterprises under republican control, but this did not improve the management of production. The reasons for that, Khrushchev explained, were organizational flaws incorporated into the ministerial system and the unwillingness of the ministries to correct those flaws. The flaws were known and had been previously addressed: over-centralized decision making along branch lines, and departmentalism. Ministries formed huge *apparat* and, all the way down the administrative vertical, driven by the intention to improve management, they drained qualified specialists from the periphery to the centre.

Departmentalism that developed in the minds and practices of the ministries prevented them from cooperating and developing specializations. As a result, ministries used inputs irrationally and paid huge transportation costs, rising to more than 2 billion roubles annually. Ministries resisted innovations; they asked for more investment to build new factories while keeping reserve production capacity 'frozen', because 'this corresponded to their narrow departmental interests, although everyone knows that such practice is against state interests'.⁵ At the same time, idle production capacity did not always reflect a non-state attitude on the part of the ministries; sometimes the centre was simply ignorant of the available capacities of their enterprises.

If the ministries could not provide effective administration, then who could? Well, the driving force was the Party. In 1955–1956, when the ministries resented placing the relevant orders, the Party had addressed the plants directly and organized supplemental production of agricultural machinery.⁶ Nonetheless, the administration of industry and construction should be transferred to new territorial administrations.

In the long-term perspective, territorial administrations could run complex industrial regions such as the Ural region. However, at the beginning they should be formed within the borders of the existing administrative units, 'because here we have established Party, trade union and Soviet organizations that in the new system would play a major role in planning and plan fulfilment'.⁷ The administrative *apparat* in *oblasti* or *kraya*, formed from the former ministerial functionaries, should be small. The industrial-economic councils should include representatives of local Party, trade union and Soviet organizations and formulate general economic policy for their region, coordinate the work of enterprises of separate branches, and so on. A technical council would solve specific technical issues, introduce new technology and rationalization, and give advice to enterprises on modernization.

The bureaucratic layers that currently existed between an enterprise and its *glavk* and the ministry would disappear. (After his August 1956 trip to the Ukrainian coal mining regions, Khrushchev argued that the *glavki* were an unnecessary administrative layer between the coal mining ministries and the trusts and mines.)[8] More importantly, 'we will erase departmental boundaries and give scope to wise management'.[9] By 'wise management', Khrushchev meant specialization and cooperation among enterprises of different branches located on the same territory, elements of what was termed complex regional development.

The new organizational structure would 'immeasurably' increase the role of the local Party and Soviet organizations and trade unions in economic administration. The Party committees would obtain real political and administrative power and would be able to influence the plan indices and the fulfilment of plans. At the same time, their responsibility for the economic situation in the region would increase. The new system would simplify planning, eliminate long cross-hauls and wasteful transportation, simplify the supply system and reduce the *apparat* currently involved in managing supplies. 'Life itself would push the word "*tolkach*" out from the lexicon as an obsolete category.'[10] The proposed system would have a positive impact on science and education. And it was more suitable in the case of a war too: the country's economy would not be paralyzed because the decision-making centres would be all over the country.[11]

What of disadvantages? A tendency towards autarky, 'to form a closed economy', said Khrushchev, was not excluded. 'How [can we] fight it? If in some region production is more expensive and of inferior quality than in the other region ..., then it is necessary to give priority to developing that production in the second region'. Here, the USSR CM and the republican governments should control the situation and USSR Gosplan and *Gosekonomkomissiya* should study the regional economy and avoid investing in enterprises that would be unprofitable.[12]

Some central organizations would remain. USSR Gosplan was to continue doing what it was doing, perspective planning, but it should communicate with the republican governments instead of the central ministries. *Gosekonomkomissiya* should review its functions and focus on coordinating the work of microeconomic regions. 'All decisions of an administrative, economic and technical nature would be made locally; there would be nobody to deal with these issues in the centre, besides, there would be no need for this.'[13] Khrushchev did not exclude, however, that the branch administrations that would be created within *Gosekonomkomissiya* and that would assume certain functions of the abolished ministries in planning and supplies would also set the general policy for branches and would coordinate technological policy.

The new system would promote horizontal, or direct, relations between the regions, although certain issues would be coordinated from the centre:

> For example, one region supplies material. Another one gives something in exchange. Such relations can be based on an appropriate agreement ... and can be maintained directly, without involving central organizations. Here in Moscow, in *Gosekonomkomissiya*, these direct supplies should only be registered.[14]

In the republics, territorial administrations should be subordinated directly to the republican governments that would administer all industry and construction.

38 *Search for efficient economic administration*

At the end of the note, Khrushchev suggested that the transfer to the new system should start with abolishing only a few ministries; territorial administrations should be first formed in such clearly defined regions as Moscow, Leningrad, Sverdlovsk, Gor'kii and some others and only then all over the country. The ministries should be abolished only after their peripheral enterprises had been transferred to the territorial administrations.

Discussion of Khrushchev's note

Khrushchev must have realized that the Presidium would not support his reorganization, so he distributed the note outside the Presidium 'to all members and candidates of the CC CPSU, members of the Central revision commission, republican, *kraya* and *oblasti* Party secretaries, USSR ministers and the heads of the CC CPSU departments'.[15] Indeed, Khrushchev proposed a radical reorganization. Still, according to the records of the Presidium proceedings, the majority of those who were present and talked at the 28 January meeting agreed with, although not necessarily supported, Khrushchev's idea. Of the 13 present, three expressed categorical disagreement with the decentralization – Pervukhin, Molotov and Voroshilov – and one abstained from expressing his position, P.N. Pospelov.[16] At the June 1957 Plenum, Khrushchev remembered that D. Shepilov was against the reorganization too, as 'he demagogically asked: and who will represent the working class in the Council of Ministers?'.[17]

On 4 February, a specially formed commission held its first meeting. The commission was chaired by Khrushchev and included, according to Khrushchev, 'the majority of the Presidium members and the CC CPSU secretaries, *obkomy*, *kraikomy* [territorial committees of the Communist Party] and republican secretaries, ministers and directors of enterprises', in particular, the head of the CC CPSU department of machine-building I. Kuz'min (who with the reform became the Chairman of USSR Gosplan), the Chairman of USSR Gosplan N. Baibakov, the head of the CC CPSU department of heavy industry A. Rudakov, chief editor of *Pravda* P. Satyukov and the head of the USSR Central Statistical Agency, or TsSU, V. Starovskii; the CC CPSU secretaries A. Aristov and L. Brezhnev, First Vice-Chairman of *Gosekonomkomissiya* and First Vice-Chairman of USSR Gosplan A. Kosygin and the USSR Minister of Finance A. Zverev took part in the discussions.[18] Unlike the January Presidium meeting, the commission meeting held on 4 February was less emotional. The commission focused on technical details but remained vague on the specific elements of the new system. Some commission members called for preserving centralized control in some areas. M. Evseenko, the USSR Minister for Site Construction of the Oil Industry and the Vice-Chairman of the RSFSR Gosplan, spoke in favour of centralized *sbyty* and for keeping specialized organizations. The USSR Minister of Chemical Industry S. Tikhomirov suggested not decentralizing the industrial branches for raw materials.[19] Zademid'ko suggested organizing regional administration according to the branch principle. Kosygin anticipated problems with supplies and recommended merging *snaby* and *sbyty*. Baibakov proposed abolishing industrial ministries for raw materials only after the machine-building ministries and the ministries for construction. Echoing his own and Saburov's idea from one year earlier,[20] he suggested that the republic should plan from the beginning to the end and USSR Gosplan should only combine the plans of all republics into one.[21]

At the February 1957 CC CPSU Plenum, the forthcoming reorganization was announced to the country.[22] After the debates, without the participation of or support for the reorganization from the Presidium members, and despite lobby talks against the reorganization,[23] the Plenum decided to publish the thesis of Khrushchev's report, to launch a public discussion of the thesis and then to discuss it in the USSR Supreme Soviet.[24] Nonetheless, the decision in principle to abolish the industrial and construction ministries and create *sovnarkhozy* had been made at the Plenum,[25] so adjusting the industrial administration to the new system started immediately after the Plenum.[26]

On 22 March, the Presidium discussed the reorganization again. By then, some of Khrushchev's original ideas had been examined and reconsidered. A.I. Mikoyan, L.M. Kaganovich, N.A. Bulganin, M.G. Pervukhin, G.M. Malenkov, B.I. Aristov and A.G. Zverev spoke for double subordination of the *sovnarkhozy*, to the centre and to the republican governments.[27] Khrushchev himself must have realized that his original idea was extreme and returned to the traditional division of industry into all-Union, Union-Republic and local.[28] (Later this classification would be reconsidered again and the final subordination of industry would be all-Union, republican and local.) By implying that the operational decision making for a number of enterprises should remain in the centre, he retreated from his original proposition that the management of all enterprises should be transferred to the peripheral managers.[29]

That the Party functionaries at all levels supported the reform was of no surprise. To them, the reform promised a considerable increase in power. The central ministerial bureaucracy rejected the idea, but kept silent in public and did not criticize the reform in newspapers.[30] Central ministries expressed their disapproval by not participating in establishing the new system. According to A. Zademid'ko, the USSR Minister of Coal Mining and then the chairman of the Kemerovo *Sovnarkhoz*, the reform was initiated and worked out by the *apparat* of the CC CPSU and *obkomy*.[31] (Petro Shelest, the First Secretary of the Kiev *obkom* at the time, insisted that the structure offered by the Ukrainians was used as the basis for the structure of the future *Sovnarkhoz*.[32]) From the start, the USSR CM addressed numerous problems either slowly or not at all. There were no new supply plans and nobody was assigned to study the problems that the *sovnarkhozy* would certainly have to deal with. At the Plenum on the Anti-Party group in June 1957, Zademid'ko remembered that on the last day of the session of the USSR Supreme Soviet,

> it was scary to find out that nobody [in the USSR CM Presidium] had any idea about anything; no propositions had been drafted except the proposal from com. Kosygin. But his proposal was mainly on the abolition of the *apparat* of the ministries, and was still incomplete.[33]

Of course, the lack of proposals from the central ministerial *apparat* could be explained by a genuine lack of ideas as to how to turn the Soviet economic administration from a branch to a territorial structure.

Among those who were cautious, even worried, about the proposed reorganization, Molotov stands out. He was so concerned that on 24 March, he submitted to the Presidium his comments on Khrushchev's project in which he insisted that it was unfinished, one-sided and that 'without considerable corrections it would seriously complicate the economic administration'.[34] Molotov warned about the dangers of extreme decentralization and the abolition of all central economic administrations except planning. Leaving only planners in the centre would weaken the directing role of the Central Committee and the central government. Molotov suggested replacing the ministries with several committees for the main branches. These committees would balance the decentralization and ensure proper administration of the industries, while the operational management (*neposredstvennoe upravlenie*) would be transferred to the periphery as proposed. Molotov also pointed to potential problems between the *sovnarkhozy* and the *oblispolkomy*, since their relations were not clearly defined in Khrushchev's project. The supply system was not clearly outlined either. On top of that, Molotov suggested counting the future administrative *apparat* all over the country, since it was not obvious that it would reduce.[35] Molotov did not reject the idea of the reorganization *per se*, at least not in writing. All he suggested was to work out the details of the reorganization before publishing it.

Two days later, Khrushchev responded. Where Molotov was constructive, Khrushchev was emotional. Khrushchev was indignant at the very fact of the disagreement and at the persistence with which Molotov defended his opinion even after the Presidium had unanimously approved the reorganization. Molotov's suggestion to create branch committees was interpreted by Khrushchev as an attempt to preserve the ministries.[36] Ironically enough, the branch committees that Molotov talked about started appearing immediately after the regional economic councils took over production and construction.

At the Presidium meeting on 27 March, Molotov heard many unpleasant comments about his note and his attitude:

> Pervukhin: ... Molotov disagrees on the very substance of the reorganization. The note is erroneous.
> Suslov: The very fact of presenting the note demands a Party protest. There is no loyalty. There is no good will. He wants to dissociate himself in advance from the Presidium ...
> Molotov: In Khrushchev's note [Khrushchev's response to Molotov], there are certain inaccuracies concerning my position. I submitted the note so that my well articulated proposals were considered.[37]

Molotov's reasoning on particular details was not heard. Everyone in the Presidium agreed that Molotov had cast aspersions on an issue of great importance.[38]

On 10 May, the USSR Supreme Soviet adopted the relevant law and introduced amendments to the USSR Constitution.[39] The territorial principle of administering industry and construction was prioritized over the branch. Ten all-Union ministries and 15 Union-Republic ministries that were located in Moscow along with 141 ministries all around the Soviet Union were abolished. Only a very small number of enterprises remained under the management of central ministries. Practically all industry and construction enterprises were transferred under the jurisdiction of the republican governments and 105 *sovnarkhozy*, which were created during May–June 1957: 70 in the RSFSR, 11 in Ukraine, nine in Kazakhstan, four in Uzbekistan and one in each of the other republics.[40] The *sovnarkhozy* were placed under sole jurisdiction of the republican governments, although the USSR CM retained the right to annul any decision of the *Sovnarkhoz* that was found economically irrational. On 29 August 1957 the central leadership issued another resolution that further enhanced the rights of the republican governments in economic and cultural issues.[41]

Conclusion

The switch in the approach to organizing the economic administration provoked by Khrushchev's January note was drastic. The policy of enhanced republican economic rights that was supplemental to the extension of the rights of the central *apparat* now dominated. The new policy prioritized territorial (republican and/or regional) development of industry and construction. Both the republics and the central *apparat* expected radical changes.

Khrushchev could not ignore the political gains that the reform would bring to him. The reform meant elevating the importance of the Party in economic decision making and consolidating the position of the republican-level authorities. At the same time, as some scholars concluded, reorganization was designed to weaken the influence of other aspirants to the position of supreme power in Moscow.[42]

Yet, regardless of whether political motivation prevailed, there was administrative logic in Khrushchev's decision to devolve economic decision making to the republics and regions, even though the organizational structure of the reform took this logic to the very extreme. By the end of 1956, after two years of increasing participation of the republics in economic administration, there was still no clear understanding as to how to effectively divide decision making between the centre and the republics. Khrushchev thought he had found a clear and simple solution: to let the peripheral managers run enterprises and let the centre work out the general policy for the branches. Khrushchev's reform, particularly its organizational structure, was indeed rather advanced for its time. It required setting a system of formal relations between the centre and the republics and the regions. The central *apparat* was not ready for this. The decentralized character of the reform did not and could not appeal to the central ex-ministerial bureaucracy, and yet it was they who were assigned to implement the reform.

Part II
Decentralization of decision making
Hopes and disillusionment

4 Setting new elements

To the Ukrainian republican authorities, the abolition of the industrial ministries was as much a surprise as it was to the central *apparat*. Like their counterparts in central offices, the Ukrainian ministries showed little enthusiasm for the new system.[1] Discussion of the reform started in the Party, the Soviets and Gosplan of Ukraine. Of a number of organizational issues which had to be resolved before the ministries ceased their managerial activity, two were most urgent: defining the new regionalization and setting a new system for channelling information from peripheral enterprises to Kiev and Moscow. The first issue was resolved almost successfully. The regions were determined, although in July–August there remained unfilled staff positions in the *sovnarkhozy* and Gosplan of Ukraine. The second issue was not resolved by the beginning of the reform, causing additional difficulties to the new managers and planners at both central and republican level.

Regionalization

By the time the reform was announced, the new regionalization had already been discussed on the pages of the Soviet press. At the end of 1956, in *Planovoe khozyaistvo* P. Alampiev pointed out that the existing regional net formed in 1939 had become obsolete.[2] It corresponded neither to the territorial nor to the economic complexes that had been formed since then, nor did it reflect the economic growth of the country. Guided by the Directives for the FYP which promoted development of complex regions and regional specialization, Alampiev proposed large regions that would not cross the boundaries of the republics, but which would unite several neighbouring small republics.[3] With the *Sovnarkhoz* reform, Alampiev's project could not be applied, as it would treat the republican governments unequally and thus contradict the republican policy announced at the XX Congress. The government of a small republic would have less influence on the *Sovnarkhoz* which would manage the industry of more than one republic than the government of a large republic where the *Sovnarkhoz* would not be concerned with the neighbouring economy.

As the reform was announced, a number of specialists and the *obkomy* secretaries proposed small regions, almost within the boundaries of the *oblasti*. Others, by contrast, took a more moderate approach and suggested forming one

Sovnarkhoz in each republic and dividing only large republics into several sovnarkhozy, 10–12 in the RSFSR, 3–4 in Ukraine, 2–3 in Kazakhstan.[4] Political considerations aside, the new regionalization had to consider the following aspects: specialization of the regions on an all-Union scale; the development of complex regions and interdependence of the industrial branches within them; and cooperation of enterprises inside the regions to avoid excessive transportation.[5]

Based on these principles, in Ukraine there were three projects. In February, the CC CPUk suggested eight regions.[6] Gosplan of Ukraine considered six. Ukrainian academics divided Ukraine into five large regions.[7] The numbers of the sovnarkhozy proposed by the Ukrainian organizations reflected their interest in the reform, or their lack of it. Party functionaries preferred forming as many economic regions consisting of one oblast' (oblasti-regions) as possible, building head-to-head relations with the sovnarkhozy and not competing over resources with other oblasti and, of course, imposing tight Party control over the sovnarkhozy. Three oblasti in the Party project formed separate economic regions: Voroshilovgrad, Stalino and Zaporozh'e. For the ex-ministerial bureaucracy whose interests were represented by Gosplan of Ukraine, the more oblasti that composed one economic region, the more industry they would run and the more solid their position would be in their relations with the obkomy, so no oblast' formed a separate economic region in their proposal. Ukrainian academics had no interests to pursue; like the planners, they proposed that none of the oblasti form a separate economic region.

By the end of April, all three projects were studied and rejected and to the CC CPSU, the CC CPUk submitted the final project where the number of the economic regions was eleven.[8] (Table 4.1)

Why was the number of regions for Ukraine changed? The documents do not give a definite answer. However, some explanation can be offered if we analyse the composition of the economic regions and the chairmen of the sovnarkhozy.

Eight out of 11 economic regions fell under tight control of the Party and/or a central appointee. Five economic regions consisted of one oblast' (Voroshilovgrad, Stalino, Dnepropetrovsk, Zaporozh'e and Odessa), of which the sovnarkhozy of

Table 4.1 Economic administrative regions of Ukraine, 1957

	Name of Sovnarkhoz	Oblasti included
1	Voroshilovgrad	Voroshilovgrad
2	Stalino	Stalino
3	Khar'kov	Khar'kov, Poltava, Sumy
4	Dnepropetrovsk	Dnepropetrovsk
5	Zaporozh'e	Zaporozh'e
6	Odessa	Odessa
7	Kherson	Kherson, Nikolaev, Crimea
8	Kiev	Kiev, Chernigov, Zhitomir, Cherkassy, Kirovograd
9	Vinnitsa	Vinnitsa, Khmel'nitskii
10	L'vov	L'vov, Ternopol', Volyn', Rovno
11	Stanislav	Stanislav, Drogobych, Zakarpat'e, Chernovtsy

Setting new elements 47

Dnepropetrovsk and Zaporozh'e were chaired by appointees coming from Moscow. The three other *sovnarkhozy* consisted of more than one *oblast'* (Khar'kov, Kherson and Kiev), but their chairmen also came from the centre (see Table 4.2).

Table 4.2 Chairmen of the Ukrainian *sovnarkhozy*, 1957

Name	Sovnarkhoz	Place of last job	Previous position
N.A. Tikhonov	Dnepropetrovsk	Moscow	Head of the main administration of pipe industry of the USSR Ministry of Ferrous Metallurgy
S.A. Skachkov	Khar'kov	Moscow	USSR First Deputy Minister of Transport Engineering
I.S. Pribyl'skii	Kherson	Moscow	USSR First Deputy Minister of the Shipbuilding Industry
P.Ya. Lysnyak	Kiev	Moscow	RSFSR Deputy Minister of the Automobile Transport Industry
V.N. Valuev	L'vov	Kiev	Vice-Chairman of the CM of Ukraine
P.V. Rudnitskii	Odessa	Kiev	Ukrainian Minister of the Food Industry
I.I. Dyadyk	Stalino	Stalino	Second secretary of Stalino *obkom*
A.P. Eremenko	Stanislav	Kiev	Chairman of the Union of industrial cooperation of Ukraine
V.V. Yapaskurt	Vinnitsa	Kiev	Head of *Ukrglavsakhar*
A.S. Kuz'mich	Voroshilovgrad	Kiev	Ukrainian Minister of Coal Mining
G.I. Ivanovskii	Zaporozh'e	Moscow	USSR Deputy Minister for Site Construction of the Metallurgical and Chemical Industry

Note: The first and second columns of this table are based on the Resolution of the CC CPUk 'On chairmen of *sovnarkhozy* of UkSSR', 28 May 1957, TsDAGOU, f. 1, op. 6, d. 2643, ll. 3–4. Information on Tikhonov and Skachkov in A.A. Fursenko (ed.), *Prezidium TsK KPSS. 1954–1964. Chernovye protokol'nye zapisi zasedanii. Stenogrammy. Postanovleniya. T. 1: Chernovye protokol'nye zapisi zasedanii. Stenogrammy*. Moscow: ROSSPEN, 2004, pp. 1281, 1288; on Pribyl'skii, *Spravochnik po istorii Kommunisticheskoi partii i Sovetskogo Soyuza 1898–1991*, available HTTP: http://www.knowbysight.info/PPP/04986.asp (accessed 10 August 2010); on Lysnyak, *Spravochnik po istorii Kommunisticheskoi partii i Sovetskogo Soyuza 1898–1991*, available HTTP: http://www.knowbysight.info/LLL/04988.asp (accessed 10 August 2010); on Valuev, in *Politicheskoe rukovodstvo Ukrainy 1938–1989*, sost. V.Yu. Vasil'ev [et al.], Moscow: ROSSPEN, 2006, p. 477; on Rudnitskii and Kuz'mich, in Minutes of the meeting of the CC CPUk Secretariat held on 6 January 1956, TsDAGOU, f. 1, op. 8, d. 2217, l. 3; on Dyadyk, *Spravochnik po istorii Kommunisticheskoi partii i Sovetskogo Soyuza 1898–1991*, available HTTP: http://www.knowbysight.info/DDD/04878.asp (accessed 10 August 2010); on Eremenko, *Spravochnik po istorii Kommunisticheskoi partii i Sovetskogo Soyuza 1898–1991*, available HTTP: http://www.knowbysight.info/YeYY/04978.asp (accessed 10 August 2010); on Yapaskurt, in Proposition to invite employees of the abolished all-Union ministries to work in the Ukrainian ministries made by N. Podgornyi and O. Ivashchenko to A. Kirichenko, 13 March 1956, TsDAGOU, f. 1, op. 24, d. 4294, l. 65; TsDAGOU, f.1, op. 6, d. 2643, l. 4; on Ivanovskii, Personal file of Ivanovskii Georgii Ivanovich, 10 October 1961, State archive of Zaporozh'e *oblast'*, f. P2540, op. 25, d. 186.

The economic importance of the *sovnarkhozy* in question was very high. More than 92 per cent of coal mining in Ukraine was concentrated in Voroshilovgrad and Stalino *oblasti* and almost 93 per cent of the extraction of iron-ore was concentrated in Dnepropetrovsk and Zaporozh'e.[9] At the same time, by 1957, the share of Ukraine in the all-Union production of coal was almost 33 per cent and iron-ore was 56.1 per cent. The eight economic regions produced 50 per cent of the all-Union output of cast iron, 38.4 per cent of steel and 40.3 per cent of rolled metal.[10] As for Odessa, it accounted for half of Ukraine's export of machine-building and for more than 50 per cent of all Soviet exports by sea.[11] In 1955, the Khar'kov economic region generated 15.4 per cent of gross Ukrainian output, including 25.5 per cent of the output of the Ukrainian machine-building industry; Kherson and Kiev *sovnarkhozy* combined generated 30.5 per cent of gross Ukrainian output. The total economic value of the eight regions in the Fifth FYP was estimated at about 88 per cent of gross output of Ukraine, including 100 per cent of iron-ore production; 76.7 per cent of the Ukrainian machine-building industry; 79 per cent of agricultural production; 73 per cent of meat production; about 60 per cent of investment; and about 89 per cent of state investments. The value of the remaining 'unsupervised' three regions was about 12 per cent of gross output and 11 per cent of investment.[12]

On the basis of what has been stated above, regionalization that divided Ukraine into eleven economic regions appears to have been a consensus between the Party's interest to have as many *oblasti*-regions as possible and the interests of the *central* ex-ministerial bureaucracy that sought to retain control over the most important industrial centres. However, at the same time, the fact that none of the new *sovnarkhozy* obtained total management control of all the major production sources points to the Party as the body that dictated the new regionalization.[13]

Staff for the sovnarkhozy

The *sovnarkhozy* had republican jurisdiction and so were subordinated solely to the republican governments. The selection, proposal and approval of staff for the *sovnarkhozy* was formally done by the CC CPUk and the *obkomy*, depending on the position of the appointee, but was discussed with the ministries.[14] The five chairmen sent from Moscow must have been proposed by the CC CPSU and/or the USSR CM, although it is equally possible that they were proposed by the CC CPUk, since all of them had worked in Ukraine before.[15] The second secretary of Donetsk *obkom* A. Lyashko described the procedure:

> *Obkomy* second secretaries prepared personnel lists for the newly created economic administrations. Candidates for the key positions were then introduced to the first and other *obkom* secretaries. After the *obkom* bureau approved them, they became members of the *obkom nomenklatura*.[16]

Candidates for the chairmen and vice-chairmen of *sovnarkhozy* were proposed to the CC CPUk by the second secretary of the CC CPUk N.V. Podgornyi (at the

Setting new elements 49

end of 1957 he replaced A.I. Kirichenko and became the First Secretary) and the CC CPUk secretaries O.I. Ivashchenko and I.I. Vivdychenko.[17] The candidatures of all members of the *Sovnarkhoz* had then to be approved by the CC CPUk. The chairmen of *sovnarkhozy* were also members of the CC CPSU Presidium nomenclature.[18] Therefore the CC CPSU Presidium had to approve them as well. All chairmen of the Ukrainian *sovnarkhozy* came from the ministerial *apparat*, except one, Ivan Dyadyk. Dyadyk was the only chairman of *Sovnarkhoz* in Ukraine who was local and had previously worked in the Party organization.[19]

Positions within the *sovnarkhozy* were to be filled mainly by locals, which was a problem since there was a shortage of qualified staff in the republic. The staff of the *sovnarkhozy* could be, and were to some small extent, filled by ex-ministerial functionaries. Functionaries from Kiev and Moscow generally resisted moving to the periphery and the local authorities did not insist on them coming for one simple reason, the shortage of housing. The total staff of the *sovnarkhozy* was put at 8,094 people in June 1957 and 8,192 people in August when the *sovnarkhozy* of Voroshilovgrad, L'vov and Stalino obtained additional staff posts. By July 1957, 85.8 per cent of staff posts in the *sovnarkhozy* had been filled and by 1 August the figure was 92.4 per cent (Table 4.3)[20]

Wages in the *sovnarkhozy* differed depending on the category of the *Sovnarkhoz*. The 103 *sovnarkhozy* all over the country were divided into four categories. Two others, the *sovnarkhozy* of Moscow and Moscow *oblast'*, were not assigned to any of the categories and paid the highest wages. Five Ukrainian *sovnarkhozy* were in the first category with the highest wages: Voroshilovgrad, Dnepropetrovsk, Kiev, Stalino and Khar'kov. In the second category, there were the *sovnarkhozy* of Zaporozh'e and Kherson and in the third, Vinnitsa, L'vov, Odessa and Stanislav.[21]

Table 4.3 Information on the staff of the Ukrainian *sovnarkhozy* on 18 June 1957

Name of Sovnarkhoz	Required No. of employees	Already selected	Including from				Approved employees	
			Moscow	Kiev	Dnepr*	Stalino	No.	Per cent
Vinnitsa	380	182		45			122	32.11
Voroshilovgrad	1050	741	3			201	610	58.10
Dnepropetrovsk	860	549	2		547		148	17.21
Zaporozh'e	590	207	9	17	7		197	33.39
Kiev	950	661	6	655			350	36.84
L'vov	410	184		20			137	33.41
Odessa	390	155	1	9			75	19.23
Stalino	1648	1356	1	1	20	1334	1356	82.28
Stanislav	446	137	1	26			129	28.92
Khar'kov	910	384	9	9			348	38.24
Kherson	460	205	2	25			155	33.70
Total:	8094	4761	34	807	574	1536**	3627	44.81

Note: Information on the staff of the Ukrainian *sovnarkhozy* available on 18 June 1957, TsDAGOU, f. 1, op. 31, d. 872, l. 17.
* Dnepropetrovsk.
** This number is in the document.

50 *Decentralization of decision making*

No Ukrainian *Sovnarkhoz* was in the fourth category with the lowest salaries. This classification prompted lots of *sovnarkhozy* to petition the CC CPSU to transfer them to a category with higher salaries.[22]

Staff for Gosplan of Ukraine

Similarly to the *sovnarkhozy*, Gosplan of Ukraine also lacked qualified personnel. With the reform, the number of professional staff increased from 465 to 1750 people[23] and by July 1957, 73.7 per cent of the staff posts had been filled.[24] Top positions were not hard to fill. According to Hough, Gosplan of Ukraine 'contained one former USSR minister, two former USSR deputy ministers, five deputy chairmen of the CMUk and six Ukrainian ministers'.[25] However, to fill the positions in the branch departments for coal mining, the metallurgical, chemical, mechanical engineering industries and the department for site construction of the metallurgical industry, Gosplan of Ukraine struggled to find planners and managers. Coming from Moscow, Stalino or Dnepropetrovsk to work in Kiev, the majority of them had to accept lower salaries. Moreover, in 1957, the wages of the top employees of Gosplan of Ukraine (including heads of the departments and their deputies) were 10 per cent lower than the wages of employees of the same category of Gosplan of RSFSR.[26] The Vice-Chairman of Gosplan of Ukraine Petr Rozenko tried to obtain an increase for the specialists in at least the coal and metallurgical industries, arguing that the output volumes of these industries in Ukraine were no smaller than those in the RSFSR.[27]

Information: statistical agencies

Along with the ministries, the reform also abolished their statistical departments which had collected and processed information on the performance of industry and construction. At the February 1957 Plenum, it was decided to address this by extending the functions and the network of the TsSU. The original idea for channelling information was quite straightforward. Production information had to be transferred from the production unit directly to the centrally controlled vertical chain of statistical agencies: *oblstatupravlenie* (*oblast'* statistical agency)/ *raistatupravlenie* (*raion* statistical agency), *Ukrstatupravlenie* (Ukrainian statistical agency which until 1960 stayed under the direct jurisdiction of the TsSU), the TsSU. The *Sovnarkhoz*, the *obkom* and the *oblispolkom* would obtain information from the *oblstatupravlenie*, and the CC CPUk, the CMUk and Gosplan of Ukraine would report to the *Ukrstatupravlenie*. However, as the first months of the reform had shown, before it could be developed, the system had to be created practically from scratch.

By 1957, each ministry had its established system for reporting indices of a general and specific nature. Information that was collected by the statistical agencies was of secondary importance to the ministries, as well as to the USSR Gosplan and *Gosekonomkomissiya*. As a result, during the 5–6 years preceding the reform, the TsSU insisted that the peripheral statistical offices reduced the size of their reports and included as few economic indices as possible. With the *Sovnarkhoz* reform, local statistical agencies were instructed to do the opposite and include as many indices in the reports as possible, to restore what had been taken out during the last 5–6 years.[28]

As the reform started, Ukrainian peripheral statisticians were not up to the task. At their meeting in Kiev in August 1957, regional statisticians discussed a number of difficulties they had faced, from the simplest to the most complicated. In some regions, Odessa for example, data processing centres had not been formed. Where they had been formed, they could not start functioning because they lacked equipment. In certain cases, statisticians did not have enough calculators.[29] More serious difficulties were related to the methodology of calculations. From the TsSU, the local agencies received instructions that were hardly applicable. To quote Denisova from the Kiev statistical office:

> Lately they [the TsSU] write entire books on major construction, three books in six months, in fact. Physically we cannot read and study all these instructions. They describe everything to the last paragraph, but the content of each paragraph, how to calculate it, this you will not find in any instruction. Everyone is calculating in his own way and there are tonnes of mistakes.[30]

Besides, the instructions arrived with enormous delays, leaving no time for the local agents to study and apply them.[31] So, the methods for calculating indices were individualized. Furthermore, local statisticians had to apply different methods for calculating the same indices for different industries: 'For industrial statistics, there is an applied method of drafting reports according to the branch principle; for major construction works, according to the territorial'.[32]

The most acute problem was nonetheless the availability of data from enterprises. Moscow was not specific on who should draft what, and enterprises were not informed on which data they should provide to the *oblstatupravleniya*. Khar'kov statistician, Chernyavskii, described the situation:

> We are required to obtain information, or supplementary data, that enterprises, at least lots of them, had never calculated. We are forced now, under the pressing demand of the *Ukrstatupravlenie*, to get these data. But it is not so simple. Try to get information on tools. In the instruction, it is stated that we should show all instruments. We decided to ask the TsSU whether we should collect data on all tools or just on commercial tools. They replied, just on commercial. It is the same with lathes and hundreds of other products. Eighty per cent of the products listed in the TsSU reference book are produced in our *oblast'*; and all these data we should collect from enterprises in other *oblasti*.[33]

So, how reliable could the information provided by *oblstatupravleniya* possibly be? Well, it was not reliable and this was not a secret. The head of Odessa *oblstatupravlenie* Zhitkevich stated this out loud at a meeting in August:

> We are spending all our time on drafting reports. As for the audits, we have started to forget about them. At the same time, the *glavki* are no longer there and the *sovnarkhozy* do not make audits. Quite often they include upward distortions. Sometimes they add, or include in planned or commercial production what is not supposed to be included. We have simply no time to take care of this. And it should be taken care of. ... The engineering industry is reporting 100–100.1 per cent [of the fulfilment of the plan], whereas it is clear that they are not even close to 100 per cent. In any case, there is an upward distortion there.[34]

It was common practice to communicate corrected indices after the scheduled report had been submitted. The notions of 'correct' or 'actual' data thereby became relative. Which data should ultimately be considered in the case of the Stanislav statistical agency if data on production for the first half of 1957 were changed three times?[35] Still, correcting information was not the hardest part of the work of the statisticians. The hardest part was to obtain any information at all. Markin from the *Ukrstatupravlenie* complained about the head of the department for industrial statistics of the Stanislav statistical agency:

> Comrade Kats is acting most unworthily. Our employees call him, they request information by phone. Comrade Kats usually asks them to wait a minute so that he can get the material. He leaves the phone, time passes, com. Kats does not come back to the phone. Then the line is disconnected. All this is repeated many times.[36]

Reliance solely on information collected by the local statistical agencies complicated decision making and control over the performance of peripheral managers for republican and all-Union economic authorities. To reduce their dependence on the statisticians, they immediately adopted the practice of directly approaching enterprises for the necessary information. Direct contacts contributed to the growth of administrative *apparat* in the *sovnarkhozy* and in the republican and central planning and controlling agencies.

Sovnarkhozy: functions and rights

At the beginning of 1957, Ukrainian industry was run by 34 all-Union ministries and departments, 18 Union-Republic and 15 Republic ministries. Construction works were performed by 1,712 construction-assembling organizations of 50 ministries and departments.[37] On 1 July 1957, almost all of them (all industrial) ceased to exist. Their operational authority was transferred to eleven councils of the national economy, *sovnarkhozy*, that had been created in each economic administrative region, the CMUk, but mainly Gosplan of Ukraine, and USSR

Gosplan. All necessary information on the supplies and funds assigned to the enterprises and construction sites for 1957 was communicated to the *sovnarkhozy*.[38]

Ukrainian *sovnarkhozy* included functional departments, branch departments, trusts and groups of enterprises (*kombinaty*). On top of each *Sovnarkhoz* there was a council, *Sovet*. It was planned that the councils of *sovnarkhozy* would have 7–10 members;[39] however, eventually the size of the councils increased to 9–11 members. The Stalino *Sovnarkhoz*, for example, had 13 members. The council of a *Sovnarkhoz* included a chairman, his deputies (from two to four, depending on the size of the economic administrative region) and heads of the branch departments. The *sovnarkhozy* also had technical and economic councils.[40] From April 1960, according to the USSR CM resolution, the councils of the *sovnarkhozy* included directors of the largest enterprises and construction sites. Importantly, among the members of the councils of the *sovnarkhozy* there were no *obkom* secretaries, despite the fact that the Party was key in introducing the *sovnarkhozy*.[41]

The main task for the *sovnarkhozy* was to ensure the fulfilment of all targets fixed in the state production and construction plans by all enterprises and construction organizations under their jurisdiction.[42] At the same time, from the very start of the reform, the economic plan of an enterprise or an organization was considered unfulfilled if the contractual (*kooperativnye*) deliveries envisaged by the state plans, or by specific resolutions of the USSR CM or the CM of the Union republic, or by the plans of the ministries, were not made. 'The bonus assigned for the fulfilment of the plan will not be paid in this case'.[43]

The *Sovnarkhoz* was expected to establish rational economic relations inside the region; use natural resources in the most rational way; develop specialization and cooperation with due regard to the already existing production relations inside the economic region; use the available production capacities to manufacture above-plan volumes of the materials, spare parts and equipment for construction; determine current and future demand for specialists with higher and specialized education; replace old production norms in a timely manner; improve the administration and eliminate superfluous departments; and so on.[44] At the same time, the *sovnarkhozy* had to obtain approval from a higher authority when establishing economic relations with enterprises from other regions, setting the norms for the utilization of materials, fuel and electric energy in production and construction or the norms for production reserves, or drafting proposals on prices of production that had to be priced only by higher authorities.[45] Almost 90 paragraphs in the Regulations on a *Sovnarkhoz* stated the rights of the *sovnarkhozy* in planning, major construction works, deliveries, financing and credit, and labour and wages. The most important paragraphs are mentioned very briefly below. Given the absence of restraining mechanisms, they permitted the *sovnarkhozy* to prioritize their own economic interests.

In planning, the *sovnarkhozy* could establish and modify the targets for their enterprises within the limits set by the state plans; they could also assign supplementary targets in addition to those already adopted. They could modify, in agreement with the customer, the volume and terms of deliveries of certain types of production, although all changes had to be introduced into the plan and communicated to the republic Gosplan and could not affect the budget.[46]

In material and technical supply, the *sovnarkhozy* could distribute and redistribute raw materials, materials, fuel, equipment and means of transportation among the regional enterprises, organizations and administration.[47] (In 1959, this right was revoked and the *sovnarkhozy* were no longer authorized to redistribute materials, fuel, equipment and the means of transportation between the branches or construction sites.) The *sovnarkhozy* also had the right to sell production that was not sold to the holders of the funds and to redistribute or sell unused and surplus material, equipment and other valuables. An important paragraph concerned the right to use funded materials, spare parts, finished products and equipment produced above the plan. This production could only go towards the needs of public housing or municipal construction, for mechanization of production processes or towards the improvement of work conditions in industry and construction. However, the Ukrainian government revised the last paragraph and allowed the *sovnarkhozy* to keep only 50 per cent of the above-plan production.[48]

In finance and credit, the *sovnarkhozy* had the right to redistribute savings at the end of the year among enterprises and to create a reserve fund to provide financial help to enterprises and organizations.[49] Paragraphs 108, 109 and 110 allowed the *sovnarkhozy* to improve their financial situation: the *sovnarkhozy* could fix, in accordance with the main consumer (a ministry or another *Sovnarkhoz*), temporary wholesale prices of new mass production, although these prices had to be approved by a higher authority. The *sovnarkhozy* could fix, in accordance with planning organs of the republic or *oblast'*, temporary wholesale prices valid for a period up to six months for new consumer goods if these goods were not yet priced. They could also fix wholesale prices for production manufactured for enterprises of the same economic region, if that production had not been already priced.[50] These particular paragraphs provided the *sovnarkhozy* with a legitimate basis to increase profits without introducing any technological innovations.

The area where the *sovnarkhozy* were least flexible was labour and wages. Considering that the workers and employees were no longer attached to the enterprises and were free to leave at any time, the *sovnarkhozy* were still not granted any rights that would allow them to attract more labour. As in other areas, the *sovnarkhozy* had to stay within the limits of the allotted funds and follow centrally approved estimates within the budget. However, the chapter on labour and wages was the one in which the central organizations are mentioned most often. No matter what a regional economic organization decided on the issue of labour or wages, it had to be approved by the USSR CM State Committee for Labour and Wages, the USSR Ministry of Finance and various departments of *Gosbank* or the All-union Central Council of Trade Unions (VTsSPS).[51]

The Regulations on a *Sovnarkhoz* only formally and indicatively defined the margins of authority of the *sovnarkhozy*. As shown below, their real power, particularly during the first three years of the reform, extended further.

5 First disillusionment
Plan for 1958

The *Sovnarkhoz* reform targeted the problem of unbalanced planning that had been broadly discussed in 1956 and was supposed to resolve the inapplicability of plans. According to the economic journal *Planovoe khozyaistvo*, shortcomings in planning were supposed to be eliminated by reinforcing planning and increasing the role of USSR Gosplan.[1] USSR Gosplan, in charge of both perspective and current planning after the abolition of *Gosekonomkomissiya*,[2] would concentrate on ensuring the proportional development of the industrial branches, republics and economic regions and on planning production investment. It should communicate its decisions on the most rational economic relations, specialization, cooperation and investments, only through these plans.[3] At the same time, it was up to the republics and *sovnarkhozy* to propose the best utilization of local resources and the specialization of the regions, as well as pointing to the economic, geographical and cultural peculiarities of each republic or region.[4] In response to republican demands from previous years, volume targets for industrial production, wages and cost price would now be assigned to each republic without specifying separate targets for each industrial branch. The targets for gross output and commercial production would also be assigned to the republics in total. It was now the responsibility of the republican CM to assign the targets to the *sovnarkhozy* and *oblispolkomy* for local industry.[5]

The transfer of most current and perspective planning to the republics inevitably promoted republic Gosplans to a key position in the Soviet economic administration. Before the reform Ukraine fully planned only one-tenth of its own production; now it had to plan more than 96 per cent of the republic's gross output.[6] Before the reform Gosplan of Ukraine distributed funded materials for only a limited number of Ukrainian ministries and departments. Now it was in charge of supplying practically the entire republican economy.

The Ukrainian leadership was very enthusiastic about the centrality of Gosplan of Ukraine's new role. Suffice to say, in a very early proposal on the new administrative system, the CC CPUk defined Gosplan of Ukraine as 'the main organization for state planning in the republic', with no mention of USSR Gosplan's authority over Gosplan of Ukraine.[7] Of course, in spring 1958 when USSR Gosplan legalized the status of Gosplan of Ukraine, this perception was corrected. Gosplan of Ukraine was characterized as the sole representative of

USSR Gosplan in the republic with vast functions, as a scientific organ of republican planning which, following the tasks announced in the economic plan of the USSR and through the plans of the economic development of the republic, had to ensure that the interests of the economic development of the entire Soviet Union were pursued.[8] This role for Gosplan of Ukraine corresponded far more to Khrushchev's rhetoric at the 7th Session of the Supreme Soviet in May 1957 than the statement of the CC CPUk. 'If the question is studied more closely', said Khrushchev, 'there can be but one conclusion: it is only a matter of transferring the centralism nearer to the localities where the immediate economic process develops, i.e., not less, but more centralization'.[9] Yet, regardless of the status that the centre assigned to it, Gosplan of Ukraine took over its new responsibilities under the perception that it was the ultimate economic – not just planning – authority in the republic and that the *Sovnarkhoz* reform had been launched for the benefit of the republics. This perception manifested itself most vividly during the preparation of the production plan for 1958.

1958: planning 'from below'

The 1958 plan had to be drafted 'from below'. To Ukraine, USSR Gosplan communicated only indicative limits for certain products.[10] The enterprises and *sovnarkhozy* were expected to discover new and reveal previously concealed resources and production capacities and establish real investment needs. Along the chain, the draft plans were to be submitted by enterprises to the combines (*kombinaty*), then to the *Sovnarkhoz*. The draft plans of the *sovnarkhozy* would then be examined in the republic Gosplans and finally in the USSR Gosplan. The USSR Gosplan and the republic Gosplans would discuss the drafts and, after the USSR CM had adopted the final draft, it would be sent back to the republics. The republic Gosplans would disaggregate the targets among the branches, the *sovnarkhozy* and soviets of the *oblasti* and *kraya*.[11]

In practice, the compilation of the 1958 draft plan for Ukraine followed a different scenario. As envisioned, drafting of the 1958 plan started at the enterprises. But already in July 1957, at the early stage of compiling the plan, the planners from the general department of current plans of Gosplan of Ukraine travelled to the economic regions in order to supervise the peripheral planners, recommend how to eliminate the problems that were revealed and assist the *sovnarkhozy* and *oblispolkomy* in compiling the plans.

In the regions, they discovered several problems. First, not all *sovnarkhozy* had a clear idea of the production capacity of their enterprises. Many enterprises were not registered. So the lists of enterprises, construction sites and organizations under the management of the *sovnarkhozy* were not complete and it was not always clear to which branch enterprises belonged. Second, despite the fact that they did not have complete information about regional industry, the *sovnarkhozy* continued the tradition of the abolished ministries and for 1958 asked for substantially more investment than their regions received in 1957. Third, peripheral planners lacked information on demand, which complicated planning for some

First disillusionment 57

industries, namely engineering. Fourth, statistical agencies were not ready to keep track of inventories and thus could not provide necessary data. Fifth, the *sovnarkhozy* failed to uncover any additional production capacity.[12]

Under the circumstances, the simplest and fastest way for Gosplan of Ukraine to submit a draft of the 1958 plan for the republic to USSR Gosplan in time was to compose the plan generally, disregarding the targets proposed by the *sovnarkhozy*, with minimum assistance from the regional planners and relying on the information that they already had and received directly from the enterprises and plants. This is what Gosplan of Ukraine did.[13] Neglecting the targets proposed by the *sovnarkhozy* caused the first major conflict between the regional and the republican planners. These disagreements were discussed at a meeting in the CMUk held on 7 January 1958. Gosplan of Ukraine argued that it had superior competence. The *sovnarkhozy* argued that the republican planners had exceeded their authority (although at the moment of the January discussion, contrary to the *sovnarkhozy* whose authority had by then been enshrined in statute (by the *Sovnarkhoz* Regulations of 26 September 1957), the margins of authority of Gosplan of Ukraine and the regulative authority governing relations between Gosplan of Ukraine and the *sovnarkhozy* and USSR Gosplan had not been determined).

According to Gosplan of Ukraine, the *sovnarkhozy* were simply not ready for their first planning assignment and the republican planners had to save the situation. The main complaint about the draft plans composed by the *sovnarkhozy*, *oblispolkomy* and the remaining Ukrainian ministries was that they did not consider the needs of the republican economy, not to mention the needs of the country, and proposed indices based on the production volumes of the previous year.[14] In other words, they did not demand higher outputs and lower inputs. At the same time, the republican planners had reasons to argue that they were more competent to set the production targets for the *sovnarkhozy* than the *sovnarkhozy* themselves. Soon after the February 1957 CC CPSU Plenum, Gosplan of Ukraine had carried out a study of the republican regions, since it had been instructed to compose the production plan for these territories back in 1957. At that time, the republican planners had gone to the major *oblasti* and analysed the possibilities for the development of complex regions and the elimination of irrational transportation and wasteful construction costs, as well as for improved cooperation within the *oblasti* and uncovering unused reserves.[15]

The chairmen of the *sovnarkhozy* saw the situation differently. They saw it as a conflict of power between them and Gosplan of Ukraine. From their perspective, Gosplan of Ukraine attempted to undermine their authority in the regions and establish centralized management at the level of Kiev, which contradicted the newly promulgated system that the *sovnarkhozy* had the ultimate economic authority in the regions. As the Chairman of the Khar'kov *Sovnarkhoz* put it: 'Under no circumstances should Gosplan of Ukraine contact enterprises directly and communicate its decisions directly to them, but this had happened'.[16] The *sovnarkhozy* were equally frustrated with the fact that to some of them, Gosplan of Ukraine had not even bothered to communicate the new plan.[17] The Chairman of the Kherson *Sovnarkhoz* I. Pribyl'skii complained that for some products of machine-building, the plan was completely changed and discussions on this had been held on the telephone just a few days before.[18]

The second problem for the chairmen of the *sovnarkhozy* was the organizational structure of Gosplan of Ukraine: it was different from the structure of the *sovnarkhozy*. Branch barriers were eliminated in the *sovnarkhozy*, but in Gosplan, industrial enterprises were distributed according to the branch principle, which meant that the *sovnarkhozy* had to address numerous departments and sub-departments.[19] Thereby, since the work of a large number of production sites had to be planned by several branch departments, the complex development of these sites was impossible for Gosplan of Ukraine.[20] The chairmen of the *sovnarkhozy* did not dispute that their draft plans were unacceptable, but they strongly objected to Gosplan of Ukraine's intention to overrule their authority. As the former Ukrainian Minister of Coal Mining, now the Chairman of the Voroshilovgrad *Sovnarkhoz*, A. Kuz'mich put it, the problem was that Gosplan of Ukraine got too much authority and attempted to establish tutelage over the regional economic councils.[21]

What both republican and peripheral planners failed to mention was the lack of professional planners in Kiev, and particularly in the regions, although at this stage of the reform this problem was unavoidable. In spring 1957, A. Omarovskii from the Institute of Scientific Research of USSR Gosplan explained that the petty tutelage of enterprises practised by USSR Gosplan and the ministries during the Second World War resulted in a reduction in the number of peripheral specialists qualified in planning. 'Even today, there are no textbooks on general economic planning, or planning of industrial branches, or planning for economic regions'.[22]

1958 production plan drafted by Gosplan of Ukraine

Comments by the republican planners on the flaws in the draft plans compiled by their regional colleagues implied that such mistakes would be avoided in their draft plan for the republic. Yet the examination of the Ukrainian draft plan in USSR Gosplan in September 1957 demonstrated that this was not the case. Similarly to the situation inside Ukraine, where the conflict of power manifested between the *sovnarkhozy* and Gosplan of Ukraine, in Moscow a conflict of interests was apparent between USSR Gosplan and Gosplan of Ukraine, the latter being supported by the CC CPUk. In the draft plan for the republic, Gosplan of Ukraine prioritized republican needs, whereas USSR Gosplan adjusted the republican draft to the needs of the entire country.

In particular, according to USSR Gosplan, Ukraine underestimated its gross output by 4.7 billion roubles in 1957 and, consequently, by 6 billion roubles in the 1958 draft plan. Commercial production was underestimated by 5.3 billion roubles in 1957 and by 5.7 billion roubles in the draft plan for 1958.[23] Ukraine a) understated production targets for heavy industry and overstated production targets for the light and food industries and machine-building; b) understated

Table 5.1 Some 1958 plan indices presented by Ukraine and rejected by USSR Gosplan

	Planned increase of production in comparison to 1957		Planned increase of consumption in comparison to 1957	
	Thousand tonnes	Per cent	Thousand tonnes	Per cent
Cast iron	747	4	1457	Almost 10
Rolled metal	785	4.9	1810	21.5
Fertilizer	269	8.4	Doubled	200
Cement	629	N/a	2850 or 5 times	500

Note: Based on the Report of USSR Gosplan from 24 January 1958. Chapter 'On manifestations of *mestnichestvo* and other shortcomings in the work of the *sovnarkhozy*', RGAE, f. 4372, op. 57, d. 203, ll. 61–2.

investment targets for heavy industry and overstated investment targets for consumer goods, the food industry and machine-building; c) reduced deliveries of meat and milk to the all-Union funds;[24] and d) increased production and consumption of certain products but reduced deliveries of these products to other republics and the all-Union funds.

The Ukrainian leadership clearly indicated what it expected from the reform: to change the balance between the industries of groups 'A' and 'B' and meet the demand of the Ukrainian population for consumer goods and food, but also to meet the needs of Ukrainian industry in inputs of Ukrainian origin (see Tables 5.1 and 5.2). Effectively, Ukraine proposed changing the existing practice whereby outputs were distributed by central agencies to one that allowed the republic to meet domestic demand with domestic products.

USSR Gosplan could not accept the Ukrainian draft plan. If the Ukrainian figures were accepted, USSR Gosplan explained, deliveries of rolled metal to other republics would decrease by more than 1 million tonnes, deliveries of cement by almost 2 million tonnes and of fertilizer by more than 1 million tonnes. The republican turnover of consumer goods and food products would increase by 12.4 per cent in 1958 but the supplies of these products to other republics would

Table 5.2 Planned domestic supply and export of some consumer goods, 1957

	Increase of domestic supply compared to 1957 (per cent)	Decrease of deliveries outside the republic compared to 1957 (per cent)
Motorcycles	10	30
Electric irons	47	51
Electric lamps	9.5	32
High-quality china	5	23
Enamel and iron cooking ware	7	23
Vacuum cleaners	10	13

Note: RGAE, f. 4372, op. 57, d. 167, l. 10; RGAE, f. 4372, op. 57, d. 203, l. 62.

decrease by an unknown figure.[25] Increasing consumption at the expense of deliveries to other republics was unacceptable 'because that would force other republics to set up production which is more profitable in Ukraine',[26] the central planners insisted.

A sensitive issue for USSR Gosplan was Ukraine's intention to change the balance between heavy and light industries. To respond to the USSR Gosplan's concerns, the Ukrainian government 'found it possible' to launch in 1958 three blast-furnaces and increase the production of cast iron, steel, rolled metal and ore, but they disagreed that this increase should be funded from the republican budget. The Ukrainian leadership pointed to the fact that since the purpose of the reform was to uncover concealed production capacity, for 1958 Ukraine had already been assigned much less capital investment than for 1957. Increasing capital investment by 138.2 per cent in ferrous metallurgy and the ore industry, by 133.5 per cent in the oil and gas industry, by 130.3 per cent in the chemical industry and 120.8 per cent in the sugar industry, as requested by the central planners, meant cutting investments for other branches and areas of social and cultural life in the republic. Investment in machine-building would then fall to 81.2 per cent of the investments made in 1957, to 63 per cent in the defence industry, to 62.1 per cent in the industry of construction materials, to 52 per cent in the municipal economy, to 70 per cent in education and culture, to just above 75 per cent in public health and to 70 per cent in science.[27] Equally alarming was Ukraine's intention to redirect centrally allocated funds into areas where the centre did not intend to make any allocations. For example, Ukraine wanted to spend a share of the funds assigned for coal production and ferrous metallurgy on communal (*kommunal'noe*) construction.[28] (The argument that the funds were urgently needed in construction was disregarded by the central planners.)

USSR Gosplan disagreed with the proposal that Ukraine should produce more electricity and fixed the republic's growth target at 13.5 per cent for 1958, or 5 per cent less than in 1956. This target left Ukraine, which produced 19 per cent of the all-Union gross output and which was home to a quarter of the Union's population, with 9 per cent less energy per person than the all-Union average.[29] For agricultural production, USSR Gosplan expected Ukraine to deliver 56 per cent of its state meat reserves to the all-Union fund, a considerable increase from the 42 per cent contributed by Ukraine in 1957. The new quota reduced planned state supplies of meat to the Ukrainian population from 16.3 kg per person in 1957 to 12.2 kg in 1958. USSR Gosplan also expected Ukraine to increase deliveries of milk to the all-Union fund: Ukraine proposed delivering 40 per cent of its production; USSR Gosplan insisted on 48 per cent.[30]

Ukraine was not alone in concluding that during the *Sovnarkhoz* reform it would direct economic development. Other republics concluded the same. For example, in the 1958 draft plan composed by the RSFSR, USSR Gosplan saw the same tendencies: the growth of production of some goods was not high enough, the volume of construction and assembly works (*stroitel'no-montazhnykh*) exceeded the established limits, capital investments into construction were dispersed, growth targets for labour productivity and reduction of production costs were understated and supplies were not correlated with the manufacture of the most important products. The RSFSR also hoped to reduce supplies to other republics in 1958 and also underestimated its gross output in 1957.[31] In Latvia, some prominent functionaries in the governmental and Party *apparat* did not give up on the idea until 1960 and insisted that the investment in and consumption of the output of consumer goods industries inside the republic should be increased, whereas the development of machine-building and car-building industries, the output of which was necessary for the whole country, was slowed down. Their position was shared by some economists from the Latvian Gosplan and the Latvian Academy of Sciences' Institute for Economy.[32]

Conclusion

The republics proved Khrushchev wrong when relying on peripheral managers to reveal production capacities previously concealed by the ministries. Similarly to the ministries, the republics prioritized their own economic comfort. They also proved him wrong when relying on the republic-level authorities to maintain the existing economic complex, which from the perspective of the centre meant the integrity of the Soviet economy. At the first opportunity, they sought to reduce their dependence on the centre and increase consumption of their own output. The policy of prioritizing their own economic development thus took on strong political connotations.

The central planners understood that. Indeed, given mere lack of time or resources to verify the plan indices proposed by the republics or to study the new model of inter-republican and centre–republican economic relations that the republics proposed in their plans, the central planners could not objectively insist on the economic inapplicability of the new model. So USSR Gosplan's rhetoric about 'unhealthy and parasitical' tendencies 'to build closed economies inside the *sovnarkhozy*, inside the republics',[33] or cutting out economic ties with non-domestic customers, was first and foremost a political response to the republics.[34]

The experiment with compiling the 1958 plan was a unique experience in which the republican governments were given an opportunity to express their vision about the development of their economies and centre–republic economic relations. It had also demonstrated, at the very beginning of the reform, that the rhetoric and aims of the reform contradicted the interests of the principal executive or the architect of the reform, USSR Gosplan. The reform called for the development of complex economic regions and republics and for cutting out irrational long-distance deliveries.[35] The interests of USSR Gosplan lay in maintaining the existing balance between the branches and the existing dependence of the republics on each other.

The planning experiment did not cause any economic damage: USSR Gosplan corrected the republican indices. In Ukraine's draft plan the targets for 120 types of the most important products were set higher than those in 1957, while for more than 100 types of products the targets were reduced.[36] In their conclusions, central planners diplomatically stated that the ubiquitous underestimate of production

62 *Decentralization of decision making*

targets and overestimation of investment claims by enterprises and *sovnarkhozy* were the result of a lack of control figures.[37] Ukrainian planners agreed that if indicative figures were communicated to them in advance, over- and underestimates would have been largely avoided. So subsequent plans were compiled on the basis of control figures fixed by the centre. The ideas of the republican authorities about the future of their economies were not that important after all. The practice of 'planning from below' was abandoned.

6 Republican budgetary rights

Since 1954, when enterprises started being transferred from the all-Union to republican jurisdiction, the republics had argued that the extension of their economic rights should be comprehensive and spread to such areas as pricing, credit and finances and, in particular, the budget. In 1955, the republics asked for the right to compile republican and local budgets based on limits set by Moscow, and for some flexibility to manipulate the budget.[1] In 1956, at the peak of the reorganization of the ministerial system, the centre and the republics jointly drafted a project 'On the budgetary rights of the Union republics'. With the *Sovnarkhoz* reform, the margins of republican authority outlined in the 1956 project were no longer satisfactory. So work continued and in spring 1958, the USSR CM presented drafts of two documents designed to regulate centre–republic relations in the budget area: the Law on budgetary rights of the USSR and Union republics (hereafter 'Budget Law') and Regulations on compiling and fulfilling the state budget (hereafter Budget regulations). By June 1958, the CMUk finished its comments on both of these documents. Compared to 1956, the expectations of the Ukrainian leadership had grown.

In 1956, when 78.6 per cent of Ukrainian industry was under republican management, Ukraine suggested that the USSR Ministry of Finance fix the total revenue and expenditure figures for the republic in the state budget of the USSR, allowing the republic to fix allocations for the economy, culture, state administrations, salaries and subsidies. Ukraine asked that the republic be permitted, in agreement with the USSR Ministry of Finance, to determine the amounts and sources (!) of the payments in the all-Union budget, to retain the above-plan revenues and create a reserve fund of 5–7 per cent of the republican budget. Ukraine hoped to get the right to fix the turnover tax on the consumer goods manufactured by republican and local industry which had not been priced by the central government, to set the procedure for fixing wholesale and retail prices of the production of republican, local and cooperative industry and, in exceptional cases, to finance certain construction works. The CMUk also asked for the authority to give financial subsidies to theatres and concert associations of republican and local status and to fix the prices of the tickets.[2]

In 1958, the claims of the CMUk were more substantial. By then, of course, its share of industry as well as its functions and responsibilities had increased

64 *Decentralization of decision making*

as well. First of all, echoing the 1956 requests, Ukraine insisted that the new Budget Law grant to the republics the right to determine the size of the reserve fund and the right to use the reserve fund on the basis of the legislation of the Union republic. Ukraine repeated its request to retain the republic's above-plan revenue and to spend it the following year according to the legislation of the Union republic. At the same time, the CMUk requested that because the *sovnarkhozy* had republican jurisdiction, a share of the deductions from the profits made by *Sovnarkhoz* enterprises and economic organizations that was transferred to the all-Union budget should remain within the republic. The same was proposed regarding the income tax collected from the population. It should also come to the budget of the Union republic: it would provide more revenue for local budgets. Finally, the Ukrainian government insisted on being compensated in all cases when the revenues or expenditures of the republican budgets were changed as a result of new laws or resolutions introduced by central government.

> It should be obligatory that these modifications are agreed with the USSR Ministry of Finance and the CM of the Union republic, and that modifications to wholesale prices and rates of turnover tax are prepared during the current year and applied with effect from 1 January of the following year.[3]

With regard to the procedures for compiling and fulfilling the budget, the Ukrainian government insisted that the all-Union agencies were as duty bound to perform their functions by the deadlines set as were the republics.[4] The Ukrainian government found the new procedure for presenting the budget-drafts to be complicated, and did not agree that the republics should present their drafts to the USSR Ministry of Finance more than once, or include detailed calculations in the financial plans and summary estimates. Ukraine also disagreed with the new procedure for assigning the volume of cash circulating in the republics during the adoption of the USSR State budget. Ukraine argued that the existing procedure should remain where the amount of cash in circulation was determined during the adoption of the budget by the CM of the republic.[5]

Moscow's reaction to Kiev's comments

By the end of September 1958, the USSR Ministry of Finance, USSR Gosplan and the USSR CM Legal Commission finished their response to the comments of all those organizations involved in the composition of the budget. The four most important requests of the Ukrainian government – that the republic keep the income tax paid by the population, that the republic determine the amount of deductions from the profits of the *sovnarkhozy*, that the republic keep any above-plan revenues and that the size of the reserve fund be determined by the republic – were rejected by the USSR Ministry of Finance and the Legal Commission. USSR Gosplan found it possible to make one concession and leave the profits of the *sovnarkhozy* to the republics.[6]

Ukraine was not the only republic that made these four claims. According to the statement (*spravka*) from the USSR Ministry of Finance that explained the Ministry's refusal to grant the above-listed rights to the republics, each of the claims had been made by several other republics and even some all-Union agencies. Thus, the claim for income tax was made not only by Ukraine, but also by Byelorussia, Uzbekistan, Moldavia, the USSR Ministry of Commerce and the TsSU. (Income tax was rather modest in the Soviet Union. The marginal rate on income above 100 roubles per month was 13 per cent. The tax on 100 roubles income was 5.92 per cent.[7]) 'We cannot agree to that', wrote the USSR Ministry of Finance. 'If we transfer income tax of the population to the budgets of the Union republics, the most stable income of the Union budget would fall.' The Ministry of Finance agreed to leave 50 per cent of the income tax paid by the republican population to the republic.[8]

The right of the republics to retain the profits of the *sovnarkhozy* was claimed by the RSFSR and Moldavia, USSR Gosplan and the USSR Ministry of Commerce. The USSR Ministry of Finance disagreed. The new law, explained the Ministry of Finance, would increase the revenues of the republican budgets from the all-Union budget. The republics would keep the forestry tax, income tax from *kolkhozy*, agricultural tax, tax on bachelors, single women and on citizens with small families, and the above-mentioned 50 per cent of the income tax paid by the population. 'A further reduction in revenue for the all-Union budget should not be planned.'[9]

In the claim about the reserve fund, Ukraine was joined only by the RSFSR and Estonia. The USSR Ministry of Finance explained that it was necessary to fix the size of republican reserve funds simultaneously with the adoption of the USSR State budget in order to correlate the budget with available resources. Some resources could be taken from the all-Union budget for republican reserve funds.[10] On spending above-plan revenue, all republics except Kazakhstan, Uzbekistan and Kirghizia insisted on the right to retain and spend above-plan revenue according to the republican legislation. The USSR Ministry of Finance agreed to the solution proposed by USSR Gosplan of continuing the practice adopted in 1957 and 1958 when the spending of above-plan revenue was determined by resolutions issued by the USSR CM.[11]

As for the Ukrainian comments on the new Budget regulations, the one of major importance – to continue with the existing practice and allow the republics to determine the volume of cash in circulation – was supported by the RSFSR, Latvia, Armenia, Byelorussia, Turkmenistan and Estonia. This claim was refused.[12] A few days after the Ukrainian leadership received the Statement from the Ministry of Finance, the head of the CC CPUk department for planning, commerce and finance organizations V. Starunskii received joint comments from his department, from Gosplan of Ukraine and from the Ukrainian Ministry of Finance, unanimous in the opinion that the CMUk should insist to the USSR CM that the Ukrainian comments be included in the new Budget Law and Budget regulations. However, the Ukrainian leadership was repeatedly refused.[13] (In the Law of 30 October 1959, article 35, 50 per cent of the income tax collected from

Table 6.1 Proposals of shares of *rayon* and *oblast'* profits to be left for the local budgets, 1958

Name of organization	Share of rayon *profit to be left for the local budget (per cent)*	Share of oblast' *profit to be left for the local budget (per cent)*
USSR Ministry of Finance	60	30
USSR Gosplan	40	40
CM and Gosplan of Ukraine	60	60
RSFSR CM	60	60

Note: The table is based on the shorthand record report of the meeting in the office of the Vice-Chairman of the CMUk M.S. Grechukha held on 1 August 1958, TsDAVOU, f. 2, op. 9, d. 4306, ll. 47, 48.

the population was left to the republics; according to article 41, the above-plan revenue remained for the republics, but the republics were not completely free to spend it at their discretion.) Furthermore, to firm up the all-Union budget, in summer 1958 the central government instructed the USSR Ministry of Finance and USSR Gosplan to examine the possibility of redistributing the profits of local industry (see Table 6.1).

Both the USSR Ministry of Finance and USSR Gosplan found it necessary to increase payments from local industry to the all-Union budget. The USSR Minister of Finance A. Zverev also proposed reviewing the turnover tax on the production of local industry, which in the case of Ukraine would have reduced its income by about 1 billion roubles. Ukraine and the RSFSR insisted that the *oblispolkomy* and *raiispolkomy* kept 60 per cent of their profits, 'otherwise the situation in local industry would drastically deteriorate'.[14]

Having expanded republican budgets, the central leadership also tightened control over their expenditures, which was all the more necessary since the republics tended to overspend their budgets, whereas the Union budget was increasingly underspent.[15] Such a solution could not satisfy the republics. The republican governments expected more funds and more autonomy in managing them, but also shared responsibility with the central agencies for the fulfilment of the budget.

7 Decentralizing the supply system
Losing control over resources

The organizational structure of the new supply system

Like planning itself, the new supply system was designed by the planners.[1] The opinion of the *sovnarkhozy* was taken into consideration much later, in spring 1958. Resource management was divided between central, republican and regional managers. USSR Gosplan, with its *Glavsbyty*, *Glavnye upravleniya po postavkam* (main administrations for sales), managed two essential groups of products: a) products for inter-republican deliveries, and deliveries into the all-Union funds and for export; and b) all types of materials and equipment. USSR Gosplan also assigned the totality of funds for other production to the republic Gosplans, and performed controlling and regulating functions, set principal terms for deliveries and drafted standard delivery contracts.[2]

The newly empowered Gosplan of Ukraine, with staff numbers almost four times greater than before the reform, now had in its structure 12 general-economic (*svodno-ekonomicheskie*) departments, 34 branch departments and 19 Ukrainian main administrations for supplies and sales, or *Ukrglavsnabsbyty*, that corresponded to the *Glavsbyty* of USSR Gosplan.[3] Merging supplies and sales offices cut their number from 170 before the reform to 136 in 1958.[4] *Ukrglavsnabsbyty* were in fact mini-ministries. They worked along branch lines and played a crucial role in the *Sovnarkhoz* system. *Ukrglavsnabsbyty* were positioned between the *Glavsbyty* and the *sovnarkhozy*. They channelled information from the regions to the centre and in the opposite direction, and distributed centrally assigned funds among the Ukrainian *sovnarkhozy*, *oblispolkomy* and non-industrial ministries. They drafted supply plans for production managed by the republic and controlled the fulfilment of all supply plans, particularly for inter-republican and inter-regional deliveries and deliveries for export. It was their responsibility to suppress manifestations of *mestnichestvo* in the deliveries. The *Ukrglavsnabsbyty* were assigned control over the fulfilment of deliveries to Ukraine from other republics. In the very first project on Gosplan of Ukraine that was drafted in spring 1957, the CC CPUk expected that the *Ukrglavsnabsbyty* would assign production targets for inter-republican deliveries, deliveries to the all-Union funds and for exports; however, that function was given to the *Glavsbyty*.[5] The heads of the *Ukrglavsnabsbyty* were granted ministerial ranks.

The staff of *Ukrglavsnabsbyty* largely consisted of ex-functionaries of the *snaby* and *sbyty* of the abolished ministries and their peripheral offices.[6]

To assist Gosplan of Ukraine in Moscow, the Ukrainian government initiated the opening of a Moscow office of Gosplan of Ukraine.[7] The Moscow office had to ensure the realization of those funds assigned to Ukrainian enterprises by suppliers located outside Ukraine, to assist the Ukrainian *sovnarkhozy* in obtaining decentralized supplies, and to solve all supply problems with USSR Gosplan.[8] The office was also responsible for providing additional resources by organizing decentralized supplies or manufacturing at enterprises in Moscow and in nearby areas.[9] The tasks that the Ukrainian government assigned to the Moscow office quite clearly indicated that the republic did not count on the smooth working of the new supply system.

The *sovnarkhozy* managed supplies delivered to and from their economic regions, except for the supplies of local industry administered by the *oblispolkomy*. The highest authority on supplies in the region was the main supply and sales department of the *Sovnarkhoz*, or *glavsnabsbyt*. It included departments for material funds which planned the inputs for the enterprises of the *Sovnarkhoz* and defended these plans in Gosplan of Ukraine, distributed funds between the branch departments of the *Sovnarkhoz*, controlled fulfilment of the deliveries, and so on. *Glavsnabsbyty* carried out all operational activity in supplying and selling through a network of self-financing departments and specialized warehouses. The latter provided substantive inputs to all economic organizations of the region, based on the funds assigned to them. The *Sovnarkhoz* could also create self-financing offices to supply products that were not supplied by Kiev, or place orders with various customers for industrial processing within the enterprises of the *Sovnarkhoz*.[10] Depending on the industrial complex of the region, the *glavsnabsbyt* could organize from nine to 17 branch *sbyty*, each corresponding to an *Ukrglavsnabsbyt*.[11]

Each trust, combine and enterprise of the *Sovnarkhoz* had its own supply and sales department (*snabsbyt*). In 1957 they were not abolished, to avoid interruptions of deliveries during the transitory period. At the beginning of 1958, the USSR Ministry of Finance suggested abolishing the self-financing supply offices of the *sovnarkhozy*, their branch *sbyty* and the *snabsbyty* of enterprises and trusts. Gosplan of Ukraine found this idea premature, but promised to consider it in the future.[12]

With the reform, the original extension of the rights of republican and regional managers in matters of supply was considerable. For example, both Gosplan of Ukraine and the Ukrainian *sovnarkhozy* obtained the right to redistribute material funds between regions and enterprises. Gosplan of Ukraine obtained the right to manipulate funds for contractual deliveries inside the republic: it was the fundholder.[13]

At the same time, several formal mechanisms were established to ensure that the centre retained control over resources. First of all, even though the reform introduced the territorial management of industry, supplies continued to be distributed along branch lines.[14] The branch principle in supplies was also maintained by continuing contractual deliveries that dominated in machine-building branches. Second, USSR Gosplan retained full control of materials, equipment and machinery, and of other products that crossed the borders of the republics, by setting production targets and issuing orders for deliveries (*naryady na postavki*). For Ukraine this meant that more than 80 per cent of domestic production was to some extent managed by USSR Gosplan and its *Glavsbyty*.[15] Third, to prevent the *sovnarkhozy* from changing the branch balance in their regions without authorization, the *sovnarkhozy* were not allowed to redistribute capital investments between branches.[16] At the same time, their contracts with other *sovnarkhozy* had to be assigned and approved either by Gosplan of Ukraine if the *Sovnarkhoz* was Ukrainian, or by USSR Gosplan if the partner was situated outside Ukraine.[17] Finally, as early as 1958, USSR Gosplan extended the list of centrally distributed products and included products that were originally in the list of Gosplan of Ukraine.[18] Until 1959, USSR Gosplan also retained control over planned production (not always covered with inputs and accounted by volume, or rouble) and funded production (always covered with inputs).[19]

Formally, the new supply system balanced the decentralization of resource management with centralized control over essential inputs, regardless of whether they crossed the boundaries of the economic regions or republics or not, as well as the inter-republican flow of all goods. In practice, however, that balance was far from satisfactory and, from the start, the centrifugal tendencies prevailed. By the end of 1957, USSR Gosplan had sufficient information to assert that the tendency to rely on native suppliers and direct contacts for inputs was ubiquitous among the *sovnarkhozy* and republic Gosplans. At the December 1957 meeting held at USSR Gosplan, the Ukrainian *sovnarkhozy* of Stalino and Dnepropetrovsk were criticized for systematically prioritizing their own needs in metal production and violating the delivery plans of metal, particularly pipes, beams and channels to other *sovnarkhozy*, despite the fact that the latter were fulfilling important state tasks. Thus the Chairman of the Stalino *Sovnarkhoz* I. Dyadyk ordered that until the end of 1957 it would only supply the coal industry of its *Sovnarkhoz*. To make sure that customers from outside the Stalino *Sovnarkhoz* received metal, the head of *Glavmetallosbyt* Gorbasev contacted the directors of metallurgical mills directly and set a new schedule of deliveries. Yet Dyadyk annulled this schedule. Only after the CC CPSU department of heavy industry intervened was the new schedule re-established. The Zaporozh'e *Sovnarkhoz* failed to deliver sheet metal, reported Gorbasev, and the Khar'kov *Sovnarkhoz* reduced production and deliveries of spare parts for tractors.[20]

Ukraine was also criticized for reviewing production plans of certain goods. Vinnitsa *Sovnarkhoz*, for example, with the authorization of Gosplan of Ukraine, approved the cessation of manufacture of about 400 units of different installations for the food industry made at the Barskii engineering works.[21] Regarding the consumption of very scarce deficit production, USSR Gosplan registered that the Voronezh *Sovnarkhoz* (RSFSR) delivered 100 tonnes of synthetic rubber to a Khar'kov plant without an order from *Glavkhimsbyt*, and 3,137 units of automobile tyres to the customers of the local *Sovnarkhoz*, thus exceeding the funds assigned to the Voronezh *Sovnarkhoz* by 1,062 units for one quarter. 'The latter decision was made in violation of the regulation that the distribution of automobile tyres, synthetic rubber, metal and other materials in acute deficit was in the exclusive purview of the USSR CM.'[22]

Although USSR Gosplan accused the *sovnarkhozy* of *mestnichestvo* and called the actions of some chairmen of the *sovnarkhozy* illegal – that is how the actions of Dyadyk were qualified – neither the central or Ukrainian government nor the CC CPSU or CPUk punished the chairmen who violated state discipline. The explanation for this can only be that central planners understood very well that the reasons for non-delivery lay outside issues of personalities; non-deliveries were not a new phenomenon and customers knew what to do to obtain the supplies needed for the fulfilment of their production plans (to send a *tolkach* directly to the supplier or to pressurize the supplier through the Party organization). After all, as stated at the December meeting of USSR Gosplan, the metallurgical mill of the Stalino *Sovnarkhoz Azovstal'* violated its delivery plans back in 1957 when industry was still run by the ministries.[23]

At the same time, the economic growth rate in 1957 did not make it possible to insist that *mestnichestvo* in deliveries undermined fulfilment of the production plan. The growth rate of Ukraine, the customer and supplier to tens of thousands of enterprises all over the country, was 10 per cent in 1957. Officially, Ukrainian planners explained high growth and the over-fulfilment of the original production plan of gross output by almost 3 per cent by bringing into production materials accumulated within enterprises over several years.[24] The contribution of the tendency towards localism in this growth was not mentioned.

The power effect of non-deliveries to USSR Gosplan, however, *was* alarming. The chairmen of the *sovnarkhozy*, particularly of such industrially developed ones as Stalino, felt comfortable in overruling the procedures and instructions of USSR Gosplan. That could not but concern the central planners. The constraining mechanisms and the mechanisms to enforce delivery plans were clearly ineffective. USSR Gosplan was forced to seek assistance from the Party.

Further decentralization: a push from below

Ukrainian planners and managers could not deny that they prioritized local economic needs, but they could not agree with the accusations of ill intentions or *mestnichestvo* either. From the standpoint of the *sovnarkhozy*, under conditions of scarcity and the lack of any new mechanisms that would guarantee that supplies arrived on time or arrived at all, they had to choose between creating a shortage in their own regions or in others. As for the republican planners, they could not prevent or fight *mestnichestvo* because they often had no information on all resources available in the republic, or on what was delivered and what was not. This information was dispersed between the centre and the regions. The two systems that channelled this information, the network of peripheral supply offices of the abolished ministries and the statistical agencies, both remained under Moscow's control at the beginning of the reform. Besides, the usefulness of information collected through statistical agencies was rather low. Their information had an 'archival', outdated character, which was unsuitable for operational decision making. A more reliable source of information was the peripheral supply offices. Obtaining control over that network was therefore essential if Gosplan of Ukraine was to establish its authority in the republic. Yet, to the *sovnarkhozy*, control over this network was equally important.

In May 1957, the Ukrainian government anticipated that with the abolition of the ministries, their peripheral network of supply offices and warehouses would be transferred directly to the *sovnarkhozy* and *oblispolkomy*.[25] This was a reasonable expectation, since the *sovnarkhozy* and *oblispolkomy* were taking over industry. However, as the reform got under way, the peripheral supply offices remained under the centralized control of USSR Gosplan and *Glavsbyty*, the USSR Ministry of Chemical Industry and the USSR Ministry of Radio-Engineering Industry. USSR Gosplan explained that leaving the peripheral supply offices under centralized control would ensure that interruptions in deliveries were prevented. Neither the *sovnarkhozy* nor *Ukrglavsnabsbyty* had finished organizing the *snabsbyty*, nor were they fully staffed with qualified personnel, so they could not take over this network.[26]

On 12 November 1957, USSR Gosplan transferred the network of peripheral supply offices from central jurisdiction to the jurisdiction of the CMUk.[27] By this time, however, after the trial period of the reform, the Ukrainian government had changed its original intention of transferring the peripheral supply offices to the *sovnarkhozy* and decided to place them under the centralized republican control of Gosplan of Ukraine. After all, control over the network of peripheral supply offices meant not only first-hand access to information on fulfilled and non-fulfilled deliveries and on realized and non-realized funds, but it meant control over all resources assigned to the regions: peripheral offices supplied information to all economic actors in the *oblasti*, including producers of agricultural production and commercial organizations.[28] This decision led to the second, after drafting the 1958 plan, major conflict between the *sovnarkhozy* and Gosplan of Ukraine.

Gosplan of Ukraine, namely *Ukrglavsnabsbyty*, explained that first of all, placing the supply offices under centralized republican control would reduce their total number.[29] Second, the share of the *sovnarkhozy* in deliveries distributed through the *Ukrglavsnabsbyty*, i.e., planned and funded production, was estimated at 65 per cent, while 35 per cent was consumed by the *oblispolkomy*, ministries and departments, agriculture and trading organizations. Making the *sovnarkhozy* responsible for delivering 35 per cent of the funds 'would distract the *glavsnabsbyty* of the *sovnarkhozy* from their direct responsibilities and create serious difficulties'[30] (not to mention that in this case, the *sovnarkhozy* would control 100 per cent of supplies). Moreover, the peripheral offices should service several regions. If they were subordinated to the *sovnarkhozy*, then it would be necessary to create supply offices in each *Sovnarkhoz*, which would lead to an increase in personnel and the accumulation of materials in the regions. *Ukrglavsnabsbyty* would not be able to manoeuvre resources on a republican scale.[31]

72 *Decentralization of decision making*

Sovnarkhozy, surprising as it might seem, were not unanimous about the jurisdiction of the network of peripheral supply offices or even the role of the *Ukrglavsnabsbyty* in the new supply system. The majority – at least seven out of 11 chairmen – spoke in favour of the transfer of the supply offices to the *sovnarkhozy*.[32] They sought to obtain leverage in their relations with the *Glavsbyty* and *Ukrglavsnabsbyty*. The Vinnitsa *Sovnarkhoz* spoke in favour of leaving the peripheral network to the *Ukrglavsnabsbyty* but reducing their number; and the Khar'kov *Sovnarkhoz* did not consider it necessary to bring the peripheral network under republican control at all, but to leave it under the jurisdiction of the *Glavsbyty*.[33]

The argument for the transfer of the peripheral network to the *sovnarkhozy* was straightforward: the responsibility for supplies could not be separated from the responsibility for production, and, as Valentinov from the Stalino *Sovnarkhoz* explained, according to the Regulations on a *Sovnarkhoz*,[34] the *Sovnarkhoz* was responsible for fulfilling the production plan, providing regular supplies to the enterprises, and for the sales of production manufactured by the enterprises of the *Sovnarkhoz*.[35] *Ukrglavsnabsbyty*, he insisted, were incapable of ensuring supplies and sales. They had no influence on production and almost no influence over supplies and sales. So they could not be responsible for supplying the economy.[36]

The *sovnarkhozy* shared the view that the *Ukrglavsnabsbyty* had abused their power in 1957 when by-passing the *sovnarkhozy* and contacting Ukrainian enterprises directly, yet they were powerless to solve practical problems with supplies. The chairmen of the *sovnarkhozy* agreed that they needed a regulating and enforcing centre which would guarantee the fulfilment of supplies, yet only a few of them viewed *Ukrglavsnabsbyty* as being even potentially capable of doing this. The *Ukrglavsnabsbyty* had no decision-making power; all decisions on inter-republican deliveries, funds and limits were made in Moscow. For the same reason, *Ukrglavsnabsbyty* could not assist the *sovnarkhozy* in establishing direct relations with the non-Ukrainian *sovnarkhozy*.[37] Moreover, Gosplan of Ukraine, they said, viewed the supply system of Ukraine as a separate system, whereas they viewed the republican supply system as an integrated part of the supply system of the entire country: 'Ukraine cannot have a closed cycle for chemical or metal production'.[38] Viewed from this perspective, the *sovnarkhozy* would manage industry more efficiently if their *glavsnabsbyty* were subordinated directly to Moscow, suggested the majority. The *Ukrglavsnabsbyty* were superfluous.

Further decentralization: a push from above

In 1958, the central leadership did not consider non-deliveries, and thereby the tendency towards *mestnichestvo*, a threat to the economic integrity of the country and continued with further decentralization of the supply system. In June, the network of peripheral supply offices, warehouses, shops and enterprises of 12 *Ukrglavsnabsbyty* was transferred to the jurisdiction of the *sovnarkhozy*. (However, the payments for the deliveries realized through this network remained centralized, prompting Podgornyi to address the CC CPSU asking for the peripheral offices to be allowed to manage the payments.[39]) Kiev retained control over the supply offices for non-ferrous metallurgy, salvage metal, automobiles and tractors, bearings, wood and paper, oil, equipment and production of the defence industry.[40]

The resolution of 17 April 1958 compelled USSR Gosplan to transform *Glavsbyty* into *Glavnye upravleniya po mezhrespublikanskim postavkam produktsii* (hereafter GlUMPP), or main administrations for inter-republican deliveries, and limit their authority to planning, managing and controlling inter-republican deliveries and deliveries for export, deliveries to the all-Union funds and to the all-Union ministries and departments.[41] Control over the fulfilment of interrepublican deliveries had to be performed through the republican *snabsbyty*. Direct contact between the GlUMPP and enterprises of the *sovnarkhozy* was not planned. The new supply system formally prioritized direct relations between enterprises, so the *sovnarkhozy* were instructed to intensify the work of setting direct relations inside their regions, republic Gosplans inside their republics and USSR Gosplan at the all-Union level. The importance of contracts between the suppliers and customers and the responsibility of the suppliers for untimely deliveries had to be increased. Republican governments, Gosplans and the *sovnarkhozy* bore full responsibility for deliveries.[42]

If applied, these changes would have decentralized the supply system to an unprecedented degree. Stable direct relations, if indeed prioritized, would have increased the power of the *sovnarkhozy* and enterprises, since the volume of production under the control of the central and republican planners would have been reduced, as would the dependence of the producers on their issuing the delivery orders. With regard to Ukraine, the April 1958 resolution compelled the transfer of six *Glavsbyty* from central to republican jurisdiction. 'These *sbyty* will manage production and issue warrants to all enterprises, without exception',[43] explained republican planners. The resolution, if applied, promised to reduce Ukrainian dependence on the centre for six branches.

Indeed, with this resolution Khrushchev was instructing the planners to reduce their own influence over the movement of resources. As a result, since it was up to the central planners themselves to put the resolution into practice, the April resolution was never fully implemented. In 1959, direct deliveries were included for centralized distribution, and the system that would tie consumers to suppliers for long periods of time, allowing the latter to 'organize regular supplies, study demand and improve the quality of the goods supplied', and was much expected in the regions, was never fully established.[44]

Decentralization in practice: the growing autonomy of the *sovnarkhozy*

The modifications to the supply system that were introduced in 1958 further increased the flexibility of the *sovnarkhozy* in managing resources. The side effect of their flexibility in resource management was the withdrawal of resources from the control of planners and the growing dependence of the planners on the producers. The *sovnarkhozy* were certainly dependent on the planners for funds and delivery orders; however, the fact that their enterprises actually manufactured inputs and could always send a *tolkach* to provide the necessary materials allowed the *sovnarkhozy* to effectively modify plans and thus challenge the authority of the planners.

The *sovnarkhozy* had several ways of increasing their material stocks. One mentioned previously was non-delivery. *Sovnarkhozy* re-directed supplies and prioritized local customers over non-local ones. The status of deliveries did not guarantee their fulfilment. Contractual deliveries, deliveries for export or to the all-Union funds were as likely to be unfulfilled as inter-republican or inter-regional regular deliveries. Control over the fulfilment of deliveries on the part of *Ukrglavsnabsbyty* was complicated by the mere fact of an absence of information. The *sovnarkhozy* often failed to inform Kiev of the non-fulfilment of delivery contracts.[45] At the same time, the *sovnarkhozy* could use funded materials, supposedly scarce and assigned exclusively by the centre, to increase the output of production for which these funds were not originally assigned. 'We have incidents', said M.A. Lesechko at the meeting in Gosplan of Ukraine in spring 1958, 'when, with funded materials, plans are fulfilled by 120 per cent'. He believed that there was no demand for production manufactured above the plan.[46] When the *sovnarkhozy* did not need inputs, they did not hesitate to return them directly to their suppliers without informing the planning authorities, thus depriving planners of the opportunity of redistributing these resources, whereas 'funds for contractual deliveries of casts, punching, forging and other forms of production are assigned to the republic and the republic has the right to re-allocate them'.[47]

The power of planners over regional managers was further reduced when, in order to meet local demand for certain inputs, the *sovnarkhozy*, instead of developing cooperation with other economic regions, which was coordinated by Gosplan of Ukraine at the republican level and USSR Gosplan at the all-Union level, developed small workshops, *tsekhi*.[48] In those cases when inputs or information about planned production were not available, the *sovnarkhozy* could change the types and volumes of production. The output they produced was not necessarily required by the plan but was often required for local needs.[49]

Redistribution of capital investment

In summer 1958, the CC CPUk discussed the problem of unauthorized redistribution of capital investment between economic branches by the *sovnarkhozy*. Some *sovnarkhozy*, as Podgornyi described the situation, 'reduced investment assigned by the 1958 plan for the development of the coal, metallurgical, coal mining, chemical, gas and other important branches and channelled them for local needs and other purposes'.[50] The *sovnarkhozy* used available funds to credit under-financed areas, and construction in particular, without any authorization from the CMUk or USSR Gosplan.

Thus, the Lugansk *Sovnarkhoz* reduced investment in the coal mining industry by 76.7 million roubles and directed 43.7 million roubles into the construction industry and 33 million roubles into actual construction, including 5.5 million roubles in the construction of an administrative building for the *Sovnarkhoz*. The Stalino *Sovnarkhoz* withdrew 24.4 million roubles of investment designated for the coal mining industry without permission and used them to build housing, kindergarten, a holiday home and other objects. The L'vov *Sovnarkhoz* reduced capital investment in the coal mining industry by 39.6 million roubles and directed them to the industry of construction materials. The Odessa *Sovnarkhoz* distributed 17.2 million roubles originally assigned for the fishing industry among various branches. Some *sovnarkhozy* reduced investment in the food industry: Kiev by 6.2 million roubles, L'vov by 9.7 and Vinnitsa and Khar'kov by 5 million roubles each.[51]

Having established these facts of unauthorized redistribution of capital investment, Podgornyi did not explain the economic damage that the *sovnarkhozy* caused to the Soviet economy. He made it clear, however, that such unauthorized redirection of investments 'became possible because *obkomy* did not properly control the economic activity of the *sovnarkhozy*'.[52] To correct the situation, the *sovnarkhozy* were compelled to return the redirected investments to the originally designated branches. Gosplan of Ukraine, Commission of Soviet control, *Prombank*, *Gosbank*, *Torgbank* and *Sel'khozbank* were instructed to increase control over the correct usage of financial funds and report to the CC CPUk and the CMUk on any violations discovered.[53]

Pricing

Another considerable problem for the planners was the accumulation of financial and material resources in the *sovnarkhozy* through pricing. Prices were fixed at all levels, all-Union and republican, by the *sovnarkhozy* and enterprises.[54] 'Yet our comrades went further', said the head of the department of light industry of Gosplan of Ukraine D. Kostenko, 'the Ukrainian Minister of Commerce G. Sakhnovskii, despite the fact that he had consulted the TsK, allowed any commercial organization together with the directors of enterprises to set retail prices. ... As a result, the mark-up on the same product varied from branch to branch; sometimes the mark-up was as high as 50 per cent or 60 per cent. The highest mark-up was on production from the food industry.'[55]

Due to the bureaucratic delays in Kiev and Moscow, temporary prices were turning into permanent ones.[56] Moreover, to fix a new temporary price for a product, it was sufficient to move manufacturing of the product from one enterprise to another and 'modify' it.[57] The more cash in the hands of the *sovnarkhozy*, the more inputs could be provided through officially authorized decentralized deliveries or by organizing supplementary production, and thus more production that was not on the list of any of the Gosplans could be released into circulation directly by the *sovnarkhozy*.

76 Decentralization of decision making

In Gosplan of Ukraine, they recognized that high prices were often caused by the incentive of the *sovnarkhozy* to fulfil the profit plan, although the general understanding was that the *sovnarkhozy* exceeded their power because of the lack of control in pricing on the part of the planners and the Party. Indeed, from 1957 until 1959, the actual profits of industry recorded by Gosplan of Ukraine exceeded the planned figures by 5.9 per cent in 1957, by 6.3 per cent in 1958 and by 8.6 per cent in 1959. However, starting from 1960, after the memorandum (*dokladnaya zapiska*) of the TsSU 'On the level and modifications of prices in 1959 and shortcomings in pricing' and the subsequent restrictive measures taken by the CMUk on the matter, until the end of the reform, the *sovnarkhozy* never over-fulfilled the profit plan.[58] (Of course, another explanation for the difference in the level of fulfilment of the profit plan before and after 1959 could be higher profit targets after 1959.)

Lack of control over pricing was due to several factors. The system of price control was complicated and lots of time was required for full auditing. The department of prices in Gosplan of Ukraine was understaffed: to check the wholesale prices of metal, coal, rolled metal and the production of machine-building industries in the two-month term, the department needed 46 people, but had only 26.[59] At the same time, to turn temporary prices into permanent ones, the *sovnarkhozy* had to submit relevant documents to a number of departments and consider their 'often irrelevant' remarks. So the procedure slowed down the entire process of fixing permanent prices. The fact that even in 1958, a standard pricing policy did not exist and the methodology for composing prices included lots of exceptions from the existing rules did not speed up the process either.[60]

A substantial source of additional material stocks was *production manufactured above the plan*. Strictly speaking, during the *Sovnarkhoz* reform, above-plan production should not have existed: all production capacities and resources had to be included by the *sovnarkhozy* in their plans. However, the experiment with planning 'from below' failed and planning 'from above' made the above-plan production unavoidable. Producing above the plan up to a certain point was in the interest of enterprises, *sovnarkhozy* and the republics. Above-plan production was remunerated at a higher rate than planned production,[61] management received bonuses, respect from the authorities, and a share of the above-plan output was left for the producer.[62] The share of above-plan production in total output, however, was kept relatively low, since it was included in the production targets for the following year.

The authorities generally encouraged production above the plan and regularly ordered above-plan production, although the central leadership promoted the idea that above-plan production should be the result of introducing technological innovations and increasing productivity, not using more material inputs or labour. Then the bonuses and higher salaries would be justified. The *sovnarkhozy*, however, had no incentives to increase their production by advancing production technology and continued the tradition of producing above the plan by negotiating the actual plan and then increasing the inputs and labour.

In 1959, the central government decided to review its policy of distributing above-plan production. It sought to meet two ends: to economize on the wages fund and to bring a larger share of above-plan production under centralized control. A larger wages fund was necessary for the Eastern parts of the country where industrial development was intended to be accelerated.[63] In 1958 the fund was overdrawn. To replenish it, the government, among other measures, deprived regional managers of personal incentives for above-plan manufacture. On 26 February 1959, the USSR CM issued a resolution according to which the production of scarce goods above the plan had to be ignored when evaluating the work of enterprises or when assigning bonuses to the management staff and engineers.[64] 'After 1959', Zaleski writes, 'bonuses were paid only for fulfilment or overfulfilment of the plan for costs; and they were also made contingent on fulfilment of plans for gross output, assortment, and all the other principal productive indexes'.[65] As a result, 'The share of bonus payments in the basic salaries of engineers and technicians fell from 26.4 per cent in 1959 to 19 per cent in 1960, to 13.2 per cent in 1961, and to 11.6 per cent in 1962'.[66] The summer 1959 resolution 'On procedures for using above-plan industrial production, both manufactured and stored' increased the share of above-planned production for tractors, automobiles, agricultural machines and spare parts for them, certain types of steel, steel pipes, certain types of coal, iron and manganese ore, cement, mineral fertilizers, certain types of soda, chemical fibre, leather production, paper, carton, all types of glass table- and kitchenware for central distribution.[67] The two resolutions effectively aimed to de-incentivize enterprises from above-plan production at the existing high rate and aimed to reduce the share of the above-plan production in total output.

The Ukrainian leadership saw the problem not in above-plan production *per se*, but in the irresponsibility of the central planners when assigning above-plan production: the central planners should assign supplementary production and delivery tasks only for goods and equipment with specific purposes, including the development of new technologies. Furthermore, control over resources would increase and the cost of above-plan production would decrease if the republics were allowed to keep between 50 and 100 per cent of the above-plan production, which would be sold to the population and used for major construction and for the production of scarce goods and for other republican needs.[68]

The resolution on distribution of production manufactured above the plan and stocked above the approved norms was ready by December 1959. The list of the products that the republics were authorized to keep was much shorter than the list that the Ukrainians composed and did not include any products that the republics could keep entirely. The largest share of the above-plan production that the republics could keep was 60 per cent of ferroalloy. They could also keep 50 per cent of construction materials made from local raw materials; 50 per cent of the above-plan production of the wood processing industry; 50 per cent of mineral fertilizers (the May 1955 resolution left 25 per cent to the republics); 25 per cent of cable production, steel pipes and automobile tyres. The republics could not keep any Donetsk anthracites of high quality, any production of machine-building, electro-technical or instrument-making industry, any vegetable oil, any starch or agricultural raw materials (wool, raw silk), any leather production or any type of glass table- and kitchenware, any accessories for shoes or clothing or any furniture mirrors. The republics could not keep anything that would allow them to increase their output of consumer goods.[69] The next time the republics would get an opportunity to review the volumes of above-plan production for domestic consumption would be in 1965.

Resources that the *sovnarkhozy* accumulated had several applications. They could be used directly for production inside the region,[70] or for informal exchange with other regions. Of course, some share of the accumulated stocks was indeed defective, waste or obsolete. According to the results of the audit conducted by Gosplan of Ukraine, by the end of 1958 the total value of unmarketable production that was stocked above the norms in industry and commerce was about 5 billion roubles.[71] Leaving aside speculation as to what share of this production was indeed obsolete, of unacceptably low quality or defective, and what share was only classified as unmarketable on paper, the fact of the matter was that to manufacture this production the *sovnarkhozy* had paid salaries and used materials. For the Ukrainian budget this constituted losses: the turnover taxes, or any other transfers normally received from profits, were not paid and considerable amounts of cash were withheld from official circulation, since the goods were never officially sold.[72] At the same time, 5 billion roubles constituted about one-fifth of the investments that the USSR CM allocated to Ukraine for 1958; total investments constituted about 26.5 billion roubles. In fact, the difference between the amount of investment approved for Ukraine for 1958 and the amount that Ukraine asked for was 6 billion 760 million roubles.[73] *De facto* or *de jure*, unmarketable and obsolete production was a loss to the official economy.

The new system had enough loopholes through which regional managers could withdraw resources from the control of planners and use them for their own purposes. In the official rhetoric, prioritizing one's own needs was qualified as *mestnichestvo* and a violation of state discipline. To the *sovnarkhozy*, prioritizing one's own needs was an objective necessity dictated by the economy of scarcities and uncertainties about incoming supplies. Moreover, 'the combination of regional underdevelopment and the heightened burden of personal responsibility on party and Sovnarkhoz leaders for the performance of their regions'[74] made prioritizing one's own economic needs inevitable. Establishing control over resources was the priority issue for the planners and the republican and central authorities.

8 Gosplan of Ukraine
Setting its authority in the republic

To keep control over resources, starting in 1958, the central and Ukrainian leadership continuously put pressure on the *sovnarkhozy* to stop *mestnichestvo* in supplies, mainly with legislative acts.[1] To Gosplan of Ukraine, gaining control over resources was particularly important. Gosplan of Ukraine gained institutional weight only with the *Sovnarkhoz* system. Its authority in the republican administrative system depended on access to the resources managed by the *sovnarkhozy* and GlUMPP, on access to information generated in the regions and accumulated in the centre, and on *de facto* administrative power to influence decision making in the regions, which could be obtained only in Moscow. At the same time, republican planners believed that possessing resources and information would enable them to bring the *sovnarkhozy* under control and would ensure that the republic fulfilled its all-Union obligations. In 1958–1959, Gosplan of Ukraine put pressure on Moscow to expand the margins of its authority.

Inputs and railways

In 1958, providing resources for the regions in sufficient volume was particularly hard for Gosplan of Ukraine. By 1 January 1958, the Soviet economy was running a deficit of 50 billion roubles.[2] Part of the deficit was supposed to be covered by putting into practice the new policy of uncovering concealed, or 'frozen', production capacities. So the inputs and investments assigned to the republic for 1958 did not fully correspond to the production targets. The production targets for 1958 were higher than in 1957 and the inputs were lower than in 1957. For Ukraine, the growth rate for gross output was planned at 108.1 per cent, including 113 per cent for machine-building, whereas the funds for rolled metal constituted 99.3 per cent of the funds in 1957 and the funds for some chemical materials constituted 25–60 per cent of the required inputs. At the same time, subsidising of the coal-mining industry, which represented 7.5 per cent of Ukrainian industry, was stopped.[3] (Of all Ukrainian branches, coal-mining remained unprofitable until 1965; metallurgy, after the introduction of a 7-hour working day, became unprofitable in 1959.[4]) At the same time, a number of goods that since 1955 had remained for republican distribution were now in central distribution.[5] Growth of output had to be provided by producers: by attracting accumulated resources, increasing productivity, promoting advanced technologies and by using decentralized investment.

The Ukrainian leadership did not believe in its ability to put into practice the policy of increasing growth by uncovering concealed production capacities. So in December 1957 and January 1958 Gosplan of Ukraine approached USSR Gosplan asking, amongst other things, for authorization to provide the necessary inputs a) by setting supplementary production targets for much-needed rolled metal, pipes, rails, cast iron, cord, cable, non-ferrous metals, sodium, starch, equipment and other materials to Ukrainian enterprises; and b) by leaving to the republic all above-plan residues of ferrous and non-ferrous metals, metal and cable production, wood and construction materials and chemicals. Ukraine asked for inputs that could not be manufactured by the republic to be provided by other republics through USSR Gosplan setting supplementary production targets. Interestingly, the Chairman of the USSR Gosplan Kuz'min had first signed an authorization for Gosplan of Ukraine to set supplementary plan targets of its own, but later annulled it,[6] prompting Gosplan of Ukraine to address the CC CPUk with the problem.

The situation with the inputs for 1959 was similar: USSR Gosplan did not provide resources in sufficient amounts to fulfil the approved production targets.[7] However, at the end of 1958, along with traditionally asking USSR Gosplan for additional supplies and the authorization to set supplementary production and make use of above-plan production, Gosplan of Ukraine proposed making some systemic changes. Ukrainian planners argued that the 1959 plans for production and material and technical supplies should be approved simultaneously to ensure that production targets matched available resources.[8] The regions would not necessarily reveal their true production capacities, but they would not use lack of inputs as an excuse for the non-fulfilment of the production plan or delivery plan. At the same time, insisted Gosplan of Ukraine, it was necessary to change the entire principle of distribution of industrial and agricultural production.

The existing procedure for distributing agricultural production compelled the republic to supply first the all-Union funds and only then to keep the residue. A similar mechanism worked for industrial production distributed by the republic. So Gosplan of Ukraine and the *sovnarkhozy* had incentives to increase output. 'However, with production for centralized distribution there is no incentive to increase output',[9] explained the Vice-Chairman of Gosplan of Ukraine G.P. Onishchenko. No matter how much a Ukrainian enterprise produced, its output was distributed by the centre and the centre determined how much of that production the republic received back. So if the centre sought to increase the output, the principle of distribution had to be changed. The republic should decide how much it could produce, how much of its production it needed, and how much it could deliver outside the republic. 'You can check our needs, whether we determined them correctly, and whether we have distributed the rest correctly'.[10] (In their March 1958 proposals 'On further improving the administration of industry and construction', the *sovnarkhozy* argued that keeping enough domestic production for their own needs, particularly wood, consumer goods and other finished products, and then delivering the rest outside the region, would reduce transportation cross-hauls.[11]) In 1958 and 1959 Gosplan of Ukraine also objected to the inclusion on the list of centrally distributed products the production of local industry, which had previously been administered by the Ukrainian Ministry of Local and Fuel Industry and which was now managed partly by the *sovnarkhozy* and partly by the *oblispolkomy* and district committees of the Communist Party (*raikomy*).[12]

Along with arguing that the republic should have priority in consuming and distributing production of its enterprises, in 1958 the Ukrainian leadership raised a rather unexpected issue, from Moscow's perspective, which was that of decentralizing control over *railway transportation*. The Ukrainian leadership promised that under republican administration, the work of the six Ukrainian railways and the fulfilment of delivery plans would improve. The idea of decentralizing the administration of railway transportation could have first come to the minds of the republican leaders, but it was the *sovnarkhozy* who at the end of 1957 alerted the CC CPUk that 'formal and bureaucratic relations' had been established between the *sovnarkhozy* and the administrations of railways. The latter often ignored the requests of the *sovnarkhozy* to provide them with wagons or to change traffic direction, and so on.[13]

In April 1958, the CC CPUk tried to implement Khrushchev's idea from August 1953 and suggested to the central leadership that it should transform the all-Union Ministry of Railways into a Union-Republic one and create a Ukrainian Ministry of Railways. Podgornyi explained to the CC CPSU that the average daily railway loading in Ukraine constituted 30 per cent of the total loading in the Union, 85 per cent of which stayed inside Ukraine. A substantial share of cargo transport was seasonal agricultural production. Centralized management of the railways only complicated the administration of the economy.[14]

Ukraine was refused. Khrushchev must have been no longer in favour of the idea and administration of the railways remained centralized. In February 1959, Gosplan of Ukraine tried to initiate changes in transportation planning, arguing that the existing procedure, whereby the Ministry planned all traffic on the basis of the requests of the republic Gosplans, and where the *sovnarkhozy*, *oblispolkomy* and the remaining ministries had to submit one set of the documents to the railway administrations and another set to their Gosplans, complicated and slowed the planning process and the administration of traffic. Ukraine suggested that local transportation should be planned locally, by the railway administration.[15]

Information and inter-republican deliveries

Providing a sufficient volume of inputs for the *sovnarkhozy* to (relatively) effortlessly meet production targets, or obtaining control over railway transportation, would have certainly consolidated the authority of the Ukrainian republican planners and increased their power vis-à-vis the *sovnarkhozy* and enterprises. However, obtaining control over the railways was impossible and obtaining the necessary inputs was not always guaranteed. The centre could not and, furthermore, did not consider it necessary to provide all producers with the appropriate supplies. After all, the *Sovnarkhoz* reform was designed to boost economic growth by increasing productivity, not inputs, and relied on the administrative skills of peripheral managers. Under these circumstances, Gosplan of Ukraine could provide the required inputs only by increasing the number of products distributed by the republic. The simplest way to increase this list was to reduce the list of Ukrainian production for inter-republican deliveries, or 'to optimize the long-distance economic relations', in the terminology of the time.

The optimization of inter-republican deliveries was complicated from the very start. The aim of the reform in cutting irrational long-distance transportation cross-hauls was not supported by the new organizational structure. The administration of inter-republican deliveries, particularly contractual deliveries in the machine-building branches,[16] remained centralized and was provided by the *Glavsbyty*. Whereas the republics sought to reduce the number of inter-republican deliveries and replace their distantly located partners with local ones, the *Glavsbyty* did not and could not have such an interest. Reducing long-distance inter-republican deliveries meant increased volumes of resources under the control of the *sovnarkhozy* and increased self-sufficiency for the territorial economies. The influence of the central planners on the republics and branches would subsequently be reduced. In setting and managing inter-republican deliveries, *Glavsbyty* and Gosplan of Ukraine were motivated by opposing pressures.

In addition to these opposing pressures, there were technical problems to optimizing economic relations. First, the terms for deliveries and procedures for concluding contracts were not unified, which complicated the revision of existing inter-republican relations.[17] Second, Gosplan of Ukraine could do very little to optimize inter-republican deliveries for republican enterprises without the relevant information.

With the *Sovnarkhoz* system, work on the optimization of contractual and other inter-republican deliveries had to be held at three levels: all-Union, republican and regional. It might be assumed that the *sovnarkhozy* would have collected information on the regional economies quite promptly, given their proximity to production. However, as the composition of the 1958 draft plans demonstrated, in 1957 the *sovnarkhozy* did not have complete knowledge of the industrial complex of their regions. Of course, with time, the *sovnarkhozy* learned their economies and could increase inner-regional cooperation, but in 1957 and 1958, despite the new opportunities to cut transportation costs, the *sovnarkhozy* generally maintained old relations for their enterprises. The head of the department of Gosplan of Ukraine for specialization and cooperation N.F. Dolzhenko illustrated this tendency:

> If you check the requests (*zayavki*) of the *sovnarkhozy* you will clearly see a narrow departmental tendency: Vinnitsa tool-making plant is getting up to 10 tonnes of casts from the Leningrad tool-making plant because both of them were run by the same ministry. And there are plenty of examples like this one.[18]

However, Dolzhenko admitted that after the *sovnarkhozy* thought through this problem they sent their requests to Gosplan of Ukraine asking to change their suppliers.[19] Collecting information in manual mode could not solve the problem of optimizing economic relations in the short term.

Gosplan of Ukraine was in a better position to redesign economic relations inside the republic than the *sovnarkhozy* were in the regions. It started working on the problem even before Khrushchev presented his idea of reform.[20] Information on 78.6 per cent of Ukraine's industry was obtained by the *Ukrglavsnabsbyty* from the Ukrainian ministries. For information on the 17.6 per cent of Ukrainian industry and construction which was transferred to Ukrainian control with the reform, Kiev was at the mercy of the *Glavsbyty*. Yet even without information from the *Glavsbyty*, Gosplan of Ukraine could say already in October 1957 that for the transportation of imported equipment from other republics and from abroad, Ukraine incurred 350 million roubles of unproductive expenditures in 1957. Ukraine 'ordered and imported 2/3 of the equipment of the same name (*odnoimennoe oborudovanie*)', although still, in the 1958 draft plan, Gosplan of Ukraine could eliminate only 8 per cent of the long-distance deliveries qualified as irrational.[21]

USSR Gosplan and *Glavsbyty* had complete information on inter-republican contractual deliveries since they had access to all the data of the abolished ministries. But the *Glavsbyty* often refused to provide the necessary information to the republican planners. When the *Ukrglavsnabsbyty* received information from the *Glavsbyty* and other central agencies, they still needed to spend time matching classifications of enterprises. USSR Gosplan, the Ministry of Finance, *Gosbank* and the TsSU each classified enterprises according to their own system.[22] An enterprise classified by the Ministry of Finance as belonging to one branch could be classified by USSR Gosplan as belonging to a different branch. Even goods for contractual deliveries were categorized according to different systems all over the country. One standard system for classifying components did not exist. So in 1958, Gosplan of Ukraine had to work out its own system, based on which the *Ukrglavsnabsbyty* and the *sovnarkhozy* would select products for contractual deliveries.[23]

The absence of a common information system left the republics and regions highly dependent on USSR Gosplan's efficiency in coordinating and regulating inter-republican deliveries. At the end of November 1959, at the meeting of the chairmen of the *sovnarkhozy* in USSR Gosplan, it was stated that 'the time had come to study contractual relationships and develop those that proved to be most beneficial',[24] which meant that the *sovnarkhozy* could not review contractual relationships without coordination from the centre.

Managing inter-republican deliveries

To manage inter-republican deliveries efficiently and to control their implementation by the *sovnarkhozy*, Gosplan of Ukraine also lacked information. 'The main problem for us is the absence of a plan for inter-republican deliveries.

Soyuzglavmetallosbyt [Main department for sales of metallurgical production] persistently refuses to give us the plan, in spite of the recent resolution of the Government. We are managing deliveries, in fact, in the dark',[25] commented Slysh from the Ukrainian main administration for supplies and sales of metal production (*Ukrglavmetallosnabsbyt*) in May 1959 on the state of communication between the republican and central planners. By the end of that year, nothing had changed: 'We do not have a plan for inter-republican deliveries and we never had it. Yet responsibility [for the fulfilment of the plan] lies with the republic'.[26]

Strictly speaking, a situation where Gosplan of Ukraine was ignorant of the plan for the republic should not have occurred since the main indices were negotiated between Kiev and Moscow. In practice, however, the negotiated targets were not included in the final plan. The reason for that was shared planning inside USSR Gosplan. The Ukrainian government negotiated inter-republican deliveries with the USSR Gosplan general departments according to group categories. Yet decomposing the group categories into specific products was done by GlUMPP, which did not always accurately adhere to the figures that were negotiated between USSR Gosplan and the republic. Such practices certainly complicated control over the fulfilment of inter-republican deliveries by the *sovnarkhozy*, but at the same time provided both the *sovnarkhozy* and Gosplan of Ukraine with an explanation if inter-republican deliveries were not fulfilled.

Why did GlUMPP not communicate the modified plan to the republic? According to the USSR CM resolution of 22 January 1959, they did not have to. GlUMPP were compelled to coordinate the placement of production orders with the republic Gosplans but were not specifically compelled to coordinate with the republics the changes that they introduced to the plan through the delivery orders.[27] Yet GlUMPP complicated the management of the supply system further when, in addition to arbitrarily modifying the plans, they exceeded the margins of their authority and issued delivery orders for internal republican supplies. Here they violated the above-mentioned resolution.

In June 1959, Gosplan of the RSFSR described the situation to the Head of the USSR CM Legal department Mishunin:

> In direct violation of the established order [by the resolution of 22 January 1959], by 10 June 1959 *Soyuzglavtyazhmash* [the USSR Gosplan main department for inter-republican deliveries of production of heavy machine-building industry] has issued hundreds of orders and continues issuing them directly to the mills-suppliers of the RSFSR for the mills-consumers of the RSFSR as well as for the mills-consumers in other republics. ... *Soyuzglavtyazhmash*, again in violation of the established procedures set by the USSR CM, leaves *Rosglavtyazhmashsnabsbyt* of Gosplan of the RSFSR [main department for supplies and sales of production of heavy machine-building industry] uninformed of the cancellations and changes in the orders that it communicates directly to the producers, and gives instructions to the mills-suppliers of the RSFSR about deliveries to other republics and for all-Union needs as well as to the mills-consumers of the RSFSR, without

discussing and coordinating these issues with *Rosglavtyazhmashsnabsbyt* of Gosplan of the RSFSR.²⁸

By the beginning of 1960, the functions of the supply and sales agencies were still not clearly defined. By then, the Ukrainian government could assert that some GlUMPP personnel used the lack of clarity in the functions of the central, republican and *sovnarkhozy snabsbyty* to recentralize the supply system and to consolidate their own power; instead of curtailing their functions, they enhanced them.

> The majority of GlUMPP did not fulfil the USSR CM resolution on the composition of plans for inter-republican deliveries or fulfilled it completely unsatisfactorily. ... *Soyuzglavmetal* [USSR Gosplan State Committee for Metallurgy] interpreted the 22 January 1959 USSR CM resolution as an instruction to withdraw sales from the jurisdiction of the Union republics and return it to the previously existing system of centralized sales. Whereas in 1958 *Slyuzglavmetal* composed the plans for inter-republican deliveries of non-ferrous metals, in 1959 it did not. ... A similarly unregulated situation exists with other GlUMPP.

Some GlUMPP, however, did share the plans with the republics, did not issue centralized delivery orders and created the conditions necessary for fulfilling the delivery plans of the republics.²⁹

Direct communication between GlUMPP and the producers might have been effective had GlUMPP been efficient. However, as the economy grew, GlUMPP could not physically cope with the paperwork. For example, in April 1959, the GlUMPP that managed sales of electronic equipment was behind schedule with 1,195 orders for equipment to be exported by six Ukrainian *sovnarkhozy*.³⁰ At the same time, the absence of delivery plans and their replacement with delivery orders often meant that the total volume of production orders was either too large for the available inputs or too small. The chairman of the Stalino *Sovnarkhoz* N. Sobol' called such planning 'a great evil' for the supplier-enterprises as well as for the consumers: GlUMPP issuing orders for volumes exceeding their production targets 'leads to irresponsibility among suppliers and deprives consumers of their right to receive production that is assigned to them'.³¹ Furthermore, central planners did not always operate with accurate production information about the enterprises to which they gave orders. In February 1959, Gosplan of Ukraine had to explain to USSR Gosplan that Ukrainian plants could not manufacture 1,201 cranes as was agreed in the plan because production of the cranes at the Zhdanov metal construction plant, which was one of two producers, was unrealistic, as its production capacities were overloaded with production of metal constructions for mining machine-building.³²

All in all, GlUMPP clearly indicated that they aimed to minimize the participation of *Ukrglavsnabsbyty* in managing supplies. Such a policy certainly undermined the power and authority of the *Ukrglavsnabsbyty* vis-à-vis the *sovnarkhozy* and their ability to assist Moscow in controlling and ensuring inter-republican supplies. It equally contributed to conflict between the central and republican planners. Inevitably, to build up their administrative weight, the *Ukrglavsnabsbyty* channelled their energy to orchestrating resources of republican origin. Now the lack of detailed and up-to-date delivery plans constituted a legitimate excuse for the *Ukrglavsnabsbyty* to satisfy the demands of the Ukrainian customers in the production of Ukrainian origin and allowed them to consolidate their administrative position. The *sovnarkhozy*'s craving for inputs and the *Ukrglavsnabsbyty*'s craving for power were allied.

A symptomatic situation was created in 1960 with the deliveries of metal. Ukrainian metallurgical mills were the major suppliers of metal production,[33] and over-fulfilled production plans, over-fulfilled delivery plans and supplied volumes of metal and pipes that exceeded the volumes for which Moscow had issued delivery orders. However, only Ukrainian customers benefited from the achievement of the Ukrainian mills as they received supplementary thousands of tonnes of metal and steel pipes based on delivery orders issued by *Ukrglavmetallosnabsbyt*. In contrast, the deliveries managed by USSR Gosplan for the RSFSR, Kazakhstan, Georgia, Azerbaijan, Moldavia and Estonia; USSR Ministries and departments of Railways, of Power Plants Construction and of Marine Fleet; USSR State Committees for chemical production, automation and machine-building, shipbuilding, grain production, aircraft engineering and radio electronics; *Glavgaz* and other all-Union consumers remained under-fulfilled.[34] USSR Gosplan blamed *Ukrglavmetallosnabsbyt* and the *sovnarkhozy* concerned for the difficulties experienced by non-Ukrainian customers and asked the Ukrainian government for assistance in enforcing the delivery plan.

Conclusion

By the end of 1959, Gosplan of Ukraine, which had been reorganized for the purpose of running the republican economy, still had only limited and non-systemic authority over production.[35] The Ukrainian planners did not possess any effective administrative or economic levers to protect all-Union interests in the republic. They did not have sufficient mechanisms or the staff to monitor the *sovnarkhozy*, regularly obtain and process information on resources available in the regions and force the *sovnarkhozy* to share their surpluses with others. Branch departments of Gosplan of Ukraine had no directive rights: they could only recommend that the *sovnarkhozy* accept goods for production; the *sovnarkhozy* were free to refuse.[36]

The authority of Gosplan of Ukraine was further undermined by the lack of clarity in the functions of the *snabsbyty* and poor communication between the central and republican planners. The conditions for the *sovnarkhozy* to pursue localism therefore remained most favourable. Under these circumstances, the Ukrainian authorities urged the central leadership to formalize the administrative system and align responsibility for production and deliveries with decision-making authority. The fact that GIUMPP made decisions on production for

Gosplan of Ukraine 87

inter-republican deliveries but were not held accountable for the failures of the deliveries complicated control over regional *mestnichestvo* and increased the uncertainty about the fulfilment of contracts on the part of the *sovnarkhozy*. The decision making of GlUMPP had to be constrained and controlled. Gosplan of Ukraine insisted that by establishing direct control over the fulfilment of inter-republican deliveries, assigning production targets and contacting local warehouses directly, GlUMPP usurped the republican and regional *snabsbyty* and disorganized the production process and control over supplies.

To simplify the administration of supplies, Gosplan of Ukraine suggested that USSR Gosplan compose a single list of goods for inter-republican deliveries: it should extend the list of goods that was composed jointly by USSR Gosplan and the republic Gosplans, including the detailed list of the GlUMPP and excluding the products that should be transferred to the republics. Instead of two plans there should be one. This plan should be the only document regulating inter-republican deliveries. This would make it unnecessary for GlUMPP to issue orders. The principle of assigning priority status to deliveries should change as well. Inter-regional or local deliveries were sometimes as or more important than inter-republican deliveries.[37]

By the end of 1959, the conflict of obligations that was originally incorporated in the duties of Gosplan of Ukraine – to ensure the fulfilment of the production plan by the republic and to enforce the fulfilment of the supply plans by the *sovnarkhozy* in an economy of scarcity – reached its culmination. By this time, the Ukrainian planners had developed strong incentives to protect republican interests and Moscow had to deal with *mestnichestvo* on two different levels: *mestnichestvo* at the regional level and *mestnichestvo* at the republican level. For Moscow, the latter tendency was unquestionably more alarming. The efforts of Gosplan of Ukraine to centralize economic authority at the republican level, supported by the CC CPUk, had unpredictable implications for the Soviet economy and for the power of the central *apparat* over the republican economy in particular. Without ever testing the ability of Gosplan of Ukraine to control the *sovnarkhozy*, USSR Gosplan moved from tacit to open curtailment of the process of decentralizing decision making.

Part III
Recentralizing economic administration

9 The turning point

Two years into the *Sovnarkhoz* reform, the new institutional system still lacked transparency. The central *apparat*, the republican authorities and the *sovnarkhozy* remained driven by contradictory aims and incentives. Whilst the republic authorities sought to formalize the system of economic administration and maximize the devolution of economic decision making, the central *apparat* concentrated its efforts on keeping the republics and regions dependent on its own decision making. As a result, the implementation of the decentralization policy was full of inconsistencies. The institutional mechanisms, so necessary for the policy of decentralization to take full effect, were either not installed or were rendered ineffective. Formally centralized distribution of materials and equipment, and centralized management of inter-republican deliveries, proved insufficient for the central planners to retain control over resources and induced the central *apparat* to impose informal control over resources. The *sovnarkhozy*, particularly the highly industrialized ones, had more leverage over the planners than the planners had over the *sovnarkhozy*. In 1959, before it had had a chance to prove itself, the policy of decentralization of economic decision making entered a U-turn.

In March 1959 the central government decided to close the Moscow office of *Ukrglavsnabsbyty* of Gosplan of Ukraine, following a proposal from the Commission of Soviet Control that was also supported by USSR Gosplan. In April, Podgornyi objected to the idea of closing the Moscow office of *Ukrglavsnabsbyty*, arguing that the supply system could not guarantee supplies.

> Given that at present, orders are issued centrally by GlUMPP for all inter-republican deliveries that include 11 thousand categories, maintaining regular communication with the all-Union *sbyty* is a necessary condition without which it would be impossible to ensure the placement of orders according to the required specifications and by the required deadlines.[1]

The confrontation between the Ukrainian authorities and USSR Gosplan in 1959–1960 might have ended in Kiev's favour, to a certain extent, had USSR Gosplan not obtained a new chairman. In 1959 the 'indecisive', *nereshitel'nyi*, Iosif Kuz'min was replaced by the 'experienced and talented manager' Aleksei Kosygin.

Kuz'min had come to USSR Gosplan from the Central Committee, where he was the head of the department of machine-building. For his reform, Khrushchev wanted someone new, someone not from the ex-ministerial *apparat*: 'all of them [the ministers] did not see an alternative to the branch vertical, did not understand the need for the reform',[2] Sergei Khrushchev remembered. Kuz'min supported the idea of the *sovnarkhozy* and worked with Khrushchev from the start. At the same time, to Khrushchev 'Kuz'min appeared industrious, taking the initiative, and thinking'.[3] However, once in USSR Gosplan, Kuz'min did not manage to impose his authority over the ministers; according to Sergei Khrushchev, Kuz'min lacked the knowledge and experience of running the entire economy. By 1959, Khrushchev understood that assigning Kuz'min to head USSR Gosplan was a mistake, and so he entrusted USSR Gosplan to Kosygin, someone who had the requisite experience and knowledge.[4]

Kosygin was assigned to USSR Gosplan after the XXI Party Congress (27 January–5 February 1959), which was called to approve the Seven Year Plan (1959–1965). The criticism of the unsatisfactory work of USSR Gosplan that was heard at the Congress was followed by the separation of perspective planning from current planning and the organization of a new planning agency, the USSR CM State Scientific and Economic Council, or *Gosekonomsovet*, for perspective planning. The former Chairman of USSR Gosplan Kuz'min was transferred to head *Gosekonomsovet*.[5]

Compared to Kuz'min, Kosygin was indeed better qualified to run USSR Gosplan, and as a result, 'with the arrival of Kosygin, the performance of Gosplan improved',[6] Sergei Khrushchev recalled. But Kosygin was someone from the ex-ministerial *apparat* who was also perfectly qualified to restore centralized control over regional economies. Brought up in the strict Stalinist system of vertical power, Kosygin truly believed in the ministerial system as the only effective system of economic administration, 'the system that had proved itself during the years of industrialization and war'.[7] Kosygin was a man of discipline and tolerated the *sovnarkhozy*, but he was suspicious of any manifestations of liberty in managing the economy.[8]

So does the replacement of Kuz'min by Kosygin mean that Khrushchev sought to curtail the reform already in 1959? Or, as Sergei Khrushchev suggests, did Khrushchev simply replace Kuz'min with the best available candidate because he was tired of the quarrels between Kuz'min and the ministers in USSR Gosplan, expecting that the new candidate would continue the policy of decentralization? After all, economic growth in 1958 was higher than the previous year, which indicated the success, rather than the failure, of the *Sovnarkhoz* system.

It seems unlikely that Khrushchev intended to curtail the reform as early as 1959. At the same time, as a new chairman of the government (since March 1958), Khrushchev might have sought to restore centralized control over resources. In any event, Kosygin, as a man of discipline, worked vigorously to impose discipline over the peripheral managers, which in his interpretation meant nothing else but restoring the central *apparat*'s confidence in recentralizing administration of the economy. After one year of re-tuning USSR Gosplan,

Kosygin left the chairmanship of USSR Gosplan to another disciplined *apparatchik* and a true believer in the strict Stalinist system of vertical administration, Vladimir Novikov.[9] In July 1962, Novikov was replaced by Veniamin Dymshits, a friend of Khrushchev, but also another man reared by the ministerial system.

As a result of Kosygin's arrival in USSR Gosplan, starting in 1959, the tacit resistance of the central *apparat* to decentralization became loud and well articulated and the central *apparat* increasingly pressured Khrushchev to curtail the economic rights of the peripheral managers. Exerting such pressure would not have been difficult. After his term in USSR Gosplan, Kosygin became the First Vice-Chairman of the USSR CM and was, therefore, well placed to share with Khrushchev his arguments in favour of recentralizing economic administration. Besides, the *sovnarkhozy* and republican governments persisted in prioritizing their own interests. For Khrushchev, the true believer in the union of the republics, the tendency towards *mestnichestvo* was unacceptable. By the November 1962 CC CPSU Plenum, Khrushchev fully supported the consolidation of the centralized branch administration. For the central *apparat*, this meant nothing less than Khrushchev's backing of the policy of recentralization.

The present chapter addresses the events of that transition period from 1959 until 1962. Khrushchev still advocated the *Sovnarkhoz* reform, leaving the republican governments with the hope that the recentralization pursued by USSR Gosplan was reversible, and letting them believe that the non-procedural practices of the central planners and informal curtailment of republican economic rights were random violations of separate departments rather than a systematic policy. Ukraine more than other republics had reasons to believe this was the case. During this period the Ukrainian republican authorities, although they could not shield republican planners and managers from the informal managerial practices of the central planners, had nonetheless successfully retained control over the republican administrative system. Furthermore, as Koropeckyj observed:

> [The Ukrainian leadership] started to stress the importance of the republic in international trade of the USSR. ... Officials heading the international department of the Ukrainian Gosplan were identified for the first time. The Ukraine was visited by several economic delegations from foreign countries. ... The republic began to participate separately from the USSR in various international fairs.[10]

The November 1959 meeting at USSR Gosplan

At the beginning of November 1959, in the middle of his chairmanship, Kosygin called a meeting of the functionaries of USSR Gosplan and Gosplan of the RSFSR and chairmen of the *sovnarkhozy* who had come to Moscow to participate in the 3rd session of the USSR Supreme Soviet. The fact that the meeting was called spontaneously, as Kosygin put it, makes one wonder whether it would have been called at all. Regardless, the meeting was held and the participants discussed their problems. In particular, the discussion turned around two issues: USSR and RSFSR Gosplans wanted to know why the plans were not being fulfilled; the *sovnarkhozy* wanted to find out why their rights were curtailed.

The chairman of the *sovnarkhozy* had rather similar understandings of the reasons for the non-fulfilment of plans. Among the most commonly mentioned causes were a) the lack of correlation between production and investment plans; b) the inapplicability of the investment plans, when either the equipment or the machinery was available but the funds for its installation were not, or the funds were available but the equipment was not delivered, or the deadlines for launching new production were unrealistic; and c) modified production tasks that exceeded the originally assigned production targets. To ensure the fulfilment of production targets, USSR Gosplan should correlate production and supply plans. Supplementary production tasks should be eliminated, but if they were necessary, they should be discussed with the *sovnarkhozy* first. Aleksandr Zademid'ko from the Kemerovo *Sovnarkhoz* gave an example when, in addition to the plan targets, his plant was instructed to produce certain materials and equipment. As it was later discovered, the Kemerovo *Sovnarkhoz* could not fulfil the order because the plant in question did not belong to the Kemerovo *Sovnarkhoz*. GlUMPP should not contact enterprises directly for at least one simple reason: when ordering production directly from an enterprise, the director could choose what was easier and simpler for the enterprise to manufacture, but not what was necessary. GlUMPP might also order from a plant that had no capacity to fulfil the order. The same should be applied to the *sovnarkhozy*: if during the year the planners needed certain goods, the *sovnarkhozy* should be given a specific order and not 'the volume', *bezob'emnyi val*, that permitted them to choose what to produce. The *sovnarkhozy* might also choose what was not needed.

The chairman of the *sovnarkhozy* considered it necessary that the *sovnarkhozy* should again be allowed to re-distribute inputs between construction sites. They had had this right in 1958, but not in 1959. *Glavkomplekty* should concern themselves only with the most important construction sites and unique installations. The *sovnarkhozy* should manage the absolute majority of products. Investments should be assigned to the *sovnarkhozy* in total and the *sovnarkhozy* should be allowed to distribute and redistribute investments between the branches and merely inform Gosplan of their final decisions.

The supply system in the periphery and in the centre had become cumbersome, according to the chairman of the *sovnarkhozy*, so USSR Gosplan should distribute only the scarcest production. The *sovnarkhozy* should be allowed to stop manufacturing goods which were not in demand. In theory the *sovnarkhozy* had this right, but since the targeted production volume, *val*, was not reviewed, they could not exercise it. The *sovnarkhozy* should also be allowed to reduce the prices of products that were not in demand. In order to increase output, 25 per cent of production manufactured above the plan should remain for the *Sovnarkhoz*. *Sovnarkhozy* also craved more information and asked Kosygin to improve the quality of statistical reporting.

Kosygin spoke against the redistribution of investments between branches: the CC CPSU planned the development of one branch but investment went into another. As for leaving 25 per cent of the above-plan production to the *sovnarkhozy*, Kosygin was also against this: some over-fulfil the plan, others under-fulfil. Kosygin promised to think about the redistribution of supplies and agreed with the criticism of the practice of assigning supplementary production targets: plans should be specific and accurate. At the same time, he complained that the *sovnarkhozy* were curtailing or ceasing production of some consumer goods that remained in demand.[11]

The November 1959 meeting at USSR Gosplan marked the turning point of the reform. After Kosygin's explanation that the curtailment of managerial authority for regional managers was part of a policy that aimed at restoring centralized control over resources, the illusion that the *sovnarkhozy* cherished about boosting the policy of decentralization started to fade. Disillusionment continued as the central leadership initiated a new regionalization and the creation of Republican *Sovnarkhozy* for the RSFSR, Kazakhstan and Ukraine.

New regionalization

The Soviet press started preparing the public for a new regionalization at the beginning of 1960.[12] In the February edition of *Voprosy ekonomiki*, the author of an article described as 'posing a problem' argued that since economic complexes spread beyond the frontiers of the republics, the time had come to merge economic regions. 'Already at present, a new type of economic region has been outlined, an inter-republican region that embraces separate Union republics and several economic administrative regions of the RSFSR.'[13]

In April 1960, the central leadership announced the forthcoming reorganization which, however, did not merge the republics or the economic administrative regions but regrouped them in large regions with economic councils at the top. The new economic councils were supposed to 'further develop and consolidate economic relations between the *sovnarkhozy* and develop specialization and cooperation in production'.[14] Above all, they were supposed to bring the economic regions closer to the central planners.

The new administrative structure was to be elaborated by USSR Gosplan in cooperation with the governments of the Union republics. The work on the proposal advanced rather slowly and whether it was because the *sovnarkhozy* and *obkomy* opposed the idea, or because there was no real need for these councils, it took almost eight months for USSR Gosplan to submit to the USSR CM its final draft that regrouped 78 economic regions into 13 large regions.[15] The new councils were not envisioned for Ukraine, Kazakhstan, Moldavia, and three Russian *sovnarkhozy*.[16] For them, with the exception of Moldavia, which geographically could not be united with any other republic but Ukraine, the central authorities created Republican *Sovnarkhozy*.

With the new economic councils, the role of the *obkomy* in economic management would reduce. Local Party functionaries were not included in the new councils and they were not invited to participate at any stage of the work of the economic council of the enlarged region.[17] They were not included in the councils of the original *sovnarkhozy* either, but in 1957, far fewer *oblasti* composed one

96 *Recentralizing economic administration*

economic region, so the *obkomy* could and did form close relations with the *sovnarkhozy*. With a much larger number of *oblasti*, it became harder for the *obkomy* to protect the economic interests of their *oblasti*.

According to Conyngham's interpretation of the events of 1960, the new councils for enlarged economic regions and the pronounced intention to debar Party functionaries from economic management reflected the growing power of governmental functionaries in the crucial period of their conflict with the Party *apparat*.

> The crucial period of the conflict was probably between the June 1959 and July 1960 plena of the Central Committee. The 1959 plenum, the first since the adoption of the Seven-Year Plan, was more sharply critical of the managers' technological conservatism and the inefficiencies of the system of management than at any time since the reorganization. The decision to maximize the pressure of the Party apparatus in economic decision making, however, met such opposition that it was reversed by the July 1960 plenum, which, like the December 1956 plenum, was dominated by state economic officials. Of the thirty-three speakers, only seven were Party officials.[18]

Planners from *Gosekonomsovet* also worked on the new regionalization. In order to compose a general perspective plan for the economic development of the USSR for the period until 1980, they suggested dividing the country into 16 regions. Contrary to the regionalization proposed by USSR Gosplan, *Gosekonomsovet* included Ukraine, Kazakhstan, Moldavia and three Russian *sovnarkhozy* in its regionalization.[19]

New regionalization in Ukraine: three new *sovnarkhozy*

As the centre sought to bring control over production sites closer to USSR Gosplan and prepared the ground for the future merging of economic regions, the Ukrainians moved in the opposite direction. They increased the number of the economic regions, bringing their total to 14, and, as analysed below, debarred the newly organized Ukrainian Republican *Sovnarkhoz* from participating in economic administration. The three new economic regions formed in Ukraine in 1960 were of Crimea, which consisted of one *oblast'*; Poltava, which also consisted of one *oblast'*; and Cherkassy, which united two *oblasti*, Kirovograd and Cherkassy. The formal reason for creating separate economic regions out of these *oblasti* was poor management of their current *sovnarkhozy*, Kherson, Khar'kov and Kiev respectively, and the fact that a large share of their enterprises was administered by local trusts.

Thus, for example, the secretary of the Crimean *obkom* V. Komyakhov and the Deputy of the Crimean *oblispolkom* N. Moiseev, in their request addressed to N. Podgornyi in January 1960, explained that functionaries of the Kherson *Sovnarkhoz* visited Crimea rarely, preferring to 'govern by phone', so in order to resolve the problems, Crimean managers had to interrupt their immediate work and travel to Kherson. At the same time, the Crimean *oblast'* provided 50 per cent of the industrial output of the Kherson *Sovnarkhoz* and consumed 50 per cent of the total investment for major construction works. In particular, 58 per cent of enterprises in the fish-processing industry and 70 per cent of the fishing industry, 70 per cent of wine-making, 90 per cent of production of the construction materials industry and 65 per cent of energy production were in the Crimean *oblast'*. All enterprises of the metallurgical, chemical, volatile oils and tobacco industries of the Kherson *Sovnarkhoz* were located in the Crimean *oblast'*. Four out of six construction trusts of the Kherson *Sovnarkhoz* were located in Crimea.[20]

According to the Crimean authorities, the creation of the Crimean *Sovnarkhoz* would not affect the administration of the Kherson *Sovnarkhoz* much, because it would manage what the Crimean *oblast'* was already managing. Only 34 out of 134 enterprises were run directly by the Kherson *Sovnarkhoz*; others were run by trusts located in Crimea. Furthermore, the organization of the Crimean *Sovnarkhoz* would allow for a reduction of personnel in the Crimean trusts and in the administration of the Kherson *Sovnarkhoz*.[21]

In March 1960, the CC CPSU approved the creation of the *sovnarkhozy* of Crimea, Poltava and Cherkassy, and in May Ukraine's administrative map changed. (In 1962, Sumy and Chernigov *oblasti* would request separate *sovnarkhozy* for their *oblasti*, but their requests would be rejected by Gosplan of Ukraine at the initial stage of the examination.[22]) The new chairmen were former second secretary of the Crimea *obkom* N.P. Surkin in the Crimea *Sovnarkhoz*, V.N. Yakovlev in the Poltava *Sovnarkhoz* and A.S. Chernegov in the Cherkassy *Sovnarkhoz*. Why did Khrushchev approve the creation of three new economic regions in Ukraine at a time when USSR Gosplan was working on effectively merging the regions? Here we can only speculate, as the documents do not clarify this point.

According to Borys Lewytzkyj, it was in the context of a vehement campaign against localism that the new economic regions aimed 'to improve the organic structure of other regions'.[23] Howard R. Swearer explained that in the case when a *Sovnarkhoz* included several *oblasti* the coordination between the *oblispolkom* and *Sovnarkhoz* became complicated. Poltava complained, as early as the end of 1958, that the Khar'kov *Sovnarkhoz* was favouring Khar'kov *oblast'* with supplies. So, Poltava officials wished to organize a separate economic region.[24]

Indeed, the creation of three new economic regions in Ukraine could have been part of the campaign against *mestnichestvo*. However, there were other factors that must have contributed to the positive decision about the new economic regions and should not be disregarded. First, because the economy was growing in this period – the industrial output of the Ukrainian *sovnarkhozy* increased by 22.5 per cent from 1957 to 1959 – it must indeed have been harder for the *sovnarkhozy* to keep control over production located in remote territories, which also explains why only a quarter of Crimean enterprises were managed directly from Kherson. Second, the Ukrainian leadership enjoyed the support of Khrushchev who had warm feelings towards the republic, and the CPUk had a solid position in the system. In May 1960, the First Secretary of the CC CPUk

N. Podgornyi (1957–1963) was elected to the CC CPSU Presidium. Podgornyi had a good relationship with Khrushchev as well as with other Presidium members and must have pushed this idea in the Presidium and the Central Committee.[25]

Increasing the number of economic regions was a small victory for the Ukrainian leadership. Nonetheless, it demonstrated that whereas in Moscow, USSR Gosplan was gradually imposing its policy upon the Party *apparat*, in Ukraine the Party retained a strong position and did not have any drastic confrontation with Gosplan of Ukraine. The ability of the CC CPUk and Gosplan of Ukraine to cooperate in order to protect common interests became crucial in the republic's efforts to retain control over the republican administrative system after Moscow had installed the Ukrainian Republican *Sovnarkhoz*.

Ukrainian Republican *Sovnarkhoz*, *Ukrsovnarkhoz*

Officially, the Republican *Sovnarkhozy* were formed for the same purpose as the economic councils for enlarged economic regions: to develop specialization and cooperation in the entrusted territory, consolidate branch development and tighten control over local managers. The literature generally interprets the creation of the Republican *Sovnarkhozy* in the RSFSR, Kazakhstan and Ukraine as 'gradual vertical centralization of the *Sovnarkhoz* system'.[26] Yet, if it was control over the Ukrainian *sovnarkhozy* that the centre expected from the *Ukrsovnarkhoz*, then it was integrated in Ukraine's administrative system rather incompetently.

With *Ukrsovnarkhoz*, Gosplan of Ukraine was supposed to be no longer responsible for controlling the *sovnarkhozy* or assisting them in solving problems related to the fulfilment of the production or delivery plans. Its functions were to be reduced to a) drafting annual and perspective plans and b) studying problematic aspects of the economic development of the republic and drafting scientific conclusions, forecasts and propositions.[27] In other words, Gosplan of Ukraine had to work on the economic development of the republic in theory and *Ukrsovnarkhoz* on the practical application of the plans.

Two of the major problems that *Ukrsovnarkhoz* was designed to target were not denied in Ukraine. One problem was uncoordinated decision making at the level of the republican authorities. As the Ukrainian *sovnarkhozy* described it, they had to knock on the doors of the CM for some questions and of Gosplan of Ukraine for others, but it was the CC CPUk that was very often the most helpful. They would prefer to solve all issues in one place. Another problem was the growing regional *mestnichestvo*. Gosplan of Ukraine openly stated that it was losing control over the economic regions. Yet neither Ukrainian *sovnarkhozy* nor Gosplan of Ukraine wished for another organization in the republic. The *sovnarkhozy*, in all likelihood, realized that if 'one place' had the authority to solve all their problems it would also use its power to control them; therefore 'one place' was not desirable. Whereas what Gosplan of Ukraine wished for was the extension of its own authority to be able effectively to influence the decision making of the *sovnarkhozy*. So, from the perspective of the Ukrainian republican and regional managers, the creation of *Ukrsovnarkhoz* was undesirable and unnecessary.[28]

Moscow anticipated that Ukraine would not agree to another organization in the republic, so the decision on *Ukrsovnarkhoz* was not discussed with the republic and was made by, but not necessarily suggested by, the CC CPSU Presidium.[29] This fact, combined with the functions of *Ukrsovnarkhoz*, implies that the centre counted on *Ukrsovnarkhoz* to deliver what Gosplan of Ukraine could not: namely, to bring all resources into controlled circulation and guarantee the fulfilment of inter-republican delivery plans by Ukrainian producers. Yet, to fulfil its recentralization mission, *Ukrsovnarkhoz* lacked two elements from the very start. First, *Ukrsovnarkhoz* was subordinated directly and only to the CMUk.[30] It was not accountable to USSR Gosplan or any other all-Union agency, so Ukraine was not losing its *de jure* authority over republican industry and construction. Second, *Ukrsovnarkhoz* started its administrative life without clearly defined rights and responsibilities and with no economic or administrative authority over the *sovnarkhozy* or the republic-level agencies. The republican status of *Ukrsovnarkhoz*, in combination with its lack of authority, made it relatively easy for the CC CPUk and the Ukrainian government to minimize the participation of the new organization in the economic life of the republic.

Instalment of *Ukrsovnarkhoz*

The first conflict that *Ukrsovnarkhoz* had to settle with the Ukrainian republican authorities was about personnel. Between August 1960, when the first chairman of *Ukrsovnarkhoz* N. Sobol'[31] submitted a proposal on the structure and staff of *Ukrsovnarkhoz*, and 11 March 1961 when the Statute 'On *Ukrsovnarkhoz*' was adopted by the CMUk, the staff of *Ukrsovnarkhoz* was reduced by almost 40 per cent[32] and its structure shrank. Out of five territorial departments, 14 main branch departments, 14 main functional departments and offices, and 79 organizations that *Ukrsovnarkhoz* expected to have in its structure, the CMUk agreed to 14 branch departments, 14 functional, two administrative and no territorial departments. Only 38 organizations were transferred under the jurisdiction of *Ukrsovnarkhoz*. The remaining 41 were left with Gosplan of Ukraine.[33]

The strategy that *Ukrsovnarkhoz* chose to fit within the republican economic administration was not to become a trouble-shooter for the *sovnarkhozy*, even though this was one of its main functions, but to establish petty tutelage over the *sovnarkhozy*. *Ukrsovnarkhoz* followed the path of Gosplan of Ukraine when, in 1957–1958, it tried to bypass the *sovnarkhozy* and establish direct contacts with the most important industrial sites. But in 1960–1961, such an approach was much more frustrating for the *sovnarkhozy*, which by now had accumulated managerial experience and qualified staff. The frustration of the *sovnarkhozy* grew when they had to respond to uncoordinated actions of Gosplan of Ukraine and *Ukrsovnarkhoz* when a decision of Gosplan of Ukraine was disapproved by *Ukrsovnarkhoz* and vice versa.

In May 1961, in the office of the CC CPUk secretary I.P. Kazanets, the chairmen of the *sovnarkhozy* and *Ukrsovnarkhoz* were given an opportunity to exchange opinions on their cooperation so far. Thus, the Vice-Chairman of

Ukrsovnarkhoz B.G. Tsomaya complained that the *sovnarkhozy* and the republic-level agencies were silently resisting the authority of *Ukrsovnarkhoz* and there was no contact between them and *Ukrsovnarkhoz*: 'The majority did not recognize *Ukrsovnarkhoz*, although since this organization already exists, the central republican organs should provide the necessary support'.[34] The new chairman of *Ukrsovnarkhoz* A.S. Kuz'mich disagreed on the division of functions between *Ukrsovnarkhoz* and Gosplan of Ukraine, in which Gosplan of Ukraine drafted the plans and managed resources whereas *Ukrsovnarkhoz* was held accountable for the fulfilment of plans. At the same time, Kuz'mich admitted that *Ukrsovnarkhoz* had no decision-making power and was powerless to punish the *sovnarkhozy* for violations or to solve problems for them.[35]

Republican and regional planners and managers were unanimous in their unwillingness to work with *Ukrsovnarkhoz*. In May 1961, *Ukrsovnarkhoz* was just another organization to correspond with.[36] Still, the abolition of *Ukrsovnarkhoz* was not an option, so Kazanets called on the participants in the meeting to accept *Ukrsovnarkhoz* and find ways to cooperate with it.

After this discussion in Kazanets's office, having assumed that the CC CPUk supported it, *Ukrsovnarkhoz* tried out its powers as it redistributed the investments that were assigned to the republic for special purposes. Kuz'mich and his deputy V.F. Garbuzov, without consulting Gosplan of Ukraine or the CMUk, reduced the investment for the construction of a Poltava plant that was supposed to produce fluorescent lighting.[37] This decision was wrong and it came to the attention of Moscow; the order for fluorescent lighting was supported by a special joint resolution of the CC CPSU and the USSR CM. As a result, Kuz'mich got a severe reprimand and a warning. But more importantly, he demonstrated that *Ukrsovnarkhoz* was not fully involved with the republican administration.

After this incident, the CC CPUk did not clarify or enhance the functions and authority of *Ukrsovnarkhoz* and, for months, the place and role of *Ukrsovnarkhoz* in the administrative hierarchy remained marginal. On all problems that *Ukrsovnarkhoz* was formally authorized to deal with – in planning, supplies, financing and credit and work regulations – it had to consult with one or more of Gosplan of Ukraine, the CMUk or the Ukrainian Ministry of Finance.[38] In addition to the constraints imposed on its activity by the republican administrative system, *Ukrsovnarkhoz* had to deal with the chronic problem that existed for all economic actors: the lack of information and communication between agencies. In September 1961, the head of the planning and economic department of *Ukrsovnarkhoz*, N.E. Drogichinskii, drew a rather sombre picture as he described the state of planning:

> Unfortunately, the plan for a number of items is unknown not just to the *Sovnarkhoz* or to a branch department or any other department of the *Sovnarkhoz*. It is unknown to Gosplan of Ukraine that is introducing corrections into this plan. We have come across examples when we instructed change to plan indices for certain products but these changes were applied to different plan indices. ... In order to talk about the fulfilment of the plan,

each department should get a clear picture of what the plan *is*, how much of the plan is fulfilled and define what each index means. The changes are made not just by *Ukrsovnarkhoz*, but by Gosplan and all *sovnarkhozy*. ... We discover only now that the manufacturing of certain products has been moved to the 4th quarter. We have not received all such corrections. There is a lot of work to do in order to specify all indices for all economic branches.[39]

Ukrsovnarkhoz and the delivery system

One of the main tasks of *Ukrsovnarkhoz* was to organize supplies for industry and construction. However, by September 1961, it could not demonstrate any achievements in this area. In October 1961, the CC CPSU and the USSR CM issued a resolution 'On regulating material supplies and setting norms of using material resources' which confirmed the responsibility of the republican *Sovnarkhozy* and republican *snabsbyty* for the fulfilment of inter-republican deliveries and the proper use of the material resources by the *sovnarkhozy*.[40] Inspired by this support from the centre, at the end of October B. Tsomaya and the head of the department of material and technical supplies and sales of *Ukrsovnarkhoz* A. Mikhalyov 'revealed' to V.V. Shcherbitskii, the CMUk chairman since February 1961, that the organization of material supplies during 1961 had not been simplified or improved but had become more complicated. However, the situation with the supplies could improve if 'proper administrative conditions' were created for *Ukrsovnarkhoz* to perform its functions. By 'proper conditions' Tsomaya and Mikhalyov meant independence in managing supplies.

> In the existing system, in order to solve any minor problem when allocating small amounts of metal or other materials for the immediate needs of the *sovnarkhozy*, *Ukrsovnarkhoz* has to address Gosplan of Ukraine. Being often on business trips, the supervisory personnel of *Ukrsovnarkhoz* are incapable of solving any problems until they return to Kiev and consult Gosplan of Ukraine. *Ukrsovnarkhoz* does not establish needs and does not distribute material resources. Thus it is deprived of the possibility of practising its right to make the necessary modifications to supply plans. A system where *Ukrsovnarkhoz* is responsible for coordinating the work of the *sovnarkhozy* and fulfilling production and construction plans by the republic, whereas Gosplan of Ukraine is responsible for distributing essential funded material resources, complicates industrial administration and causes an inevitable duplication of work. The situation becomes more complicated due to the fact that without material resources, *Ukrsovnarkhoz* cannot manipulate resources and make urgent decisions.[41]

In their petition to Shcherbitskii, the *Ukrsovnarkhoz* officials referred to the experience of the Republican *Sovnarkhozy* of Kazakhstan and the RSFSR: both agencies managed supplies independently. In order to improve the delivery system in the republic, *Ukrsovnarkhoz* proposed to a) limit the responsibilities of

Gosplan of Ukraine to those problematic issues that required contacts with USSR Gosplan since Gosplan of Ukraine was already working with USSR Gosplan on general calculations for Ukraine, and b) transfer full control over spplies to *Ukrsovnarkhoz*. *Ukrsovnarkhoz* should determine republican needs in raw materials, materials and equipment based on production and construction plans adopted by Gosplan of Ukraine; draft plans of distribution of material resources among the *sovnarkhozy*; control deliveries and establish priority over deliveries; and manage resource reserves.[42]

Strictly speaking, the functions that *Ukrsovnarkhoz* asked for should have been accorded to it, if not in 1960, then in spring 1961, and the frustration of its officials was understandable, particularly considering that their counterparts from Kazakhstan and the RSFSR did not face the same resistance in their republics. Nonetheless, at a meeting held on 9 November 1961, the CC CPUk Presidium stood by Gosplan of Ukraine as it effectively refused to support the claims of *Ukrsovnarkhoz* and left it to Gosplan of Ukraine and *Ukrsovnarkhoz* to settle the conflict between them.[43] Gosplan of Ukraine, well in power, was clearly not going to place itself below *Ukrsovnarkhoz* in the administrative hierarchy and allow *Ukrsovnarkhoz* to monopolize communication with the regions on supplies.

In 1961, *Ukrsovnarkhoz*'s isolation had several explanations. First, the CC CPUk did not believe that another agency could improve economic administration in the republic. Besides, delegating any power to *Ukrsovnarkhoz* meant sharing, or dispersing, the decision-making authority at the republican level, which contradicted the aim of the Ukrainian leadership to consolidate control over the republican economy in the fewest possible administrations. As for the argument of *Ukrsovnarkhoz* that the Republican *Sovnarkhozy* of RSFSR and Kazakhstan managed deliveries independently, it must have spoken against the cause of *Ukrsovnarkhoz*. By the end of 1961, it was known that the high authority of the Republican *Sovnarkhozy* in these republics led to more red tape and confusion, causing 'parallelism' and 'two-step planning'.[44] The Ukrainian leadership, apparently, was determined to avoid that.

The second explanation lay with the personalities of the chairmen of *Ukrsovnarkhoz* and Gosplan of Ukraine. The latter was certainly more integrated with the republican *apparat* and appeared to have been more competent to run the republican economy. In 1961–1962, the chairman of *Ukrzovnarkhoz* was Anton Kuz'mich and the chairman of Gosplan of Ukraine was Petr Rozenko. In 1954, Kuz'mich and Rozenko had briefly worked together in the Ukrainian Ministry of Coal Mining, Kuz'mich as the First Vice-Chairman and Rozenko as a Vice-Chairman. However, as early as the same year, the career paths of Kuz'mich and Rozenko separated: Kuz'mich was promoted to the post of the Minister of Coal Mining and Rozenko was moved to the CMUk as a Vice-Chairman. With the *Sovnarkhoz* reform in 1957, Kuz'mich effectively stayed in the branch as he was assigned to head the Voroshilovgrad economic region where the coal-mining industry was prevalent. Rozenko, on the other hand, remained involved with the Ukrainian economy as a whole, now in the capacity of First Vice-Chairman of Gosplan of Ukraine. Kuz'mich returned to Kiev in 1960 as a Vice-Chairman of *Ukrsovnarkhoz*. By that time, Rozenko was the Chairman of Gosplan of Ukraine (since 14 April 1959). The career paths of Kuz'mich and Rozenko suggest that by 1961, Rozenko had had an opportunity to build solid relations with the CMUk and the CC CPUk, not to mention that he had accumulated the experience of running a republican economy. Kuz'mich, on the other hand, after three years in the Voroshilovgrad *Sovnarkhoz*, could not have had the same quality of relations with the republican *apparat* and his managerial experience lay primarily in coal mining.

In March 1962, *Ukrsovnarkhoz* made another attempt to adapt to the system. This time, it used the report of the Commission of State Control of the CMUk regarding business trips. The commission discovered that in violation of the government's resolutions and instructions that established the procedures for business trips, *sovnarkhozy* continued spending considerable financial resources on sending their employees, *tolkachi*, to Kiev and Moscow. Nothing was left to finance the trips to far-located enterprises and construction sites.[45]

On the basis of this report, Garbuzov promised Shcherbitskii that *Ukrsovnarkhoz* would solve the problem. According to Garbuzov, at the root of the problem lay plan modifications, changes in investment, financing or supplies introduced by Gosplan of Ukraine, the Ministry of Finance and other Ukrainian republican agencies. So, the procedures for introducing changes to the plans and for contacting the *sovnarkhozy* should be reviewed. Regional and republican managers should communicate with each other only through *Ukrsovnarkhoz*. The republic-level agencies should call representatives of the *sovnarkhozy* only with the approval of *Ukrsovnarkhoz* and they should not call the *sovnarkhozy* on issues related to personnel or modifications to production, financial and delivery plans. These modifications should be discussed with *Ukrsovnarkhoz* and not directly with the *sovnarkhozy*. The CMUk should compel Gosplan and the Ministry of Finance to make necessary modifications to the plans in time, and only once. The Ukrainian Ministry of Finance should discuss the drafts of financial plans with *Ukrsovnarkhoz* before presenting them to higher authorities. Finally, *Ukrsovnarkhoz* should obtain the authority for planning and distributing material resources from the list of products that were managed centrally by USSR Gosplan and GlUMPP. The existing order, explained Garbuzov, where supplies of the main funded material resources were managed by Gosplan of Ukraine and supplies of resources from the lists that were compiled by GlUMPP were managed by *Ukrglavsnabsbyty* of *Ukrsovnarkhoz*,[46] led to duplication and parallelism in work and wasteful expenditures.[47]

How could the CMUk respond to *Ukrsovnarkhoz*? At this particular moment – spring 1962 – not with much. In Ukraine, *Ukrsovnarkhoz* was still considered unnecessary. Furthermore, at a meeting on 22 March 1962, the CC CPSU Presidium decided to reorganize the economic administration and invited the republics to submit their proposals. Based on the ideas proposed at the meeting – to increase the influence of the Party on industrial administration in the economic regions and in the centre, to increase the responsibility of the *sovnarkhozy* and USSR Gosplan and *Gosekonomsovet*, to enforce the decisions of the Party on the central *apparat* and to increase centralized administration over the branches – the purpose of the new reorganization was to fight growing *mestnichestvo* by strengthening centralized control over economic branches, and to increase Party control over the central *apparat*.[48]

For the Ukrainian Ministry of Finance, the forthcoming reorganization represented a chance to get rid of a useless organization. So in its proposal for improving the administration of industry there was no place for *Ukrsovnarkhoz* at all. The Ministry of Finance proposed that, because planning and general administration of separate branches would be transferred to the all-Union and republican branch committees, it was reasonable to abolish Republican *Sovnarkhozy* both in Ukraine and the RSFSR.[49] Curiously, by the beginning of April, Gosplan of Ukraine completely changed its attitude towards *Ukrsovnarkhoz* and suggested keeping *Ukrsovnarkhoz* but modifying its structure and functions. '*Ukrsovnarkhoz* should ... ensure the fulfilment of production and delivery plans and coordinate and control the work of the *sovnarkhozy*. Its structure should be reorganized accordingly: the functional departments should be reduced in number and the production departments [branch] should be replenished [with skilled personnel]'.[50]

The USSR Gosplan commission, which by the end of April had finished checking the *sovnarkhozy* of Dnepropetrovsk and Donetsk, shared the opinion of the Ukrainian Ministry of Finance: *Ukrsovnarkhoz* should be abolished.[51] Instead, in Ukraine, where 'industry was located closely on a relatively small territory with a well established transport system and a high concentration of production in large enterprises', it was necessary to enlarge the *sovnarkhozy* and reduce their number to three. Gosplan of Ukraine should provide administration of these *sovnarkhozy* and, consequently, should be 'reinforced with qualified staff'.[52]

In view of the forthcoming reorganization, on 10 July 1962 the CC CPUk Presidium instructed Gosplan of Ukraine and *Ukrsovnarkhoz* to 'divide their functions more clearly' and specify their duties and responsibilities.[53] In the meantime, a joint commission of the CC CPUk and CMUk finished its report 'On the work of *Ukrsovnarkhoz*'. The general conclusion of the commission was that *Ukrsovnarkhoz* had not proved to be a valuable organization for coordinating and controlling the *sovnarkhozy*. In particular, its functionaries drowned themselves in paperwork producing lots of reports, notes and other 'often useless documents'. They regularly went to Moscow for business trips and rarely to the periphery, so they were poorly informed on the situation in the enterprises and construction sites. *Ukrsovnarkhoz* was unable to ensure export deliveries. For the first quarter of 1962, out of the 99 most important commodities that Ukraine exported, deliveries of 34 items were not fulfilled. *Ukrsovnarkhoz* did not control the fulfilment of resolutions issued by the CC CPUk and the CMUk: in 1961, out of 2,590 resolutions and instructions the fulfilment of which had been checked, only 69 per cent were executed on time. Nor was it improving the structure of its *apparat*. There were more than 130 departments in *Ukrsovnarkhoz* but the majority of them consisted of 4–5 functionaries. As for positive achievements in the work of *Ukrsovnarkhoz*, according to the commission, there were none.[54]

The turning point 105

It is possible that the CC CPUk was preparing to address the CC CPSU with a request to abolish *Ukrsovnarkhoz*. However, after the 26 July CC CPSU Presidium discussion on 'further improving economic administration' when, among other issues, the Presidium rejected the idea of USSR Gosplan embracing both planning and management, the request to abolish *Ukrsovnarkhoz* would not have been supported.[55] The Ukrainian authorities had to find a way to reorganize *Ukrsovnarkhoz* and fit it into the Ukrainian administrative economic system.

Conclusion

In October 1962, work on the distribution of authority between Gosplan of Ukraine and *Ukrsovnarkhoz* was still in progress when the CC CPUk Presidium instructed everyone involved in the project to postpone their work until the end of the November 1962 Plenum of the CC CPSU.[56] Following this Plenum, the separation of the functions and responsibilities of Gosplan of Ukraine and *Ukrsovnarkhoz* became a most urgent task: *Ukrsovnarkhoz* was to take over the administration of the republican economy. Still, it was not until spring 1963, when the central leadership had finished establishing the new organizational vertical hierarchy, creating the Supreme Council of the National Economy (VSNKh), and had given Union-Republic status to USSR *Sovnarkhoz*, *Ukrsovnarkhoz*, USSR Gosplan and Gosplan of Ukraine, that the position of *Ukrsovnarkhoz* in the Ukrainian system was consolidated.[57] Until then, *Ukrsovnarkhoz* effectively remained an outsider in the system: it was poorly informed on the reorganization process, and its efforts to obtain the appropriate authority from the Ukrainian government were futile.[58]

The success of the Ukrainian republican authorities in resisting recentralization was limited to the regionalization policy and the isolation of *Ukrsovnarkhoz* from active participation in the system, and was largely due to several factors. First and foremost, the CPUk had a solid position in the Soviet system and enjoyed the support of Khrushchev. In addition to that, in the period from 1960 until 1962, the policy of recentralization was not yet dominant and the organizational structure through which the central *apparat* could implement the policy of recentralization was not yet set. So, preventing creation of three new economic regions in Ukraine was not a matter of principle on which the central *apparat* considered it necessary to focus; and in the case of *Ukrsovnarkhoz*, the system could not yet provide it with the necessary framework to allow it to enforce the policy of recentralization in the republic.

We can certainly suggest that had Khrushchev remained as enthusiastic about the idea of the devolution of decision making in 1961 as he was in 1956–1957, the success of the Ukrainian authorities might have spread beyond the two above-mentioned matters. After all, according to Taubman, the XXII CPSU Congress held in October 1961 was 'the period of Khrushchev's sole stewardship', 'his "time in the sun"' when he enjoyed the support of 'everyone',[59] which implies that he could have imposed his decisions upon the central planners. But by the end of 1961, Khrushchev's dedication to the policy of decentralization had weakened. Khrushchev still seemed to believe in the potential benefits of decentralization, but he started becoming disillusioned about the ability of the system to extract these benefits, or to suppress *mestnichestvo* while continuing to devolve economic decision making from the centre to the periphery.[60] USSR Gosplan, on the other hand, systematically demonstrated its ability to impose its own policy.

As a result, although Khrushchev still supported the idea of the *sovnarkhozy* and remained in principle faithful to the policy of decentralization, he could provide little assistance to the Ukrainian leadership on the matter of actual resource management. Here the Ukrainian leadership had little leverage over USSR Gosplan and the GlUMPP, which successfully continued the practice of limiting the access of *Ukrglavsnabsbyty* to resources. Supply plans continued to be drafted by USSR Gosplan for the limited and most important products and by GlUMPP for the extended list of products. The 4 May 1955 USSR CM resolution that allowed Union republics to retain a 5 per cent reserve of capital investment had little effect due to the fact that the investments could be redistributed between branches of the economy only with the permission of the USSR CM or USSR Gosplan. Funds for the construction of republican status projects and from republican materials were transferred by USSR Gosplan to the republics not directly but through the *Soyuzglavkomplekty*. Starting in 1962, USSR Gosplan required that the lists of new construction projects and the reconstruction of objects valued between 1.5 and 2.5 million roubles should be coordinated with USSR Gosplan, even though by April 1962 USSR Gosplan had not finished examining the list submitted by Ukraine in 1961 for 1962. Also starting in 1962, the share of decentralized financing in above-plan capital investment was considerably reduced and the difference was not compensated for in the 1962 plan.[61] From 1960, the share of Ukrainian enterprises transferred back under centralized management would gradually increase, from the lowest 2.9 per cent in 1959, to 3.05 per cent in 1960, 3.1 per cent in 1961, 3.3 per cent in 1962, 3.5 per cent in 1963 and 4.25 per cent in 1964.[62]

10 November 1962 CC CPSU Plenum

Giving up on the reform?

For the central governmental *apparat*, but not the Party, the 19–23 November 1962 CC CPSU Plenum must have brought a certain comfort and relief about the future. At the Plenum, although still supporting the principle of territorial administration of production and still believing in the advantages of decentralized over centralized decision making, Khrushchev emphasized the importance of the branch approach in scientific and engineering work.[1] This change of emphasis immediately translated into another reorganization. The day after the Plenum ended, on 24 November, USSR *Sovnarkhoz* appeared and *Gosekonomsovet* disappeared. With the abolition of *Gosekonomsovet*, USSR Gosplan took over perspective planning but transferred current planning to USSR *Sovnarkhoz*.[2] USSR *Gosstroi* regained control over construction and was to become, as Khrushchev said, 'very centralized, Union-Republic, with strict centralization'.[3] A number of state branch committees were formed in order to centrally orchestrate the development of certain industries. The reorganization of the governmental *apparat* was substantial, but its general trend corresponded to the long-cherished aspiration of the ex-ministerial bureaucracy in Moscow to recentralize control over the economy.

The Party was less fortunate. At the November 1962 Plenum, Khrushchev announced his second reform designed 'to shake party members out of the disciplined lethargy into which they had been plunged under Stalin's terrifying rule'.[4] The first reform had been initiated at the XXII Party Congress in 1961. The new Party Rules adopted at that Congress included a provision for compulsory and regular renewal of the Party cadres. No fewer than a quarter of the members of the Central Committee and its Presidium had to be replaced at each Party Congress; one-third of the members had to be replaced in the republican and *oblasti* Party organs and one-half of the members in the *raiony* Party organs. The Rules also limited the number of times that the same person could be elected to occupy the same post.[5]

The reform launched at the November 1962 Plenum divided, or bifurcated, the Party organizations in the *oblasti* and the levels below into agricultural committees and industrial committees.[6] Khrushchev believed that the specialization of the Party organizations in agriculture and industry would allow the Party functionaries to increase their expertise and professionalism and 'to make party control over these two branches of the national economy more effective, less formal, less spasmodic and less remote'.[7] 'Instead of being judged and rewarded for political skill and ideological purity, at which they were specialists par excellence, their test would be economic efficiency, which all too often eluded them.'[8]

Contrary to the new provisions of the Party Rules, the November 1962 bifurcation undermined the systemic position of regional party secretaries. With the *Sovnarkhoz* reform, the influence of the *obkomy* and *raikomy* over industry had been not as high as was originally expected. After the Plenum, Khrushchev planned to merge economic regions. Merging of the economic regions reduced the influence of the Party secretaries over industry even further.[9] Such changes could not be embraced with enthusiasm by the mass of Party functionaries and, immediately after Khrushchev was ousted from office, the old system of united Party organizations was restored.

The November 1962 CC CPSU Plenum launched a massive reorganization of the Party and state *apparat* that did not respond to the interests of the former, but generally responded to those of the latter. Creation of the VSNKh in March 1963 and a return to a branch system of economic administration in March 1963 boosted the process of recentralization of economic administration while undermining the authority and influence of the regional Party functionaries.[10]

Reorganization in the centre:
USSR Gosplan–USSR *Sovnarkhoz*

By December 1960, the recently approved Seven Year Plan[11] needed to be corrected, not necessarily because of the mistakes in the plan (which were always present), but because of the poor harvest in 1960. That year Ukraine, for example, sold 21,855,922 kg of wheat to the state. Less wheat was sold only in 1946, the first post-war year when there were no agricultural machines, no seed and there was a severe drought.[12] Khrushchev offered to tackle the agricultural problem in a traditional way, by improving the leadership and the management of agriculture, but also by increasing investment in agriculture. He planned to cultivate an additional 8 million hectares of virgin lands and increase agricultural investments at the expense of metallurgy.[13]

By 1962, the situation with agricultural production or with 'its leadership' had not improved. The increase in pensions that was not supported by agricultural production or consumer goods contributed 1.5 billion roubles to the budget deficit.[14] In order to at least partially reduce the deficit, the CC CPSU agreed to increase the prices of meat and milk products and to reduce salaries.[15] The Party leadership in industry was also recognized as weak. To increase profitability in industry, in March 1962 Khrushchev suggested focusing on improving Party leadership and introducing technological innovations. At the same time, to ensure that the technological innovations were implemented in mass production, the Presidium considered consolidating centralized administration and 'maybe increasing the role of the existing branch state committees … and maybe creating new ones'.[16] The governmental *apparat* could hardly miss these 'maybes': the next reorganization, this time to recentralize control over the economy, was approaching.

Yet Khrushchev realized that he could not rely on USSR Gosplan for its future reorganization; it was inefficient and could not control the economy. In May 1962, during discussion of the Seven Year Plan, he went beyond the traditional criticism of planners and proposed organizing an agency that would control all industry from top to bottom, from USSR Gosplan to the enterprises.

> Our Gosplan today is such that it is necessary to consider an organ which can control it. In Gosplan, there are lots of people who were already 'born' in Gosplan. Yes, yes, they were born there and their fathers and mothers got jobs there for them. And they no longer think like factories. They think like calculators. ... Apparently, it is necessary to revive the Party and state control over enterprises.[17]

Functionaries of USSR Gosplan, said Khrushchev, should get out of Gosplan and go to work in industry, to see life a bit.[18]

At the Presidium meeting on 26 July 1962, what in March was in the 'maybe' mode became certain. The resolution 'On further improving the *apparat* for administration and specialization in machine-building, construction and other branches of the economy' instructed the governmental *apparat* to improve its performance, in particular the performance of the branch committees 'that act like old ministries', and to reorganize USSR Gosplan, because 'we cannot have a universal organ'.[19] Of crucial significance was Khrushchev's directive to improve the work of the *apparat* in the context of 'breaking national frontiers'.[20]

To the experienced audience that was present at this Presidium meeting, the latter instruction indicated that Khrushchev had reached a point of no tolerance for *mestnichestvo*. He no longer insisted on prioritizing the development of complex economic regions and republics, but supported the development of complex industrial branches that could be designed and orchestrated only from Moscow and required breaking national frontiers. The central *apparat* could only conclude that Khrushchev now supported the policy of recentralization. At the November 1962 Plenum, however, Khrushchev would also promote the idea of enhancing the economic rights of the *sovnarkhozy* and enterprises, indicating that he did not completely give up on the policy of decentralization.

That the 26 July 1962 resolution would be carried through with utmost zeal raised no doubts with the central leadership. The leadership anticipated that the forthcoming reorganization would be used as a perfect excuse to return to Moscow those functionaries who had been exiled in 1957 to the periphery, but also by the central agencies to bring qualified specialists from industry to their central offices. To prevent the central *apparat* from swelling, on 4 October 1962 the USSR CM issued another resolution, 'On partial changes in the procedures for the registration (*propiska*) in Moscow'. This forbade all ministries and administrations, all directors of enterprises, departments and organizations from employing specialists and functionaries from locations other than Moscow to work in Moscow. Already after the November 1962 Plenum, USSR Gosplan would have to ask for special permission to employ 150–200 highly qualified specialists from enterprises, scientific and design offices from other cities.[21]

Continuing with the post-Plenum reorganization, the USSR *Sovnarkhoz* was established. It is not quite clear how exactly the creation of USSR *Sovnarkhoz* and the abolition of *Gosekonomsovet* were supposed to boost economic growth, but politically the organizational reshuffle gave Moscow at least one advantage. It allowed a review of the balance between the decision-making authority of the centre and the republics and regions without bringing attention to the increasing power of the central planners, who by 1962 had been the subject of an excessive number of complaints from the republics about their administrative methods. With USSR *Sovnarkhoz*, USSR Gosplan and the state branch committees in the system, Khrushchev initiated the creation of an organization to coordinate the work of all economic agencies. The organizational pyramid was completed on 13 March 1963 with the VSNKh. Ustinov was chosen to head the VSNKh.[22]

State branch committees

With the abolition of a number of industrial ministries in 1957, state branch committees were seen as a solution to maintaining centralized control of particularly important branches, such as the aircraft industry, shipbuilding, and radio electronics.[23] As the reform progressed, more branch committees were formed; for example, the committee for automation and machine-building was created in February 1959, electrical engineering in March 1961, ferrous and non-ferrous metallurgy in December 1961, fuel industry in December 1961, fishing industry in June 1962. The Ministry of the Chemical Industry that survived the 1957 reorganization was transformed into the USSR CM State Committee for the Chemical Industry in June 1958. After the November 1962 Plenum, the committees for the food industry, light industry and commerce appeared.[24] On 21 January 1963, however, some committees were abolished, namely the committees for the food industry, light industry, electrical engineering, and automation and machine-building.[25] Still, the total number of state committees for administration of industry had grown from twelve before November 1962 to thirty after this date.[26] In spring 1963, some state branch committees were transferred under the jurisdiction of the VSNKh, others remained within the structure of the USSR CM or USSR Gosplan.[27]

At the November 1962 Plenum, Khrushchev emphasized the importance of the state committees for developing the industrial branches, namely for research and the implementation of technological innovations.[28] His statement translated into the transfer of the design offices and research organizations and institutes, which in 1957 had been subordinated to the *sovnarkhozy*, *oblispolkomy*, republic ministries and republic Gosplans, back under centralized administration.[29] In 1957, bringing research close to production was supposed to boost technological modernization. In 1962, the transfer of research under peripheral control was found not to be a complete success: research institutes preferred to focus on the current problems of particular enterprises and when an innovation appeared in one region it did not always spread to other regions. The general perception of the situation was that research institutes did not communicate; thereby they could not contribute to research for the branches in general. Dispersed all over the country, research centres slowed down the implementation of new technologies in mass production.

Bringing research back under centralized administration was supposed to correct this problem. However, now the problem was to ensure that the *sovnarkhozy* followed the instructions of the branch committees. According to Khrushchev, the branch committees had to be positioned close to USSR Gosplan and communicate with the *sovnarkhozy* through the plan by translating the new technology into plan targets. The *sovnarkhozy*, guided in their decision making by the plan, would thereby implement research in practice.[30]

The central *apparat* developed Khrushchev's idea and, in 1963, invited the state branch committees to participate in the distribution of supplies.[31] But already in 1962, the committees tried to expand their authority to the areas that were under the jurisdiction of the *sovnarkhozy*. For example, in March 1962, after Khrushchev announced the forthcoming enhancement of the authority of the branch committees, some committees asked the central leadership to transfer leading industrial enterprises and design offices of the Leningrad *Sovnarkhoz* to their jurisdiction.[32] In December 1962, when Khrushchev visited Ukraine, the Ukrainian authorities complained to him that the state committees showed the intention of obtaining control over large enterprises with 5–7 thousand workers. The Ukrainian authorities were concerned not so much about the committees overstepping the limits set for them at the November 1962 Plenum, but about the fact that handing over design offices without the enterprises was indeed a senseless exercise. At the same time, if both the design offices and the enterprises were handed over to the central committees then they would turn into ministries.[33] Then what would be the point of having the *sovnarkhozy*?

The concerns of the Ukrainian leadership were not groundless. As Khrushchev responded to them, he approved of the consolidation of the branch administration.

> The branch departments should have the rights of ministries, so that they could decide on everything that is within their jurisdiction. They should finance their branches, move the funds inside the branch and report to the chairman. ... If we were saying that Dymshits[34] coped, now I would say that he is not coping, that is why the head of department should have more rights. He should decide. And when it concerns moving finances from one branch to another, then these questions should be coordinated with the Chairman of *Sovnarkhoz* [USSR *Sovnarkhoz*] or the Chairman of Gosplan [USSR Gosplan]. To put it briefly, we should give more independence to people in solving all these problems. After all, the problems are generally solved the way proposed by the branch departments. So let us consider this from the beginning.[35]

On 9 February 1963, the CC CPUk Presidium confirmed the transfer of 62 industrial research institutes, or almost half of the research institutes situated in the republic, under the jurisdiction of the state committees of the USSR Gosplan.[36] By 1965, Ukraine had transferred practically all its scientific centres under the centralized administration of the all-Union agencies and branch committees: 55 large scientific-research institutes, 49 project (*proektnye*) organizations and 20 large independent design (*konstruktorskie*) organizations. However, the centralization of scientific work did not result in common technological policy throughout the country. The most correct way of implementing common technological policy, reckoned the Ukrainian authorities in November 1964, would not have been the centralization of the administration of scientific organizations, but clearly defined specialization and coordination of their activity.[37]

Enlarging the rights of the *sovnarkhozy* and enterprises

The opposite end of the recentralization dynamic was Khrushchev's initiative to enhance the rights of the *sovnarkhozy* and enterprises. Before the November 1962 Plenum, the issue had already been discussed by the central planners and the Ukrainian republican authorities. Thus in spring 1962, before the Presidium confirmed its decision to increase the role of the state branch committees, a group of central planners that audited the Donetsk *Sovnarkhoz* suggested that the *sovnarkhozy* should acquire more flexibility in managing investments. They thought that the *Sovnarkhoz* should be allowed to keep a share of production to compensate for the introduction of any specialization. The practice whereby instructions issued by the *sovnarkhozy* were not implemented because of delays or obstruction on the part of local financial authorities was to be forbidden. The right to use a share of production that was manufactured above the plan during a quarter should be restored.[38]

When the agenda of the November Plenum was communicated to Ukraine, *Ukrsovnarkhoz* submitted to the USSR CM a set of propositions that expanded the financial flexibility of enterprises and *sovnarkhozy*. In particular, *Ukrsovnarkhoz*, supported by the CMUk, suggested cancelling or reviewing certain instructions and resolutions issued by the USSR Ministry of Finance and *Gosbank* that regulated the procedures for assigning bonuses and spending the profits that were received from selling consumer goods manufactured from waste.[39] At the end of October 1962, the Ukrainian authorities drafted another set of propositions on the rights of *sovnarkhozy* and directors of construction sites and enterprises. This time the Ukrainians focused not so much on enhancing the rights of the above-mentioned economic actors, but on restoring those rights that were granted to them, particularly to the *sovnarkhozy*, in September 1957, but which had been gradually revoked in the following years. For example, the right to redistribute the remainder of circulation funds among enterprises and construction sites, the right to fix permanent prices for all products manufactured from local inputs or production waste, or the right to redistribute capital investments between the branches, within the branches and between the enterprises.[40]

After the Plenum, several commissions were formed to enhance and specify the functions of the *sovnarkhozy* and draft regulations on enterprises. The commissions had to consider Khrushchev's statements, made in 1961, on the importance of material incentives for improving economic performance of the *sovnarkhozy* and enterprises and the new policy of combining territorial management of production with consolidated vertical administration of the branches. The commission that worked on enhancing the rights of the *sovnarkhozy* and enterprises, chaired by the Chairman of USSR *Sovnarkhoz* Dymshits, finished one version of the new regulations by the beginning of January 1963.[41] This commission reported to the USSR CM that the rights of the *sovnarkhozy* were enhanced, and certain paragraphs were re-edited to protect the *sovnarkhozy* from petty tutelage and to let the directors of enterprises exercise their rights. However, due to the reorganization of the administration of construction – Ministries for Construction were created in all republics and in Moscow and they were taking over the construction organizations – the rights and responsibilities of the *sovnarkhozy* in construction were reduced. In Dymshits's draft, two issues remained undecided: a) the USSR *Gosstroi* did not agree that *sovnarkhozy* and republic Gosplans should redistribute capital investment between industrial branches; and b) the USSR *Gosbank* and the USSR Ministry of Finance found it impossible to allow the *sovnarkhozy* to free those enterprises whose wage funds were overdrawn from repaying the previous year's overdraft.[42]

The USSR CM commission, chaired by the First Vice-Chairman of the USSR CM Kosygin, studied Dymshits's version of the new regulations on the *sovnarkhozy* and introduced important corrections that explicitly indicated a turn towards the recentralization of administration. From now on, the *sovnarkhozy* were not obliged to act through the CM of their republics or through the republican *Sovnarkhozy*, or even through the republic Gosplans when it concerned the development of new technologies. They had to communicate directly with the state branch committees. At the same time, the *sovnarkhozy* were obliged to implement those instructions issued by USSR *Sovnarkhoz* concerning the fulfilment of plans, increases in production volumes, improvements in quality and enlargements of the assortment and fulfilment of supplementary tasks on production and supplies. As for those two issues that the Dymshits commission left open, in the final draft of the regulations they were settled: the *sovnarkhozy* were not allowed to redistribute investment between branches or between the construction sites of the same branch, and they were not allowed to forgive enterprises any overdrafts in their wage funds.[43]

Along with formalizing the increased role of the state branch committees, the new regulations emphasized the elevated importance of the branch departments in the *sovnarkhozy*. They were not only held responsible for the economic activity of the enterprises and organizations subordinated to them, but they became independent in solving problems for their enterprises and organizations.[44] The *sovnarkhozy* were placed under double jurisdiction of the republic Gosplans and of the USSR *Sovnarkhoz*. This meant that the authority of the republican authorities vis-à-vis the *sovnarkhozy* formally decreased and their status vis-à-vis the central economic agencies was demoted.

After the November 1962 Plenum, some work was done on enlarging the rights of the directors of enterprises. In February 1963, the USSR CM commission, chaired by USSR Gosplan Chairman P. Lomako, presented a draft of the very first Law to establish the legal foundations of a socialist enterprise. 'The rights and responsibilities of the enterprises are regulated by numerous decisions issued by the all-Union and republican organs. The present draft of the Law on a socialist state enterprise defines the main tasks, responsibilities and rights of the enterprise'.[45] Lomako's commission was guided by Khrushchev's idea about the gradual enlargement of economic rights and responsibilities of enterprises and the involvement of workers in management.[46] How far Lomako's commission progressed in its work is hard to say. Regardless, even though Khrushchev personally promoted the idea, the enhancement of the rights of the directors of enterprises was not considered a matter of great urgency by the central or republican *apparat*. Moreover, if actually applied, the process of recentralizing the economic administration would have slowed down. The rights of enterprises would become important later, after Khrushchev's dismissal, when the leadership moved to the next reform, *Kosyginskaya*.[47]

From 1963, resisting recentralization policies became harder, and in some areas impossible. Yet, as before, the attempts of the central leadership and the central *apparat* to recentralize control over resources by applying organizational measures were economically ineffective and politically frustrating.

11 Recentralization in Ukraine

There were three major policies that Ukraine could no longer avoid implementing: merging of the *sovnarkhozy*, the administrative elevation of the status of *Ukrsovnarkhoz*, and the transferring of local industry to the *sovnarkhozy*. In 1957, local industry had been placed under the management of local executive committees (*ispolkomy*) and produced mainly for local consumption. Yet, of the three policies, only the redrawing of the administrative map could be considered as successfully implemented.

Merging Ukrainian *sovnarkhozy*

After the failure of economic councils for enlarged regions, the new regionalization provided the central *apparat* with a favourable administrative framework for consolidating branch development and cooperation and specialization. At the end of 1962 and beginning of 1963, in the RSFSR, 67 *sovnarkhozy* were merged into 24. Uzbekistan (where by 1960 there was only one *Sovnarkhoz* in the republic), Kirghizia, Tajikistan and Turkmenistan were merged into one *Sovnarkhoz*. After merging, the number of economic administrative regions was reduced to 47.[1]

In Ukraine, 14 economic administrative regions were merged into seven (see Table 11.1). It was easier to promote cooperation in seven regions and it was easier to control seven *sovnarkhozy*. Why seven *sovnarkhozy* were created and not fewer, it is hard to say with certainty. According to Ukrainian sources, the merging of the Ukrainian economic regions was related to the bifurcation of Party organs and the creation of industrial Party committees (see Chapter 10). In the proposal on the bifurcation of Party organs, the CC CPUk suggested that in the republic there should be 25 agricultural *obkomy*, based on the number of *oblasti*, and seven industrial *kraikomy* or regional committees. Thus, the existing 14 economic administrative regions had to be merged into seven. Seven economic regions were created, but the idea of creating seven industrial *kraikomy* was rejected.[2] Instead, Ukraine organized 19 industrial *obkomy*.[3]

Except for the Chairman of the Podol'skii *Sovnarkhoz* Stepanenko, all the chairmen had had previous experience of managing a *Sovnarkhoz*. According to Conyngham, however, the high level of stability among *sovnarkhozy* chairmen seen in Ukraine in 1963–1964 was not typical of other republics.[4]

Table 11.1 Ukrainian *sovnarkhozy* after 1963 merging

Name of Sovnarkhoz	Oblasti included	Chairman
1 Donetsk	Donetsk, Lugansk (formerly Voroshilovgrad)	N.M. Khudosovtsev
2 Khar'kov	Khar'kov, Poltava, Sumy	O.V. Soich
3 Pridneprovskii	Dnepropetrovsk, Zaporozh'e, Kirovograd	L.E. Lukich
4 Chernomorskii	Odessa, Kherson, Nikolaev, Crimea	I.S. Pribyl'skii
5 Kiev	Kiev, Chernigov, Zhitomir, Cherkassy	P.Ya. Lysnyak
6 Podol'skii	Vinnitsa, Khmel'nitskii Ternopol', Chernovtsy	I.D. Stepanenko
7 L'vov	L'vov, Volyn', Zakarpat'e, Rovno, Stanislav (Ivano-Frankovsk)	A.P. Eryomenko

The transfer of local industry to the *sovnarkhozy*

Local industry had to be transferred to the *sovnarkhozy* because, if not, 'there will be no specialization, it will be amateurish work, *kustarshchina*'; on this Khrushchev agreed with Kosygin at the Presidium meeting held at the end of November 1962.[5] So more than 15 thousand enterprises of local industry with 3.5 million employees were placed under the management of the *sovnarkhozy*. Municipal services remained under the management of the local *ispolkomy*. The problem with the local industry was its low level of mechanization, and Khrushchev believed that the *sovnarkhozy* would solve this problem, further increase specialization and boost economic growth.[6] This did not happen.

In Ukraine, attempts to place local industry under the management of the *sovnarkhozy* had been made since the beginning of the reform, but had been successfully blocked by the CC CPUk. The CC CPUk did not believe that the *sovnarkhozy* would run local industry more efficiently than the *ispolkomy*, and at the same time, it did not want to leave regional authorities without their own sources of revenue and thus make them totally dependent on the *sovnarkhozy*. In 1957, when industry of all-Union, Union-Republic and republican status had almost entirely been transferred to the *sovnarkhozy*, in Ukraine it was suggested that all bakeries, enterprises producing milk products, creameries, oil-mills, cheese dairies and soft-drink plants should be transferred to local industry, as well as a number of breweries and enterprises making clothing and knitted goods.[7] When the *sovnarkhozy* were physically established, they nonetheless took over the meat and milk industries. After all, in 1956, 54 per cent of meat, 69 per cent of butter and 70 per cent of cheese produced in Ukraine was delivered outside either the *oblasti*-manufacturers or the republic. The *oblasti* of Cherkassy, Kirovograd, Vinnitsa and Poltava, for example, consumed only 2–8 per cent of their meat, butter and cheese.[8] Besides, in 1957, the share of local production in

Ukraine's export of consumer goods and food products (mainly vodka and honey) constituted 18.16 per cent, and amounted to more than 20 per cent of the retail state and cooperative commerce inside the republic.[9]

Later on, at the beginning of 1959, USSR Gosplan tried to transfer a number of products, semi-products and materials manufactured by enterprises of local industry to central distribution, but Gosplan of Ukraine objected to this idea.[10] However, two years later, at the end of 1961, Gosplan of Ukraine itself suggested to Podgornyi and Shcherbitskii that local industry be transferred to the administration of the *sovnarkhozy*.[11] On the basis of a proposal from Gosplan of Ukraine, Podgornyi assigned a commission to study the issue. The commission discovered that only three *oblasti* preferred to transfer the entire local industry to the *sovnarkhozy*, L'vov, Chernigov and Crimea. The general opinion was that it would be more reasonable to transfer only part of local industry to the *sovnarkhozy*: all specialized light industrial enterprises, wood-processing factories, factories that manufactured furniture and musical instruments, certain metal-working enterprises and the largest specialized enterprises of the food industry. Those enterprises that manufactured for local consumption or provided services should remain under the management of the *ispolkomy*.[12]

The commission agreed that with enterprises of local industry the *sovnarkhozy* should in principle be better able to specialize; however, it warned about three particular difficulties that potentially undermined the success of such a transfer. First, for some time, nobody would be responsible for local industry. The *sovnarkhozy*, now the sole administrators of local industry, would not be able to take over the industry immediately, whereas local Party and Soviet organs would no longer be fully responsible for it. Second, local budgets would lose a large share of revenues which had been spent on house-building, the construction of public buildings and the improvement of living areas. Third, once in charge of local industry, the *sovnarkhozy* would be obliged to eliminate the difference between the rates of tariffs and wages paid in local industry and those in the industry originally run by the *sovnarkhozy*. The cost of equalizing these wages was estimated at 12 million roubles of annual expenditure.[13]

In March 1962, the CC CPUk Presidium had gathered sufficient arguments to reject the idea of transferring local industry to *sovnarkhozy*.[14] However, in November 1962 the decision was made in Moscow and arguing against it would have had no effect. In 1963, all Ukrainian local industrial enterprises were transferred to the *sovnarkhozy*, with no exceptions: 2,022 enterprises with 2,352 million roubles of gross output and 348 thousand employees.[15] The *oblispolkomy* kept only consumer services. More than two thousand enterprises constituted 60 per cent of all enterprises managed by the *sovnarkhozy* with only 12 per cent of the total output.[16]

As the above-mentioned commission had warned, local industry turned out to be a burden for the *sovnarkhozy*. Under *Sovnarkhoz* management, local industrial enterprises lost preferential terms in financing and supply that had been accorded to them at the beginning of the *Sovnarkhoz* reform. For example, under the jurisdiction of the *ispolkomy*, major local construction works were financed from non-centralized sources and in 1962, the volume of investment from non-centralized sources was planned to constitute 60.4 million roubles. In 1963, decentralized allocations were not anticipated. Local construction organizations experienced additional difficulties caused by the new procedure according to which they were not financed until the lists of construction sites had been approved by USSR *Gosstroi*. Yet the 'very centralized' USSR *Gosstroi* was physically incapable of responding to all of the demands coming from all over the country.[17] About a thousand enterprises lost preferential rates for paying turnover taxes, but had they remained under the management of *oblispolkomy* they would have saved 18.6 million roubles. Local enterprises lost the right to use surplus agricultural products and raw materials from *kolkhozy* and *sovkhozy* to produce food and consumer goods. For local enterprises these surplus goods had been their main, or only, source of inputs that enabled them to produce output worth more than 100 million roubles annually. Another important issue was the difference in wholesale and retail prices of some products manufactured by local industry and the *sovnarkhozy*. Local enterprises lost the right to fix preferential wholesale or retail prices. They also lost preferential terms for employing disabled people. The expenditures of the *sovnarkhozy* related to the transfer of local enterprises totalled about 20 million roubles annually.[18]

The transfer of local industry to the *sovnarkhozy* was a total failure. It did not improve specialization or increase the production of consumer goods. Things worked out just as the Ukrainian commission that worked on the issue in spring 1962 had anticipated. The *sovnarkhozy* concentrated their efforts and attention on the main industrial branches, whereas the *oblispolkomy* very soon lost their influence on this segment of industry. By 1965, more than two thousand enterprises had to cut production of certain consumer goods.[19]

Reinstalling *Ukrsovnarkhoz*

Reinstalling *Ukrsovnarkhoz* into the Ukrainian economic administrative system was far more important for the success of the recentralization policy than merging the economic regions or transferring local industry to *sovnarkhozy* administration. In March 1963, following the organizational restructuring in Moscow, *Ukrsovnarkhoz* consolidated its authority as it was now performing the functions of Gosplan of Ukraine in managing the republican economy and drafting current plans. The importance of Gosplan of Ukraine, now in charge of perspective planning, decreased. In theory, *Ukrsovnarkhoz* was finally in a position to implement the recentralization policy. In practice, however, this new vertical strand in administering the economy of Ukraine did not provide the centre with control over resources. *Ukrsovnarkhoz* housed the leading and most experienced functionaries of Gosplan of Ukraine, including the ex-Chairman of Gosplan of Ukraine Rozenko, who continued to pursue the pre-November 1962 pro-republican policies. *Ukrsovnarkhoz* was, effectively, Gosplan of Ukraine, as it had the same address, Kirova 12/2.[20]

Table 11.2 Number of professional staff (without servicing staff and security)

	By the end of 1962	Estimated increase due to the after-Plenum reorganization	1963
Gosplan of Ukraine	1261 (without staff in *sbyty*)	1261 (without staff in *sbyty*)	980
Ukrsovnarkhoz	962	1,488	1,415
Total	2,223	2,749	2,395

Note: TsDAVOU, f. 2, op. 10, d. 2524, l. 3; Resolution of the CC CPUk on the structure and staff of Gosplan of Ukraine and *Ukrsovnarkhoz*, 12 February 1963, TsDAGOU, f. 1, op. 6, d. 3517, ll. 47, 108.

Ukrsovnarkhoz: managing resources

At the November 1962 Plenum, the central leadership supported the recentralization policy but did not abandon the policy of decentralization, which allowed Ukraine to hope that republican rights in managing resources could yet be extended. This assumption was based on the Plenum decision of 23 November 1962 to increase the list of products to be managed by *Ukrglavsnabsbyty*. (It remains unclear, however, whose list would be shortened as a result, that of the GlUMPP or the *sovnarkhozy*.) Ukraine also expected that the central leadership would finally clearly define and systematize the functions of *Ukrglavsnabsbyty* and eliminate the discrepancy between the official policy that extended the functions of the republican planners and the practical application of the official policy, by which the central planners *de facto* limited the influence of *Ukrglavsnabsbyty* on the supply system. Ukraine's expectations were far too high.

In the post-Plenum supply system the dynamic of recentralization was stronger than the dynamic of decentralization. The number of central agencies involved in the distribution of resources increased: besides GlUMPP, the state branch committees were awarded a say in matters of supplies. Then, rejecting Ukraine's suggestion from previous years to expand the list of products that were managed by USSR Gosplan and negotiated between the centre and the republics and to reduce the list of products managed by the GlUMPP which was compiled without consulting the republics, in January 1963, USSR *Sovnarkhoz* did exactly the opposite. It reduced the list of centrally planned products that were negotiated between the centre and the republics, and increased the list of products managed by GlUMPP and branch committees, which would hardly simplify the adjustment of production plans to available inputs.[21] At the same time, the centre demanded that the quantity of documents involved in accounting for the circulation of resources be increased and include more information than before.[22]

There was little indication that centre–republic economic relations would be finally formalized. In September 1963, the central agencies still had not fulfilled the government instruction from 1961 that compelled them to clearly define the functions of central and republican *snabsbyty* (and this was not the first time the agencies were so instructed).²³ So the practice of managing supplies in manual mode and keeping the republican *snabsbyty* effectively debarred from setting production targets continued. For example, *Ukrglavmetallosnabsbyt* was in charge of placing production orders for cast iron, ferroalloys and coke-chemicals with the Ukrainian metallurgical mills for customers all over the country and yet the issuance of orders remained with the central *Glavmetallosbyt*.²⁴

Since 1957, no progress was made in setting up regular communication between the central and republican *snabsbyty*. GIUMPP persistently avoided providing Ukraine with information on the fulfilment of inter-republican deliveries.²⁵ Yet despite all the efforts of the central *apparat*, the situation concerning the actual fulfilment of deliveries after the November 1962 Plenum was not much different from the one during previous years: the *sovnarkhozy* continued breaking contracts with both Ukrainian and non-Ukrainian customers.²⁶ They continued concealing resources and accumulating above-norm production reserves. The central *apparat* was not yet in a position to control all resources, whereas the republic-level planners became ever less motivated to fight regional *mestnichestvo* for the sake of consolidating the power of the central planners.

Thus, in June 1963, *Ukrsovnarkhoz* sent a group of functionaries to the regions to check how the *sovnarkhozy* fulfilled the plans for inter-republican deliveries and deliveries for all-Union needs. (This fact alone points to the absence of any progress in establishing mechanisms to circulate up-to-date information between the regions and Kiev.) The audit concerned only the production of ferrous metallurgy, cast iron, rolled metal and other forms of metallurgical production. The results were not optimistic and the conclusions were neither sophisticated nor new. The irregularities in deliveries, the Ukrainian government claimed in July 1963, were caused by a lack of control and by the wilful, rather than unintentional, decisions of the *sovnarkhozy* to retain resources in the regions, or effectively *mestnichestvo*. The *sovnarkhozy* did not force enterprises to submit reports by the deadlines, so the republic-level functionaries could not react to incidents of non-fulfilment of deliveries and provide the necessary assistance to the *sovnarkhozy* customers.²⁷ However, when reporting to the central government on the non-deliveries of metal, the Ukrainian government retreated from its previous method of focusing on the failures of the *sovnarkhozy* and pointed to non-Ukrainian parties, namely the USSR *Sovnarkhoz* and *Soyuzglavmetal*, which had contributed to the problem:

> The difficulties with material supplies in 1963, in particular with the supplies of some assortments of rolled ferrous metal, are … explained by the fact that USSR *Sovnarkhoz*, after estimating the amount of unused materials by 1 January 1963, assigned to the republic 22 thousand tonnes of rolled wire less than the republic requested. USSR Sovnarkhoz had also reduced the supplies of assorted scarce types of rolled ferrous metal by 56 thousand tonnes.²⁸

Instead of making up for this shortage, 'instead of envisaging ways of solving the problem', USSR *Sovnarkhoz* reduced republican funds. The estimates of

Ukrglavmetallosnabsbyt which showed that *Soyuzglavmetal* had 'artificially cut republican funds' were ignored.

The deviation from the traditional explanation of delivery failures made by *Ukrsovnarkhoz* could hardly be missed in Moscow. Whereas during the first few years of the *Sovnarkhoz* reform the Ukrainian authorities, when talking about Ukraine's interests, demonstrated their trust in the system and central *apparat* by holding the *sovnarkhozy* responsible for interruptions in supplies, starting in 1959, but particularly after the November 1962 Plenum, the Ukrainian republican authorities insisted on holding the central planners responsible for the malfunctioning of the supply system. The *sovnarkhozy* did not deliver, but they could not be held responsible if the non-delivery was caused by a central agency. Thereby, *mestnichestvo* in its traditional interpretation was not necessarily the cause of the failed deliveries. This was the main political tone of the Ukrainian authorities when talking about inter-republican deliveries.

The Ukrainian planners arrived at the same conclusion after they analysed the problem of concealment of material resources and the accumulation of above-norm reserves by the *sovnarkhozy*. At the end of April 1963, the head of the TsSU V. Starovskii informed the CMUk that substantial inventories of uninstalled equipment and concealed material inputs had been discovered and demanded that the *sovnarkhozy* reduce the inventories and penalize those responsible for the accumulations.[29] The problem of concealed and accumulated above-norm reserves was no less acute for the planners, although not necessarily for the economy, than the problem of non-deliveries. For Moscow the problem was the absence of balance between the turnover of production and output. In 1957–1962, productive output increased by a factor of 1.6 whereas the accumulation of resources in some *sovnarkhozy* exceeded the norms by several times. For example, in the Dnepropetrovsk *Sovnarkhoz*, the stock of rolled metal was twice as large as the norm, the stock of cast-iron water pipes exceeded the norm by a factor of four, and bronze exceeded it by a factor of seven.[30] In the retail trade of the entire country in 1961–1963 inventories increased by 28 per cent, but sales by 15 per cent.[31]

By July 1964, Ukrainian enterprises accumulated inputs classified as 'unnecessary' of 57.3 million roubles, which constituted 18.5 per cent of the total above-norm material stocks, including unfinished and finished goods, or 31 per cent of total production stocks.[32] Throughout 1963, but mostly in the fourth quarter of the year, the *Ukrsovnarkhoz* worked on reducing the above-norm inventories generally by redistributing the surplus stocks both inside the same *Sovnarkhoz* and among different Ukrainian *sovnarkhozy*.[33] At the end of 1963, the *Ukrsovnarkhoz* concluded that the reasons for the accumulation of above-norm stocks of raw materials and other materials were the non-fulfilment of production plans by some enterprises; multiple modifications in the assortment plan; modifications in the design of production that were introduced when manufacturing was in progress; modifications in construction projects, which required cancelling previous orders; or deliveries of inputs ahead of the schedule.[34] (The *Ukrsovnarkhoz* did not, however, include in its information that the reason for accumulating unused equipment was a severe shortage of machine-tool operators in the early 1960s, which was due to a high labour turnover in engineering caused, in its turn, by the tighter norms imposed by the wage reform of 1956–1962.[35]) According to *Ukrsovnarkhoz*, in the majority of cases, accumulations of resources above the norms did not depend on the enterprise. The accumulations could be a result of irregular work of enterprises, *neritmichnaya rabota*,[36] which was often due to factors on which enterprises had no influence; for example, enterprises could do nothing when the all-Union *sbyty* issued orders for sale either not in time or not for the total output.[37] The Ukrainian authorities had the same arguments to explain unfulfilled deliveries and hoarding of production by enterprises: this was not entirely the fault of enterprises and *sovnarkhozy*.

Curiously, when *Ukrsovnarkhoz* analysed the problem in September 1962, it gave different reasons for the accumulation of inventories: obsolete norms and the deliberate supply of surplus amounts.[38] The enterprises chose to store above the allowed norms, and when they applied out-of-date norms they in fact had a choice not to apply them. At the same time, *Ukrsovnarkhoz* emphasized that the purposes of accumulating above the norms generally were to have the inputs 'just in case', which included changes in the plan, urgent above-plan orders or interruptions of supply, and to exchange with other enterprises. An important factor that facilitated the decision to accumulate was that those responsible for the accumulations bore only ethical responsibility;[39] the worst that could happen to them was to be denounced by society, which could in principle have a negative effect on their reputation but rarely had any impact on their career, thereby costing them very little.

In 1962, *Ukrsovnarkhoz* did not develop the logic of enterprise behaviour any further. It did not analyse why enterprises had to consider 'just in case' situations and why they had to count on exchange with other enterprises or *sovnarkhozy*. Only a year later would the reasons for *mestnichestvo* in managing resources be analysed and included in the reports submitted to Moscow. *Ukrsovnarkhoz* argued instead that economic stimulus and material incentives for workers, functionaries and directors could reduce accumulations of materials and improve the fulfilment of various plans. Before the November 1962 Plenum, the Ukrainian authorities did not find it sensible to blame the central planners for the problem. After the Plenum, however, by arguing that the causes for accumulating stocks lay outside Ukraine, Kiev tried to stop or reverse the recentralization of the economic administration.

The VSNKh learned the conclusions of *Ukrsovnarkhoz* on the reasons for accumulating surplus materials in 1964 when it asked the Ukrainian government for comments on a draft of a central resolution on this issue. At this point, the CMUk stated that in a number of cases, accumulations of the above-norm inventories of unfinished and finished products were the fault of the central planning agencies. So, in its resolution, the VSNKh should include paragraphs on the responsibility of central agencies for instructions that caused enterprises to accumulate surplus material stocks. Specifically, when USSR Gosplan, USSR *Sovnarkhoz*, the state committees or any central ministry or department interrupted production or changed the terms of delivery for production that was still in the process of being manufactured, they should advise the VSNKh on the sources of compensation for the costs incurred. The CMUk also insisted, repeatedly, that USSR *Sovnarkhoz* should ensure that the central *sbyty* issue orders on sales of planned production in time. When necessary, continued the CMUk, USSR *Sovnarkhoz* should offer credits for production that was finished but on which the orders were pending.[40] Again and again Ukraine insisted on the mutual responsibility of the republic and central planners for their decisions and the fulfilment of their obligations, something that Kosygin would call for when launching his 1965 reform.

Conclusion

The November 1962 Party Plenum had a crucial effect on two processes: a) the official switch to prioritizing branch administration and the subsequent organizational restructuring that permitted the central *apparat* to intensify the recentralization of control over resources; and b) consolidation of the position of *Ukrsovnarkhoz* in the Ukrainian administrative system. The second process was impossible without the first. The newly empowered *Ukrsovnarkhoz* was supposed to deliver what Gosplan of Ukraine failed to do: ensure that the republic fulfilled its obligations to other republics, to all-Union funds and for export. This did not happen. Most likely, if *Ukrsovnarkhoz* had been given sufficient authority when it was created in 1960 it would have worked, in contrast to Gosplan of Ukraine, to promote and protect all-Union interests within the republic. But in 1963, *Ukrsovnarkhoz*, staffed with ex-Gosplan of Ukraine functionaries, could not conduct any other policy except the policy of protecting republican interests.

The period after the November 1962 Plenum, and particularly after spring 1963 when the vertical administrative structure had been completed, is characterized as one of open recentralization of the economic administration, but it can also be characterized as the period of open confrontation between the republic and central planners. The policies outlined at the Plenum, the organizational readjustment at the centre, along with Khrushchev's changing attitude to the reform, sobered the Ukrainian authorities on the prospects of economic decentralization, although they did not completely disillusion them about the possibilities for change. Otherwise, in their analyses of the reasons for non-deliveries and the withdrawal of resources from centralized control, they would not have gone any further than complaining about a 'lack of control'. The disillusionment came later, after Khrushchev's dismissal in October 1964.

Epilogue

Along with other Khrushchev projects, the *Sovnarkhoz* system was abandoned soon after its initiator lost power. Still, despite all the effort that the central *apparat* put into recentralizing control over industry, despite all the progress that was achieved in constructing an organizational structure that legitimized the centre's direct access to manufacturing, and finally, despite the sheer disbelief of central managers and planners in the territorial administration of the economy, it took longer for the new leadership to return to the ministerial system than for Khrushchev to install the *sovnarkhozy*. Why? Why and how was the *Sovnarkhoz* system abandoned?

On 13 October 1964, the CC CPSU Presidium gathered to criticize Khrushchev and remove him from power. Khrushchev was criticized for many things, including his many initiatives. He was blamed for making a declaration on the Eight Year Plan without consulting anyone, for the bifurcation of *obkomy*, for frequent structural changes, for communication between Presidium members through notes, for a non-Party attitude towards his comrades, and so on.[1] The Presidium members focused on the issues that frustrated them personally and the *apparat* in general, pouring out their anger with Khrushchev and focusing on the negative outcomes of his projects. Khrushchev was advised to retire, which he officially did the next day.[2]

The *Sovnarkhoz* reform, and the damage that it had done to the centralized economic administration, was mentioned, but compared to his other 'sins' the *Sovnarkhoz* reform was not noted frequently and not with the same ferocity as, for example, the bifurcation of the Party. The Chairman of the newly formed Committee of *Goskontrol'* – the CC CPSU and the USSR CM Committee for Party-state control which was formed in 1962 – A.N. Shelepin reproached Khrushchev for detaching science from production. The Chairman of the VTsSPS V.V. Grishin pointed to the low technological level of industry, confusion in industrial administration, numerous committees and loss of the branch approach to industrial development. But nobody blamed Khrushchev, at least not out loud, for *creating* territorial economic councils or increasing the involvement of the republican governments with industrial administration. Why not? The reason for the comparatively mild criticism of the *Sovnarkhoz* reform and no criticism of his republican policy was the dependence of the new Presidium, of Brezhnev and others, on the support of the republican first secretaries in removing Khrushchev. Without their support, there was a risk of repeating the scenario of the June 1957 Plenum.

In 1964, as well as in 1957, the republic Party secretaries supported the side which promised them enhanced economic rights and decision-making authority. In 1957 it was Khrushchev. In 1964 it was the Presidium. The difference was that by June 1957, Khrushchev had *already extended* the republican rights, whereas in 1964, the Presidium *let the republics believe* that their rights would be extended. Most likely, those who plotted Khrushchev's dismissal made no explicit promises. Yet by stressing the importance of the republican leaders for removing Khrushchev, by pointing them to the issues that they planned to criticize Khrushchev for, among which the enhancement of republican rights was not included, Brezhnev and others indicated that the contribution of the republican First Party secretaries would not be forgotten and that the balance of power between the centre and the republics would at least not change, possibly even swing in favour of the republics.

The first indication that the leadership would default on its promise, even though it was not explicitly articulated or documented, was made at the end of October 1964 when it offered the republics two possible scenarios for the next reorganization. With both scenarios, the central government targeted two major problems generated, so it claimed, by the *Sovnarkhoz* system: a) the multi-staged structure of industrial administration and b) the absence of a common policy in administering the branches in the republic and in the USSR in general.[3] Of course, the fact that these problems were generated and developed mainly by the central *apparat* remained beyond discussion.

In the first version, Moscow suggested continuing to administer industry through republican governments and, in the Ukrainian case, through the branch departments of *Ukrsovnarkhoz*. Industry would be administered according to the plan adopted by the USSR CM. In the second version, industrial administration should be provided by the Union-Republic ministries located in Moscow and the republic ministries located in the republic capitals.[4] In both versions, there was no place for the *sovnarkhozy*. To a large extent, this did not bother Kiev. During the reform, Gosplan of Ukraine persistently claimed the right to have direct access to production. But with the second scenario, the role of the republican governments would be considerably curtailed. This did concern Kiev.

On 6 November, an *Ukrsovnarkhoz* commission formed to study the issue reported to the CC CPUk that the administration of industry through republican governments was 'the most acceptable' option. All enterprises, combines and trusts should be subordinated directly to the branch departments of *Ukrsovnarkhoz*. *Ukrsovnarkhoz*, in its turn, should be expanded. In the explanation of the advantages of keeping industry under republican control there was absolutely nothing new. The republic would be more efficient in using resources and developing the republican economic complex. It would solve organizational problems and problems related to the production process faster, and so on. Another reason for keeping all industry under republican control was to 'facilitate the administrative work

126   *Epilogue*

of the Union organs and allow them to focus on the most important issues of economic administration';[5] the Ukrainians were echoing Khrushchev's ideas at the beginning of the reform.

As for the version that offered the return of the industrial ministries, the Ukrainian commission was sure that the ministries would restore ministerial barriers and again aim at creating closed economies, causing a proliferation of effectively identical agencies. The influence of the republics on the fulfilment of production targets would be drastically reduced. It would then be impossible to provide territorial inter-branch coordination and cooperation. It would be hard to create a common supply system in the territory of the republic. The Ukrainians even appealed to the 'savings' factor: with the first scenario, the number of departments and staff in *Ukrsovnarkhoz* would be considerably smaller than with the ministries.[6]

Along with emphasizing the advantages of running industry from republican capitals, the commission suggested enlarging the decision-making authority of the republics, indicating that in Kiev they did not expect the curtailment of republican economic rights. The republics should have the authority to fix supplementary targets for producing raw materials, materials, machinery and equipment for republican needs; keep production manufactured above the plan; organize and reorganize scientific and research institutes; keep 50 per cent of the income tax received from the sales of consumer goods that were produced above the plan; and redistribute investment between all branches within a limit of 2 per cent of the total investment assigned to the republic.[7] There were no new requests in this section of the commission's document either. At some point during the reform, some rights were granted to the republic but later revoked, and some rights were discussed but never granted.

Despite the advantages that the *Sovnarkhoz* system offered, the central government made its decision and it was now a matter of time and, to some extent, of political correctness to bring all administrative levers back to Moscow. At the Plenum on 16 November 1964, the Central Committee discussed the reorganization of industrial administration and whether it was reasonable to keep the *sovnarkhozy*. The participants, wrote Pyzhikov, gave a positive evaluation of the *sovnarkhozy*. However, the reasoning for keeping the *sovnarkhozy* was disregarded and the opinion of the Presidium on the issue – to abolish them – got the majority of votes.[8] This did not, however, imply the curtailment of republican rights, at least not yet.

In the period from December 1964 until June 1965, the central leadership managed to persuade the republic Party leaders to agree to the restoration of the ministerial system. Here is what First CC CPUk secretary Shelest wrote in his diary about the discussion in the CC CPSU Presidium held on 10–12 June:

> [Kosygin's] speech was not well structured and was not convincing. The *Sovnarkhoz* system was criticized a lot, as if it was because of them [the *sovnarkhozy*] that our economy was rather slack. All this was exaggerated and did not reflect reality. It was simply necessary to reduce the role of the

sovnarkhozy in order to move to a new reorganization, to the creation of the ministries, although less than a year ago everyone was supporting the *sovnarkhozy* ... .

After Kosygin, it was Brezhnev's turn. Cautiously, he supported Kosygin. He knew that almost all the republics had agreed to the creation of the ministries with reluctance. And it was not so much because they adhered to the *Sovnarkhoz* system. Simply, there were no reasonable arguments in favour of the ministries. Nevertheless, L.I. Brezhnev made it clear that the issue was the centralization of the industrial administration. To confirm this, he gave examples of *mestnichestvo*, claiming that the Party committees were cut off from production and the work of Gosplan was unsatisfactory. But all this did not sound persuasive either. And this is how the discussion of this important problem finished. We all understood that the restoration of the ministries had been decided. There was only one thing left: to make sure that for certain industrial branches Union-Republic ministries were created and that the republic kept those agencies which influenced production ... .[9]

The CC CPSU Plenum held on 29 September 1965 brought industry back under ministerial management. CC CPUk secretary and member of the CC CPUk Presidium A. Lyashko remembered that the leaders of the republics, except the RSFSR, 'developed a taste for a certain independence from the centre and were hardly happy with the forthcoming loss of this achievement':

This was reflected in the character and tone of the speech of Shelest. He suggested, in fact demanded, that ... all industrial and construction ministries and a number of departments were organized in Ukraine. The reaction to his speech was immediately reflected on the faces of those who sat in the Presidium and was clearly malevolent. The Chairman of the RSFSR CM G.I. Voronov who spoke after Shelest confirmed this. What he hurled into the audience was remembered due to its unambiguousness and even rudeness: 'We are not going to rashly demand the organization of ministries of heavy industry and construction. Let this be administered by the Union ministries and we will cooperate with them.'

I got it immediately: Russia is giving up on administrating the basic economic branches and is devolving all responsibility for their work and their further development to the Union ministries. For the Russian government, it would certainly be much easier this way, but not for the Ukrainian. ... After us, D.A. Kunaev from Kazakhstan said that in his republic it was necessary to create ministries for non-ferrous metallurgy, geology and some other branches that would run the republican enterprises that produced a large share of the all-Union output. Other republics also came forward proposing the creation of Union-Republic ministries. So after all, the 'absolute' centre of the past could not be restored. To some extent, it was necessary to share the administration of the economy with the republics. The Ukrainians, due to their economic potential, second only to Russia's, now set ... an example for others in the aspiration for independence in administrating their economy as a part of a common country-wide economic complex, of course.[10]

Ukraine succeeded in creating ministries for the leading Ukrainian industries: the coal mining industry, ferrous metallurgy, chemical industry, construction materials, light and food industry, local industry, meat and milk industry, melioration and water industry, and some others. However, the all-Union ministries took complete control over 'the machine-building enterprises, the enterprises of the defence industry and shipbuilding plants, the instrument-making industry with its numerous scientific and production associations of radio electronics and means of communication.'[11]

Ironically, Shelest, when supporting the Presidium in October 1964, accused Khrushchev, during his leadership, of not giving the republics enough rights: they had responsibilities but no rights.[12]

Conclusions

Khrushchev's decision to abolish industrial ministries and transfer their managerial rights to peripheral authorities was dictated by the administrative logic of the first half of the 1950s. After Stalin's death, the ministerial system went through continuous reorganizations, yet as the economy grew, the ministries struggled to increase the efficiency of their *apparat*. At the same time, the involvement of the republics with economic administration grew, along with their insistence on the benefits of the devolution of administrative authority from the centre to the periphery.

By 1957, Khrushchev could hardly question the potential economic gains from transferring decision making from the centre to the periphery. Territorial economic councils were a promising alternative to the ministries, as they had the potential to correct the mistakes of the ministries and reduce the cost of the administrative *apparat*. More importantly, the territorial economic councils could provide the central *apparat* with information, allowing the latter to make better macro-economic decisions. The new system would eliminate the chronic flaw of irresponsibility. In the *Sovnarkhoz* system, the peripheral managers would make decisions and be responsible for their implementation and effect.

Khrushchev envisioned simple, well organized and centrally regulated decentralization of operational decision making and resource control, based on the unchallenged foundations of central planning and the centrality of the central planners' role in economic administration. The *sovnarkhozy*, located close to production, would make routine decisions about manufacturing and implement the instructions of the planners, republican governments would run republican economies based on the plan targets and control the *sovnarkhozy*, and the central *apparat* would concentrate its efforts and skills on fulfilling the functions that could not be transferred below central level: policy making and perspective planning for the entire country, coordination of the development of regional economies and branches, distribution of financial and essential material resources and so on. Together, the central *apparat* and peripheral managers would lead the country to prosperity. The economy would grow faster at a lower cost for the central budget.

So, the reform aimed to boost economic growth, increase efficiency and improve the structure of economic administration. By the end of 1964, all of these

130 *Conclusions*

aims remained unaccomplished: the economy was growing slower than before or at the beginning of the reform,[1] the originally simplified system of economic administration turned into something burdensome and the quality of economic decisions, although somewhat improved at the regional level, remained low at the central level. The republics' Party secretaries did not feel sufficiently grateful to Khrushchev for replacing the ministerial system with the *sovnarkhozy* to oppose his dismissal in October 1964. To them, the decentralization turned out to be excessively centralized.

Yet the reform had a promising start. The first three years, those of decentralization, showed increased annual growth rates for industry (see Table C.1). The administrative *apparat* shrunk by a third and reached its post-war minimum of 1.2 million people in 1960.[2] The organizational structure of economic administration was simplified. Instead of four categories, all-Union, Union-Republic, republican and local, industry was divided between three categories: local, run by the local Soviets; republican, run by the *sovnarkhozy*; and a very small share of all-Union. Three-quarters of all-Union production was manufactured by the *sovnarkhozy*. In Ukraine, the *sovnarkhozy* ran more than 73 per cent of industry in 1957 and more than 86 per cent in 1965; the centre retained control over a mere 3.8 per cent in 1957, 3.3 per cent in 1958 and the lowest share of 2.9 per cent of Ukraine's industry in 1959.[3] Nonetheless, in 1959, when the *sovnarkhozy* were still showing positive results, the centre reversed the direction of the reform. Why?

The reason for the recentralization was claimed to be *mestnichestvo* which was ubiquitously pursued by the *sovnarkhozy*, and its negative impact on the branch development in particular. The *sovnarkhozy* abused their economic rights, prioritized their own needs and neglected the needs of non-local customers. *Mestnichestvo* developed with decentralization, so the policy of decentralization should be curtailed and control over production should be brought back to Moscow. This was the logic that prevailed among the central *apparat*.

The reason for recentralization was indeed *mestnichestvo*, however, not its economic element. Economically, regional *mestnichestvo* was not a new phenomenon, as it was no different from ministerial departmentalism. Both the *sovnarkhozy* and the ministries prioritized their own economic needs to ensure the fulfilment of the plans. As for the presumably higher cost of *mestnichestvo* to the economy,[4] this assertion remains debatable, since to the best of my knowledge nobody has yet offered any quantitative proof of this statement. We can certainly talk about the possibly larger scale of *mestnichestvo* compared to departmentalism, but this also remains to be confirmed. Besides, the larger scale of *mestnichestvo* did not necessarily mean a larger negative effect on the economy. *Mestnichestvo*, particularly its negative effect on branch development, was certainly more *discussed* in the press than the effect of departmentalism on the regional economies and thereby it appeared more visible, tangible. But this lively discussion could have been a result of the more relaxed social atmosphere rather than the particularly damaging economic effect of localism.

Despite the territorial rhetoric, the *sovnarkhozy* were not in a position to prioritize the complex development of territorial economies to the detriment of the branches. The development of branches during the reform was orchestrated and controlled by USSR Gosplan through production plan targets, investment, financing, the supply system and, more importantly, through the branch departments in republic Gosplans and the *sovnarkhozy* that channelled the central instructions and distributed the funds. As a result, Ukraine, having the second after the RSFSR most diversified economic complex, despite all formal and informal efforts, had not managed to improve the branch balance in favour of light and food industry.[5]

The *mestnichestvo* that motivated the centre to curtail the policy of decentralization had a more complex nature than was described in the press. The tendency of protecting one's own interests spread beyond the supply system or bargaining for lower production targets along with higher investment and inputs, and above the level of the *sovnarkhozy*, and penetrated the administrative layer that was supposed to stay immune from this tendency, the level of the republican authorities. At the same time, although both regional and republican authorities prioritized their own economic needs, they were motivated by different factors, and *mestnichestvo* pursued by them had different implications.

Regional *mestnichestvo*, as already mentioned, was essentially economically driven as it was the response to the economy of scarcity and to the inefficiency of the formal supply system. It was also motivated by the rhetoric of the reform that called for the development of complex economic regions and for reductions in wasteful long-distance cross-hauls. *Mestnichestvo* among the republic-level authorities, on the other hand, in addition to the economic factor and the rhetoric of the reform, was a response to the inability of the central *apparat* to establish a system where the interests of the centre and the republics would be aligned. Contrary to regional *mestnichestvo*, *mestnichestvo* at the level of the republics' capitals had political implications. How quickly would economic claims generate political claims? The application of the reform in Ukraine, where the republican planners and authorities had a similar response to the central policies as the authorities of other republics, makes it possible to affirm that it was *mestnichestvo* at the level of republican authorities that induced the central planners, and later the central leadership, to recentralize economic administration. *Mestnichestvo* pursued by the republican authorities, fuelled by the developing informal relations between Kiev and the regions and by increasing volumes of resources withdrawn from the control of the planners, had unpredictable implications.

So, which actions or non-actions on the part of USSR Gosplan induced *mestnichestvo* among the Ukrainian republic-level authorities and why could the policy of decentralization not continue? The new organizational system put the central *apparat* in an unusual position when, except for a very small share of industry, they were formally deprived of direct access to industry and resources and could, again formally, communicate with production sites only through the republican governments. From the start, this separation from production was negatively perceived by the central *apparat* and caused tensions with the republican planners. The first conflicts manifested themselves in 1957, when USSR Gosplan overruled the new procedures and, instead of contacting republican governments, contacted the *sovnarkhozy* and mills in an attempt to force them to fulfil their inter-republican delivery obligations. The tension increased during the discussion of the 1958 draft plans composed 'from below' when it became clear that the reform rhetoric, including the very notion of all-Union interests, was interpreted differently by the republics and the central planners.

The republics explained that in the new system they did not view their role as executing central instructions without question; that decentralization was a policy that aimed to minimize the interference of the central managers and planners with the republican economies and maximize the role of the republican planners in orchestrating republican economies; that the reform was designed for their benefit and that the purpose of abolishing central ministries was to let the republican governments and *sovnarkhozy* correct the distortions that had been created in local economies. In other words, the interests of the republics *were* the interests of the entire Union. Thereby, when composing the plan for the entire country, republican opinion about the development of their economies should be fully considered. As the Ukrainian planners translated the republic's perceptions into plan targets, they composed the 1958 plan, the fulfilment of which they were ready to guarantee, and which addressed the problematic issues of the Ukrainian economy inherited from the ministries. They corrected the balance between the industries of groups 'A' and 'B' and, to respond to the inefficiency of the centre in distributing resources, they suggested changing the principle of distribution of production from 'delivering everything to the centre and then receiving what is needed from the centre' to 'keeping what is needed and delivering the excess to the centre'.

Assigned by the central leadership to guard the all-Union interest, USSR Gosplan could not accept such an interpretation of the purpose of the reform. From the perspective of the central planners, the reform was indeed designed to correct the distortions formed in local economies, but the ultimate purpose of the complex development of territorial economies was to increase economic growth of the entire economy at the lowest possible cost for the all-Union budget. The orchestration of overall growth, with all objectiveness, could be done only at the central level. Thereby, despite the rhetoric of the central leadership, the republics could not change the balance between industrial branches within the republics. Nor could they change the principle of distributing production. To let the republics conduct their own economic policies would most likely transform the economy and most definitely reduce the role of USSR Gosplan in inter-republican and centre–republican relations. Interpreting the reform as being designed for the benefit of the republics *was mestnichestvo*. Implicitly, any position taken by the republican authorities that differed from the position of the central planners was a manifestation of *mestnichestvo*.

Immediate manifestations of regional *mestnichestvo* in supplies, informal contacts between the central planners and the *sovnarkhozy* and production sites, along with the discrepancy in interpretation of the goals of the reform by the central leadership, USSR Gosplan and the republics that was demonstrated during the discussion of the 1958 draft plans, indicated that the new system

Conclusions 133

contained numerous loopholes that were used at each administrative level. Given that USSR Gosplan was assigned to implement the reform, it was up to its *apparat* to eliminate those loopholes. USSR Gosplan failed. The republics expected the policy of decentralization to be improved. USSR Gosplan preferred to retreat.

USSR Gosplan started by restoring the old planning practice whereby the centre dictated the targets. The old practice was convenient for the central and, to a lesser extent, republican planners. The so-called control figures, based on which the *sovnarkhozy* and republic Gosplans had to compose the draft plans, already reflected the all-Union interests. For USSR Gosplan, this was also the simplest and quickest way of not dealing with the problems in local economies that for the centre were of no importance.

The return to the previous planning practice left republic Gosplans with the old planning problems of input–output incoherence, incoherence between production and financial plans, production and supply plans, supply and transportation plans, and so on, all of those 'incoherencies' which would have been easier to correlate for the *sovnarkhozy* and the republics than for the entire country. At the same time, the republic Gosplans were again responsible for the fulfilment of plans in which their calculations and considerations had often been disregarded. How exactly did USSR Gosplan protect all-Union interests if it assigned production targets to a factory that was not operational or that did not have the technological capacity to fulfil the plan assignment, something that the peripheral planners would know about from the start but not have an opportunity to communicate to the centre?

Despite their differences in interpretation of the goals of the reform, USSR Gosplan and the Ukrainian authorities cordially shared their opinions on regional *mestnichestvo*. Both condemned it and qualified acts of prioritizing one's own needs over the needs of non-local customers as violation of state discipline. Both viewed tightening of control as the solution to the problem. USSR Gosplan even agreed with the premise that *mestnichestvo* should be controlled by the republics' capitals. However, when it came to empowering Gosplan of Ukraine with those levers needed to influence the *sovnarkhozy* and suppress *mestnichestvo*, the Ukrainian authorities faced resistance from the central planners, resistance that originated from their reluctance to pursue the reform and a lack of knowledge as to how to decentralize economic administration.

Of course, from the perspective of the Ukrainian leadership, which at the beginning of the reform did not question the competence of the central planners, it was the reluctance of USSR Gosplan to decentralize economic administration, or effectively implement the reform, that prevented it from empowering Gosplan of Ukraine. This perception was based on several observations. First, as Kiev saw things, the limited authority of Gosplan of Ukraine over the *sovnarkhozy*, insufficient decision-making power that did not correspond to the economic rights or responsibilities of the Ukrainian planners and their inability to correct the mistakes of the central planners had a negative economic effect. Surely, the planners from USSR Gosplan understood that. Second, there was a discrepancy between the resolutions of the central leadership and the policies of

USSR Gosplan. As the Ukrainian authorities noticed, USSR Gosplan used its exclusive position to delay or partially ignore the realization of those instructions that undermined its authority vis-à-vis the republican governments or the *sovnarkhozy*. Later on, as the policy of recentralization was gaining speed, the responsibility of the central *apparat* for their planning or managerial decisions did not increase. The functions of the central and peripheral *snabsbyty* were not clarified or formalized, allowing ambiguous interpretations and violations of procedure at all administrative levels. The system of exchange of information between the republics was not set up either, leaving Ukrainian planners managing deliveries 'in the dark'. The central planners did not rush to simplify and formalize the procedure for setting up direct relations, which would have reduced bureaucracy and increased the efficiency and responsibility of the producers, so the *sovnarkhozy* remained dependent on Moscow for suppliers and customers from non-native republics.[6] Thus in Ukraine, the volume of inter-republican contractual deliveries that prevailed in the machine-building industry fell by 30 per cent, instead of the 88 per cent that the Seven Year Plan called for.[7]

Reluctance by the central planners and ex-ministerial functionaries of the central *apparat* to empower the republics' economic authorities had its logic. The reform went against their departmental interests. The mechanisms that would permit Ukraine, or any other republic, to suppress *mestnichestvo*, such as full access to information generated in central offices, other republics and regions, a system that would allow the direct exchange of information and goods between producers and suppliers, an increase in the size of reserves at the disposition of the CMUk, and flexibility in moving material and financial resources between regions and branches, would also enable the Ukrainian authorities to pursue their own power ambitions and loosen their formal and informal dependence on the central economic agencies. The successful reduction or suppression of *mestnichestvo*, which the planners believed was possible, meant consolidating the decentralization policy, which would have translated into a further devolution of economic authority from the centre to the republican governments and the *sovnarkhozy* and liberalization of the economy. In addition to the unpredictable economic effect of this, the power of the republican authorities would have increased vis-à-vis the regions and the centre, and their dependence on central planners would have been reduced. The failure of Kiev to suppress regional *mestnichestvo*, on the other hand, justified the transfer of control over production back to the centre.

It would certainly be wrong to suggest that USSR Gosplan approved or promoted regional *mestnichestvo*. After all, the *sovnarkhozy* undermined the authority of the central managers too. Yet regional *mestnichestvo* was a familiar trend, whereas *mestnichestvo* at the level of the republican authorities was not. By 1959, the ambitions of the Ukrainian authorities to reduce the republic's economic dependence on Moscow and centralize control over the Ukrainian economy in Kiev were all too obvious.

At the same time, judging from the original distribution of authority between the centre, the republican capitals and the *sovnarkhozy* and the subsequent corrections

Conclusions 135

to the balance of authority between the centre and the periphery, we can conclude that USSR Gosplan, as the main architect of the reform, had rather vague ideas as to how to incorporate the republic-level authorities in the new system; how to share decision-making authority between the central and republican economic agencies so that the republican agencies had the power to suppress regional *mestnichestvo* but did not use it to pursue interests different from those determined by the centre; how to construct centre–republic economic relations in general to prevent centralization at the republican level and retain control over the economy; and how to organize direct inter-republican communication that would not reduce the centrality of USSR Gosplan's position in the system. For the central *apparat*, formalizing the system was something new. As the reform progressed, the understanding of the above-mentioned issues did not become any clearer. The case of *Ukrsovnarkhoz*, the precipitate turn to the recentralization policy and the very organizational system during the recentralization policy and then the abolition of the *Sovnarkhoz* system demonstrated that rather persuasively.

Lack of authority and a supporting institutional framework to fight regional *mestnichestvo* made it difficult for the Ukrainian leadership to promote all-Union interests with the *sovnarkhozy*, whereas, in order to guarantee the fulfilment of the production plan by the republic, the plan that remained the most important one, Gosplan of Ukraine and later *Ukrsovnarkhoz* had strong incentives to develop close relations with the *sovnarkhozy* and promote their interests in Moscow. The refusal of USSR Gosplan to cede authority to its Ukrainian counterpart was mirrored by formal and informal resistance from Gosplan of Ukraine to the subsequent policy of recentralization. After the November 1962 CC CPSU Plenum, as the tension between the Ukrainian and central planners transformed into an open confrontation, Ukrainian planners changed their tone from submission to affirmation and did not hesitate to challenge the decisions and procedures practised by the central planners. As Ukrainian planners gained knowledge and experience of running the republican economy, their understanding of regional *mestnichestvo* changed. Along with respecting the tradition that interpreted *mestnichestvo* as a violation of state discipline, they argued that the reasons for *mestnichestvo* often lay outside the *sovnarkhozy*. After the November 1962 Plenum, they felt confident enough to share their understanding with the central leadership and insist that *mestnichestvo* was to a large extent due to the inefficiency of the central *apparat*.

The policy of recentralization, started by USSR Gosplan and then supported by Khrushchev, was implemented in a more systematic way than the policy of decentralization. Recentralizing was more familiar and natural to the *apparat* than decentralizing. Yet the formal curtailment of economic rights of the *sovnarkhozy* did not eradicate *mestnichestvo* or make the republic-level authorities more motivated to protect all-Union interests in the republic, whereas the proliferation of central economic agencies made the system of economic administration cumbersome, ineffective and difficult to operate.

The economic results of the reform remain controversial. Although still insufficient on its own to support the view that decentralization offered advantages in the Soviet context, the Ukrainian Soviet annual data on industrial development of

136 *Conclusions*

Ukraine during the reform indicate that each recentralization impulse exacerbated the slowdown in growth (see Table C.1). (The Ukrainian statisticians, in fact, did not relate high growth rates to the decentralization policy. They explained the highest growth rate in 1958 as the result of a good harvest that allowed a considerable increase in production of food and consumer goods. The opposite reason caused the slowest growth in 1963.[8]) The CIA data on the annual growth of the all-Union industry shows the same tendency, except that for the Soviet Union the best reform year was 1959.[9]

The average annual growth rate of Ukrainian industry in 1957–1965 was 9.4 per cent, with more than 10 per cent before 1963 and almost 8 per cent in the period 1963–1965. The average growth rate of Ukrainian industry in the period 1951–1956, however, was 13.6 per cent. The slowdown during the *Sovnarkhoz* reform was attributed by Ukrainian statisticians to the particularly high growth rate before the reform.[10] During the reform, the productivity of industry fell from the average growth of 7.7 per cent in the period 1951–1956 to 5.2 per cent in 1959–1964. The productivity of light industry dropped from 5.6 per cent in 1951–1956 to 1.6 per cent in 1959–1964, and the productivity of the food industry fell from 6.8 per cent to 3.8 per cent respectively.[11]

About 900 industrial enterprises were launched in Ukraine in 1959–1964; 683 industrial enterprises became operational in the period 1951–1956.[12] Except for the coal mining industry, capital investment in Ukrainian industry had considerably increased during the *Sovnarkhoz* system.[13] By the end of the reform, Ukraine's heavy industry had increased and the republic remained highly integrated in the all-Union economic complex. The total share of Ukrainian gross output in all-Union production had increased from 16.6 per cent in 1958 to 18.1 per cent in 1964. As noted earlier, the centre had successfully retained control over the branches, so the industrial complex of Ukraine in general developed as the centre planned: by 1965 the share of the machine-building and metal-working industry had increased to 22.2 per cent from 16.8 per cent in 1958, the share of the chemical industry had increased from 3.3 per cent to 5.7 per cent, and the share of the coal mining industry had been reduced from 7.5 per cent to 5.54 per cent. The share of light industry in Ukraine's industrial complex had fallen from 2.45 per cent in 1958 to 1.75 per cent in 1965: in 1965, Ukraine, a republic with 20 per cent of the all-Union population, manufactured only 4 per cent of all-Union fabrics for clothing. The share of the food industry had fallen from 28.6 per cent to 24.6 per cent in the same years.[14]

During the *Sovnarkhoz* reform, Ukraine became better acquainted with the world. Whereas in 1957, Ukraine exported to 31 countries, in 1960 the republic exported to 41 countries, and in 1965, 722 enterprises of the Ukrainian *sovnarkhozy* exported to 81 countries, including 24 capitalist countries. The value of exported goods in 1965 had almost doubled since 1960. For some products, the share of the Ukrainian enterprises in the all-Union exports was more than substantial: 98 per cent of iron ore, 51.3 per cent of manganese ore, 81.5 per cent of cast iron, 63.7 per cent of rolled metal, 100 per cent of combustible gas, 99.8 per cent of superphosphate and 78.4 per cent of coal.[15]

Table C.1 Annual growth rate and value added of Ukrainian industry, 1957–1965

	1956	1957	1958	1959 (Kosygin in USSR Gosplan)	1960	1961	1962 (November CC CPSU Plenum)	1963	1964	1965
Gross output (%)	100	110.3	110.4	110.9	108.1	111.0	110.1	104.4	109.0	110.2
Value added (%)	100	108.3	114.8	111.1	107.3	111.9	109.7	104.9	109.9	n/a

Note: Based on TsDAVOU, f. 4820, op. 1, d. 1896, l. 15; TsDAVOU, f. 582, op. 3, d. 5011, l. 142.

138 *Conclusions*

So all in all, was the *Sovnarkhoz* system a better alternative to the ministerial system? Were the *sovnarkhozy* better managers than the *glavki* of the abolished ministries? Would Ukrainian, or all-Union, industry have grown faster had Khrushchev, instead of creating territorial economic councils, continued with the decentralization of the ministerial system in 1957? The present study did not aim to answer these questions. In 1965, however, Ukrainian statisticians tried to compare the efficiency of the *sovnarkhozy* with the pre-reform ministries, but concluded that it was impossible to make a comparative analysis of the two systems.[16] For them, there was a problem with data which simply did not exist. When describing the period from 1950 until 1964, they wrote:

> Based on the materials available to the TsSU of Ukraine, it is very hard to make judgments about general processes developed in the republican industry during a long period of time. This is due to the fact that until 1954–1957, the enterprises of all-Union jurisdiction constituted a considerable share in the Ukrainian industry and lots of indices that would have been relevant to the republican industry for these enterprises were not calculated. Generally in the Soviet Union, in 1956 (prior to the reorganization), industry under the jurisdiction of the CM of the Union republics was producing 55 per cent and industry of the Union jurisdiction 45 per cent of total industrial production. After the reorganization, the overwhelming share of production was manufactured by enterprises subordinated to the CM of the Union republics, whereas three-quarters of all production was manufactured by the *sovnarkhozy*. This makes numerous indices for these periods incomparable.[17]

In their report, the Ukrainian statisticians specified that the existing data on the volumes of gross output, the growth of labour productivity and growth of production of certain goods, as well as financial indices, only indirectly indicated the advantages and disadvantages of the administrative methods applied at different periods. Therefore, to say with certitude that the *Sovnarkhoz* system provided better economic administration required much deeper analysis than they could undertake.[18]

The results of the *Sovnarkhoz* reform are mixed. The economic slowdown by the end of the reform clearly points to its failure. However, it can be equally argued that the *sovnarkhozy* delayed the slowdown that would have come later anyway. The generally progressive idea of decentralizing economic administration and unloading petty decisions from the central *apparat* was poorly conceived and erratically implemented. The decision that predetermined the failure of the reform was made by Khrushchev himself when he entrusted people, who by the nature of their work and, on the basis of their experience until that point, could not agree with the very idea of decentralization, to elaborate a new institutional system where economic relations would be formalized and reduced between the central planners and the peripheral managers and increased between the republics. Of course, Khrushchev had hardly any choice of agencies or cadres to implement his reform, not to mention that he did not expect the decentralization of policy making, but only the decentralization of management. The central *apparat* proved more rigid than Khrushchev expected and stayed true to its values. It made a remarkable demonstration of its power to protect its own interests, which can also be interpreted as the success of the centre in retaining control over the economy.

It was equally wrong for Khrushchev to expect that with no fundamental changes to the system of incentives and restraining mechanisms, the republics would act differently from the ministries and prioritize all-Union interests over their own. Khrushchev counted on Party discipline and the conscience of the republic-level Party and government *apparat* and could not suspect that they would choose to reduce their economic dependence on the centre. The Ukrainian authorities also demonstrated an ability to resist those policies that undermined their authority.

All in all, it seems reasonable to suggest that with the *Sovnarkhoz* reform, Khrushchev was to a considerable extent outwitted by the governmental *apparat* in Moscow and the republics. From the start, the latter had the initiative over the reform in their hands and Khrushchev, instead of conducting the reform, was led by it. The explanations for that are several. First of all, as noted earlier, Khrushchev expected the *apparat* to do something it could not. Second, Khrushchev himself did not have a detailed plan that would explain how exactly to decentralize economic decision making and preserve centralized control over the economy. Yet at the same time, as much as the central *apparat* influenced Khrushchev, Khrushchev did not attempt to resist its influence. Khrushchev certainly believed in the advantages of decentralized decision making over centralized decision making, but he believed in the Union of Soviet republics more. Besides, Khrushchev himself was brought up in the strict Stalinist system of vertical power. The developing tendency towards *mestnichestvo* was a 'by-product' of the *Sovnarkhoz* reform that threatened the integrity of the state and therefore could not be tolerated.

The reform revealed, but failed to address, structural defects in the Soviet economic administration, namely the lack of mechanisms to enforce all economic actors to respect formal procedures and fulfil their obligations, and a lack of consistency between decision-making authority and responsibility for the final result. Nonetheless, the ideas that were generated during the *Sovnarkhoz* reform, and the theoretical work that had been done on the Soviet economy, were used by Kosygin for the reform that followed the abolition of the *Sovnarkhoz* system. *Kosyginskaya* reform would also address the structural problems of mutual irresponsibility and unbalanced authority.

For the Ukrainian authorities, the *Sovnarkhoz* reform did not meet the expectations that they had cherished since 1954. They did not obtain the necessary, from their perspective, flexibility in policy making and control over resources and production that was transferred directly to the regions. For them, the reform was far too conservative in its revision of the centre–republic balance of decision-making authority and far too progressive in its organizational form.

Still, the reform tested decentralization in the Soviet context of the 1950s and1960s. And even though the policy of decentralization was not fully applied, a certain decentralization of decision making and resource control was retained, informally more than formally, and the economic rights of the republics were enhanced. Informal relations actively developed between and inside the regions and republics, as proved by the increasing number of *tolkachi*. The *Sovnarkhoz* reform opened up new opportunities for peripheral managers and planners, who gained experience in running industry and construction, whereas the Ukrainian leadership gained experience and knowledge of the republican economy and became confident in their ability to run the republic. How well they ran the republic after Khrushchev is a subject for further research. The *Sovnarkhoz* reform certainly established that a return to Stalin's highly centralized ministerial system was impossible.

Notes

Introduction

1 G.M. Ivanova, *Na poroge 'gosudarstva vseobshchego blagosostoyaniya'. Sotsial'naya politika v SSSR (seredina 1950-kh-nachalo 1970-kh godov)*, Moscow: IRI RAN, 2011, pp. 53–7.
2 Ivanova, *Na poroge 'gosudarstva vseobshchego blagosostoyaniya'*, pp. 55–6.
3 Ivanova, *Na poroge 'gosudarstva vseobshchego blagosostoyaniya'*, p. 59.
4 The study of G.M. Ivanova *Na poroge 'gosudarstva vseobshchego blagosostoyaniya'* examines in detail the social policy of the Soviet government during the Khrushchev era and the beginning of the Brezhnev era.
5 *USSR: Measures of Economic Growth and Development, 1950–80: Studies prepared for the use of the Joint Economic Committee, Congress of the United States, December 8, 1982*, Washington, DC: U.S.GPO, 1982, p. 56.
6 Robert C. Allen, *Farm to Factory: A reinterpretation of the Soviet industrial revolution*, Princeton, NJ; Oxford: Princeton University Press, 2003, pp. 189, 190, 198; Robert C. Allen, 'The Rise and Decline of the Soviet Economy', *The Canadian Journal of Economics*, 34, 4, 2001, 869.
7 In 1953, to improve the dire situation in agriculture, taxes and compulsory delivery quotas from the peasants' household plots were reduced; state procurement prices for agricultural products were raised, rates of payment in kind and daily wages for collective-farm work were raised. *Kolkhozniki* were allowed to pasture their livestock on *kolkhoz* land. See Donald A. Filtzer, *The Khrushchev Era: De-Stalinization and the limits of reform in the USSR, 1953–1964*, Basingstoke: Macmillan, 1993, pp. 40–1; Philip Hanson, *The Rise and Fall of the Soviet Economy. An economic history of the USSR from 1945*, Harlow: Longman, 2003, p. 53; Alec Nove, *The Soviet Economic System*, London: George Allen & Unwin, 1977, pp. 235–6; R.G. Pikhoya, *Sovetskii Soyuz: istoriya vlasti 1945–1991*, Moscow: RAGS, 1998, p. 189.
8 Nove, *The Soviet Economic System*, p. 71; Moshe Lewin, *The Soviet Century*, G. Elliott (ed.) London: Verso, 2005, p. 223; Philip G. Roeder, *Red Sunset: The failure of Soviet politics*, Princeton, NJ: Princeton University Press, 1993, pp. 168–74; Filtzer, *The Khrushchev Era*, p. 68; William J. Conyngham, *Industrial Management in the Soviet Union: The role of the C.P.S.U. in industrial decision-making 1917–1970*, Stanford, CA: Hoover Institution Press, Stanford University, 1973, pp. 218–23; Robert F. Miller, 'Khrushchev and the Soviet economy: Management by re-organisation', in R.F. Miller and F. Fehér (eds) *Khrushchev and the Communist World*, London: Croom Helm, 1984, pp. 128–9; Roger Munting, *The Economic Development of the USSR*, London: Croom Helm, 1982, pp. 134–5.
9 Valery Vasil'ev, 'Failings of the Sovnarkhoz reform: the Ukrainian experience', in J. Smith and M. Ilic (eds) *Khrushchev in the Kremlin: policy and government in the Soviet Union, 1953–1964*, Milton Park, Abingdon, Oxon; New York, NY: Routledge, 2011, p. 127.

10 Conyngham, *Industrial Management*, pp. 105–6; W.J. Tompson, *Khrushchev: A Political Life*, Basingstoke: Macmillan in association with St Antony's College, Oxford, 1995, p. 177.
11 Stephen Whitefield, *Industrial Power and the Soviet State*, Oxford: Clarendon Press; New York: Oxford University Press, 1993, p. 25; Lewin, *The Soviet Century*, p. 221; Jacques Sapir, *Les fluctuations économiques en URSS, 1941–1985*, Paris: Ed. de l'Ecole des hautes études en sciences sociales, 1989, p. 97; Filtzer, *The Khrushchev Era*, pp. 67–70; Conyngham, *Industrial Management*, pp. 105–6, 223; David A. Dyker, *The Soviet Economy*, London: Crosby Lockwood Staples, 1976, pp. 84–9; Munting, *The Economic Development of the USSR*, pp. 134–5; Tompson, *Khrushchev: A Political Life*, pp. 174–8; Yu.A. Vedeneev, *Organizatsionnye reformy gosudarstvennogo upravleniya promyshlennost'yu v SSSR: istoriko-pravovoe issledovanie (1957–1987 gg.)*, Moscow: Nauka, 1990, pp. 38–47; Eugène Zaleski, *Planning Reforms in the Soviet Union, 1962–1966: An analysis of recent trends in economic organization and management*, trans. Marie-Christine MacAndrew and G. Warren Nutter, Chapel Hill, NC: University of North Carolina Press, 1967, p. 190.
12 Donna Bahry, *Outside Moscow: Power, politics, and budgetary policy in the Soviet republics*, New York: Columbia University Press, 1987, p. 47; Thad P. Alton, 'The Soviet economy: new expedients and persistent problems', *Proceedings of the Academy of Political Science*, 28, 1, 1965, 29–31; Nove, *The Soviet Economic System*, p. 73; Dyker, *The Soviet Economy*, p. 86.
13 Filtzer, *The Khrushchev Era*, p. 70; see also Donald A. Filtzer, *Soviet Workers and De-Stalinization: The consolidation of the modern system of Soviet production relations, 1953–1964*, Cambridge: Cambridge University Press, 2002, p. 21.
14 M.C. Kaser, 'Changes in planning methods during the preparation of the Soviet Seven Year Plan', *Soviet Studies*, 10, 4, 1959, 331.
15 Whitefield, *Industrial Power and the Soviet State*, p. 25; Filtzer, *The Khrushchev Era*, p. 68; Nove, *The Soviet Economic System*, p. 74.
16 Filtzer, *The Khrushchev Era*, pp. 68–70; Lewin, *The Soviet Century*, pp. 221, 222–3; Z. Mieczkowski, 'The 1962–1963 reforms in Soviet economic regionalization', *Slavic Review*, 24, 3, 1965, 489.
17 Alec Nove, 'The industrial planning system: reforms in prospect', *Soviet Studies*, 14, 1, 1962, 9–10.
18 Bahry, *Outside Moscow*, p. 52; Conyngham, *Industrial Management*, p. 106.
19 Nove, 'The industrial planning system', 2; Howard R. Swearer, 'Decentralization in recent Soviet administrative practice', *Slavic Review*, 21, 3, 1962, 467; Mieczkowski, 'The 1962–1963 reforms', 489.
20 Jerry F. Hough, *The Soviet Prefects: The local party organs in industrial decision-making*, Cambridge, MA: Harvard University Press, 1969, p. 57; Filtzer, *The Khrushchev Era*, pp. 68–9; Filtzer, *Soviet Workers and De-Stalinization*, p. 21; G. Grossman, 'The structure and organization of the Soviet economy', *Slavic Review*, 21, 2, 1962, 204–5, 217.
21 Conyngham, *Industrial Management*, p. 113; Hough, *The Soviet Prefects*, p. 191; John A. Armstrong, *The Politics of Totalitarianism: the Communist Party of the Soviet Union from 1934 to the present*, New York: Random House, 1961, p. 313; T.H. Rigby, 'Khrushchev and the rules of the Soviet political game', in R.F. Miller and F. Fehér (eds) *Khrushchev and the Communist World*, London: Croom Helm, 1984, pp. 57–8, 66.
22 Swearer, 'Decentralization in recent Soviet administrative practice', 466; Hough, *The Soviet Prefects*, 58.
23 David Granick, 'An organizational model of Soviet industrial planning', *The Journal of Political Economy*, 67, 2, 1959, 110, 130.
24 Aleksandr Lyashko, *Gruz pamyati. Trilogiya, Vospominaniya. Na stupenyakh vlasti*, Kyiv: Delovaya Ukraina, 1997, p. 57.

25 Swearer, 'Decentralization in recent Soviet administrative practice', 460.
26 Z. Frank and J. Waelbroeck, 'Soviet economic policy since 1953: a study of its structure and changes', *Soviet Studies*, 1965, 17, 1, 1965, 33.
27 Vedeneev, *Organizatsionnye reformy*, p. 35.
28 Yu. F. Vorob'ev (ed.), *Ocherki ekonomicheskikh reform*, Moscow: Nauka, 1993, p. 191.
29 Namely Nicholas Laskovsky, 'Reflections on Soviet industrial reorganization', *American Slavic and East European Review*, 17, 1, 1958, 47–58; Dyker, *The Soviet Economy*, p. 86; Nove, *The Soviet Economic System*, pp. 71, 72.
30 Grossman, 'The structure and organization of the Soviet economy', 217; Alton, 'The Soviet economy', 34.
31 The number of Ukrainians among the CC CPSU members had increased from 16 in 1952 to 39 by 1956 and to 59 by 1961 and constituted 18.5 per cent of all CC CPSU members and candidates. Ukrainians had now more than average representation among the members of the Central Committee. G. Simon, *Nationalism and Policy Toward the Nationalities in the Soviet Union: From totalitarian dictatorship to post-Stalinist society*, Boulder, CO: Westview Press, 1991, pp. 230, 231.

1 1953–1956

1 R.G. Pikhoya, *Sovetskii Soyuz: istoriya vlasti 1945–1991*, Moscow: RAGS, 1998, pp. 99, 100; A.V. Pyzhikov, *Khrushchevskaya 'Ottepel''*, Moscow: Olma-Press, 2002, p. 87; S.V. Korobenkov, *Dela Kremlya. Pravitel'stvennyi apparat*, tom 2, Moscow: Forum, 2004, p. 103.
2 According to H. Schwartz, the new Politburo cut the number of the ministries in order to consolidate the power in fewer hands of those whom its members trusted. Yoram Gorlizki considered that the second merging in particular, the one on 15 March, was Malenkov's solution 'to untangle the cross-cutting lines of authority that had characterized the late Stalin period.' Apparently, the strategy was not new for Malenkov: on his initiative, in 1948 the number of ministries was reduced from 59 to 48. See H. Schwartz, *The Soviet Economy Since Stalin*, London: Victor Gollancz Ltd, 1965, p. 67; Yoram Gorlizki, 'Anti-Ministerialism and the USSR Ministry of Justice, 1953–1956: A study in organisational decline', *Europe–Asia Studies*, 48, 8, 1996, 1291, 1307.
3 After the Second World War, the ministries were often either split or merged. See T.P. Korzhikhina, *Sovetskoe gosudarstvo i ego uchrezhdeniya. Noyabr' 1917–Dekabr' 1991*, Moscow: RGGU, 1995, pp. 228–30; Pikhoya, *Sovetskii Soyuz: Istoriya Vlasti*, pp. 235–6; V.I. Ivkin, *Gosudarstvennaya vlast' SSSR. Vysshie organy vlasti i upravleniya i ikh rukovoditeli. 1923–1991 gg. Istoriko-biograficheskii spravochnik*, Moscow: ROSSPEN, 1999, pp. 42–187.
4 Our calculations are based on the information provided by Ivkin. See Ivkin, *Gosudarstvennaya Vlast' SSSR*, pp. 42–187.
5 It is significant, for example, that the ministers became more flexible in fixing salaries and rewards and in distributing investments between the enterprises of their branches; or that they got the right to approve and modify construction project targets and estimate the cost for construction of enterprises (up to 100 million roubles, in certain cases up to 150 million roubles) and housing (up to 15 million roubles). See 52 paragraphs in the Resolution of the USSR CM from 11 April 1953. *Resheniya Partii i Pravitel'stva po khozyaistvennym voprosam (1917–1967)*, tom 4, Moscow: Izdatel'stvo politicheskoi literatury, 1968, pp. 5–14.
6 List of the Ukrainian ministries and departments after the 1953–1954 reorganization, TsDAVOU, f. 2, op. 8, d. 10234, l. 59.
7 See A.N. Yakovlev (ed.), *Lavrentii Beria. 1953. Stenogramma iyul'skogo plenuma TsK KPSS i drugie dokumenty*, Moscow: MFD, 1999; Pikhoya, *Sovetskii Soyuz: istoriya vlasti*, pp. 113–8.
8 See Yakovlev (ed.), *Lavrentii Beria. 1953*, pp. 133–4, 170–3.

9 However, at the CC CPSU Plenum held on 22–29 June 1957 'On the Anti-Party group of Malenkov, Molotov, Kaganovich and Shepilov "who had joined them"', the USSR Minister of Internal Affairs N.P. Dudorov held Malenkov and Beria responsible for the March 1953 amalgamation of ministries. See A.N. Yakovlev (ed.), *Molotov, Malenkov, Kaganovich. 1957. Stenogramma iyun'skogo plenuma TsK KPSS i drugie dokumenty*, Moscow: MFD, 1998, pp. 45, 735.
10 In the periods from 29 July 1948 until 28 December 1950 and later from 15 March 1953 until 8 February 1954, the USSR Ministry of the Metallurgical Industry administered both ferrous and non-ferrous metallurgy. From 28 December 1950 until Stalin's death and from 8 February 1954 until 10 May 1957, ferrous and non-ferrous metallurgy industries were administered by separate ministries. Ivkin, *Gosudarstvennaya vlast' SSSR*, pp. 64, 65, 66.
11 Report of A. Kirichenko to N. Khrushchev on the discussion of the June 1953 CC CPSU Plenum. Submitted on 3 August 1953, TsDAGOU, f. 1, op. 24, d. 2775, l. 439.
12 From March 1953 until February 1954, I.F. Tevosyan was the USSR Minister of Metallurgical Industry. Ivkin, *Gosudarstvennaya vlast' SSSR*, p. 554.
13 Report of A. Kirichenko to N. Khrushchev, TsDAGOU, f. 1, op. 24, d. 2775, l. 440.
14 Ibid.
15 Ibid.
16 The speakers, however, criticized the work of local Party organizations. They pointed out, for example, that *obkomy* showed a lack of interest in the work and problems of primary Party organizations at the enterprises, that they had weak liaisons with masses and workers, that they did not organize a sufficient amount of quality lectures for the population, etc. In other words, they were not always performing their direct duties. See Report of A. Kirichenko to N. Khrushchev, TsDAGOU, f. 1, op. 24, d. 2775, ll. 434–5, 436.
17 Report of A. Kirichenko to N. Khrushchev, TsDAGOU, f. 1, op. 24, d. 2775, l. 444.
18 Report of A. Kirichenko to N. Khrushchev, TsDAGOU, f. 1, op. 24, d. 2775, ll. 442–6.
19 See 'Information on the measures taken by the Ukrainian Party and Soviet organs in order to fulfil the tasks declared in the speech of G. Malenkov and in the resolutions of the 5th Session of the USSR Supreme Soviet', TsDAGOU, f. 1, op. 24, d. 3063, ll. 50, 57, 58.
20 Yakovlev (ed.), *Lavrentii Beria. 1953*, pp. 91–2.
21 N.G. Tomilina (ed.), *Nikita Sergeevich Khrushchev: dva tsveta vremeni: dokumenty iz lichnogo fonda N.S. Khrushcheva: V 2-kh tomakh. Tom 2*, Moscow: MFD, 2009, p. 232.
22 Tomilina (ed.), *Nikita Sergeevich Khrushchev: dva tsveta vremeni. Tom 2*, pp. 232, 233, 235.
23 Tomilina (ed.), *Nikita Sergeevich Khrushchev: dva tsveta vremeni. Tom 2*, p. 232.
24 Tomilina (ed.), *Nikita Sergeevich Khrushchev: dva tsveta vremeni. Tom 2*, p. 233.
25 Tomilina (ed.), *Nikita Sergeevich Khrushchev: dva tsveta vremeni. Tom 2*, pp. 233–4.
26 Tomilina (ed.), *Nikita Sergeevich Khrushchev: dva tsveta vremeni. Tom 2*, pp. 232, 234, 235.
27 Tomilina (ed.), *Nikita Sergeevich Khrushchev: dva tsveta vremeni. Tom 2*, pp. 234, 237.
28 On Malenkov's policies, see G.M. Ivanova, *Na poroge 'gosudarstva vseobshchego blagosostoyaniya'. Sotsial'naya politika v SSSR (seredina 1950-kh-nachalo 1970-kh godov)*, Moscow: IRI RAN, 2011, pp. 56–9.
29 Pikhoya, *Sovetskii Soyuz: istoriya vlasti 1945–1991*, p. 131; Pyzhikov, *Khrushchevskaya 'Ottepel''*, pp. 89–90; D.A. Vanyukov, *Khrushchevskaya ottepel'*, Moscow: Mir knigi, 2007, pp. 21–2.
30 Vanyukov, *Khrushchevskaya ottepel'*, p. 23.
31 In his August 1953 speech, Khrushchev was inaccurate. The September 1953 Plenum resolution (*Postanovlenie*) specified that out of 350 thousand specialists with higher and secondary education, 18.5 thousand worked in *kolkhozy* and 50 thousand at the MTS. See extract from the shorthand record report of Khrushchev's speech, 10

August 1953, RGASPI, f. 17, op. 165, d. 131, ll. 84–90, in Pyzhikov, *Khrushchevskaya 'Ottepel'*', pp. 339–41; *Resheniya Partii i Pravitel'stva*, tom 4, p. 23.
32 Extract from Khrushchev's August 1953 speech, in Pyzhikov, *Khrushchevskaya 'Ottepel'*', p. 341.
33 Resolution of the CC CPSU from 25 January 1954 'On considerable shortcomings in the work of the Party and Soviet *apparat*', TsDAGOU, f. 1, op. 24, d. 4295, l. 322.
34 V.A. Shestakov, *Sotsial'no-ekonomicheskaya politika sovetskogo gosudarstva v 50e – seredine 60-kh godov*, Moscow: Nauka, 2006, p. 249.
35 a) The CC CPSU resolution from 3 June 1954; b) The CC CPSU and USSR CM resolution from 21 August 1954 'On the role and tasks of the USSR State Bank'; c) The CC CPSU and USSR CM resolution from 14 October 1954, 'On considerable shortcomings in the structure of the USSR ministries and departments and measures on the improvement of the functioning of the governmental *apparat*'. See *Resheniya Partii i Pravitel'stva*, tom 4, pp. 129–50.
36 *Resheniya Partii i Pravitel'stva*, tom 4, p. 146.
37 During the Second FYP (1933–1937), *Gosbank* was instructed to 'carry out "the day to day rouble control over the fulfilment of the plans in production and circulation of goods, of the fulfilment of the financial plans and the process of accumulation in the socialized sector of the national economy".' S. Tsakunov, 'The People's Commissariat of Finance' in E.A. Rees (ed.) *Decision-making in the Stalinist Command Economy, 1932–1937*, Houndmills, Basingstoke, Hampshire: Macmillan, New York, NY: St Martin's Press, 1997, p. 77.
38 *Resheniya Partii i Pravitel'stva*, tom 4, p. 73.
39 *Resheniya Partii i Pravitel'stva*, tom 4, p. 148.
40 Yu. Aksyutin, *Khrushchevskaya 'ottepel'' i obshchestvennye nastoreniya v SSSR v 1953–1964 gg.*, 2nd edn, Moscow: ROSSPEN, 2010, p. 247.
41 By 1956, the Ukrainian share in all-Union production of cast iron was 48 per cent, steel 37.7 per cent, metal rolling almost 39 per cent, iron ore 56 per cent, coal 32 per cent. The first Ukrainian Minister of Ferrous Metallurgy was S.I. Tishchenko, previously director of Zhdanov metallurgical mill *Azovstal'*; the first Ukrainian Minister of Coal Industry was K.I. Pochenkov, previously USSR First Deputy Minister of Coal Industry and the head of the *Stalinugol'* combine. See A.A. Fursenko (ed.), *Prezidium TsK KPSS. 1954–1964. Chernovye protokol'nye zapisi zasedanii. Stenogrammy. Postanovleniya. T. 1: Chernovye protokol'nye zapisi zasedanii. Stenogrammy.* Moscow: ROSSPEN, 2004, p. 1289; Tomilina (ed.), *Nikita Sergeevich Khrushchev: dva tsveta vremeni. Tom 2*, p. 234; Proposals of the Ukrainian government on the extension of the rights and responsibilities of the governmental organs at the republican, *oblast'* and *raion* levels, 8 May 1954, TsDAVOU, f. 2, op. 9, d. 3088, l. 99 *oborot*; Letter of the CC CPUk to the CC CPSU (no date), TsDAGOU, f. 1, op. 24, d. 4474, l. 9.
42 In 1921–1922, the administration of coal industry of the South region was moved closer to production, from Khar'kov, the capital of the Ukrainian republic in 1917–1934, to Bakhmut (the name of Artemovsk, Donetsk *oblast'*, until 1924).
43 The creation of the two ministries did not increase the influence of Ukrainian managers on these branches and consequently, argued Ukrainians, did not bring the expected improvement in the administration of these industries. The sales and supplies of coal and metal remained managed by the central *apparat*, so republican offices for supplies and sales were not even created. The two new Ukrainian ministers did not have any say in planning either: the development of the Ukrainian branches was outlined and coordinated in Moscow. In financial issues, due to the absence of theUkrainian offices of *Gosbank* or *Prombank*, Ukrainian ministers also remained totally dependant on the centre. Nonetheless, Ukrainian authorities argued that the everyday management of coal and ferrous metallurgical enterprises did become more efficient. Letter of A. Kirichenko to the CC CPSU Presidium, 2 February 1956, TsDAGOU, f. 1, op. 24, d. 4294, l. 2.

146   Notes

44 Suggestions of the Ukrainian Minister of Construction of Enterprises for the Coal Industry G. Krasnikovskii on the rights that should be granted to the Ukrainian ministers. Submitted to the CC CPUk on 25 January 1957, TsDAGOU, f. 1, op. 31, d. 873, l. 21.
45 Proposals on the extension of the rights and responsibilities of the governmental organs, 8 May 1954, TsDAVOU, f. 2, op. 9, d. 3088, l. 101.
46 Ibid.
47 In the matter of allowing Ukraine access to statistical information, Moscow showed remarkable reluctance. The Statistical Agency of Ukraine got Union-Republic status only in 1960. TsDAVOU, f. 2, op. 9, d. 3088, l. 99.
48 TsDAVOU, f. 2, op. 9, d. 3088, ll. 100–1.
49 TsDAVOU, f. 2, op. 9, d. 3088, ll. 102, 104.
50 TsDAVOU, f. 2, op. 9, d. 3088, ll. 114, 115.
51 TsDAVOU, f. 2, op. 9, d. 3088, ll. 123–4.
52 The replacement of Malenkov with Bulganin was initiated by Khrushchev. At the end of 1954, Khrushchev criticized the style of work and the politics of Malenkov. In the resolution of the CC CPSU Presidium from 31 January 1955, Malenkov was characterized as an incompetent politician and administrator. After the January 1955 Plenum, Khrushchev visibly dominated the economic policy. In his memoirs, Baibakov illustrated the influence that Khrushchev had. One of Khrushchev's projects at the end of 1955 was to reconstruct the railway system and replace steam traction with electric and thermal traction during the following three Five Year Plans. Kaganovich opposed the idea. Nonetheless, the project was realized. 'At this time, planning in our country was under permanent supervision of the First Secretary of the CC CPSU and then of the Chairman of the USSR CM N.S. Khrushchev', wrote Baibakov. On the removal of Malenkov see, for example, Fursenko (ed.), *Prezidium TsK KPSS. 1954–1964, tom 1*, p. 886; Pyzhikov, *Khrushchevskaya 'Ottepel''*, p. 90; see also Philip Hanson, *The Rise and Fall of the Soviet Economy. An economic history of the USSR from 1945*, Harlow: Longman, 2003, p. 51; N.K. Baibakov, *Sorok let v pravitel'stve*, Moscow: Respublika, 1993, p. 67. On modernization of the railways, see John Westwood, 'The Modernization of Soviet railways traction in comparative perspective', in J. Smith and M. Ilic (eds) *Khrushchev in the Kremlin: policy and government in the Soviet Union, 1953–1964*, Milton Park, Abingdon, Oxon; New York, NY: Routledge, 2011, pp. 190–201.
53 Report of the Vice-Chairman of the CMUk V. Valuev to the CMUk on the conclusions of the commission headed by A. Kosygin on the republican rights. Submitted in April–first half of May 1955, TsDAVOU, f. 2, op. 9, d. 329, l. 97.
54 *Resheniya Partii i Pravitel'stva*, tom 4, pp. 200–17.
55 *Resheniya Partii i Pravitel'stva*, tom 4, p. 200.
56 When explaining the removal of Malenkov, Khrushchev reproached Malenkov for forcing the development of light industry and for the failures in agriculture, thus implying that investment in the light and food industries would not be increased. The paragraphs in the May resolution that dealt with food products and consumer goods aimed to allow the republics to increase supplies for local population without injecting considerable investment. *Resheniya Partii i Pravitel'stva*, tom 4, pp. 201–2; Report of V. Valuev, TsDAVOU, f. 2, op. 9, d. 329, l. 98.
57 Report of V. Valuev, TsDAVOU, f. 2, op. 9, d. 329, ll. 108–11, 115–6.
58 Thirty-two out of 36 paragraphs of the May 1955 resolution that enhanced the rights of the republican ministers repeated 32 out of 47 paragraphs of the April 1953 resolution that extended the authority of the all-Union ministers.
59 The first time Ukraine asked to create republican branches of the mentioned banks in 1954 it was refused. In 1955, *Gosbank* and the USSR Minister of Finance supported Ukraine's request. Ukraine, however, was the only republic where *Gosbank* and the Ministry of Finance agreed to create republican branches. Proposals on the extension of the rights and responsibilities of the governmental organs from 8 May 1954, TsDAVOU, f. 2, op. 9, d. 3088, l. 101; TsDAVOU, f. 2, op. 9, d. 329, l. 99.

60 TsDAVOU, f. 2, op. 9, d. 329, l. 99; TsDAGOU, f. 1, op. 31, d. 873, l. 26.
61 The housing problem in the Soviet Union was widespread and had, as Bulganin admitted, a negative effect on the economy since it caused high circulation of the workforce. Report of Bulganin, 1955. RGANI. F.2, op.1, d. 148, ll. 74–105. The document is annexed in Pyzhikov, *Khrushchevskaya 'Ottepel'*, p. 366. On the housing program, see Shestakov, *Sotsial'no-ekonomicheskaya politika sovetskogo gosudarstva*, pp. 266–74.
62 By 1955, a large share of Ukraine's pre-war housing supply was either not restored or old. In 12 out of 26 *oblast'* centres, the housing supply was 1.5 million m² less than before the war. More than 300 thousand m² were in dire need of repair and that amount increased by 50 thousand m² each year. At the same time, in 1954–1955, Ukraine was going through massive migration of population. In 1954–1958, 17,800 families of *kolkhozniki* were scheduled to be moved from all over Ukraine to the southern *oblasti* of Ukraine and Crimea – transferred to Ukraine in 1954 – to work in agriculture. The state planned to cover 40 per cent of the cost of housing for the new migrants. Yet that the new migrants would have to endure hardships was clear to the Ukrainian leadership from the experience of previous migrants who came to the region in 1944–1946 and in 1949–1954 and who were still unsettled. By 1 September 1954, out of 108.4 thousand families that moved in 1949–1954, only 81.6 thousand had stayed, whereas 26.8 thousand could no longer tolerate the poor housing conditions and returned to the places they came from. To solve the housing problem for the migrants, Ukraine suggested that the USSR Ministry of Finance provide them with long-term construction loans for five years.Starting in 1955, Ukrainian Donbas expected 15 thousand workers and young professionals from all over the republic to work in the mines.The housing problem in the Western *oblasti* was no less acute. From 1953 onwards, 'amnestied bandits, former members of the Organization of Ukrainian Nationalists (OUN) and priests of the Uniate Church' started returning from the camps and exile. By September 1956, their number reached 40 thousand. Their housing, however, was long occupied by those who moved from all over the Union to build up this region after 1945. Letter of A. Kirichenko to G. Malenkov, 2 January 1955, TsDAGOU, f. 1, op. 24, d. 4022, l. 1; Letter of N. Kal'chenko and A. Kirichenko to the USSR CM, 10 April 1954, TsDAGOU, f. 1, op. 24, d. 3755, l. 96; Draft of the Resolution of the USSR CM and the CC CPSU 'On measures to further develop agriculture, towns and resorts of the Crimean *oblast'* of the Ukrainian SSR', TsDAGOU, f. 1, op. 24, d. 3755, l. 119; Information on settlement of migrants into southern *oblasti* of the Ukrainian SSR, TsDAGOU, f. 1, op. 24, d. 3587, l. 41; Letter of A. Kirichenko to N. Khrushchev, 11 April 1955, TsDAGOU, f. 1, op. 24, d. 4023, l. 225; Letter of N. Podgornyi to the CC CPSU, 25 September 1956, TsDAGOU, f. 1, op. 24, d. 4250, l. 293.
63 Letter of A. Kirichenko to N. Khrushchev, 2 February 1955, TsDAGOU, f. 1, op. 24, d. 4023, l. 61.
64 TsDAGOU, f. 1, op. 24, d. 4023, l. 60.
65 Remarks of the CC CPUk and the CMUk on the USSR CM resolution 'On the transfer of brickworks and lime plants and granite mining and processing enterprises situated in the SSR of Ukraine under the jurisdiction of the Ukrainian Ministry of Construction Materials', submitted to N. Bulganin on 26 February 1955, TsDAGOU, f. 1, op. 24, d. 4022, l. 5.
66 Based on the remarks of the CC CPUk and the CMUk from 26 February 1955, TsDAGOU, f. 1, op. 24, d. 4022, ll. 4–5.
67 TsDAGOU, f. 1, op. 24, d. 4022, l. 1.
68 Letter of A. Kirichenko to N. Khrushchev, 2 February 1955, TsDAGOU, f. 1, op. 24, d. 4023, ll. 60–62; Letter of the First Secretary of the CC CPUk Kirichenko, the Chairman of the CMUk Kal'chenko and the USSR Minister of Construction N. Dygai to Khrushchev, 22 April 1955, TsDAGOU, f. 1, op. 24, d. 4023, ll. 277–8.
69 In 1956, in Ukraine there were created Union-Republic Ministries of Construction, for Site Construction of the Metallurgical and Chemical Industry and for Site Construction of the Coal Mining Industry. Draft of the Resolution of the CC CPSU Presidium from

March 1956, TsDAGOU, f. 1, op. 24, d. 4248, l. 138; Resolutions of the Presidium of the Supreme Soviet of Ukraine regarding the organization of the Ukrainian Ministry of Construction, 4–9 August 1956, TsDAGOU, f.1, op. 6, d. 2465, ll. 78–82.
70 Until the *Sovnarkhoz* reform, the USSR Ministry of Construction, for example, retained control over 71 Ukrainian enterprises with annual production worth 1.9 billion roubles. Letter of A. Kirichenko to the CC CPSU Presidium, 2 February 1956, TsDAGOU, f. 1, op. 24, d. 4294, l. 1.
71 Report of Bulganin, 1955, RGANI, f. 2, op. 1, d. 148, l. 74, in Pyzhikov, *Khrushchevskaya 'Ottepel''*, p. 362.
72 RGANI, f. 2, op. 1, d. 148, ll. 74–105, in Pyzhikov, *Khrushchevskaya 'Ottepel''*, pp. 362–4.
73 RGANI, f. 2, op. 1, d. 148, ll. 74–105, in Pyzhikov, *Khrushchevskaya 'Ottepel''*, p. 365.
74 RGANI, f. 2, op. 1, d. 148, ll. 74–105, in Pyzhikov, *Khrushchevskaya 'Ottepel''*, pp. 367–8.
75 Korzhikhina, *Sovetskoe gosudarstvo i ego uchrezhdeniya*, pp. 231–2.
76 Information of Gosplan of Ukraine and the TsSU of Ukraine 'On economic development of the Ukrainian SSR in 1951–1955', May–June 1956, TsDAGOU, f. 1, op. 31, d. 573, l. 59.
77 At least seven resolutions extending the decision-making powers of all-Union ministers were issued in 1955, six by the USSR CM and one jointly by USSR CM and the CC CPSU. TsDAGOU, f. 1, op. 31, d. 873, l. 21.
78 The last request was accepted by the Kosygin commission at the beginning of 1955 for submission to the Presidium, but the Presidium rejected it. TsDAVOU, f. 2, op. 9, d. 329, l. 99.
79 The economic regions were first defined before the creation of the Soviet Union, in 1920 in the plan GOELRO. The country was divided between eight regions. This regionalization remained until the Third FYP. In 1939, there were nine economic regions in the RSFSR only. The general plan of the economic development of the country for 15 years (1943–1957), which was composed before World War II, envisaged complex development of nine large economic regions of the USSR (the republics were included). Later, the network of the economic regions was reviewed and included nine regions of the RSFSR and four that incorporated the republics. See P. Alampiev, 'O setke ekonomicheskikh raionov SSSR', *Planovoe khozyaistvo*, 6, 1956, 26–7.
80 N.G. Tomilina (ed.), *Nikita Sergeevich Khrushchev: dva tsveta vremeni: dokumenty iz lichnogo fonda N.S. Khrushcheva: V 2-kh tomakh. Tom 1*, Moscow: MFD, 2009, p. 552.
81 Tomilina (ed.), *Nikita Sergeevich Khrushchev: dva tsveta vremeni. Tom* 2, p. 313.
82 The note of the Chairman of the USSR Gosekonomkomissiya M.Z. Saburov and the Chairman of USSR Gosplan N.K. Baibakov was attached to the report. See A.A. Fursenko (ed.), *Prezidium TsK KPSS. 1954–1964. Chernovye protokol'nye zapisi zasedanii. Stenogrammy. Postanovleniya. T. 2: Postanovleniya. 1954–1958*, Moscow: ROSSPEN, 2006, pp. 160, 162.
83 Fursenko (ed.), *Prezidium TsK KPSS. 1954–1964, tom 1*, p. 910.
84 Fursenko (ed.), *Prezidium TsK KPSS. 1954–1964, tom 1*, p. 76.

2 XX CPSU Congress – December 1956 CC CPSU Plenum

1 Yu. Aksyutin, *Khrushchevskaya 'ottepel'' i obshchestvennye nastoreniya v SSSR v 1953–1964 gg.*, 2nd edn, Moscow: ROSSPEN, 2010, p. 248.
2 *Resheniya Partii i Pravitel'stva po khozyaistvennym voprosam (1917–1967), tom 4*, Moscow: Izdatel'stvo politicheskoi literatury, 1968, p. 281.
3 Donna Bahry, *Outside Moscow: Power, politics, and budgetary policy in the Soviet republics*, New York: Columbia University Press, 1987, p. 29.

4 Memorandum of the Ukrainian Deputy Minister of Commerce A. Romanov to A. Kirichenko 'To the problem of the improvement of controlling the economic development of the republic', 6 February 1956, TsDAGOU, f. 1, op. 31, d. 573, ll. 31–2.
5 TsDAGOU, f. 1, op. 31, d. 573, l. 32.
6 TsDAGOU, f. 1, op. 31, d. 573, l. 33.
7 TsDAGOU, f. 1, op. 31, d. 573, ll. 33–4.
8 Proposal of the Ukrainian Minister of Finance N. Shchetinin to A. Kirichenko on the transfer of the control–inspection department for Ukraine of the USSR Ministry of Finance to republican jurisdiction, 5 March 1956, TsDAGOU, f. 1, op. 24, d. 4294, l. 54.
9 TsDAGOU, f. 1, op. 24, d. 4294, ll. 54–5.
10 *XX S'ezd Kommunisticheskoi Partii Sovetskogo Soyuza 14–25 fevralya 1956 goda, Stenograficheskii otchet, tom 1*, Moscow: Gosudarstvennoe izdatel'stvo politicheskoi literatury, 1956, p. 94.
11 In particular, the *Goskontrol'* considered that in addition to 45 thousand staff that had been made redundant, an additional 10 thousand could go. Furthermore, Ukrainian ministries set inflated salaries for their personnel by giving the titles of heads of the departments, deputies or senior specialists to regular executives. In the Ukrainian Ministry of Coal, for example, there were 1.7 positions of higher staff per one ordinary position. Its economic department, *kantselyariya* (the department in charge of clerical work: preparation of documents and correspondence), the minister's secretariat, legal department, accounting and financial departments employed 10 per cent of all specialists working in the coal industry, yet their personal wages fund was 2 million roubles, or 55.5 per cent, of the 3.6 million rouble specialist wage fund that was fixed for the entire industry. Annex to the CC CPUk Presidium Protokol no. 60, meeting of 6 January 1956, TsDAGOU, f. 1, op. 8, d. 2217, ll. 37, 38–9, 40–1.
12 TsDAGOU, f. 1, op. 8, d. 2217, l. 43.
13 Letter of the Ukrainian Minister of Commerce G. Sakhnovskii to N. Podgornyi 'To the problem of the improvement of economic work in the UkSSR', 20 February 1956, TsDAGOU, f. 1, op. 31, d. 573, ll. 35, 36.
14 TsDAGOU, f. 1, op. 31, d. 573, ll. 37, 38.
15 Materials 'On reorganization of Union-Republic ministries of Ukraine', 20 February 1953–29 November 1954, TsDAVOU, f. 2, op. 8, d. 10234, l. 14; Proposition to invite employees of the abolished all-Union ministries to work in the Ukrainian ministries made by N. Podgornyi and O. Ivashchenko to A. Kirichenko, 13 March 1956, TsDAGOU, f. 1, op. 24, d. 4294, l. 65.
16 Propositions of Gosplan of Ukraine to A. Kirichenko 'To the problem of the improvement of economic work in the republic', 5 March 1956, TsDAGOU, f. 1, op. 31, d. 573, ll. 43, 44.
17 TsDAGOU, f. 1, op. 31, d. 573, ll. 45–46.
18 In September 1958, the magazine *Ekonomika Radyans'koi Ukrainy* (The Economy of Soviet Ukraine) began publication. TsDAGOU, f. 1, op. 31, d. 573, l. 46. See also, 'Ekonomika Sovetskoi Ukrainy', *Planovoe khozyaistvo*, 4, 1959, 87–90.
19 Remarks of A. Kirichenko regarding sending specialists to international exhibitions and fairs, submitted to the CC CPSU Presidium on 22 February 1956, TsDAGOU, f. 1, op. 24, d. 4248, l. 111.
20 Ibid.
21 Report of G. Sakhnovskii on the XI session of the UN Economic conference for Europe, TsDAGOU, f. 1, op. 24, d. 4248, l. 190.
22 Ibid.
23 Ibid.
24 TsDAGOU, f. 1, op. 24, d. 4248, l. 191.
25 Ibid.
26 Note of A. Kirichenko attached to the Report of G. Sakhnovskii on the XI session of the UN Economic conference for Europe, submitted to the CC CPSU on 8 May 1956, TsDAGOU, f. 1, op. 24, d. 4248, l. 188.

27 Protocol of the meeting of V. Valuev commission of 13 March 1956, TsDAVOU, f. 2, op. 9, d. 1744, l. 66.
28 The higher number in 1956 must have been due to the increase of the share of industry under republican and local jurisdiction. In 1955, it constituted 67 per cent of all planned industrial production, whereas in 1950 it was 35 per cent. By the end of 1956, it reached 78.6 per cent. Information of Gosplan of Ukraine and the TsSU of Ukraine 'On the economic development of the Ukrainian SSR in 1951–1955', May–June 1956. TsDAGOU, f. 1, op. 31, d. 573, l. 59; Main results of the work of Ukrainian *sovnarkhozy* in the period 1957–1965. *Ukrsovnarkhoz*, Liquidation commission, TsDAVOU, f. 4820, op. 1, d. 1896, l, 14.
29 Proposals on enhancing the authority of the CMUk, drafted by the CMUk and submitted to the CC CPUk on 3 April 1956, TsDAGOU, f. 1, op. 24, d. 4294, ll. 329–52.
30 At the Presidium meeting held on 26 April (chaired by Mikoyan, Khrushchev being absent) that discussed the forthcoming reorganization, very few spoke for the enhancement of republican economic rights, namely Shepilov, who suggested transferring maximum functions to the republics, and Mikoyan who proposed to transfer local industry to the republics without delay: 'It is impossible to tolerate such a horde of functionaries in Moscow.' The prevailing majority discussed the reorganization of the central *apparat*. A.A. Fursenko (ed.), *Prezidium TsK KPSS. 1954–1964. Chernovye protokol'nye zapisi zasedanii. Stenogrammy. Postanovleniya. T. 1: Chernovye protokol'nye zapisi zasedanii. Stenogrammy*. Moscow: ROSSPEN, 2004, pp. 109, 125, 126; A.A. Fursenko (ed.), *Prezidium TsK KPSS. 1954–1964. Chernovye protokol'nye zapisi zasedanii. Stenogrammy. Postanovleniya. T. 2: Postanovleniya. 1954–1958*, Moscow: ROSSPEN, 2006, pp. 208–9.
31 On the USSR Ministry of Justice, see Yoram Gorlizki, 'Anti-Ministerialism and the USSR Ministry of Justice, 1953–1956: A study in organisational decline', *Europe–Asia Studies*, 48, 8, 1996, 1307, 1279–1318.
32 Fursenko (ed.), *Prezidium TsK KPSS. 1954–1964, tom 2*, pp. 304–5.
33 Remarks of the CMUk on the draft of the resolution 'On the transfer of a number of economic branches under control of the Union republics', TsDAGOU, f. 1, op. 24, d. 4257, l. 215.
34 TsDAGOU, f. 1, op. 24, d. 4257, ll. 215–16.
35 TsDAGOU, f. 1, op. 24, d. 4257, ll. 216–17.
36 Republican proposals were submitted to the USSR CM, the USSR Gosplan and *Gosekonomkomissiya*. See the USSR CM resolution from 31 May 1956 'On procedure and deadlines for composing drafts of the USSR production plans and the USSR State budget for 1957', TsDAGOU, f. 1, op. 24, d. 4347, ll. 89, 91.
37 Ukraine's latest experience of the 'unchallenged' authority of the central planners was the composition of the draft of the Directives for the Sixth FYP. USSR Gosplan disregarded a number of indices that were approved for Ukraine at the January 1956 Plenum and fixed new, higher indices. Remarks of the CC CPUk on the Directives for the Sixth FYP for Ukraine, addressed to the CC CPSU on 6 February 1956, TsDAGOU, f. 1, op. 24, d. 4248, ll. 63, 64.
38 Fursenko (ed.), *Prezidium TsK KPSS. 1954–1964, tom 2*, p. 378.
39 Fursenko (ed.), *Prezidium TsK KPSS. 1954–1964, tom 1*, p. 160; Fursenko (ed.), *Prezidium TsK KPSS. 1954–1964, tom 2*, p. 410.
40 Fursenko (ed.), *Prezidium TsK KPSS. 1954–1964, tom 1*, pp. 165, 166.
41 There are various opinions as to what caused the revision of the FYP. According to I.A. Kulev, cited by Schwartz, 'the Central Committee had met and been informed it faced a major capital investment crisis. ... Soviet economic administrators had presented requests for capital investment allocations' totalling 37 billion roubles more than had been fixed in the FYP for the entire period and 7 billion roubles more than had been fixed for 1957. Aksyutin talks specifically about investments in housing: 'Khrushchev explained at the December 1956 CC CPSU Plenum that it was necessary to correct or

Notes 151

at least review the Five Year Plan of the economic development of the USSR for 1956–1960 and find more financing for housing construction. The necessary financing could be obtained only by reducing investment in heavy industry.' According to Shestakov, 'At the end of summer 1956, the CC CPSU Presidium considered the possibility of buying metal in the USA. It was the feeling of impending catastrophe that made the CC CPSU Presidium seriously correct the Sixth Five Year Plan at the December 1956 Plenum.' See H. Schwartz, *The Soviet Economy Since Stalin*, London: Victor Gollancz Ltd, 1965, p. 86; Yu. Aksyutin, *Khrushchevskaya 'ottepel'' i obshchestvennye nastroenya v SSSR v 1953–1964 gg.*, Moscow: ROSSPEN, 2004, p. 200; V.A. Shestakov, *Sotsial'no-ekonomicheskaya politika sovetskogo gosudarstva v 50e – seredine 60-kh godov*, Moscow: Nauka, 2006, p. 252.

42 Fursenko (ed.), *Prezidium TsK KPSS. 1954–1964, tom 1*, p. 209; Fursenko (ed.), *Prezidium TsK KPSS. 1954–1964, tom 2*, p. 488.
43 Fursenko (ed.), *Prezidium TsK KPSS. 1954–1964, tom 1*, p. 984.
44 Fursenko (ed.), *Prezidium TsK KPSS. 1954–1964, tom 1*, p. 214.
45 Fursenko (ed.), *Prezidium TsK KPSS. 1954–1964, tom 2*, pp. 511, 512.
46 On 13 December, the Presidium approved a draft of the CM USSR resolution 'On the improvement of economic administration and the reorganization of the work of the USSR *Gosekonomkomissiya*'. See Fursenko (ed.), *Prezidium TsK KPSS. 1954–1964, tom 2*, p. 978.
47 Ibid.
48 Report of Bulganin, 1956. RGANI, f. 2, op.1, d. 203, l. 69, in A.V. Pyzhikov, *Khrushchevskaya 'Ottepel''*, Moscow: Olma-Press, 2002, pp. 370, 371; See also Shestakov, *Sotsial'no-ekonomicheskaya politika sovetskogo gosudarstva*, pp. 252–4.
49 RGANI. f.2, op.1, d. 203, l. 69. Annex in Pyzhikov, *Khrushchevskaya 'Ottepel''*, p. 371.
50 Ibid.
51 V.I. Ivkin, *Gosudarstvennaya vlast' SSSR. Vysshie organy vlasti i upravleniya i ikh rukovoditeli. 1923–1991 gg. Istoriko-biograficheskii spravochnik*, Moscow: ROSSPEN, 1999, pp. 143, 466, 509.
52 Ivkin, *Gosudarstvennaya vlast' SSSR*, p. 144.
53 Critical notes on the work of USSR Gosplan and USSR *Gosekonomkomissiya*, compiled by Gosplan of Ukraine and submitted to A. Kirichenko on 19 December 1956, TsDAGOU, f. 1, op. 31, d. 573, ll. 109–10, 112.
54 TsDAGOU, f. 1, op. 31, d. 573, l. 119.
55 TsDAGOU, f. 1, op. 31, d. 573, l. 113.
56 See also the resolution of the December 1956 Plenum. *Resheniya Partii i Pravitel'stva, tom 4*, pp. 326, 327, 328.
57 On the rivalry of the Party and governmental *apparat* see, for example, Leonard Schapiro, *The Communist Party of the Soviet Union*, 2nd edn, London: Eyre & Spottiswoode Publishers Ltd, 1970, pp. 559–63; Pyzhikov, *Khrushchevskaya 'Ottepel''*, pp. 89–92.
58 The CC CPUk took his proposal into consideration and asked Krasnikovskii for a detailed note specifying the rights that should be granted to the Ukrainian ministries. Two weeks later, on 8 February, A. Burmistrov, the head of the CC CPUk department of heavy industry, received the detailed note, yet by then it had become known that the ministerial system would be abolished. See additional information drafted by the office of G. Krasnikovskii for the CC CPUk department of heavy industry on the rights that should be given to the Ukrainian ministers, 8 February 1957, TsDAGOU, f. 1, op. 31, d. 873, ll. 37, 38–48; Note of the head of the CC CPUk department of heavy industry A. Burmistrov to A. Kirichenko, 9 February 1957, TsDAGOU, f. 1, op. 31, d. 873, l. 18; Suggestions of G. Krasnikovskii, the Ukrainian Minister for Site Construction of the Coal Mining Industry, on the rights that should be granted to the Ukrainian ministers. Submitted to the CC CPUk on 25 January 1957, TsDAGOU, f. 1, op. 31, d. 873, ll. 20, 21.

59 Zasyad'ko sought to extend the authority of his ministry in planning of production and capital construction, statistical reporting, financing of main activities and capital construction, organizational structure of the ministry, project documentation and in introducing changes in the annual plans for capital construction, labour norms and payments for certain categories of workers, procedure for assigning leading personnel, the delivery system, and other areas. Ideas of the Ukrainian Minister of Coal Industry A. Zasyad'ko on devolving a number of functions of the central ministries to the CMUk and the Ukrainian Ministry of Coal, submitted to the CC CPUk on 29 January 1957, TsDAGOU, f. 1, op. 31, d. 873, ll. 22–34.
60 TsDAGOU, f. 1, op. 31, d. 873, l. 23.
61 TsDAGOU, f. 1, op. 31, d. 873, l. 26.
62 TsDAGOU, f. 1, op. 31, d. 873, l. 27.
63 S.N. Khrushchev, *Nikita Khrushchev: Reformator*, Moscow: Vremya, 2010, p. 807.
64 The post of the USSR Minister of the Coal Mining Industry was given to A.N. Zademid'ko, Ivkin, *Gosudarstvennaya vlast' SSSR*, pp. 73, 313.
65 Khrushchev remembers Zasyad'ko in his memoirs. See S.N. Khrushchev (ed.), *Memoirs of Nikita Khrushchev, vol. 2; Reformer (1945–1964)*, University Park, PA: The Pennsylvania State University Press, 2006, pp. 260, 465.
66 Fursenko (ed.), *Prezidium TsK KPSS. 1954–1964, tom 1*, p. 151.
67 Like Zasyad'ko, Kuz'mich was moved to the Ukrainian Ministry of Coal from the USSR Ministry of Coal, in 1954. Before 1954, he worked with Zasyad'ko as his Deputy and later First Deputy. Fursenko (ed.), *Prezidium TsK KPSS. 1954–1964, tom 1*, p. 954; On Kuz'mich, see *Spravochnik po istorii Kommunisticheskoi partii i Sovetskogo Soyuza 1898–1991*, available HTTP: http://www.knowbysight.info/KKK/04989.asp (accessed 5 December 2010).
68 For more details see Fursenko (ed.), *Prezidium TsK KPSS. 1954–1964, tom 1*, p. 1221.
69 Propositions of the Ukrainian Minister of Construction N. Gorbas' on the improvement of the supply system in Ukraine, submitted to the CC CPUk on 1 February 1957, TsDAGOU, f. 1, op. 24, d. 4520, l. 230.
70 TsDAGOU, f. 1, op. 24, d. 4520, l. 231.
71 TsDAGOU, f. 1, op. 24, d. 4520, l. 232.
72 Ibid.
73 Before the reform, Ukraine was the only republic that did not have a supply department in its Council of Ministers. N. Gal'perin, 'Sovremennye zadachi organizatsii material'no-tekhnicheskogo snabzheniya proizvodstva', *Voprosy ekonomiki*, 4, 1957, 86; TsDAGOU, f. 1, op. 24, d. 4520, l. 233.
74 TsDAGOU, f. 1, op. 24, d. 4520, ll. 233–4.

3 The *Sovnarkhoz* reform

1 See the entire document in A.A. Fursenko (ed.), *Prezidium TsK KPSS. 1954–1964. Chernovye protokol'nye zapisi zasedanii. Stenogrammy. Postanovleniya. T. 2: Postanovleniya. 1954–1958*, Moscow: ROSSPEN, 2006, pp. 522–39.
2 Yu. Aksyutin, *Khrushchevskaya 'ottepel'' i obshchestvennye nastoreniya v SSSR v 1953–1964 gg.*, 2nd edn, Moscow: ROSSPEN, 2010, pp. 248, 249.
3 N.G. Tomilina (ed.), *Nikita Sergeevich Khrushchev: dva tsveta vremeni: dokumenty iz lichnogo fonda N.S. Khrushcheva: V 2-kh tomakh. Tom 2*, Moscow: MFD, 2009, p. 322.
4 Aksyutin, *Khrushchevskaya 'ottepel''*, 2nd edn, p. 250.
5 Fursenko (ed.), *Prezidium TsK KPSS. 1954–1964, tom 2*, p. 527.
6 Fursenko (ed.), *Prezidium TsK KPSS. 1954–1964, tom 2*, p. 525.
7 Fursenko (ed.), *Prezidium TsK KPSS. 1954–1964, tom 2*, p. 530.
8 Tomilina (ed.), *Nikita Sergeevich Khrushchev: dva tsveta vremeni. Tom 2*, pp. 315–16.
9 Fursenko (ed.), *Prezidium TsK KPSS. 1954–1964, tom 2*, p. 532.

10 According to Harry Schwartz, *tolkachi* were illegal expediters employed by the managers of their suppliers in order to get raw materials and components that were not available through legal channels. *Tolkachi* 'knew how to use bribes or connections to get supplies.' Alec Nove explains: '*Tolkach* (literally 'pusher') is a breed of unofficial supply agent, whose job is to agitate, nag, beg, borrow, sometimes bribe, so that the necessary materials, components and equipment arrive.' See Fursenko (ed.), *Prezidium TsK KPSS. 1954–1964, tom 2*, p. 534; Alec Nove, *The Soviet Economic System*, London: George Allen & Unwin, 1977, p. 100; H. Schwartz, *The Soviet Economy Since Stalin*, London: Victor Gollancz Ltd, 1965, p. 23.
11 Fursenko (ed.), *Prezidium TsK KPSS. 1954–1964, tom 2*, p. 535.
12 Fursenko (ed.), *Prezidium TsK KPSS. 1954–1964, tom 2*, pp. 535–6.
13 Fursenko (ed.), *Prezidium TsK KPSS. 1954–1964, tom 2*, p. 537.
14 Fursenko (ed.), *Prezidium TsK KPSS. 1954–1964, tom 2*, p. 538.
15 Aksyutin, *Khrushchevskaya 'ottepel''*, 2nd edn, p. 250.
16 Fursenko (ed.), *Prezidium TsK KPSS. 1954–1964, tom 1*, p. 221–3.
17 A.N. Yakovlev (ed.), *Molotov, Malenkov, Kaganovich. 1957. Stenogramma iyun'skogo plenuma TsK KPSS i drugie dokumenty*, Moscow: MFD, 1998, p. 457.
18 Yakovlev (ed.), *Molotov, Malenkov, Kaganovich*, pp. 458, 767, 768, 771, 786, 797, 798, 820, 822, 825.
19 Fursenko (ed.), *Prezidium TsK KPSS. 1954–1964, tom 1*, p. 225–6.
20 See the report on the audit of enterprises in the regions of Transbaïkalie and Far East submitted by Baibakov and Saburov to the Presidium on 24 December 1955. Fursenko (ed.), *Prezidium TsK KPSS. 1954–1964, tom 2*, pp. 160–4.
21 Fursenko (ed.), *Prezidium TsK KPSS. 1954–1964, tom 1*, p. 226–7.
22 *KPSS v rezolyutsiyakh i resheniyakh s''ezdov, konferentsii i plenumov TsK (1898–1986)*; tom 9, 1956–1960, Moscow: Politizdat, 1986, pp. 167–74.
23 Yakovlev (ed.), *Molotov, Malenkov, Kaganovich*, pp. 336, 459.
24 Yakovlev (ed.), *Molotov, Malenkov, Kaganovich*, p. 731.
25 N.K. Baibakov, *Sorok let v pravitel'stve*, Moscow: Respublika, 1993, p. 74.
26 Fursenko (ed.), *Prezidium TsK KPSS. 1954–1964, tom 1*, p. 990.
27 Fursenko (ed.), *Prezidium TsK KPSS. 1954–1964, tom 1*, pp. 236–8.
28 Fursenko (ed.), *Prezidium TsK KPSS. 1954–1964, tom 1*, p. 239.
29 Tompson argues that the reform differed from the original proposals by weakening the powers of the centre more than originally suggested and by allowing decentralization to a far greater degree than Khrushchev originally intended. (W.J. Tompson, *Khrushchev: A Political Life*, Basingstoke: Macmillan in association with St Antony's College, Oxford, 1995, p. 174.) It is hard to say to what degree the applied concept of the reform had a more or less decentralized character, since Khrushchev's note was vague. The commission that worked out the details included representatives from the regions and it is quite possible that they succeeded in enhancing the original frames of regional authority. But this remains to be confirmed. The fact that the technical application of the reform was entrusted to USSR Gosplan, however, suggests that regardless of the level of decentralization agreed upon between the centre and the regions by May 1957, the centre intended to apply as much decentralization as USSR Gosplan would tolerate.
30 Tompson, *Khrushchev: A Political Life*, p. 176.
31 Yakovlev (ed.), *Molotov, Malenkov, Kaganovich*, p. 707.
32 Shelest was the chairman of the Ukrainian commission that worked on the *Sovnarkhoz* reform. P. Shelest, *Spravzhnii sud istorii shche poperedu. Spohady, Shchodennyky, Dokumenty, Materialy* (The True Judgment of History Still Awaits Us), Ju. Shapoval (ed.) Kyiv: Heneza, 2003, pp. 119–20.
33 Yakovlev (ed.), *Molotov, Malenkov, Kaganovich*, p. 707.
34 Fursenko (ed.), *Prezidium TsK KPSS. 1954–1964, tom 2*, p. 614.
35 Fursenko (ed.), *Prezidium TsK KPSS. 1954–1964, tom 2*, pp. 613–15.

154 *Notes*

36 In his original note, however, Khrushchev anticipated that the branches of the economy would be administered from the centre. The disagreement between Khrushchev and Molotov must have been about the subordination and the margins of authority of the branch committees, or administrations in Khrushchev's project. Khrushchev placed them under the roof of the central planners, and Molotov viewed them separately from planners. Fursenko (ed.), *Prezidium TsK KPSS. 1954–1964, tom 2*, pp. 615–19.
37 Fursenko (ed.), *Prezidium TsK KPSS. 1954–1964, tom 1*, p. 243.
38 Fursenko (ed.), *Prezidium TsK KPSS. 1954–1964, tom 1*, pp. 244–6.
39 Yakovlev (ed.), *Molotov, Malenkov, Kaganovich*, p. 707.
40 These numbers of *sovnarkhozy* are cited from Fursenko (ed.), *Prezidium TsK KPSS. 1954–1964, tom 1*, p. 990. Different numbers are presented in a collection of statistical data for 1957: 68 *sovnarkhozy* were created in the RSFSR; 11 regions were created in Ukraine, nine in Kazakhstan, five in Uzbekistan, one in each of the rest of the republics. See *SSSR v tsyfrakh, Statisticheskii sbornik*, Moscow: Gosudarstvennoe statisticheskoe izdatel'stvo, 1958, p. 52.
41 *Resheniya Partii i Pravitel'stva po khozyaistvennym voprosam (1917–1967), tom 4*, Moscow: Izdatel'stvo politicheskoi literatury, 1968, pp. 370–5.
42 For example, Tompson pointed out that the reorganization deprived Khrushchev's rivals of a political base and provided his supporters in the territorial Party apparatus with control over economic administration (W.J. Tompson, 'Industrial Management and Economic Reform under Khrushchev', in W. Taubman, S. Khrushchev and A. Gleason (eds) *Nikita Khrushchev*, trans. David Gehrenbeck, Eileen Kane and Alla Bashenko, New Haven, CT; London: Yale University Press, 2000, p. 142). 'The decisions of the December Plenum threatened to cut Khrushchev off completely from the making of economic policy. The Sovnarkhoz reform was his attempt to keep that from happening', he asserts (Tompson, *Khrushchev: A Political Life*, p. 177). William Taubman is also inclined to interpret the reform in a political context rather than economic: if the reform had only economic aims, Khrushchev could have proceeded gradually, 'but because the reform was political and because he was incapable of containing himself anyway, he brooked no delay' (William Taubman, *Khrushchev: The Man and His Era*, London: Free Press; New York, NY: W.W. Norton, 2003, p. 304). For Rigby and Armstrong the reform was closely connected to the power struggle in the Presidium and was Khrushchev's way to secure his primacy (T.H. Rigby, 'Khrushchev and the rules of the Soviet political game', in R.F. Miller and F. Féhér (eds) *Khrushchev and the Communist World*, London: Croom Helm, 1984, p. 66; John A. Armstrong, *The Soviet Bureaucratic Elite, A Case Study of the Ukrainian Apparatus*, New York, Frederick A. Praeger, Inc.: 1959, p. 69.)

4 Setting new elements

1 According to the secretary of the Dnepropetrovsk *obkom* V.V. Shcherbitskii, in the Ministry of Ferrous Metallurgy, for example, 'they sit and wait while their destiny is being decided, everyone is guessing who will go where and they talk of scandal.' Shorthand record report of the meeting of the first *obkom* secretaries and the chairmen of *oblispolkomy* held on 20 February 1957, TsDAGOU, f. 1, op. 24, d. 4570, l. 68.
2 In 1939, the USSR was divided into 13 economic regions, nine in the RSFSR and four that regrouped other republics. P. Alampiev, 'O setke ekonomicheskikh raionov SSSR', *Planovoe khozyaistvo*, 6, 1956, 27.
3 Alampiev, 'O setke ekonomicheskikh raionov SSSR', 33–4.
4 A. Omarovskii, 'O nekotorykh voprosakh organizatsii upravleniya i planirovaniya v promyshlennosti SSSR', *Voprosy ekonomiki*, 4, 1957, 71.
5 Alampiev, 'O setke ekonomicheskikh raionov SSSR', 30–3.

6 'Propositions on the economic administrative regions of the Ukrainian SSR' compiled by the CC CPUk and submitted to the CC CPSU between 15 February and 4 March 1957 (Old version), TsDAGOU, f. 1, op. 24, d. 4520, l. 11–12.
7 Propositions on the economic regionalization drafted by the Institute of the Economy of the Ukrainian Academy of Science for the CC CPUk, submitted on 11 March 1957, TsDAGOU, f. 1, op. 31, d. 867, ll. 52, 59; I. Kugukalo, 'Ekonomicheskie raiony Ukrainskoi SSR', *Voprosy ekonomiki,* 4, 1957, 47.
8 Propositions of the CC CPUk to the CC CPSU on the improvement of the organization of administration of industry and construction of the UkSSR, TsDAGOU, f. 1, op. 24, d. 4475, ll. 2–14.
9 Attachment to the note of Gosplan of Ukraine 'On economic regionalization of the UkSSR', 18 March 1957. Department of perspective planning of Gosplan of Ukraine, February 1957, TsDAGOU, f. 1, op. 24, d. 4518, l. 24.
10 Calculations based on the report of the TsSU of Ukraine 'Production growth of most important industrial goods in the USSR and Ukrainian SSR', October 1958, TsDAVOU, f. 582, op. 2, d. 1187, l. 169.
11 Shorthand record report of the meeting of the Chairmen of the Ukrainian *sovnarkhozy* in the CC CPUk held on 6 December 1957, TsDAGOU, f. 1, op. 31, d. 762, l. 36; P. Yu. Shelest, *Ukraino nasha Radyans'ka,* Kyiv: Vydavnytstvo politychnoi literatury Ukrainy, 1970, p. 191.
12 TsDAGOU, f. 1, op. 24, d. 4518, ll. 24–25.
13 According to Roeder, Khrushchev allowed the republics to determine the number of the *sovnarkhozy.* Philip G. Roeder, *Red Sunset: The failure of Soviet politics,* Princeton, NJ: Princeton University Press, 1993, p. 168.
14 Minutes of the meeting of the CC CPUk Presidium held on 9–10 April 1957. On selection of leading staff for the Ukrainian *sovnarkhozy,* TsDAGOU, f. 1, op. 6, d. 2622, ll. 7–8. On the role of the Party in personnel selection see Jerry F. Hough, *The Soviet Prefects: The local party organs in industrial decision-making,* Cambridge, MA: Harvard University Press, 1969, pp. 154–88.
15 N. Tikhonov studied in Dnepropetrovsk. Before he moved to the USSR Ministry of Ferrous Metallurgy in 1950, he was director of *Yuzhnotrubnyi* plant in Nikopol' (Dnepropetrovsk *oblast'*); S. Skachkov, in 1930–1941, worked at plant No. 183 in Khar'kov; I. Pribyl'skii, in 1954–1956, worked as the director of *Chernomorskii* Shipbuilding Yard in Nikolaev; G. Ivanovskii, in 1937–1939, was director of the *Krivorozhskii* (Dnepropetrovsk *oblast'*) and then *Makeevskii* (Donetsk *oblast'*) metallurgical mills; he was a member of the CC CPUk. I do not have information on Lysnyak. However, assuming that those appointed to the republic had previous experience there, it is likely that Lysnyak had also worked in Ukraine before.
16 Aleksandr Lyashko, *Gruz pamyati. Trilogiya, Vospominaniya. Put' v nomenklaturu,* Kyiv: Delovaya Ukraina, 1997, p. 362.
17 TsDAGOU, f. 1, op. 6, d. 2622, l. 7.
18 Lyashko, *Gruz pamyati. Put' v nomenklaturu,* p. 362.
19 In Ukraine, 45 per cent of the *sovnarkhozy* chairman came from Moscow. Roeder, with reference to Nove, indicated that in the Soviet Union, 30 per cent of the *sovnarkhozy* chairmen were former ministers or deputy ministers assigned from Moscow and 35 per cent came from Union-Republic ministries. (Roeder, *Red Sunset,* p. 168). For more information on the chairmen of the *sovnarkhozy,* see Donald R. Kelley, 'Interest Groups in the USSR: The Impact of Political Sensitivity on Group Influence', *The Journal of Politics,* 34, 3, 1972, 881; Hough, *The Soviet Prefects,* pp. 58–9.
20 Information on the staff of the Ukrainian *sovnarkhozy* as of 10 July 1957, TsDAGOU, f. 1, op. 31, d. 872, l. 79; Information on the staff of the Ukrainian *sovnarkhozy* as of 1 August 1957, TsDAGOU, f. 1, op. 31, d. 872, l. 95.

21 Groups of the *sovnarkhozy* according to the wages of employees. Attachment No 2 to the USSR CM resolution, composed in the period 25 May 1957–12 June 1957, TsDAGOU, f. 1, op. 24, d. 4521, ll. 8–12.
22 In Ukraine, for example, Dyadyk argued that, based on the industrial complex, the volume of investment and output, his *Sovnarkhoz* should be rated as the *sovnarkhozy* of Moscow and Moscow *oblast'*. See Letter of the Chairman of the Stalino *Sovnarkhoz* I. Dyadyk to N. Khrushchev and A. Kirichenko, 22 June 1957, TsDAGOU, f. 1, op. 24, d. 4519, ll. 68–71. On the *sovnarkhozy* in the RSFSR, see RGASPI, f. 556, op. 21, d. 48, ll. 66–9, also in *Regional'naya politika N.S. Khrushcheva: TsK KPSS i mestnye partiinye komitety, 1953–1964 gg.*, sost. O.V. Khlevnyuk [et al.], Moscow: ROSSPEN, 2009, pp. 174–8.
23 Originally, the number of staff for Gosplan of Ukraine was 1,900. See report 'On results of the inspection of organization of work on composition of the draft plan of economic development of the UkSSR for 1958' submitted to the Vice-Chairman of USSR Gosplan G.V. Perov, signed by M. Yampol'skii, V. Ivanchenko, D. Potanin, M. Bulavko, 7 August 1957, RGAE, f. 4372, op. 57, d. 206, l. 5.
24 Ibid.
25 Hough, *The Soviet Prefects*, pp. 56–7.
26 Information on wages of employees of Gosplan of Ukraine, mid-July, TsDAGOU, f. 1, op. 31, d. 873, l. 234.
27 Letter of P. Rozenko to A. Kirichenko and N. Kal'chenko, 29 June 1957, TsDAGOU, f. 1, op. 31, d. 872, ll. 51–2.
28 Shorthand record report of the meeting of employees of the Statistical Agencies of Ukraine and Moldavia held on 27–28 August 1957, TsDAVOU, f. 582, op. 2, d. 1058, ll. 42, 52, 83.
29 TsDAVOU, f. 582, op. 2, d. 1058, l. 30.
30 TsDAVOU, f. 582, op. 2, d. 1058, l. 89.
31 TsDAVOU, f. 582, op. 2, d. 1058, l. 68.
32 TsDAVOU, f. 582, op. 2, d. 1058, l. 43.
33 TsDAVOU, f. 582, op. 2, d. 1058, ll. 83–4.
34 TsDAVOU, f. 582, op. 2, d. 1058, l. 33.
35 TsDAVOU, f. 582, op. 2, d. 1058, l. 9.
36 Ibid.
37 TsDAGOU, f. 1, op. 24, d. 4520, l. 18.
38 Resolution of the CMUk 'On the reorganization of the material-technical supply system in the Ukrainian SSR', TsDAGOU, f. 1, op. 24, d. 4521, l. 80.
39 'Propositions of the CC CPUk to the CC CPSU on the improvement of the organization of administration of industry and construction of the RSS of Ukraine', 30 April 1957, in *Politicheskoe rukovodstvo Ukrainy 1938–1989*, p. 223.
40 Ibid.
41 R.G. Pikhoya, *Sovetskii Soyuz: istoriya vlasti 1945–1991*, Moscow: RAGS, 1998, p. 238.
42 The Regulations on a *Sovnarkhoz*, RGAE, f. 4372, op. 76c, d. 110, l. 158.
43 This regulation was highly neglected by the *sovnarkhozy* and in 1958 the central leadership issued a separate resolution that aimed to enforce the fulfilment of the deliveries. RGAE, f. 4372, op. 76c, d. 110, l. 160, § 26.
44 RGAE, f. 4372, op. 76c, d. 110, ll. 158, 159, 161, 162, §§ 16, 18, 19, 32, 34, 36, 38, 40.
45 RGAE, f. 4372, op. 76c, d. 110, ll. 158, 160, 161, §§ 16, 17, 30, 31, 32.
46 RGAE, f. 4372, op. 76c, d. 110, ll. 163, 164, §§ 48, 49, 50.
47 RGAE, f. 4372, op. 76c, d. 110, l. 170, § 83.
48 RGAE, f. 4372, op. 76c, d. 110, ll. 170, 171, §§ 84, 86, 90, 91; Propositions of the L'vov *obkom* secretary M. Lazurenko and Vice-Chairman of the L'vov *Sovnarkhoz* S. Lokot' on further improvement of economic administration submitted to the CC CPUk on 3 March 1958, TsDAGOU, f. 1, op. 24, d. 4727, l. 59.
49 RGAE, f. 4372, op. 76c, d. 110, ll. 171, 172: §§ 95, 97.

50 RGAE, f. 4372, op. 76c, d. 110, ll. 174–5: §§ 108, 109, 110.
51 RGAE, f. 4372, op. 76c, d. 110, ll. 177–80: §§ 121–135.

5 First disillusionment

1 'Perestroika upravleniya promyshlennost'yu i stroitel'stvom i zadachi planovykh organov', *Planovoe khozyaistvo*, 5, 1957, 7–8.
2 In 1957, *Gosekonomkomissiya* was abolished and Gosplan changed its status from commission to committee.
3 'Zadachi Gosplana SSSR v novykh usloviyakh upravleniya promyshlennost'yu i stroitel'stvom', *Planovoe khozyaistvo*, 7, 1957, 6.
4 'Zadachi Gosplana SSSR', 5.
5 'Zadachi Gosplana SSSR', 7–8.
6 Shorthand record report of the meeting held in the CMUk on 7 January 1958, TsDAVOU, f. 2, op. 9, d. 4308, l. 17; in another document, the number is 96.2 per cent. See Main results of the work of Ukrainian *sovnarkhozy* in the period 1957–1965. *Ukrsovnarkhoz*, Liquidation commission, TsDAVOU, f. 4820, op. 1, d. 1896, l. 14.
7 'Propositions on the economic administrative regions of the Ukrainian SSR' drafted by the CC CPUk and submitted to the CC CPSU between 15 February and 4 March 1957 (Old version), TsDAGOU, f. 1, op. 24, d. 4520, l. 27.
8 Draft of the Statute of Gosplan of Ukraine, TsDAGOU, f. 1, op. 24, d. 4685, l. 324.
9 *Soviet Union. Verkhovnyi Sovet: On the further improvement of management in industry and construction in the U.S.S.R.: materials of the seventh session of the Supreme Soviet of the U.S.S.R., May 7–10, 1957*, Moscow: Foreign Languages Pub. House, 1957, p. 68.
10 Ukrainian planners did not communicate those limits to the regions and largely disregarded them in the draft plan for the republic. Some indices, like the target for construction works, Gosplan of Ukraine ignored, while others it simply could not apply, which was the case with the production target for casts, for example. In Ukraine some plants that manufactured casts remained under the management of the all-Union Ministry of Railways. Without knowing the target for the all-Union plants, Ukraine could not set the targets for the republican plants. See Minute No. 6 of the meeting of the USSR Gosplan held on 1 November 1957, RGAE, f. 4372, op. 56, d. 1, l. 45; Shorthand record report of the meeting of the board of Gosplan of Ukraine, held on 8 October 1957. Discussion of the draft of the 1958 delivery plan, TsDAVOU, f. 337, op. 2, d. 719, l. 478.
11 'Zadachi Gosplana SSSR', 7; 'Perestroika upravleniya promyshlennost'yu i stroitel'stvom', 9.
12 Report of A. Baranovskii to N. Kal'chenko, 30 July 1957, TsDAVOU, f. 2, op. 9, d. 2700, ll. 133–4.
13 TsDAVOU, f. 2, op. 9, d. 4308, ll. 50, 81, 87.
14 TsDAVOU, f. 2, op. 9, d. 4308, l. 46.
15 Minutes of the meeting of Gosplan of Ukraine held on 28 February 1957 'On economic regionalization of the Ukrainian SSR', TsDAVOU, f. 337, op. 2, d. 716, l. 6.
16 TsDAVOU, f. 2, op. 9, d. 4308, l. 50.
17 TsDAVOU, f. 2, op. 9, d. 4308, l. 81.
18 TsDAVOU, f. 2, op. 9, d. 4308, l. 87.
19 The *oblispolkomy* experienced the same problem with the local industry and culture. For example, the Drogobych *oblast'* committee for local industry and fuel had to present its plans to seven departments of Gosplan of Ukraine. The plans of food products and construction materials that were produced in the *oblast'* were examined in 3–4 departments. Propositions of the Drogobych *obkom* secretary V. Druzhinin on the improvement of work of Gosplan of Ukraine, submitted to the CC CPUk on 1 March 1958, TsDAGOU, f. 1, op. 24, d. 4727, l. 143. See also TsDAVOU, f. 2, op. 9, d. 4308, l. 58; Propositions of the Vinnitsa *Sovnarkhoz* 'On abolition of existing industrial

158 *Notes*

ministries and the modifications in the structure of Gosplan of Ukraine and the CMUk', 4 February 1958, TsDAVOU, f. 2, op. 9, d. 3947, ll. 28–9.
20 TsDAVOU, f. 2, op. 9, d. 4308, l. 52.
21 TsDAVOU, f. 2, op. 9, d. 4308, l. 65.
22 A. Omarovskii, 'O nekotorykh voprosakh organizatsii upravleniya i planirovaniya v promyshlennosti SSSR', *Voprosy ekonomiki,* 4, 1957, 71.
23 Information on changes in the 1958 draft plan compiled by the CMUk made by USSR Gosplan, 28 February 1958. RGAE, f. 4372, op. 57, d. 167, ll. 8, 9.
24 This particular intention was only partly a response to annual increases of delivery quotas of agricultural products for the all-Union fund. On the basis of the decisions of the January 1955 CC CPSU Plenum, in 1956 the centre started changing the principle of distributing meat products to the population. Previously, deliveries were made regardless of production volumes, volumes of state deliveries and the capacities used. Now all meat resources were divided into two parts, one for the all-Union needs, and the other for the republican funds. However, the new procedure did not establish any objective criteria to determine the share or the size of deliveries that each republic should contribute to the all-Union fund. The size and the share were left to be determined by the central planners in the annual plans. Ukraine argued that the share of meat production for the all-Union fund should be equal to the republic's share in the all-Union state purchase of meat. Ukraine also argued that the republic should be allowed to decide which products to produce with the meat, milk and eggs that were left to the republic. Comments of the CC CPUk on the draft plan of state purchases of agricultural products for 1956 and 1957 compiled by *Gosekonomkomissiya*, 4 October 1955, TsDAGOU, f. 1, op. 24, d. 4024, l. 261; Conclusions of the CC CPUk and the CMUk on suggestions of the USSR *Gosekonomkomissiya*, USSR Ministry of Commerce, USSR Ministry of State Purchases and USSR Ministry of Agriculture on changes in supplying the population with meat production, TsDAGOU, f. 1, op. 24, d. 4248, ll. 130–3; The CC CPUk draft of the resolution 'On changes of procedures of supplying meat products', March–April 1956, TsDAGOU, f. 1, op. 24, d. 4310, ll. 35, 42.
25 RGAE, f. 4372, op. 57, d. 203, l. 62.
26 RGAE, f. 4372, op. 57, d. 167, l. 10.
27 RGAE, f. 4372, op. 57, d. 167, l. 11; Letter of the CMUk to the USSR CM and the Chairman of the USSR Gosplan I. Kuz'min, 26 September 1957, RGAE, f. 4372, op. 57, d. 167, ll. 118, 119, 120, 121.
28 RGAE, f. 4372, op. 57, d. 203, l. 63.
29 In some *oblasti,* less than 35 per cent of *kolkhozy* had electricity; in the Volyn' *oblast',* only 8.6 per cent *kolkhozy* had electricity. Shorthand record report of the meeting of the board of Gosplan of Ukraine held on 26 September 1957. Discussion of the 1958 draft plan of electrification of the Ukrainian SSR, TsDAVOU, f. 337, op. 2, d. 719, ll. 226, 229, 234.
30 Shorthand record report of the meeting of the board of Gosplan of Ukraine held on 3 October 1957. Discussion of the 1958 draft plan of the state agricultural procurements and purchases, TsDAVOU, f. 337, op. 2, d. 719, ll. 433, 434.
31 RGAE, f. 4372, op. 56, d. 1, ll. 43, 45.
32 G. Simon, *Nationalism and Policy Toward the Nationalities in the Soviet Union: From totalitarian dictatorship to post-Stalinist society,* Boulder, CO: Westview Press, 1991, p. 253.
33 RGAE, f. 4372, op. 57, d. 203, l. 61.
34 Optimization of inter-republican deliveries is discussed in Chapter 8.
35 This aim of the reform was confirmed by a separate resolution of the USSR CM from 6 September 1957. TsDAVOU, f. 337, op. 2, d. 714, l. 27.
36 RGAE, f. 4372, op. 57, d. 167, ll. 8, 9.
37 Remarks of the USSR Gosplan on the 1958 draft plans submitted by the Ukrainian and Moldavian SSR, 11 January 1958, RGAE, f. 4372, op. 57, d. 167, l. 49.

6 Republican budgetary rights

1. Report of V. Valuev to the CMUk on the conclusions of the commission headed by A. Kosygin on the republican rights. Submitted in April–first half of May 1955, TsDAVOU, f. 2, op. 9, d. 329, l. 97.
2. Proposals on enhancing the authority of the CMUk, drafted by the CMUk and submitted to the CC CPUk on 3 April 1956, TsDAGOU, f. 1, op. 24, d. 4294, ll. 334, 335, 336, 337, 339.
3. Comments of the CMUk to the USSR CM on the draft of the Law on Budgetary Rights of the USSR and the Union republics and draft of the Regulations on Composition and Fulfilment of the State Budget, 10 June 1958, TsDAVOU, f. 2, op. 9, d. 4313, ll. 197–9. Article 34 of the 30 October 1959 Law 'On Budgetary Rights of the Union of the SSR and Union republics' legalized the principle of contribution.
4. TsDAVOU, f. 2, op. 9, d. 4313, ll. 199–200.
5. TsDAVOU, f. 2, op. 9, d. 4313, ll. 201, 203.
6. Note of G. Esipenko to the CC CPUk and the CMUk, 20 September 1958, TsDAGOU, f. 1, op. 24, d. 4794, l. 92.
7. Alec Nove, *The Soviet Economic System*, London: George Allen & Unwin, 1977, p. 234.
8. Besides, explained the USSR Ministry of Finance, it was necessary to consider that the income tax of the military servicemen was paid centrally and it could not be transferred to the republican budgets. 'If we transfer to the republican budgets all income tax paid by the population except the taxes paid by military servicemen, it will be possible to make approximate calculations of the wage fund of the servicemen and of their number.' See Information attached to a draft of the Law on Budgetary Rights of the USSR and Union republics and draft of the Regulations on Composition and Fulfilment of the State Budget, 13 September 1958, TsDAGOU, f. 1, op. 24, d. 4794, ll. 95–6.
9. TsDAGOU, f. 1, op. 24, d. 4794, l. 96.
10. TsDAGOU, f. 1, op. 24, d. 4794, l. 97.
11. TsDAGOU, f. 1, op. 24, d. 4794, l. 98.
12. TsDAGOU, f. 1, op. 24, d. 4794, l. 97.
13. TsDAGOU, f. 1, op. 24, d. 4794, ll. 89, 90, Remarks of the head of the CC CPUk department for commercial, financial and planning organs V. Starunskii 'On the report of Esipenko', submitted to the CC CPUk in October 1958. On financial decentralization during the *Sovnarkhoz* reform, see, for example, Raymond Hutchings, *The Soviet Budget*, Albany, NY: State University of New York Press, 1983, pp. 74–5, 92–4, 103–4, 183.
14. Extract from the shorthand record report of the meeting at the office of the Vice-Chairman of the CMUk M.S. Grechukha held on 1 August 1958, TsDAVOU, f. 2, op. 9, d. 4306, l. 48.
15. The tendency reached its culmination in 1959–1960. See Hutchings, *The Soviet Budget*, p. 92.

7 Decentralizing the supply system

1. Report of V. Valuev to the CMUk on the conclusions of the commission headed by A. Kosygin on the republican rights. Submitted in April–first half of May 1955, TsDAVOU, f. 2, op. 9, d. 329, l. 97.
2. Letter of N. Podgornyi to the CC CPSU on the measures planned to be taken in order to improve the supply system of Ukraine, 14 March 1958, TsDAGOU, f. 1, op. 24, d. 4727, l. 317.
3. In 1958, the number of *Ukrglavsnabsbyty* was reduced to 15, which, due to the abolition of some other departments, allowed Gosplan of Ukraine to reduce its *apparat* by 35 per cent. Ibid.
4. Merging the supply and sales offices was practised for many years before the reform, although it was not widely applied. The main department for sales of oil, for example,

managed all deliveries of oil products for the suppliers and customers of the same region. In his proposal after the December 1956 Plenum, Gorbas' proposed to spread this practice. Later, during the discussion of the reform in February 1957, Kosygin pointed to that experience (see Chapter 3). Shorthand record report of the meeting held in the CMUk on 7 January 1958, TsDAVOU, f. 2, op. 9, d. 4308, ll. 18, 33, 40, 41.

5 Draft of Gosplan of Ukraine 'On organization of the material–technical supply system due to the reorganization of administration of industry and construction', TsDAGOU, f. 1, op. 24, d. 4475, l. 58; TsDAGOU, f. 1, op. 24, d. 4727, l. 316.

6 TsDAVOU, f. 2, op. 9, d. 4308, l. 40; Resolution of the CMUk 'On the reorganization of the material–technical supply system in the Ukrainian SSR', TsDAGOU, f. 1, op. 24, d. 4521, l. 75; Shorthand record report of the meeting of the board of Gosplan of Ukraine of 6 September 1957 'On the procedures of composing reports on industry and construction for July–September 1957', TsDAVOU, f. 337, op. 2, d. 716, l. 103.

7 According to the resolution of the Ukrainian CM from 24 July 1957, No 820.

8 Decentralization of supplies was widely practised by the *sovnarkhozy* when centrally allocated funds were insufficient. In Ukraine, this was the case with wine production, food and light industries, meat and milk, the transport industry and some other industries. Decentralized supplies of construction materials were used for non-centralized capital constructions where funded materials covered only 10–15 per cent of the necessary inputs. Main results of the work of Ukrainian *sovnarkhozy* in the period 1957–1965. *Ukrsovnarkhoz*, Liquidation commission, TsDAVOU, f. 4820, op. 1, d. 1896, ll. 161–2.

9 Letter of N. Kal'chenko to the Chairman of the Moscow city *Sovnarkhoz* K. Petukhov, January 1958, TsDAVOU, f. 2, op. 9, d. 3947, l. 8; Letter of N. Kal'chenko to the USSR CM, 1 October 1957, GARF, f. 5446, op. 92, d. 826, l. 63.

10 Draft of the CMUk 'On organization of the supply system with regard to the reorganization of the administration of industry and construction', July 1957, TsDAVOU, f. 2, op. 9, d. 3084, ll. 263–5; TsDAVOU, f. 2, op. 9, d. 4308, l. 43.

11 Nine main *sbyty* that Gosplan of Ukraine suggested to organize in each *Sovnarkhoz* were *metallosbyt* (of metals), *khimsbyt* (of chemical production), *stankoinstrumentsbyt* (of machine-tools and instruments), *elektrosbyt* (of electricity), *stroisbyt* (of construction materials), *legsbyt* (of consumer goods), *pishchesbyt* (of food production), *vtormet* (of salvage metal) and *avtotraktorosbyt* (of automobiles and tractors). TsDAGOU, f. 1, op. 24, d. 4475, l. 61.

12 TsDAVOU, f. 2, op. 9, d. 3084, l. 261; TsDAVOU, f. 2, op. 9, d. 4308, l. 44.

13 Shorthand record report of the meeting of the board of Gosplan of Ukraine 'On the fulfilment of contractual deliveries in the first quarter of 1958 and measures to be taken to ensure the fulfilment of the deliveries in the second quarter', April 1958, TsDAVOU, f. 337, op. 2, d. 771, l. 165.

14 TsDAVOU, f. 2, op. 9, d. 4308, l. 35.

15 This percentage refers to 1959. In 1957–1958, the number must have been smaller, given that direct deliveries were not included in the plan. Shorthand record report of the meeting of the board of Gosplan of Ukraine held on 10 December 1958 'On procedure and deadlines for specifying and clarifying 1959 production and supply plans for the products managed by USSR Gosplan and republican Gosplans', TsDAVOU, f. 337, op. 2, d. 774, l. 176.

16 Information on the comments of com. N.G. Ignatov to the draft of Regulations on Council of economic administrative region, by Vice-Chairman of USSR Gosplan G. Perov, RGAE, f. 4372, op. 76c, d. 110, l. 152.

17 TsDAVOU, f. 2, op. 9, d. 3084, l. 265.

18 Letter of Vice-Chairman of the CMUk N. Gureev to A. Kosygin, 1 September 1957, GARF, f. 5446, op. 92, d. 826, l. 151.

19 At the January 1958 meeting, the chairmen of the *sovnarkhozy* pointed to the difficulties that the division into funded production and planned production caused for

Notes 161

providing supplies when one component was funded and another planned. If supplies for the planned component were not provided, the goods could not be manufactured. The Chairman of USSR Gosplan Kuz'min agreed that this division was artificial: 'It was invented by *Gossnab* [the USSR CM State Committee for Supplies of Means of Production] that knew how to feed everyone with one round loaf of bread.' In 1959, the division into planned and funded production was dropped. TsDAVOU, f. 2, op. 9, d. 4308, l. 206; Remarks of the USSR Gosplan on the 1958 plan drafts submitted by the Ukrainian and Moldavian SSR, 11 January 1958, RGAE, f. 4372, op. 57, d. 167, l. 51.*Gossnab* was abolished on 15 March 1953. Subsequently, deliveries were managed by the ministries and USSR Gosplan. V.I. Ivkin, *Gosudarstvennaya vlast' SSSR. Vysshie organy vlasti i upravleniya i ikh rukovoditeli. 1923–1991 gg. Istoriko-biograficheskii spravochnik*, Moscow: ROSSPEN, 1999, p. 105.
20 Report of the First Vice-Chairman of Gosplan of Ukraine A. Baranovskii on the issues discussed at the meeting of the chairmen of republican Gosplans and chairmen of the *sovnarkhozy* held in USSR Gosplan on 27–28 December 1957, submitted to N. Podgornyi on 3 December 1957, TsDAGOU, f. 1, op. 24, d. 4764, ll. 9–10.
21 Report of USSR Gosplan from 24 January 1958. Chapter 'On manifestations of *mestnichestvo* and other shortcomings in the work of the *sovnarkhozy*', RGAE, f. 4372, op. 57, d. 203, l. 60.
22 RGAE, f. 4372, op. 57, d. 203, l. 59.
23 RGAE, f. 4372, op. 57, d. 203, l. 57.
24 In 1957, Ukraine manufactured above-plan production for 7 billion roubles, whereas in 1956 it was for 3.3 billion roubles. TsDAVOU, f. 2, op. 9, d. 4308, l. 3. Letter from the Chairman of the Voroshilovgrad *Sovnarkhoz* A. Kuz'mich to the Chairman of the CMUk N. Kal'chenko on the problems with supplies, 12 December 1957, TsDAVOU, f. 2, op. 9, d. 3947, l. 2.
25 TsDAGOU, f. 1, op. 24, d. 4521, l. 79.
26 According to the USSR CM resolution of 26 June 1957, the network of peripheral supply offices could be transferred to the republican CM only after they had set up a system of *snabsbyty*. Resolution of the CC CPUk and the CMUk 'On measures to improve the management of supplies', 23 May 1958, TsDAGOU, f. 1, op. 6, d. 2786, l. 59; Letter of the CMUk to the CM of RSFSR 'On organization of material–technical supply', 4 October 1957, TsDAVOU, f. 2, op. 9, d. 2700, l. 190.
27 Comments of Gosplan of Ukraine on the resolution of the CMUk 'On organization of the supply system in the UkSSR', 24 July 1957, TsDAGOU, f. 1, op. 31, d. 762, l. 68.
28 TsDAVOU, f. 2, op. 9, d. 2700, ll. 190–1; TsDAVOU, f. 2, op. 9, d. 4308, l. 34.
29 Comments of the Stalino *Sovnarkhoz* on the supply system in Ukraine, 15 November 1957, TsDAGOU, f. 1, op. 31, d. 762, l. 54; TsDAGOU, f. 1, op. 31, d. 762, l. 67.
30 TsDAVOU, f. 2, op. 9, d. 4308, ll. 35–6.
31 TsDAGOU, f. 1, op. 31, d. 762, l. 66.
32 Interestingly, in the report sent by Gosplan of Ukraine to the CMUk, it is stated that eight *sovnarkhozy* supported the project of Gosplan of Ukraine and only three *sovnarkhozy* – Stalino, Voroshilovgrad and Odessa – spoke for the transfer of the network of peripheral supply offices to the *sovnarkhozy*. Unfortunately, there is no date on the document and it is impossible to say whether Gosplan of Ukraine concluded this from the meeting held in the CC CPUk on 6 December, or before. If before, then by 6 December, some of the *sovnarkhozy* had clearly changed their opinion on the issue. TsDAGOU, f. 1, op. 31, d. 762, l. 65.
33 The opinion of the *sovnarkhozy* of Dnepropetrovsk and Zaporozh'e was not documented in the source. Shorthand record report of the meeting of the Chairmen of the Ukrainian *sovnarkhozy* in the CC CPUk held on 6 December 1957, TsDAGOU, f. 1, op. 31, d. 762, ll. 1–49.
34 Legalized by the USSR CM resolution from 26 September 1957. TsDAGOU, f. 1, op. 31, d. 762, l. 51.

35 Ibid.
36 TsDAGOU, f. 1, op. 31, d. 762, l. 52; Opinion of the Voroshilovgrad *Sovnarkhoz* in Letter from the Chairman of the Voroshilovgrad *Sovnarkhoz* A. Kuz'mich to the Chairman of the CMUk N. Kal'chenko on the problems with supplies, 12 December 1957, TsDAVOU, f. 2, op. 9, d. 3947, l. 6.
37 TsDAGOU, f. 1, op. 31, d. 762, l. 39.
38 TsDAGOU, f. 1, op. 31, d. 762, l. 14.
39 TsDAGOU, f. 1, op. 24, d. 4727, l. 318.
40 Administration of the defence industry was decentralized in December 1957. The ministries of the aviation industry, defence industry, radio electronics industry and shipbuilding industry were transformed into the state committees and the majority of their enterprises were transferred to the *sovnarkhozy*. The state committees were in charge of the planning, scientific research and management of a share of production which included experimental production. In Ukraine, Gosplan of Ukraine formed the Administration of Defence Industry. It planned for enterprises that manufactured military equipment and for the 83 Ukrainian plants that officially did not belong to the defence industry but produced military equipment. In 1958, this Administration also managed 30 Ukrainian enterprises that produced for the Ministry of the Mid-Level Machine-Building Industry. In the *sovnarkhozy*, one of the deputy-chairmen of *Sovnarkhoz* was held personally responsible for production for defence. Supplies for the defence enterprises were supervised by Gosplan of Ukraine and the CC CPUk. See draft of the CC CPSU and the USSR CM resolution on reorganization of administration of defence industrial branches presented by a specially assigned CC CPSU commission to the CC CPSU, around 9 July 1957, RGAE, f. 4372, op. 76c, d. 110, ll. 3, 4–6; Ivkin, *Gosudarstvennaya vlast' SSSR*, pp. 58, 59, 60, 61, 62–3, 80, 81; Letter of the Vice-Chairman of Gosplan of Ukraine N. Lesechko to the CC CPUk secretaries V. Shcherbitskii and O. Ivashchenko, 25 January 1958, TsDAGOU, f. 1, op. 24, d. 4727, ll. 18, 19; Propositions on the improvement of the administration of the defence industry of Ukraine, compiled by the CC CPUk commission, signed by N. Kal'chenko, I. Senin and V. Shcherbitskii, submitted to the CC CPUk Presidium on 11 March 1958, TsDAGOU, f. 1, op. 24, d. 4727, l. 299; Resolution of the CC CPUk on the structure and staff for Gosplan of Ukraine from 24 June 1958, TsDAGOU, f. 1, op. 6, d. 2794.
41 Ten GIUMPP were organized in 1958; by 1960, there were 17.
42 TsDAGOU, f. 1, op. 6, d. 2786, ll. 59–60.
43 Shorthand record report of the meeting of the board of Gosplan of Ukraine held on 8 July 1958 'On the structure of the departments of Gosplan of Ukraine and their personnel', TsDAVOU, f. 337, op. 2, d. 772, l. 85.
44 TsDAVOU, f. 337, op. 2, d. 774, l. 174; 'Propositions on the improvement of the supply system' presented by the Chairman of *Ukrsovnarkhoz* N. Sobol' to the CC CPUk on 16 November 1959, TsDAGOU, f. 1, op. 24, d. 4968, l. 101.
45 TsDAVOU, f. 337, op. 2, d. 771, l. 165.
46 Shorthand record report of the meeting of the board of Gosplan of Ukraine held on 16 April 1958 'On the results of the fulfilment of the production plan and major construction works in the first quarter and on measures to be taken to ensure the fulfilment of the plan in the second quarter of 1958', TsDAVOU, f. 337, op. 2, d. 771, l. 145.
47 Gosplan of Ukraine, the fund-holder for the republic, did not succeed in persuading the *sovnarkhozy* that they should inform the republic Gosplan on such refusals, so complaints addressed to the *sovnarkhozy* were regularly sounded in Gosplan. TsDAVOU, f. 337, op. 2, d. 771, l. 165; Shorthand record report of the meeting of the board of Gosplan of Ukraine held on 12 May 1959 'On the fulfilment of the delivery plan in the first quarter of 1959', TsDAVOU, f. 337, op. 2, d. 874, l. 111.
48 Shorthand record report of the meeting of the board of Gosplan of Ukraine held on 25 June 1958 'On specialization and contractual relationships', TsDAVOU, f. 337, op. 2, d. 772, l. 319.

Notes 163

49 Report of the head of the CC CPUk department of consumer goods and foodstuffs Kurilenko to N. Podgornyi 'On planning consumer goods and foodstuffs', 30 January 1958, TsDAGOU, f. 1, op. 31, d. 1117, l. 65.
50 Report of the First Secretary of the CC CPUk N. Podgornyi 'On unauthorized reductions of investment by the *sovnarkhozy* of the UkSSR', 22 July 1958, TsDAGOU, f. 1, op. 6, d. 2800, l. 8.
51 Ibid.
52 Ibid.
53 Ibid.
54 The rights of the *sovnarkhozy* in pricing were declared in paragraphs 108–110 of the Regulations on a *Sovnarkhoz*. See Part 2, Chapter 4.
55 Shorthand record report of a meeting of the board of Gosplan of Ukraine held on 15 December 1958 'On violations of the procedures of establishing prices for industrial production in the *sovnarkhozy* of Kiev and Khar'kov', TsDAVOU, f. 337, op. 2, d. 774, ll. 201, 202.
56 TsDAVOU, f. 337, op. 2, d. 774, ll. 207–8.
57 Shorthand record report of a meeting of the board of Gosplan of Ukraine held on 18 October 1958 'On the draft of the budget of the UkSSR', TsDAVOU, f. 337, op. 2, d. 774, l. 84.
58 Letter of Gosplan of Ukraine to the CMUk 'On prices in 1959 and shortcomings in the pricing policy', 22 June 1960, TsDAVOU, f. 2, op. 9, d. 7204, l. 255. Calculations based on TsDAVOU, f. 4820, op. 1, d. 1896, l. 246.
59 TsDAVOU, f. 337, op. 2, d. 772, l. 86.
60 TsDAVOU, f. 337, op. 2, d. 774, ll. 203, 204–5, 206, 207, 208.
61 Viktor Andriyanov, *Kosygin*, Moscow: Molodaya gvardiya, 2004, pp. 137, 138.
62 In May 1955, along with enhancing administrative rights of republican ministers, Moscow allowed the republics to keep 100 per cent of consumer goods produced above the plan, 50 per cent of certain construction materials, agricultural products and agricultural equipment, 25 per cent of the above-plan production of certain food products, gas pipes, wood, mineral fertilizers and radiators to be sold inside the republic. Information to a draft of the USSR CM resolution 'On further transfer of economic and cultural issues into jurisdiction of the CM of Union republics', 12 July 1957, TsDAGOU, f. 1, op. 24, d. 4489, l. 139.
63 As N.A. Mukhitdinov declared at the XXI Party Congress, 'the seven-year investment plan marks a new stage in the progress of Central Asia and the Transcaucasus towards parity with the European area of the Soviet Union.' J. Miller, 'Summary of XXI (Extraordinary) Party Congress', *Soviet Studies*, 11, 1, 1959, 93.
64 Note of the USSR TsSU to the TsSU of the Union republics accompanying the list of the production forbidden for above-plan production in 1964, TsDAVOU, f. 582, op. 3, d. 5002, l. 1.
65 Eugène Zaleski, *Planning Reforms in the Soviet Union, 1962–1966: An analysis of recent trends in economic organization and management*, trans. Marie-Christine MacAndrew and G. Warren Nutter, Chapel Hill, NC: University of North Carolina Press, 1967, p. 67.
66 Ibid.
67 Letter of N. Podgornyi to the CC CPSU containing Ukraine's remarks on a draft of the resolution 'On procedures of using industrial production manufactured and stocked above the plan', 21 July 1959, TsDAGOU, f. 1, op. 24, d. 4910, l. 164.
68 TsDAGOU, f. 1, op. 24, d. 4910, ll. 164, 165.
69 Annex to the letter of P. Shelest to the CC CPSU, 13 April 1965, TsDAGOU, f. 1, op. 24, d. 5990, ll. 168–9.
70 The *sovnarkhozy* were often required to produce above the plan, but did not always have the inputs to do so. In such cases, the *sovnarkhozy* were instructed to re-distribute the already available resources, although modifications to the plans were not or could

164   *Notes*

not be introduced. Propositions of the Ukrainian *obkomy* and *sovnarkhozy* on the improvement of administration and work of the *sovnarkhozy* and Gosplan, TsDAGOU, f. 1, op. 24, d. 4727, l. 232.
71 Report of the Vice-Chairman of Gosplan of Ukraine P. Rozenko to the CMUk on the measures that had been taken to reduce the stocks of unmarketable production, 24 January 1959, TsDAVOU, f. 2, op. 9, d. 5761, l. 13.
72 In 1958, the Ukrainian population held on hand 3 billion roubles in cash. By comparison, at the beginning of 1957, the entire Soviet population had 6.37 billion roubles in savings accounts. 'In 1957, the state expected 1.1 billion roubles to be put into saving accounts by the population. This amount would almost entirely cover the additional pension expenses related to the new Law on state pensions.' See Ivanova, *Na poroge 'gosudarstva vseobshchego blagosostoyaniya'*, p. 127.
73 TsDAVOU, f. 2, op. 9, d. 5761, l. 25; Information of the USSR Gosplan on the changes made in the 1958 draft plan submitted by the CMUk, 28 February 1958, RGAE, f. 4372, op. 57, d. 167, l. 11. (8–12)
74 Robert F. Miller, 'Khrushchev and the Soviet economy: Management by reorganisation', in R.F. Miller and F. Fehér (eds) *Khrushchev and the Communist World*, London: Croom Helm, 1984, p. 127.

8 Gosplan of Ukraine

1 At the beginning of 1958, soon after the December 1957 meeting at USSR Gosplan, the Ukrainian and the central governments attempted to regulate inter-republican deliveries by administrative means. On 3 January 1958, the CC CPUk Presidium issued the resolution 'On responsibility of the chairmen of *sovnarkhozy*, of the enterprises and *snabsbyty* for unauthorized deliveries of production'. On 26 April, the USSR Supreme Soviet Presidium legalized the regulation which stated that the failure to deliver outside the economic region was considered a serious violation of state discipline which entailed disciplinary, financial or criminal responsibility. Some understanding of correlation between the incentives of the *sovnarkhozy* to prioritize the fulfilment of the production plan over the delivery plan was even reflected in the new – modified in April 1958 – paragraph 26 of the Regulations on a *Sovnarkhoz*. It now stated that the inter-republican deliveries and deliveries to the all-Union funds had to be ensured regardless of the fulfilment of the production plans. These resolutions had limited, if any, practical effect. A year later, in 1959, Gosplan of Ukraine reported that the *sovnarkhozy* continued to neglect the resolutions of the Party and the government about prioritizing inter-republican deliveries, deliveries to the all-Union funds and for export, and prioritized their own needs in inputs. Annex to the resolution of the CMUk from May 1958 on the measures taken with regard to those who violated state discipline when not fulfilling delivery plans, TsDAGOU, f. 1, op. 31, d. 1117, l. 136; Request of USSR Gosplan to ensure the fulfilment of deliveries by the Ukrainian metallurgical mills sent to the CMUk on 25 July 1960, TsDAVOU, f. 2, op. 9, d. 7206, l. 43; I. Evenko, 'Proverka i ekonomicheskii analiz vypolneniya planov', *Planovoe khozyaistvo*, 10, 1958, 1.
2 Shorthand record report of the meeting held in the CMUk on 7 January 1958, TsDAVOU, f. 2, op. 9, d. 4308, l. 196.
3 In 1957, the Ukrainian coal industry enjoyed vast privileges for supplying to coal mines and constructions. As a result, for the first time since WW II, the coal industry fulfilled the plan for capital construction and considerably increased its output. Letter from the Chairman of the Voroshilovgrad *Sovnarkhoz* A. Kuz'mich to the Chairman of the CMUk N. Kal'chenko on the problems with supplies, 12 December 1957, TsDAVOU, f. 2, op. 9, d. 3947, l. 3; Main results of the work of Ukrainian *sovnarkhozy* in the period 1957–1965. *Ukrsovnarkhoz*, Liquidation commission, TsDAVOU, f. 4820, op. 1, d. 1896, ll. 34–5.

4 Shorthand record report of a meeting of the board of Gosplan of Ukraine held on 18 October 1958 'On the draft of the budget of the UkSSR', TsDAVOU, f. 337, op. 2, d. 774, l. 81.
5 Letter of the Vice-Chairman of Gosplan of Ukraine A. Lalayants to N. Podgornyi, 12 March 1958, TsDAGOU, f. 1, op. 31, d. 1117, l. 112.
6 TsDAGOU, f. 1, op. 31, d. 1117, ll. 113–4.
7 Shorthand record report of the meeting of the board of Gosplan of Ukraine held on 3 January 1959, TsDAVOU, f. 337, op. 2, d 873a, l. 25; Shorthand record report of the meeting of the board of Gosplan of Ukraine held on 10 December 1958 'On procedure and deadlines for specifying and clarifying 1959 production and supply plans for the products managed by USSR Gosplan and republican Gosplans', TsDAVOU, f. 337, op. 2, d. 774, l. 186; Request to modify certain indices in the 1959 supply plan for Ukraine, submitted by A. Lalayants on 15 December 1958, TsDAGOU, f. 1, op. 31, d. 1117, ll. 158–64.
8 TsDAVOU, f. 337, op. 2, d 873a, l. 25; TsDAVOU, f. 337, op. 2, d. 774, l. 186.
9 TsDAVOU, f. 337, op. 2, d. 774, ll. 179–80.
10 TsDAVOU, f. 337, op. 2, d. 774, l. 180.
11 Propositions of the Drogobych *obkom* secretary V. Druzhinin on the improvement of work of Gosplan of Ukraine, submitted to the CC CPUk on 1 March 1958, TsDAGOU, f. 1, op. 24, d. 4727, l. 146.
12 Information drafted by Kal'chenko regarding the transfer of the meat and dairy industry to the *sovnarkhozy*, TsDAGOU, f. 1, op. 24, d. 4520, l. 235; Letter of the CC CPUk secretaries Burmistrov and Kurilenko to Kirichenko on the advantages of transferring the meat and dairy industry to the jurisdiction of the *sovnarkhozy*, TsDAGOU, f. 1, op. 24, d. 4520, ll. 236–8.
13 Letter of the head of the CC CPUk department of machine-building Savel'ev to A. Kirichenko, December 1957, TsDAGOU, f. 1, op. 24, d. 4519, l. 141.
14 Propositions of the CC CPUk to the CC CPSU on reorganization of administration of railways, April 1958, TsDAGOU, f. 1, op. 24, d. 4727, ll. 427–8.
15 Letter of the Vice-Chairman of Gosplan of Ukraine A. Lalayants to the Chairman of USSR Gosplan I. Kuz'min, 2 February 1959, TsDAVOU, f. 337, op. 2, d. 878, ll. 84–5.
16 Contractual relationships between enterprises were set for the branches that manufactured complex production which consisted of numerous components, such as machine-building. Components, manufactured by specialized enterprises located all over the country, were delivered to the plant that assembled them into one piece of machinery. Contractual relationships were supposed to optimize cost-effectiveness by applying specialization and division of labour. Contractual relationships between enterprises were set by the ministries and were rarely established between enterprises belonging to different ministries. Effectively, this is what angered Khrushchev: the unwillingness of the ministries to cooperate on the same territories, causing transportation cross-hauls of thousands of kilometres. For definition of contractual relationships see A.M. Prokhorov (ed.), *Bol'shaya Sovetskaya Entsiklopediya*, 13 tom, 3rd edn, Moscow: Izdatel'stvo 'Sovetskaya Entsiklopediya', 1973, p. 116.
17 Letter of N. Podgornyi to the CC CPSU on the measures planned to be taken in order to improve the supply system of Ukraine, 14 March 1958, TsDAGOU, f. 1, op. 24, d. 4727, l. 317.
18 Shorthand record report of the meeting of the board of Gosplan of Ukraine, held on 8 October 1957. Discussion of the draft of the 1958 delivery plan, TsDAVOU, f. 337, op. 2, d. 719, l. 476.
19 Ibid.
20 Instruction of the Vice-Chairman of Gosplan of Ukraine A. Selivanov to Gosplan of Ukraine, 24 January 1957, TsDAVOU, f. 337, op. 2, d. 714, l. 1.
21 TsDAVOU, f. 337, op. 2, d. 719, ll. 479, 487.

22 Propositions of the Ukrainian *obkomy* and *sovnarkhozy* on the improvement of administration and work of the *sovnarkhozy* and Gosplan, TsDAGOU, f. 1, op. 24, d. 4727, l. 233.
23 Shorthand record report of the meeting of the board of Gosplan of Ukraine 'On the fulfilment of contractual deliveries in the first quarter of 1958 and measures to be taken to ensure the fulfilment of the deliveries in the second quarter', April 1958, TsDAVOU, f. 337, op. 2, d. 771, l. 166.
24 Minutes of the meeting of the leading employees of the USSR Gosplan and the RSFSR Gosplan with the chairmen of *sovnarkhozy*, participants in the 3rd session of the USSR Supreme Soviet, regarding eliminating shortcomings in planning and improving work of the planning organs, held in USSR Gosplan on 2 November 1959, RGAE, f. 4372, op. 58, d. 736, l. 80.
25 Shorthand record report of the meeting of the board of Gosplan of Ukraine held on 12 May 1959 'On the fulfilment of the delivery plan in first quarter of 1959', TsDAVOU, f. 337, op. 2, d. 874, l. 112.
26 Shorthand record report of a meeting of the board of Gosplan of Ukraine held on 22 December 1959 'On improvement of the supply of the economy', TsDAVOU, f. 337, op. 2, d. 876, l. 257.
27 Letter of the Chairman of Gosplan of Ukraine I. Senin to the Chairman of USSR Gosplan A. Kosygin, 6 April 1959, TsDAVOU, f. 337, op. 2, d. 878, l. 209; Letter of the Chairman of the RSFSR Gosplan main department for supply and sales of production of the heavy, transport and construction industries M. Mikhailov to the head of the legal department of the USSR CM P. Mishunin, 15 June 1959, GARF, f. 5446, op. 93, d. 1213, ll. 122, 122 *oborot*.
28 GARF, f. 5446, op. 93, d. 1213, ll. 122–1.
29 Remarks of the Ukrainian government on the 1960 delivery plan for Ukraine, submitted to the USSR CM on 9 February 1960, TsDAVOU, f. 2, op. 9, d. 7201, ll. 76–8, 82.
30 Letter of the Vice-Chairman of Gosplan of Ukraine A. Lalayants to the Chairman of USSR Gosplan A. Kosygin, 27 April 1959, TsDAVOU, f. 337, op. 2, d. 878, l. 268.
31 'Propositions on the improvement of the supply system' presented by the Chairman of *Ukrsovnarkhoz* N. Sobol' to the CC CPUk on 16 November 1959, TsDAGOU, f. 1, op. 24, d. 4968, ll. 101–2; TsDAVOU, f. 2, op. 9, d. 7201, ll. 74, 76, 78.
32 Letter of the Vice-Chairman of Gosplan of Ukraine N. Babich to the Vice-Chairman of USSR Gosplan S. Vasilenko, 10 February 1959, TsDAVOU, f. 337, op. 2, d. 878, ll. 80–2.
33 By 1962 Ukraine's share in the country's total production comprised 51.1 per cent of rolled ferrous metal and 70.5 per cent of steel pipes. TsDAVOU, f. 4820, op. 1, d. 1896, l. 165.
34 With other products of metallurgy, the situation was similar. TsDAVOU, f. 2, op. 9, d. 7206, ll. 43–5.
35 TsDAVOU, f. 337, op. 2, d. 874, ll. 112, 123; TsDAVOU, f. 337, op. 2, d. 876, ll. 249, 250; Letter of the Vice-Chairman of Gosplan of Ukraine A. Lalayants to the Vice-Chairman of USSR Gosplan S. Vasilenko, 15 January 1960, TsDAVOU, f. 337, op. 2, d. 987, ll. 89–90; TsDAVOU, f. 2, op. 9, d. 7201, ll. 74, 77–8.
36 TsDAVOU, f. 337, op. 2, d. 873a, l. 22.
37 TsDAVOU, f. 2, op. 9, d. 7201, ll. 83, 84; Comments of the CMUk on the draft of the USSR CM resolution 'On procedure and deadlines for compiling the draft of the state plan of economic development of the USSR and the State budget of the USSR for 1961', 2 April 1960, TsDAVOU, f. 2, op. 9, d. 7201, l. 246.

9 The turning point

1 Letter of N. Podgornyi to the USSR CM, 3 April 1959, TsDAGOU, f. 1, op. 24, d. 4911, l. 4.

Notes 167

2 S.N. Khrushchev, *Nikita Khrushchev: Reformator*, Moscow: Vremya, 2010, p. 398.
3 Ibid.
4 Khrushchev, *Nikita Khrushchev*, p. 399.
5 A.A. Fursenko (ed.), *Prezidium TsK KPSS. 1954–1964. Chernovye protokol'nye zapisi zasedanii. Stenogrammy. Postanovleniya. T. 1: Chernovye protokol'nye zapisi zasedanii. Stenogrammy*. Moscow: ROSSPEN, 2004, pp. 420, 1070; J. Miller, 'Summary of XXI (Extraordinary) Party Congress', *Soviet Studies*, 11, 1, 1959, 84–109; V.I. Ivkin, *Gosudarstvennaya vlast' SSSR. Vysshie organy vlasti i upravleniya i ikh rukovoditeli. 1923– 1991 gg. Istoriko-biograficheskii spravochnik*, Moscow: ROSSPEN, 1999, pp. 144, 147.
6 Khrushchev, *Nikita Khrushchev*, p. 401.
7 R. Belousov, *Ekonomicheskaya istoriya Rossii: XX vek, kniga 5, Dramaticheskii krizis v kontse stoletiya*, Moscow: IzdAT, 2006, p. 39.
8 Khrushchev, *Nikita Khrushchev*, p. 401.
9 On Novikov, see Khrushchev, *Nikita Khrushchev*, pp. 753, 756, 811.
10 I.S. Koropeckyj (ed.), *The Ukraine Within the USSR: An Economic Balance Sheet*, New York, NY: Praeger, 1977, p. 29.
11 Shorthand record report of the meeting of the leading employees of the USSR Gosplan and the RSFSR Gosplan with the chairmen of *sovnarkhozy*, participants in the 3rd session of the USSR Supreme Soviet, regarding eliminating the shortcomings in planning and improving the work of the planning organs, held in USSR Gosplan on 2 November 1959, RGAE, f. 4372, op. 58, d. 738, ll. 2–56; Minutes of the meeting of the leading employees of the USSR Gosplan and the RSFSR Gosplan with the chairmen of *sovnarkhozy*, participants in the 3rd session of the USSR Supreme Soviet, regarding eliminating shortcomings in planning and improving the work of the planning organs, held in USSR Gosplan on 2 November 1959, RGAE, f. 4372, op. 58, d. 736, ll. 72–89.
12 Also at the beginning of 1960, the central leadership assigned a commission to clearly separate the functions of USSR Gosplan and *Gosekonomsovet*. On the basis of the conclusions of that commission, the central leadership issued a resolution that aimed to elevate the importance of perspective planning. USSR Gosplan had to draft annual state plans based on the targets fixed in the perspective plans composed by *Gosekonomsovet*. The resolution had no effect on economic administration or planning practices whatsoever. Fursenko (ed.), *Prezidium TsK KPSS. 1954–1964, tom 1*, pp. 420, 1070; Introduction to the *opis'*, RGAE, f. 4372, op. 79c, p. 6.
13 A. Vedishchev, 'Voprosy ekonomicheskogo raionirovaniya SSSR', *Voprosy ekonomiki*, 2, 1960, 25–35.
14 Note by P. Ivanov, N. Strokin, V. Dymshits, A. Podugol'nikov and P. Furduev, attached to the Proposal of the commission of USSR Gosplan on organization of economic councils for coordinating and planning the work of the *sovnarkhozy* in large regions, 22 July 1960, TsDAVOU, f. 2, op. 9, d. 7206, l. 218.
15 Note of the Chairman of USSR Gosplan to the USSR CM of 11 November 1960 attached to the draft of the resolution on the economic councils for enlarged regions, TsDAVOU, f. 2, op. 9, d. 8130, l. 15; Final draft of the resolution on the economic councils composed jointly by USSR Gosplan and CM of the republics, 11 November 1960, TsDAVOU, f. 2, op. 9, d. 8130, ll. 20–2.
16 Ibid. See also Z. Mieczkowski, 'The 1962–1963 reforms in Soviet economic regionalization', *Slavic Review*, 24, 3, 1965, 487.
17 TsDAVOU, f. 2, op. 9, d. 8130, ll. 15, 16–22.
18 William J. Conyngham, *Industrial Management in the Soviet Union: The role of the C.P.S.U. in industrial decision-making 1917–1970*, Stanford, CA: Hoover Institution Press, Stanford University, 1973, pp. 100–1.
19 In the original proposal of *Gosekonomsovet*, Ukraine and Moldova formed one economic region, *Yuzhnyi* or Southern. The CC CPUk disagreed and insisted, with success, that Ukraine was divided between three regions. The CC CPUk explained that the regionalization of *Gosekonomsovet* did not reflect the reality of the Ukrainian

economy. By February 1963, the three new councils had not made any progress in perspective planning for Ukraine and when the central leadership merged the *sovnarkhozy*, the councils for the coordination and planning of the work of *sovnarkhozy* in Ukraine and the RSFSR were abolished. Letter to the CC CPUk Presidium from secretaries of the CC CPUk O. Ivashchenko and A. Baranovskii with remarks on the project of *Gosekonomsovet* 'On the economic regionalization of the USSR in connection with the elaboration of a general perspective plan of the economic development of the USSR for the period until 1980', August 1960, TsDAGOU, f. 1, op. 24, d. 5109, l. 152; Letter of Podgornyi to the CC CPSU and the USSR CM containing Ukrainian remarks on the project of *Gosekonomsovet* 'On the economic regionalization of the USSR in connection with the elaboration of a general perspective plan of the economic development of the USSR for the period until 1980', 15 August 1960, TsDAGOU, f. 1, op. 24, d. 5109, l. 100; Letter of USSR Gosplan to the VSNKh, 2 April 1963, GARF, f. 5446, op. 97, d. 1, l. 1. On the regionalization in 1962 see, for example, G. Grossman, 'The structure and organization of the Soviet economy', *Slavic Review*, 21, 2, 1962, 217; Mieczkowski, 'The 1962–1963 reforms', 479–96.

20 Letter of the secretary of the Crimean *obkom* V. Komyakhov and deputy of the Crimean *oblispolkom* N. Moiseev to Podgornyi, 30 January 1960, TsDAGOU, f. 1, op. 31, d. 1607, ll. 28, 29.
21 TsDAGOU, f. 1, op. 31, d. 1607, ll. 30, 31.
22 Project of Gosplan of Ukraine 'On the improvement of economic administration and planning' submitted to the CC CPUk on 10 April 1962, TsDAGOU, f. 1, op. 31, d. 2102, l. 171.
23 B. Lewytzkyj, *Politics and Society in Soviet Ukraine, 1953–1980*, Edmonton, Alta.: Canadian Institute of Ukrainian Studies, University of Alberta; Downsview. Ont., Canada: Distributed by the University of Toronto Press, 1984, p. 79.
24 Howard R. Swearer, 'Administration of Local Industry After the 1957 Industrial Reorganization', *Soviet Studies*, XII, 3, 1961, 223.
25 A.A. Fursenko (ed.), *Prezidium TsK KPSS. 1954–1964. Chernovye protokol'nye zapisi zasedanii: Stenogrammy. Postanovleniya: V 3 tomakh. T.3: Postanovleniya. 1959–1964*, Moscow: ROSSPEN, 2008, p. 127. See also *Politicheskoe rukovodstvo Ukrainy 1938–1989*, sost. V.Yu. Vasil'ev [et al.], Moscow: ROSSPEN, 2006, p. 11; William Taubman, *Khrushchev: The Man and His Era*, London: Free Press; New York, NY: W.W. Norton, 2003, p. 609.
26 See, for example, Yu.A. Vedeneev, *Organizatsionnye reformy gosudarstvennogo upravleniya promyshlennost'yu v SSSR: istoriko-pravovoe issledovanie (1957–1987 gg.)*, Moscow: Nauka, 1990, p. 28; Lewytzkyj, *Politics and Society in Soviet Ukraine, 1953–1980*, p. 79. According to Conyngham, Republican *sovnarkhozy* culminated 'a process of recentralization of administrative power.' Conyngham, *Industrial Management*, p. 105.
27 Resolution of the CC CPUk Presidium 'On the creation of *Ukrsovnarkhoz*', 5 July 1960, TsDAGOU, f. 1, op. 6, d. 3116, ll. 8–9.
28 Shorthand record report of the meeting of the chairmen of *sovnarkhozy* at the office of the CC CPUk secretary I. Kazanets held on 15 May 1961, TsDAGOU, f. 1, op. 31, d. 1880, ll. 179, 180.
29 TsDAGOU, f. 1, op. 31, d. 1880, l. 180.
30 Statute on *Ukrsovnarkhoz*, 11 March 1961, TsDAVOU, f. 4820, op. 1, d. 200, l. 1.
31 N.A. Sobol', former Chairman of the Khar'kov *Sovnarkhoz*, occupied the chair of the first Chairman of *Ukrsovnarkhoz* until March 1961 when he was moved to the post of the First Secretary of the Khar'kov *obkom*. The chairmanship of *Ukrsovnarkhoz* was given to A.S. Kuz'mich, Sobol's deputy and a former Chairman of the Lugansk (Voroshilovgrad until 1958) *Sovnarkhoz*. See N. Kibita, 'The "Sovnarkhoz" Reform in Ukraine: evolution of the economic administrative system (1957–1965)', unpublished PhD thesis, University of Geneva, pp. 370–3; *Regional'naya politika N.S. Khrushcheva: TsK*

KPSS i mestnye partiinye komitety, 1953–1964 gg., sost. O.V. Khlevnyuk [et al.], Moscow: ROSSPEN, 2009, p.715.
32 Note of the Chairman of *Ukrsovnarkhoz* N. Sobol' to Podgornyi and Kal'chenko from 4 August 1960, attached to the proposal on the structure of *Ukrsovnarkhoz*, TsDAGOU, f. 1, op. 31, d. 1607, l. 128; Letter of the Chairman of *Ukrsovnarkhoz* A. Kuz'mich to O. Ivashchenko, 11 April 1961, TsDAGOU, f. 1, op. 31, d. 1880, ll. 101–2; Letter of the CMUk commission to the First Vice-Chairman of the CMUk 'On envisaged structure and personnel for the *sovnarkhozy* of enlarged economic regions', 23 December 1962, TsDAVOU, f. 2, op. 10, d. 2524, l. 3.
33 Proposal of *Ukrsovnarkhoz* on the structure of *Ukrsovnarkhoz*, 4 August 1960, TsDAGOU, f. 1, op. 31, d. 1607, ll. 129, 130, 131–5; Resolution of the CMUk from 30 August 1960 on the structure and staff of *Ukrsovnarkhoz*, TsDAVOU, f. 4820, op. 1, d. 12, ll. 2, 3, 4.
34 TsDAGOU, f. 1, op. 31, d. 1880, l. 194.
35 TsDAGOU, f. 1, op. 31, d. 1880, l. 205.
36 TsDAGOU, f. 1, op. 31, d. 1880, l. 155.
37 According to paragraphs 10 and 11 of the Statute, *Ukrsovnarkhoz* had the right to redistribute material resources and capital investment, but it was obliged to communicate its decision to Gosplan of Ukraine. TsDAVOU, f. 4820, op. 1, d. 200, ll. 9, 10. Card index of the resolutions of the CC CPUk, TsDAGOU, f. 1, op. 6, d. 3280.
38 Shorthand record report of the meeting of the heads of main branch departments of *Ukrsovnarkhoz* and *glavsnabsbyty* held on 23 September 1961, TsDAVOU, f. 4820, op. 1, d. 198, ll. 6, 7.
39 TsDAVOU, f. 4820, op. 1, d. 198, l. 14.
40 Letter of B. Tsomaya and A. Mikhalyov to V. Shcherbitskii on the functions of *Ukrsovnarkhoz*, 30 October 1961, TsDAVOU, f. 2, op. 9, d. 9497, l. 27.
41 TsDAVOU, f. 2, op. 9, d. 9497, ll. 27–8.
42 TsDAVOU, f. 2, op. 9, d. 9497, ll. 29, 30, 31.
43 Information on the letter of B. Tsomaya and A. Mikhalyov (from *Ukrsovnarkhoz*) compiled by O. Gordenyuk to V. Shcherbitskii on 20 November 1961, TsDAVOU, f. 2, op. 9, d. 9497, l. 33.
44 Alec Nove, 'The industrial planning system: reforms in prospect', *Soviet Studies*, 14, 1, 1962, 8.
45 Letter of the Vice-Chairman of *Ukrsovnarkhoz* V. Garbuzov to V. Shcherbitskii, 12 March 1962, TsDAVOU, f. 4820, op.1, d. 1629, l. 63.
46 In July 1961, 19 *Ukrglavsnabsbyty* of *Ukrsovnarkhoz* with 1,549 employees managed supplies and sales of industrial production manufactured by the Ukrainian enterprises. Information on the staff of *Ukrsovnarkhoz*, 25 July 1961, TsDAVOU, f. 2, op. 9, d. 9497, l. 6.
47 TsDAVOU, f. 4820, op. 1, d. 1629, ll. 64, 65, 66.
48 Fursenko (ed.), *Prezidium TsK KPSS. 1954–1964, tom 1*, pp. 550–1. The new organizational structure took shape after the November 1962 CC CPSU Plenum. However, as early as July 1962, Khrushchev had replaced Novikov with 'his old friend' Veniamin Dymshits as the Chairman of USSR Gosplan. Sergei Khrushchev remembers that this replacement was caused by the ongoing conflict between Novikov and the Chairman of *Gosekonomsovet* Zasyad'ko. 'Father had enough of regularly reconciling Zasyad'ko with Novikov.' See more on the relations between Zasyad'ko and Novikov in Khrushchev, *Nikita Khrushchev*, p. 811.
49 Propositions of the Ukrainian Ministry of Finance on the improvement of industrial administration, TsDAGOU, f. 1, op. 31, d. 2102, ll. 303–6.
50 TsDAGOU, f. 1, op. 31, d. 2102, l. 167.
51 The USSR Gosplan collected material on 15 *sovnarkhozy* for the report 'On the tasks of the *sovnarkhozy* when fulfilling the decisions of the XXII CPSU Congress on further development of industry, construction and transport'. The notes on the work of the

sovnarkhozy of Dnepropetrovsk and Donetsk included suggestions on the improvement of the administration of economy. USSR Gosplan. Information on the work of 15 sovnarkhozy. Information on the work of the Dnepropetrovsk *Sovnarkhoz* during 1958–1961, 27 April 1962, RGAE, f. 4372, op. 64, d. 941, l. 222; USSR Gosplan. Information on the work of the Donetsk *Sovnarkhoz* and suggestions on further improvement of the administration of industry and construction, 29 April 1962, RGAE, f. 4372, op. 64, d. 941, l. 259.
52 RGAE, f. 4372, op. 64, d. 941, l. 221.
53 Card index of the resolutions of the CC CPUk, TsDAGOU, f. 1, op. 6, d. 3422.
54 Report of the CMUk 'On the work of *Ukrsovnarkhoz*', submitted to the CC CPUk, 26 July 1962, TsDAGOU, f. 1, op.31, d. 2103, ll. 187–98.
55 Fursenko (ed.), *Prezidium TsK KPSS. 1954–1964, tom 1*, p. 573.
56 TsDAGOU, f. 1, op. 6, d. 3422.
57 Our analysis shows that with regard to Ukraine, Alec Nove's observation about duplication in the big republics between the republican *Sovnarkhoz* and the republic Gosplan was not the case. Nove, 'The industrial planning system', 8.
58 One month after the November 1962 Plenum, *Ukrsovnarkhoz* drafted new regulations that would have finally increased its authority. Yet the functions, structure and staff claimed in the document contradicted three central resolutions that were issued two weeks later, 'On the organization of the work of USSR *Sovnarkhoz*', 'On the increasing role of the state committees and their responsibilities for the development of industrial branches' and 'On the further improvement of the organization of planning of economic development'. The inconsistencies were pointed out by the Ukrainian Ministry of Finance and Gosplan of Ukraine. Gosplan of Ukraine analysed the submitted document and concluded that 42 out of 83 paragraphs drafted by *Ukrsovnarkhoz* were inconsistent either with the three resolutions or with the existing procedures that were not envisaged to be changed. The Ukrainian Ministry of Finance noticed that certain paragraphs in the new regulations contradicted the existing legislation. Importantly, *Ukrsovnarkhoz* envisaged taking control over a share of financial reserves of the *sovnarkhozy*. Remarks of the Ukrainian Minister of Finance 'On the draft of Regulations, structure and staff of *Ukrsovnarkhoz*' submitted to the CMUk, 28 January 1963, TsDAVOU, f. 2, op. 10, d. 2524, ll. 307–8; Conclusions of Gosplan of Ukraine on the draft of the 'Regulations on *Ukrsovnarkhoz*', TsDAVOU, f. 2, op. 10, d. 2524, ll. 328–44.
59 Taubman, *Khrushchev: The Man and His Era*, pp. 513, 514.
60 Sergei Khrushchev remembers that in 1961, his father was very concerned with developing localism, and, as we may add on the basis of the records of the Presidium meeting on 22 March 1962, with the disobedience of the central *apparat*. Thereby, although in the fight between the proponents of the policy of decentralization and the proponents of the policy of recentralization in 1961 Khrushchev was inclined to support the former, he avoided taking sides. (Khrushchev, *Nikita Khrushchev*, pp. 746, 773.) Khrushchev might have avoided taking sides, but he obviously could not resist his instinct to establish centralized control over the economy.
61 TsDAGOU, f. 1, op. 31, d. 2102, ll. 160, 161, 163, 164.
62 Main results of the work of Ukrainian *sovnarkhozy* in the period 1957–1965. *Ukrsovnarkhoz*, Liquidation commission, TsDAVOU, f. 4820, op. 1, d. 1896, l. 14.

10 November 1962 CC CPSU Plenum

1 A.A. Fursenko (ed.), *Prezidium TsK KPSS. 1954–1964. Chernovye protokol'nye zapisi zasedanii. Stenogrammy. Postanovleniya. T. 1: Chernovye protokol'nye zapisi zasedanii. Stenogrammy*. Moscow: ROSSPEN, 2004, pp. 584, 649.
2 Fursenko (ed.), *Prezidium TsK KPSS. 1954–1964, tom 1*, p. 1104.

3 USSR *Gosstroi* was formed in 1950. With the *Sovnarkhoz* reform it was not abolished, and even the head of the committee was not replaced; however, its functions were curtailed. See Fursenko (ed.), *Prezidium TsK KPSS. 1954–1964, tom 1*, p. 649; V.I. Ivkin, *Gosudarstvennaya vlast' SSSR. Vysshie organy vlasti i upravleniya i ikh rukovoditeli. 1923–1991 gg. Istoriko-biograficheskii spravochnik*, Moscow: ROSSPEN, 1999, pp. 92, 93.
4 Leonard Schapiro, *The Communist Party of the Soviet Union*, 2nd edn, London: Eyre & Spottiswoode Publishers Ltd, 1970, p. 596.
5 See details in Schapiro, *The Communist Party of the Soviet Union*, 597–8; Donald A. Filtzer, *The Khrushchev Era: De-Stalinization and the limits of reform in the USSR, 1953–1964*, Basingstoke: Macmillan, 1993, pp. 78–9; R.G. Pikhoya, *Sovetskii Soyuz: istoriya vlasti 1945–1991*, Moscow: RAGS, 1998, pp. 238–9.
6 On the Party bifurcation see also, for example, John A. Armstrong, 'Party Bifurcation and Elite Interests', *Soviet Studies*, 17, 4, 1966, 417–30; John A. Armstrong, *The Politics of Totalitarianism: the Communist Party of the Soviet Union from 1934 to the present*, New York: Random House, 1961; Robert Conquest, *Power and Policy in the USSR: the study of Soviet dynastics*, London: Macmillan, 1961; William J. Conyngham, *Industrial Management in the Soviet Union: The role of the C.P.S.U. in industrial decision-making 1917–1970*, Stanford, CA: Hoover Institution Press, Stanford University, 1973, pp. 135–54.
7 Schapiro, *The Communist Party of the Soviet Union*, p. 600.
8 William Taubman, *Khrushchev: The Man and His Era*, London: Free Press; New York, NY: W.W. Norton, 2003, p. 587.
9 See also S.N. Khrushchev, *Nikita Khrushchev: Reformator*, Moscow: Vremya, 2010, pp. 780, 816–17.
10 See more in Conyngham, *Industrial Management*, pp. 151–2.
11 The Seven Year Plan (1959–1965) was approved at the extraordinary XXI CPSU Congress in 1959.
12 Speech of Khrushchev at the January 1961 CC CPUk Plenum, TsDAGOU, f. 1, op. 24, d. 5363, ll. 7–89. See this document also in *Politicheskoe rukovodstvo Ukrainy 1938–1989*, sost. V.Yu. Vasil'ev [et al.], Moscow: ROSSPEN, 2006, p. 259.
13 Fursenko (ed.), *Prezidium TsK KPSS. 1954–1964, tom 1*, pp. 451, 452; *Politicheskoe rukovodstvo Ukrainy 1938–1989*, pp. 259–61.
14 For details of the pension policy, see G.M. Ivanova, *Na poroge 'gosudarstva vseobshchego blagosostoyaniya'. Sotsial'naya politika v SSSR (seredina 1950-kh-nachalo 1970-kh godov)*, Moscow: IRI RAN, 2011, pp. 87–8, 96–9, 132–5.
15 On 1 June, after the Soviet press announced an increase in retail prices of agricultural products, 5,000 workers from the Novocherkassk plant of electric locomotive building went out onto the streets to protest against the increase of prices and the revision of their production norms that reduced their pay. On the causes of the tragedy in Novocherkassk, see Ivanova, *Na poroge 'gosudarstva vseobshchego blagosostoyaniya'*, pp. 146–7; see also Taubman, *Khrushchev: The Man and His Era*, pp. 518–22; Yu. Aksyutin, *Khrushchevskaya 'ottepel'' i obshchestvennye nastroenya v SSSR v 1953–1964 gg.*, Moscow: ROSSPEN, 2004, pp. 411–13; Fursenko (ed.), *Prezidium TsK KPSS. 1954–1964, tom 1*, p. 566.
16 Fursenko (ed.), *Prezidium TsK KPSS. 1954–1964, tom 1*, p. 551.
17 Fursenko (ed.), *Prezidium TsK KPSS. 1954–1964, tom 1*, p. 560.
18 Fursenko (ed.), *Prezidium TsK KPSS. 1954–1964, tom 1*, p. 561.
19 Fursenko (ed.), *Prezidium TsK KPSS. 1954–1964, tom 1*, pp. 573, 1104.
20 Fursenko (ed.), *Prezidium TsK KPSS. 1954–1964, tom 1*, p. 573.
21 Remark of the functionaries of USSR Gosplan to the Chairman of USSR Gosplan on a proposal of the resolution 'On the functions of USSR Gosplan', 15 December 1962. RGAE, f. 4372, op. 65, d. 53, l. 8.

172 *Notes*

22 Previously, Ustinov was the Chairman of the USSR CM Presidium commission for the military industry. Ivkin, *Gosudarstvennaya vlast' SSSR*, pp. 38, 39, 564.
23 Ivkin, *Gosudarstvennaya vlast' SSSR*, pp. 59, 62–3, 80–1.
24 Ivkin, *Gosudarstvennaya vlast' SSSR*, pp. 83, 56, 66, 70, 81, 122, 125, 128, 132.
25 Fursenko (ed.), *Prezidium TsK KPSS. 1954–1964, tom 1*, p. 1097.
26 G. Simon, *Nationalism and Policy Toward the Nationalities in the Soviet Union: From totalitarian dictatorship to post-Stalinist society*, Boulder, CO: Westview Press, 1991, p. 256.
27 Ivkin, *Gosudarstvennaya vlast' SSSR*, p. 38; Fursenko (ed.), *Prezidium TsK KPSS. 1954–1964, tom 1*, pp. 1123–4, 1130.
28 There were state branch committees and state production committees. Vedeneev explains that before the November 1962 Plenum, the state branch committees were in charge of branch planning; after the Plenum they were instructed to provide 'technical administration' (*tekhnicheskoe rukovodstvo*). They did not have any industry under their management. State production committees (seven by the end of the reform) directly managed some industry and organizations, planned their economic activity and were responsible for the performance of their branches to the VSNKh and *Gosstroi* (see more in Yu.A. Vedeneev, *Organizatsionnye reformy gosudarstvennogo upravleniya promyshlennost'yu v SSSR: istoriko-pravovoe issledovanie (1957–1987 gg.)*, Moscow: Nauka, 1990, pp. 31–4); Shorthand record report of the meeting of the Party, Soviet and state functionaries of Ukraine with the CC CPSU Secretary N.S. Khrushchev held on 24 December 1962 in Kiev, TsDAGOU, f. 1, op. 24, d. 5550, ll. 46–7.
29 Resolution of the CC CPUk Presidium on the transfer of design offices and research institutes in the jurisdiction of the *sovnarkhozy*, *oblispolkomy*, Ukrainian ministries and Gosplan of Ukraine, 1 July 1957, TsDAGOU, f. 1, op. 6, d. 2650, l. 3.
30 Fursenko (ed.), *Prezidium TsK KPSS. 1954–1964, tom 1*, p. 649.
31 Propositions of an *Ukrsovnarkhoz* commission on organization of the republican administration of industry and construction, submitted to the CC CPUk on 6 November 1964, TsDAGOU, f. 1, op. 31, d. 2585, l. 19. According to the editors of the 1st volume of *Presidium TsK KPSS*, the reorganization held after the November 1962 Plenum had not led to the considerable enhancement of real power of the state committees because the territorial principle of administration continued to prevail over the branch. Fursenko (ed.), *Prezidium TsK KPSS. 1954–1964, tom 1*, p. 1124.
32 Fursenko (ed.), *Prezidium TsK KPSS. 1954–1964, tom 1*, p. 1103.
33 TsDAGOU, f. 1, op. 24, d. 5550, l. 14.
34 V.E. Dymshits, in 1959–1962 worked in USSR Gosplan. In April–July 1962, he was First Vice-Chairman of USSR Gosplan, then the Chairman of USSR Gosplan. In November 1962, until 1965, he was the Chairman of USSR *Sovnarkhoz*. For more on biography of Dymshits see Fursenko (ed.), *Prezidium TsK KPSS. 1954–1964, tom 1*, p. 1215; about Dymshits, see also Khrushchev, *Nikita Khrushchev*, p. 811.
35 TsDAGOU, f. 1, op. 24, d. 5550, ll. 46–7.
36 By 1958, there were 77 scientific research institutes in the jurisdiction of Gosplan of Ukraine and 35 scientific organizations in the jurisdiction of the *sovnarkhozy*. In 1958, the CC CPUk drafted a proposal to transfer 43 research institutes from Gosplan of Ukraine to the *sovnarkhozy* and leave 33 scientific organizations of republican importance that worked on projects for other Union republics and for the foreign countries to Gosplan of Ukraine. Resolutions of the CC CPUk Presidium on the transfer of research institutes to the jurisdiction of the state committees of USSR Gosplan, 9 February 1963, TsDAGOU, f. 1, op. 6, d. 3517, ll. 55, 124, 125, 126–7, 128, 129, 130; Letter of the CC CPUk to the CC CPSU, mid-March 1958, TsDAGOU, f. 1, op. 24, d. 4727, l. 324.
37 TsDAGOU, f. 1, op. 31, d. 2585, l. 33.
38 USSR Gosplan. Information on the work of the Donetsk *Sovnarkhoz* and suggestions on further improvement of the administration of industry and construction, 29 April 1962, RGAE, f. 4372, op. 64, d. 941, ll. 257, 258.

39 In particular, *Ukrsovnarkhoz* and the CMUk mentioned the instruction of the USSR *Gosbank* of 18 June 1960, according to which the directors and other executives of enterprises that allowed the wage fund to be overdrawn were deprived of bonuses until the overdraft was paid off. Ukrainians argued that overdrafts could happen not only because of poor management, but due to the delayed launch of new production capacities caused by other enterprises or for other reasons. According to the instruction of the USSR Ministry of Finance dated 29 August 1960, the procedure for spending profits from selling consumer goods manufactured from waste was such that enterprises did not have any incentive to develop workshops that produced consumer goods. Letter of *Ukrsovnarkhoz* to the USSR CM regarding financial incentives as a means of improving economic performance of enterprises, 14 September 1962, TsDAVOU, f. 4820, op. 1, d. 1629, ll. 195, 199.

40 Paragraphs 63, 95, 109 and 110 respectively of the Regulations on the *Sovnarkhozy*. Propositions on enhancement of the economic rights of the *sovnarkhozy* and of the directors of enterprises and construction sites, October 1962, TsDAGOU, f. 1, op. 31, d. 2105, ll. 193, 194.

41 The commission included representatives of USSR Gosplan, USSR *Sovnarkhoz*, the USSR Ministry of Finance, USSR *Gosbank*, *Ukrsovnarkhoz*, *sovnarkhozy* of Sverdlovsk, Kemerovo, Leningrad and of the city of Moscow. Letter accompanying a draft of the Regulations on the *Sovnarkhozy* that was compiled by the V. Dymshits commission, sent to the USSR CM on 8 January 1963, TsDAVOU, f. 2, op. 10, d. 2523, l. 3.

42 TsDAVOU, f. 2, op. 10, d. 2523, ll. 3–4.

43 Information attached to the proposal of the Regulations on the *Sovnarkhozy*, compiled by the V. Dymshits commission, 11 February 1963, TsDAVOU, f. 2, op. 10, d. 2523, l. 168.

44 TsDAVOU, f. 2, op. 10, d. 2523, l. 169.

45 Letter of the USSR CM commission that worked on the proposal of the Law on the socialist enterprise submitted to the USSR CM, 23 February 1963, TsDAVOU, f. 2, op. 10, d. 2523, l. 104.

46 TsDAVOU, f. 2, op. 10, d. 2523, ll. 104–5. Sergei Khrushchev remembers that, by 1964, his father was deeply persuaded that the directors of enterprises should be given freedom and that it was necessary to limit their relations with the economic administrators 'on top' to the strict minimum. (See Khrushchev, *Nikita Khrushchev*, p. 961.) Yet, as we can see from the documents, Khrushchev had already, at the end of 1962, sought to formalize relations between the economic bureaucracy and the producers.

47 On the economic reform introduced after the *sovnarkhozy*, see, for example, Eugène Zaleski, *Planning Reforms in the Soviet Union, 1962–1966: An analysis of recent trends in economic organization and management*, trans. Marie-Christine MacAndrew and G. Warren Nutter, Chapel Hill, NC: University of North Carolina Press, 1967, pp. 141–83.

11 Recentralization in Ukraine

1 A.A. Fursenko (ed.), *Prezidium TsK KPSS. 1954–1964. Chernovye protokol'nye zapisi zasedanii. Stenogrammy. Postanovleniya. T. 1: Chernovye protokol'nye zapisi zasedanii. Stenogrammy*. Moscow: ROSSPEN, 2004, p. 1116; see also Z. Mieczkowski, 'The 1962–1963 reforms in Soviet economic regionalization', *Slavic Review*, 24, 3, 1965, 481–2.

2 Resolution of the CC CPUk 'On merging economic regions of Ukraine', 25 December 1962, TsDAGOU, f. 1, op. 6, d. 3432, ll. 35–6.

3 Shelest, who was at that time First Secretary of the Kiev *obkom*, described this reform as very confusing. According to him, in the CC CPUk Presidium they did not understand very well how exactly the reorganization was to be implemented. 'One could feel', wrote Shelest, 'that he [Podgornyi] himself does not master these reorganization problems. Some of his judgements clearly did not correspond to Khrushchev's

note. Podgornyi suggested that maybe they should organize Party *kraikomy* and *kraiispolkomy* in Ukraine.' P. Shelest, *Spravzhnii sud istorii shche poperedu. Spohady, Shchodennyky, Dokumenty, Materialy* (The True Judgment of History Still Awaits Us), Ju. Shapoval (ed.) Kyiv: Heneza, 2003, p. 146. See also Letter of Podgornyi to the CC CPSU on the reorganization of the Party and administrative organs, 24 October 1962 in *Politicheskoe rukovodstvo Ukrainy 1938–1989*, sost. V.Yu. Vasil'ev [et al.], Moscow: ROSSPEN, 2006, p. 277; Shorthand record report of the meeting of the Party, Soviet and state functionaries of Ukraine with the CC CPSU Secretary N.S. Khrushchev held on 24 December 1962 in Kiev, TsDAGOU, f. 1, op. 24, d. 5550, ll. 5, 18.

4 William J. Conyngham, *Industrial Management in the Soviet Union: The role of the C.P.S.U. in industrial decision-making 1917–1970*, Stanford, CA: Hoover Institution Press, Stanford University, 1973, p. 216.

5 Fursenko (ed.), *Prezidium TsK KPSS. 1954–1964, tom 1*, p. 654.

6 Ibid.

7 'Propositions on the economic administrative regions of the Ukrainian SSR' drafted by the CC CPUk and submitted to the CC CPSU between 15 February and 4 March 1957 (Old version), TsDAGOU, f. 1, op. 24, d. 4520, l. 20.

8 Information drafted by Kal'chenko regarding the transfer of the meat and dairy industry to the *sovnarkhozy*, TsDAGOU, f. 1, op. 24, d. 4520, l. 235; Letter of the CC CPUk secretaries Burmistrov and Kurilenko to Kirichenko on the advantages of transferring the meat and dairy industry to the jurisdiction of the *sovnarkhozy*, TsDAGOU, f. 1, op. 24, d. 4520, ll. 236–8.

9 List of goods for export produced by the UkSSR in 1957, TsDAGOU, f. 1, op. 24, d. 4547, ll. 45–6; Shorthand record report of the meeting held in the CMUk on 7 January 1958, TsDAVOU, f. 2, op. 9, d. 4308, l. 27.

10 Shorthand record report of the meeting of the board of Gosplan of Ukraine held on 3 January 1959, TsDAVOU, f. 337, op. 2, d. 873a, l. 12.

11 Letter of A. Tsokol' to N. Podgornyi and V. Shcherbitskii on the administration of the local industry, 20 December 1961, TsDAGOU, f. 1, op. 31, d. 1880, ll. 335, 336, 338.

12 Letter of the CC CPUk commission to Podgornyi regarding transfer of the local industry to the jurisdiction of the *sovnarkhozy*, 6 March 1962, TsDAGOU, f. 1, op. 31, d. 1880, ll. 329, 330.

13 TsDAGOU, f. 1, op. 31, d. 1880, l. 330.

14 TsDAGOU, f. 1, op. 31, d. 1880, l. 335.

15 Letter of the CMUk commission to the First Vice-Chairman of the CMUk I. Senin 'On envisaged structure and personnel for the *sovnarkhozy* of enlarged economic regions', 23 December 1962, TsDAVOU, f. 2, op. 10, d. 2524, l. 1.

16 Letter of the Chairman of *Ukrsovnarkhoz* A. Kuz'mich to the CMUk on the reorganization of the work of *Ukrsovnarkhoz* after the November 1962 Party Plenum, 29 December 1962. TsDAVOU, f. 2, op. 10, d. 2524, l. 10.

17 Shorthand record report of the meeting of the *Ukrsovnarkhoz* Presidium held on 9 February 1963 'On the fulfilment of the production and construction plan by the *sovnarkhozy* in January 1963 and measures to ensure the fulfilment of the plan in the first quarter of 1963', TsDAVOU, f. 4820, op. 1, d. 736a, l. 21.

18 Letter of V. Shcherbitskii to the USSR CM regarding problematic issues related to the transfer of local industry to the jurisdiction of the *sovnarkhozy*, 10 November 1962, GARF, f. 5446, op. 97, d. 356, ll. 2, 3, 4, 5; Proposals of *Ukrsovnarkhoz* on the extension of republican rights, TsDAGOU, f. 1, op. 31, d. 2585, l. 121.

19 Letter of P. Shelest to the CC CPSU regarding the creation of the Ukrainian Ministry of Local Industry, 2 April 1965, TsDAGOU, f. 1, op. 24, d. 5990, ll. 142, 143, 144.

20 Ukraine apparently mimicked the reorganization in Moscow when Dymshits switched the chairmanship of USSR Gosplan for the chairmanship of USSR *Sovnarkhoz*. The presidium of the *Ukrsovnarkhoz* was enlarged from 11 to 13 members. Four members

Notes 175

of its previous presidium, including the ex-Chairman Kuz'mich and his first deputy Garbuzov, were replaced by six newcomers: P. Rozenko; D. Polyakov, previously the Chairman of the Odessa *Sovnarkhoz*, now First Vice-Chairman of the *Ukrsovnarkhoz*; N. Mirgorodskii, previously head of a department in Gosplan of Ukraine, now Vice-Chairman of the *Ukrsovnarkhoz*; N. Goncharenko, head of the Main administration for the metallurgical industry, no information on his previous position; N. Drogichinskii, previously the head of the department of general current plans in Gosplan of Ukraine and, from 1961, the head of the planning and economic department in the *Ukrsovnarkhoz*; V. Yanchilin, from 1961, the head of the Main administration for the heavy engineering industry of *Ukrsovnarkhoz*. *Spravochnik po istorii Kommunisticheskoi partii i Sovetskogo Soyuza 1898–1991*, available HTTP: http://www.knowbysight.info/KKK/04989.asp (accessed 20 November 2011); Resolution of the CC CPUk 'On the members of the *Ukrsovnarkhoz* Presidium', 16 April 1963, TsDAGOU, f. 1, op. 6, d. 3527, l. 14.

21 Propositions of an *Ukrsovnarkhoz* commission on organization of the republican administration of industry and construction, submitted to the CC CPUk on 6 November 1964, TsDAGOU, f. 1, op. 31, d. 2585, l. 19.
22 Remarks of *Ukrsovnarkhoz* on a draft of the resolution 'On improvement of the work of *Ukrglavsnabsbyty*, organization of deliveries and control over spending material resources', submitted to the CMUk on 8 January 1963, TsDAVOU, f. 4820, op. 1, d. 1676, ll. 13, 15.
23 At least one similar instruction was issued in January 1959.
24 TsDAVOU, f. 4820, op. 1, d. 1676, l. 13.
25 Letter of the Chairman of the CMUk I. Kazanets to USSR *Sovnarkhoz* and the USSR Ministry of Finance on the modifications in the Ukrainian supply system after the November 1962 CC CPSU Plenum, September 1963, TsDAVOU, f. 4820, op. 1, d. 1676, l. 248; Shorthand record report of the meeting of the *Ukrsovnarkhoz* Presidium 'On fulfilment of production and supply plans for production of machine-building industry in 1st quarter and April 1963', May 1963, TsDAVOU, f. 4820, op. 1, d. 736b, l. 20.
26 TsDAVOU, f. 4820, op. 1, d. 736a, l. 19.
27 From a draft of the resolution 'On fulfilment of the delivery plans of industrial production to other Union republics and in the all-Union funds during the 1st half of 1963 and the measures taken in order to ensure the fulfilment of the annual delivery plan', July 1963, TsDAVOU, f. 4820, op. 1, d. 1676, ll. 198–9.
28 Letter of the Chairman of the CMUk I. Kazanets to the USSR CM regarding fulfilment of the production plan for the 1st half of 1963 by the republic, 17 August 1963, GARF, f. 5446, op. 97, d. 363, l. 162.
29 Letter from *Ukrsovnarkhoz* to the CMUk on concealed material resources in the *sovnarkhozy*, 24 June 1963, TsDAVOU, f. 4820, op. 1, d. 1676, l. 144.
30 USSR Gosplan. Information on the work of 15 *sovnarkhozy*. 'On fulfilment of the tasks established at the XXII CPSU Congress for the *sovnarkhozy* in the areas of further development of industry, construction and transport', RGAE, f. 4372, op. 64, d. 941, ll. 264, 321–2.
31 Thad P. Alton, 'The Soviet economy: new expedients and persistent problems', *Proceedings of the Academy of Political Science*, 28, 1, 1965, 36.
32 Letter of *Ukrsovnarkhoz* to USSR *Sovnarkhoz* on the reasons for accumulating above-norm material stocks, 15 October 1964, TsDAVOU, f. 4820, op. 1, d. 1762, l. 283.
33 Information of *Ukrsovnarkhoz* on measures taken by *Ukrsovnarkhoz* in order to reduce above-norm remains of material values in the *sovnarkhozy* of Ukraine, 30 April 1964, TsDAVOU, f. 4820, op. 1, d. 1762, l. 106.
34 TsDAVOU, f. 4820, op. 1, d. 1762, ll. 107, 108.
35 I am thankful to Donald Filtzer for pointing this out. See Donald A. Filtzer, *Soviet Workers and De-Stalinization: The consolidation of the modern system of Soviet production relations, 1953–1964*, Cambridge: Cambridge University Press, 2002,

176 *Notes*

pp. 60, 76–78. On the production norms, see also G.M. Ivanova, *Na poroge 'gosudarstva vseobshchego blagosostoyaniya'. Sotsial'naya politika v SSSR (seredina 1950-kh-nachalo 1970-kh godov)*, Moscow: IRI RAN, 2011, pp. 142–8.

36 Irregular work, *neritmichnaya rabota* or *shturmovshchina*, means that the pace of work varied a lot during a month, with high intensity at the end of the month and low intensity during the first half of the month.
37 TsDAVOU, f. 4820, op. 1, d. 1762, l. 108.
38 Letter of *Ukrsovnarkhoz* to the USSR CM regarding financial incentives as a means of improving economic performance of enterprises, 14 September 1962, TsDAVOU, f. 4820, op. 1, d. 1629, l. 198.
39 TsDAVOU, f. 4820, op. 1, d. 1629, ll. 198, 199.
40 Letter of the Vice–Chairman of *Ukrsovnarkhoz* D. Polyakov to the permanent mission of Ukraine in Moscow containing remarks of the CMUk on the resolution regarding the norms of accumulated stocks, 29 April 1964, TsDAVOU, f. 4820, op. 1, d. 1762, l. 105.

Epilogue

1 At the joint meeting of the CC CPSU Presidium and the USSR CM held on 26 September 1964, Party and governmental executives discussed the problems related to the composition of the perspective plan for 1966–1970 and the adjustment of the plan for the last two years of the Seven Year Plan (for 1964 and 1965). In the opening speech Khrushchev, without discussing it with other members of the Presidium, suggested replacing Five Year Plans with Seven or Eight Year plans. See A.A. Fursenko (ed.), *Prezidium TsK KPSS. 1954–1964. Chernovye protokol'nye zapisi zasedanii. Stenogrammy. Postanovleniya. T. 1: Chernovye protokol'nye zapisi zasedanii. Stenogrammy*. Moscow: ROSSPEN, 2004, pp. 862–72, 1178, note 11.
2 On the events of October 1964 see, for example, A.N. Artizov (ed.), *Nikita Khrushchev, 1964: Stenogrammy plenuma TsK KPSS i drugie dokumenty: sbornik dokumentov*, Moscow: MFD, Materik, 2007; William J. Tompson, 'The Fall of Nikita Khrushchev', *Soviet Studies*, 43, 6, 1991, 1101–21; R.G. Pikhoya, *Sovetskii Soyuz: istoriya vlasti 1945–1991*, Moscow: RAGS, 1998, pp. 256–71; S.N. Khrushchev, *Nikita Khrushchev: Reformator*, Moscow: Vremya, 2010, pp. 1033–41.
3 Propositions of an *Ukrsovnarkhoz* commission on organization of the republican administration of industry and construction, submitted to the CC CPUk on 6 November 1964, TsDAGOU, f. 1, op. 31, d. 2585, l. 8.
4 TsDAGOU, f. 1, op. 31, d. 2585, l. 11.
5 TsDAGOU, f. 1, op. 31, d. 2585, ll. 11–12.
6 TsDAGOU, f. 1, op. 31, d. 2585, ll. 13, 15.
7 TsDAGOU, f. 1, op. 31, d. 2585, l. 24, 25, 26.
8 A.V. Pyzhikov, *Khrushchevskaya 'Ottepel''*, Moscow: Olma-Press, 2002, p. 175.
9 P. Shelest, *Spravzhnii sud istorii shche poperedu. Spohady, Shchodennyky, Dokumenty, Materialy* (The True Judgment of History Still Awaits Us), Ju. Shapoval (ed.) Kyiv: Heneza, 2003, p. 214.
10 Aleksandr Lyashko, *Gruz pamyati. Trilogiya, Vospominaniya. Na stupenyakh vlasti*, Kyiv: Delovaya Ukraina, 1997, p. 93.
11 The CC CPUk resolutions, 6 December 1965, TsDAGOU, f. 1, op. 6, d. 3870, ll. 36, 37, 38, 39, 40, 41, 42; Lyashko, *Gruz pamyati. Na stupenyakh vlasti*, p. 93. On the reaction of the Ukrainian republican authorities, see also I.S. Koropeckyj (ed.), *The Ukraine Within the USSR: An Economic Balance Sheet*, New York, NY: Praeger, 1977, pp. 22, 23.
12 Fursenko (ed.), *Prezidium TsK KPSS. 1954–1964, tom 1*, p. 863.

Conclusions

1 According to S. Khrushchev, in October 1964 Suslov 'threw in Khrushchev's face that in 1950–1956 the annual economic growth was between 10.6 and 11.1 per cent, whereas in the 'khrushchevian' septennial 1959–1964 it fell to 6.9–5 per cent.' Moshe Lewin insists that in 1959–1960 the economic successes were beyond dispute, with annual growth rates of 8 per cent. Allen confirms that the growth began to decelerate in the 1960s. S.N. Khrushchev, *Nikita Khrushchev: Reformator*, Moscow: Vremya, 2010, p. 961; Moshe Lewin, *The Soviet Century*, G. Elliott (ed.) London: Verso, 2005, p. 221; Robert C. Allen, *Farm to Factory: A reinterpretation of the Soviet industrial revolution*, Princeton, NJ; Oxford: Princeton University Press, 2003, p. 196.
2 Yu. F. Vorob'ev (ed.), *Ocherki ekonomicheskikh reform*, Moscow: Nauka, 1993, p. 178.
3 Report of the TsSU of Ukraine on the economic development of Ukraine in 1950–1964, TsDAVOU, f. 582, op. 3, d. 5011, l. 141; Main results of the work of Ukrainian *sovnarkhozy* in the period 1957–1965. *Ukrsovnarkhoz*, Liquidation commission, TsDAVOU, f. 4820, op. 1, d. 1896, l. 14.
4 This opinion is very popular in the literature. See, among others, David A. Dyker, *The Soviet Economy*, London: Crosby Lockwood Staples, 1976, p. 86; Robert F. Miller, 'Khrushchev and the Soviet economy: Management by re-organisation', in R.F. Miller and F. Fehér (eds) *Khrushchev and the Communist World*, London: Croom Helm, 1984, p. 127; W.J. Tompson, *Khrushchev: A Political Life*, Basingstoke: Macmillan in association with St Antony's College, Oxford, 1995, pp. 174, 255.
5 TsDAVOU, f. 4820, op. 1, d. 1896, ll. 34–5.
6 Letter of the General Manager of the Republican Branch of the USSR State Bank G. Kovalenko to the Chairman of the CMUk V. Shcherbitskii, 31 July 1961, TsDAVOU, f. 2, op. 9, d. 8655, l. 1.
7 TsDAVOU, f. 4820, op. 1, d. 1896, l. 156.
8 Report of the TsSU of Ukraine 'Growth of Ukrainian gross industrial production by branches', October 1958, TsDAVOU, f. 582, op. 2, d. 1187, ll. 25–6.
9 The numbers for the USSR are taken from the CIA report and are calculated, most likely, on a different basis from the numbers that come from Ukrainian archives and are proposed here. The tendencies of growth and slowdown coincide, however, except for 1959. In 1959, the growth rate of Ukraine was lower than in 1958 but higher in the USSR. *USSR: Measures of Economic Growth and Development, 1950–80: Studies prepared for the use of the Joint Economic Committee, Congress of the United States, December 8, 1982*, Washington, DC: U.S. GPO, 1982, p. 56.
10 TsDAVOU, f. 582, op. 3, d. 5011, ll. 144, 145.
11 TsDAVOU, f. 582, op. 3, d. 5011, l. 150.
12 TsDAVOU, f. 582, op. 3, d. 5011, l. 143.
13 Ibid.
14 TsDAVOU, f. 4820, op. 1, d. 1896, ll. 34–5; Remarks of the CC CPUk and the CMUk on the FYP (1966–1970), submitted to the CC CPSU and the USSR CM on 9 June 1965, TsDAGOU, f. 1, op. 24, d. 5990, l. 271.
15 TsDAVOU, f. 4820, op. 1, d. 1896, ll. 213, 214.
16 Some time during the first half of 1965, Lyashko required a report on the economic development of Ukraine in 1950–1964. In June 1965, the TsSU of Ukraine presented it to the CC CP of Ukraine. TsDAVOU, f. 582, op. 3, d. 5011, l. 141.
17 Ibid.
18 TsDAVOU, f. 582, op. 3, d. 5011, l. 155.

Bibliography

Literature

Aksyutin, Yu., *Khrushchevskaya 'ottepel'' i obshchestvennye nastoreniya v SSSR v 1953–1964 gg.*, 2nd edn, Moscow: ROSSPEN, 2010.
Aksyutin, Yu., *Khrushchevskaya 'ottepel'' i obshchestvennye nastroenya v SSSR v 1953–1964 gg.*, Moscow: ROSSPEN, 2004.
Alampiev, P., 'O setke ekonomicheskikh raionov SSSR', *Planovoe khozyaistvo*, 6, 1956: 25–37.
Allen, R.C., 'The Rise and Decline of the Soviet Economy', *The Canadian Journal of Economics*, 34, 4, 2001: 859–81.
Allen, R.C., *Farm to Factory: A reinterpretation of the Soviet industrial revolution*, Princeton, NJ; Oxford: Princeton University Press, 2003.
Alton, Th.P., 'The Soviet economy: new expedients and persistent problems', *Proceedings of the Academy of Political Sciences*, 28, 1, 1965: 17–41.
Andriyanov, V., *Kosygin*, Moscow: Molodaya gvardiya, 2004.
Armstrong, J.A., *The Soviet Bureaucratic Elite, A Case Study of the Ukrainian Apparatus*, Frederick A. Praeger, Inc., New York, 1959.
Armstrong, J.A., *The Politics of Totalitarianism: the Communist Party of the Soviet Union from 1934 to the present*, New York: Random House, 1961.
Armstrong, J.A., 'Party bifurcation and elite interests', *Soviet Studies*, 17, 4, 1966: 417–30.
Artizov, A.N. (ed.) *Nikita Khrushchev, 1964: Stenogrammy plenuma TsK KPSS i drugie dokumenty: sbornik dokumentov*, Moscow: MFD, Materik, 2007.
Bahry, D., *Outside Moscow: Power, politics, and budgetary policy in the Soviet republics*, New York: Columbia University Press, 1987.
Baibakov, N.K., *Sorok let v pravitel'stve*, Moscow: Respublika, 1993.
Belousov, R., *Ekonomicheskaya istoriya Rossii: XX vek, kniga 5, Dramaticheskii krizis v kontse stoletiya*, Moscow: IzdAT, 2006.
Conquest, R., *Power and Policy in the USSR: the study of Soviet dynastics*, London: Macmillan, 1961.
Conyngham, W.J., *Industrial Management in the Soviet Union: The role of the C.P.S.U. in industrial decision-making 1917–1970*, Stanford, CA: Hoover Institution Press, Stanford University, 1973.
Dyker, D.A., *The Soviet Economy*, London: Crosby Lockwood Staples, 1976.
'Ekonomika Sovetskoi Ukrainy', *Planovoe khozyaistvo*, 4, 1959: 87–90.
Evenko, I., 'Proverka i ekonomicheskii analiz vypolneniya planov', *Planovoe khozyaistvo*, 10, 1958: 3–15.

Filtzer, D.A., *The Khrushchev Era: De-Stalinization and the limits of reform in the USSR, 1953–1964*, Basingstoke: Macmillan, 1993.
Filtzer, D.A., *Soviet Workers and De-Stalinization: The consolidation of the modern system of Soviet production relations, 1953–1964*, Cambridge: Cambridge University Press, 2002.
Frank, Z. and Waelbroeck, J., 'Soviet economic policy since 1953: a study of its structure and changes', *Soviet Studies*, 1965, 17, 1, 1965: 1–43.
Fursenko, A.A. (ed.) *Prezidium TsK KPSS. 1954–1964. Chernovye protokol'nye zapisi zasedanii. Stenogrammy. Postanovleniya: V 3 tomakh. T. 1: Chernovye protokol'nye zapisi zasedanii. Stenogrammy.* Moscow: ROSSPEN, 2004.
Fursenko, A.A. (ed.) *Prezidium TsK KPSS. 1954–1964. Chernovye protokol'nye zapisi zasedanii. Stenogrammy. Postanovleniya: V 3 tomakh. T. 2: Postanovleniya. 1954–1958*, Moscow: ROSSPEN, 2006.
Fursenko, A.A. (ed.) *Prezidium TsK KPSS. 1954–1964. Chernovye protokol'nye zapisi zasedanii: Stenogrammy. Postanovleniya: V 3 tomakh. T.3: Postanovleniya. 1959–1964*, Moscow: ROSSPEN, 2008.
Gal'perin, N., 'Sovremennye zadachi organizatsii material'no-tekhnicheskogo snabzheniya proizvodstva', *Voprosy ekonomiki*, 4, 1957: 84–95.
Gorlizki, Y., 'Anti-Ministerialism and the USSR Ministry of Justice, 1953–1956: A study in organisational decline', *Europe–Asia Studies*, 48, 8, 1996: 1279–318.
Granick, D., 'An organizational model of Soviet industrial planning', *The Journal of Political Economy*, 67, 2, 1959: 109–30.
Grossman, G., 'The structure and organization of the Soviet economy', *Slavic Review*, 21, 2, 1962: 203–22.
Hanson, Ph., *The Rise and Fall of the Soviet Economy. An economic history of the USSR from 1945*, Harlow: Longman, 2003.
Hough, J.F., *The Soviet Prefects: The local party organs in industrial decision-making*, Cambridge, MA: Harvard University Press, 1969.
Hutchings, R., *The Soviet Budget*, Albany: State University of New York Press, 1983.
Ivanova, G.M., *Na poroge 'gosudarstva vseobshchego blagosostoyaniya'. Sotsial'naya politika v SSSR (seredina 1950-kh-nachalo 1970-kh godov)*, Moscow: IRI RAN, 2011.
Ivkin, V.I., *Gosudarstvennaya vlast' SSSR. Vysshie organy vlasti i upravleniya i ikh rukovoditeli. 1923–1991 gg. Istoriko-biograficheskii spravochnik*, Moscow: ROSSPEN, 1999.
Kaser, M.C., 'Changes in planning methods during the preparation of the Soviet Seven-year plan', *Soviet Studies*, 10, 4, 1959: 321–38.
Kelley, D.R., 'Interest Groups in the USSR: The Impact of Political Sensitivity on Group Influence', *The Journal of Politics*, 34, 3, 1972: 860–88.
Khrushchev, S.N. (ed.) *Memoirs of Nikita Khrushchev, vol. 2; Reformer (1945–1964)*, University Park, PA: The Pennsylvania State University Press, 2006.
Khrushchev, S.N., *Nikita Khrushchev: Reformator*, Moscow: Vremya, 2010.
Kibita, N., 'The "Sovnarkhoz" Reform in Ukraine: evolution of the economic administrative system (1957–1965)', unpublished thesis, University of Geneva.
Korobenkov, S.V., *Dela Kremlya. Pravitel'stvennyi apparat*, tom 2, Moscow: Forum, 2004.
Koropeckyj, I.S. (ed.) *The Ukraine Within the USSR: An Economic Balance Sheet*, New York, NY: Praeger, 1977.
Korzhikhina, T.P., *Sovetskoe gosudarstvo i ego uchrezhdeniya. Noyabr' 1917 – Dekabr' 1991*, Moscow: RGGU, 1995.*KPSS v rezolyutsiyakh i resheniyakh s''ezdov, konferentsii i plenumov TsK (1898–1986)*; tom 9, 1956–1960, Moscow: Politizdat, 1986.

Kugukalo, I., 'Ekonomicheskie raiony Ukrainskoi SSR', *Voprosy ekonomiki*, 4, 1957: 44–63.
Laskovsky, N., 'Reflections on Soviet industrial reorganization', *American Slavic and East European Review*, 1958, 17, 1, 1958: 47–58.
Lewin, M., *The Soviet Century*, G. Elliott (ed.) London: Verso, 2005.
Lewytzkyj, B., *Politics and Society in Soviet Ukraine, 1953–1980*, Edmonton, Alta.: Canadian Institute of Ukrainian Studies, University of Alberta; Downsview. Ont., Canada: Distributed by the University of Toronto Press, 1984.
Lyashko, A., *Gruz pamyati. Trilogiya, Vospominaniya. Na stupenyakh vlasti*, Kyiv: Delovaya Ukraina, 1997.
Lyashko, A., *Gruz pamyati. Trilogiya, Vospominaniya. Put' v nomenklaturu*, Kyiv: Delovaya Ukraina, 1997.
Mieczkowski, Z., 'The 1962–1963 reforms in Soviet economic regionalization', *Slavic Review*, 24, 3, 1965: 479–96.
Miller, J., 'Summary of XXI (Extraordinary) Party Congress', *Soviet Studies*, 11, 1, 1959: 84–109
Miller, R.F., 'Khrushchev and the Soviet economy: Management by re-organisation', in R.F. Miller and F. Féhér (eds) *Khrushchev and the Communist World*, London: Croom Helm, 1984.
Munting, R., *The Economic Development of the USSR*, London: Croom Helm, 1982.
North, D.C., *Institutions, Institutional Change and Economic Performance*, Cambridge: Cambridge University Press, 2007.
Nove, A., 'The industrial planning system: reforms in prospect', *Soviet Studies*, 14, 1, 1962: 1–15.
Nove, A., *The Soviet Economic System*, London: George Allen & Unwin, 1977.
Omarovskii, A., 'O nekotorykh voprosakh organizatsii upravleniya i planirovaniya v promyshlennosti SSSR', *Voprosy ekonomiki*, 4, 1957: 64–75.
'Perestroika upravleniya promyshlennost'yu i stroitel'stvom i zadachi planovykh organov', *Planovoe khozyaistvo*, 5, 1957: 3–11.
Pikhoya, R.G., *Sovetskii Soyuz: istoriya vlasti 1945–1991*, Moscow: RAGS, 1998.
Politicheskoe rukovodstvo Ukrainy 1938 – 1989, sost. V.Yu. Vasil'ev [et al.], Moscow: ROSSPEN, 2006.
Prokhorov, A.M. (ed.) *Bol'shaya Sovetskaya Entsiklopediya*, 13 tom, 3rd edn, Moscow: Izdatel'stvo 'Sovetskaya Entsiklopediya', 1973.
Pyzhikov, A.V., *Khrushchevskaya 'Ottepel''*, Moscow: Olma–Press, 2002.
Regional'naya politika N.S. Khrushcheva: TsK KPSS i mestnye partiinye komitety, 1953–1964 gg., sost. O.V. Khlevnyuk [et al.], Moscow: ROSSPEN, 2009.
Resheniya Partii i Pravitel'stva po khozyaistvennym voprosam (1917–1967), tom 4, Moscow: Izdatel'stvo politicheskoi literatury, 1968.
Rigby, T.H., 'Khrushchev and the rules of the Soviet political game', in R.F. Miller and F. Féhér (eds) *Khrushchev and the Communist World*, London: Croom Helm, 1984.
Roeder, Ph.G., *Red Sunset: The failure of Soviet politics*, Princeton, NJ: Princeton University Press, 1993.
Sapir, J., *Les fluctuations économiques en URSS, 1941–1985*, Paris: Ed. de l'Ecole des hautes études en sciences sociales, 1989.
Schapiro, L., *The Communist Party of the Soviet Union*, 2nd edn, London: Eyre & Spottiswoode Publishers Ltd, 1970.
Schwartz, H., *The Soviet Economy Since Stalin*, London: Victor Gollancz Ltd, 1965.

Shelest, P., *Spravzhnii sud istorii shche poperedu. Spohady, Shchodennyky, Dokumenty, Materialy*, Ju. Shapoval (ed.) Kyiv: Heneza, 2003.
Shelest, P.Yu., *Ukraino nasha Radyans'ka*, Kyiv: Vydavnytstvo politychnoi literatury Ukrainy, 1970.
Shestakov, V.A., *Sotsial'no-ekonomicheskaya politika sovetskogo gosudarstva v 50e – seredine 60-kh godov*, Moscow: Nauka, 2006.
Simon, G., *Nationalism and Policy Toward the Nationalities in the Soviet Union: From totalitarian dictatorship to post-Stalinist society*, Boulder, CO: Westview Press, 1991.
Soviet Union. *Verkhovnyi Sovet: On the further improvement of management in industry and construction in the U.S.S.R.: materials of the seventh session of the Supreme Soviet of the U.S.S.R., May 7–10, 1957*, Moscow: Foreign Languages Pub. House, 1957.
Spravochnik po istorii Kommunisticheskoi partii i Sovetskogo Soyuza 1898 – 1991, available HTTP: http://www.knowbysight.info*SSSR v tsyfrakh, Statisticheskii sbornik*, Moscow: Gosudarstvennoe statisticheskoe izdatel'stvo, 1958.
Swearer, H.R., 'Administration of Local Industry After the 1957 Industrial Reorganization', *Soviet Studies*, XII, 3, 1961: 217–30.
Swearer, H.R., 'Decentralization in recent Soviet administrative practice', *Slavic Review*, 21, 3, 1962: 456–70.
Taubman, W., *Khrushchev: The Man and His Era*, London: Free Press; New York, NY: W.W. Norton, 2003.
Tomilina, N.G. (ed.) *Nikita Sergeevich Khrushchev: dva tsveta vremeni: dokumenty iz lichnogo fonda N.S. Khrushcheva: V 2-kh tomakh. Tom 1*, Moscow: MFD, 2009.
Tomilina, N.G. (ed.) *Nikita Sergeevich Khrushchev: dva tsveta vremeni: dokumenty iz lichnogo fonda N.S. Khrushcheva: V 2-kh tomakh. Tom 2*, Moscow: MFD, 2009.
Tompson, W.J., 'The Fall of Nikita Khrushchev', *Soviet Studies*, 43, 6, 1991: 1101–21.
Tompson, W.J., *Khrushchev: A Political Life,* Basingstoke: Macmillan in association with St Antony's College, Oxford, 1995.
Tompson, W.J., 'Industrial Management and Economic Reform under Khrushchev', in W. Taubman, S. Khrushchev and A. Gleason (eds) *Nikita Khrushchev*, trans. David Gehrenbeck, Eileen Kane and Alla Bashenko, New Haven, CT; London: Yale University Press, 2000.
Tsakunov, S., 'The People's Commissariat of Finance' in E.A. Rees (ed.) *Decision-making in the Stalinist Command Economy, 1932–1937*, Houndmills, Basingstoke, Hampshire: Macmillan, New York, NY: St. Martin's Press, 1997.
USSR: Measures of Economic Growth and Development, 1950–80: Studies prepared for the use of the Joint Economic Committee, Congress of the United States, December 8, 1982, Washington, DC: U.S. GPO, 1982.
Vanyukov, D.A., *Khrushchevskaya ottepel'*, Moskva: Mir knigi, 2007.
Vasil'ev, V., 'Failings of the Sovnarkhoz reform: the Ukrainian experience', in J. Smith and M. Ilic (eds) *Khrushchev in the Kremlin: policy and government in the Soviet Union, 1953–1964*, Milton Park, Abingdon, Oxon; New York, N.Y.: Routledge, 2011.
Vedeneev, Yu.A., *Organizatsionnye reformy gosudarstvennogo upravleniya promyshlennost'yu v SSSR: istoriko-pravovoe issledovanie (1957–1987 gg.)*, Moscow: Nauka, 1990.
Vedishchev, A., 'Voprosy ekonomicheskogo raionirovaniya SSSR', *Voprosy ekonomiki*, 2, 1960: 25–35.
Vorob'ev, Yu.F. (ed.) *Ocherki ekonomicheskikh reform*, Moscow: Nauka, 1993.
Westwood, J.J., 'The Modernization of Soviet railways traction in comparative perspective', in J. Smith and M. Ilic (eds) *Khrushchev in the Kremlin: Policy and Government*

182 Bibliography

in the Soviet Union, 1953–1964, Milton Park, Abingdon, Oxon; New York, NY: Routledge, 2011.

Whitefield, S., *Industrial Power and the Soviet State*, Oxford: Clarendon Press; New York: Oxford University Press, 1993.

XX S'ezd Kommunisticheskoi Partii Sovetskogo Soyuza 14–25 fevralya 1956 goda, Stenograficheskii otchet, tom 1, Moscow: Gosudarstvennoe izdatel'stvo politicheskoi literatury, 1956.

Yakovlev, A.N. (ed.) *Lavrentii Beria. 1953. Stenogramma iyul'skogo plenuma TsK KPSS i drugie dokumenty*, Moscow: MFD, 1999.

Yakovlev, A.N. (ed.) *Molotov, Malenkov, Kaganovich. 1957. Stenogramma iyun'skogo plenuma TsK KPSS i drugie dokumenty*, Moscow: MFD, 1998.

'Zadachi Gosplana SSSR v novykh usloviyakh upravleniya promyshlennost'yu i stroitel'stvom', *Planovoe khozyaistvo*, 7, 1957: 3–11.

Zaleski, E., *Planning Reforms in the Soviet Union, 1962–1966: An analysis of recent trends in economic organization and management*, trans. Marie-Christine MacAndrew and G. Warren Nutter, Chapel Hill, NC: University of North Carolina Press, 1967.

Archival sources

GARF, f. 5446, op. 92, d. 826, l. 63, Letter of N. Kal'chenko to the USSR CM, 1 October 1957.

GARF, f. 5446, op. 92, d. 826, ll. 151–49, Letter of Vice-Chairman of the CMUk N. Gureev to A. Kosygin, 1 September 1957.

GARF, f. 5446, op. 93, d. 1213, ll. 122–19, Letter of the Chairman of the RSFSR Gosplan main department for supply and sales of production of the heavy, transport and construction industries M. Mikhailov to the head of the legal department of the USSR CM P. Mishunin, 15 June 1959.

GARF, f. 5446, op. 97, d. 1, l. 1, Letter of USSR Gosplan to Supreme *Sovnarkhoz*, 2 April 1963.

GARF, f. 5446, op. 97, d. 356, ll. 2–6, Letter of the Chairman of the CMUk V. Shcherbitskii to the USSR CM regarding problematic issues related to the transfer of the local industry to the jurisdiction of the *sovnarkhozy*, 10 November 1962.

GARF, f. 5446, op. 97, d. 363, ll. 162–5, Letter of the Chairman of the CMUk I. Kazanets to the USSR CM regarding fulfilment of the production plan for the 1st half of 1963 by the republic, 17 August 1963.

RGAE, f. 4372, op. 56, d. 1, ll. 43–6, Minutes No. 6 of the meeting of the USSR Gosplan held on 1 November 1957.

RGAE, f. 4372, op. 57, d. 167, ll. 8–12, Information of the USSR Gosplan on the changes made in the 1958 plan draft submitted by the CMUk, 28 February 1958.

RGAE, f. 4372, op. 57, d. 167, ll. 49–52, Remarks of the USSR Gosplan on the 1958 plan drafts submitted by the Ukrainian and Moldavian SSR, 11 January 1958.

RGAE, f. 4372, op. 57, d. 167, ll. 118–26, Letter of the CMUk to the USSR CM and the Chairman of the USSR Gosplan I. Kuz'min, 26 September 1957.

RGAE, f. 4372, op. 57, d. 203, ll. 56–63, Report of USSR Gosplan from 24 January 1958. Chapter 'On manifestations of *mestnichestvo* and other shortcomings in the work of the *sovnarkhozy*'.

RGAE, f. 4372, op. 57, d. 206, l. 5, Extract from the report 'On the results of the inspection of organization of work on composition of the draft plan of economic development of the UkSSR for 1958' submitted to the Vice-Chairman of USSR Gosplan G.V. Perov, signed by M. Yampol'skii, V. Ivanchenko, D. Potanin, M. Bulavko, 7 August 1957.

RGAE, f. 4372, op. 58, d. 736, ll. 72–89, Minutes of the meeting of the leading employees of the USSR Gosplan and the RSFSR Gosplan with the chairmen of *sovnarkhozy*, participants in the 3rd session of the USSR Supreme Soviet, regarding elimination of the shortcomings in planning and improvement of work of the planning organs, held in USSR Gosplan on 2 November 1959.

RGAE, f. 4372, op. 58, d. 738, ll. 2–56, Shorthand record report of the meeting of the leading employees of the USSR Gosplan and the RSFSR Gosplan with the chairmen of *sovnarkhozy*, participants in the 3rd session of the USSR Supreme Soviet, regarding elimination of the shortcomings in planning and improvement of work of the planning organs, held in USSR Gosplan on 2 November 1959.

RGAE, f. 4372, op. 64, d. 941, ll. 193–224, USSR Gosplan. Information on the work of 15 *sovnarkhozy*. Information on the work of the Dnepropetrovsk *Sovnarkhoz* during 1958–1961, 27 April 1962.

RGAE, f. 4372, op. 64, d. 941, ll. 254–62, USSR Gosplan. Information on the work of the Donetsk *Sovnarkhoz* and suggestions on further improvement of the administration of industry and construction, 29 April 1962.

RGAE, f. 4372, op. 64, d. 941, ll. 263–322, USSR Gosplan. Information on the work of 15 *sovnarkhozy*. 'On fulfilment of the tasks established at the XXII CPSU Congress for the *sovnarkhozy* in the areas of further development of industry, construction and transport'.

RGAE, f. 4372, op. 65, d. 53, l. 8, Remarks of the functionaries of USSR Gosplan to the Chairman of USSR Gosplan on a proposal of the resolution 'On the functions of USSR Gosplan', 15 December 1962.

RGAE, f. 4372, op. 76c, d. 110, ll. 2–6, Draft of the CC CPSU and the USSR CM resolution on reorganization of administration of defence industrial branches presented by a specially assigned CC CPSU commission to the CC CPSU, around 9 July 1957.

RGAE, f. 4372, op. 76c, d. 110, ll. 152–3, Information to the comments of com. N.G. Ignatov to the draft of Regulations on Council of economic administrative region, by Vice-Chairman of USSR Gosplan G. Perov.

RGAE, f. 4372, op. 76c, d. 110, ll. 155–80, The Regulations on a *Sovnarkhoz*.

RGAE, f. 4372, op. 79c, p. 6, Introduction to the *opis'*.

RGANI, f. 2, op. 1, d. 148, ll. 74–105, Report of Bulganin, 1955.

RGANI, f. 2, op. 1, d. 203, l. 69, Report of Bulganin, December 1956 CC CPSU Plenum.

RGASPI, f. 17, op. 165, d. 131, ll. 84–90, Extract from the shorthand record report of Khrushchev's speech, 10 August 1953.

RGASPI, f. 556, op. 21, d. 48, ll. 66–9, Memorandum of the CM RSFSR Chairman M.A. Yasnov to the USSR CM 'On staff for the *sovnarkhozy*', 20 July 1957.

State archive of Zaporozh'e *oblast'*, f. P2540, op. 25, d. 186, Personal file of G.I. Ivanovskii, 10 October 1961.

TsDAGOU, f. 1, op. 6, d. 2465, ll. 78–82, Resolutions of the Presidium of the Supreme Soviet of Ukraine regarding the organization of the Ukrainian Ministry of Construction, 4–9 August 1956.

TsDAGOU, f. 1, op. 6, d. 2622, ll. 7–8, Extract from the minutes of the meeting of the CC CPUk Presidium held on 9–10 April 1957. On selection of leading staff for the Ukrainian *sovnarkhozy*.

TsDAGOU, f. 1, op. 6, d. 2643, ll. 3–4, Resolution of the CC CPUk 'On chairmen of *sovnarkhozy* of UkSSR', 28 May 1957.

TsDAGOU, f. 1, op. 6, d. 2650, l. 3, Resolution of the CC CPUk Presidium on the transfer of design offices and research institutes to the jurisdiction of the *sovnarkhozy*, *oblispolkomy*, Ukrainian ministries and Gosplan of Ukraine, 1 July 1957.

TsDAGOU, f. 1, op. 6, d. 2786, ll. 59–69, Resolution of the CC CPUk and the CMUk 'On measures to improve the management of supplies', 23 May 1958.

TsDAGOU, f. 1, op. 6, d. 2794, Resolution of the CC CPUk on the structure and staff for Gosplan of Ukraine, 24 June 1958.

TsDAGOU, f. 1, op. 6, d. 2800, l. 8, Report of the First Secretary of the CC CPUk N. Podgornyi 'On unauthorized reductions of investments by the *sovnarkhozy* of the UkSSR', 22 July 1958.

TsDAGOU, f. 1, op. 6, d. 3116, ll. 8–9, Resolution of the CC CPUk Presidium 'On the creation of *Ukrsovnarkhoz*', 5 July 1960.

TsDAGOU, f. 1, op. 6, d. 3280, Card index of the resolutions of the CC CPUk.

TsDAGOU, f. 1, op. 6, d. 3422, Card index of the resolutions of the CC CPUk.

TsDAGOU, f. 1, op. 6, d. 3432, ll. 35–6, Resolution of the CC CPUk 'On merging economic regions of Ukraine', 25 December 1962.

TsDAGOU, f. 1, op. 6, d. 3517, ll. 47, 104–11, Resolution of the CC CPUk on the structure and staff of Gosplan of Ukraine and *Ukrsovnarkhoz*, 12 February 1963.

TsDAGOU, f. 1, op. 6, d. 3517, ll. 55, 124–30, Resolutions of the CC CPUk Presidium on the transfer of research institutes to the jurisdiction of the State committees of USSR Gosplan, 9 February 1963.

TsDAGOU, f. 1, op. 6, d. 3527, l. 14, Resolution of the CC CPUk 'On the members of the *Ukrsovnarkhoz* Presidium', 16 April 1963.

TsDAGOU, f. 1, op. 6, d. 3870, ll. 36–42, Resolutions of the CC CPUk on the organization of Ukrainian ministries, 6 December 1965.

TsDAGOU, f. 1, op. 8, d. 2217, ll. 37–44, Annex to the CC CPUk Presidium Protokol no. 60, meeting of 6 January 1956.

TsDAGOU, f. 1, op. 24, d. 2775, ll. 432–46, Report of A. Kirichenko to N. Khrushchev on the discussion of the June 1953 CC CPSU Plenum. Submitted on 3 August 1953.

TsDAGOU, f. 1, op. 24, d. 3063, ll. 50–8, 'Information on the measures taken by the Ukrainian Party and Soviet organs in order to fulfil the tasks declared in the speech of G. Malenkov and in the resolutions of the 5th Session of the USSR Supreme Soviet'.

TsDAGOU, f. 1, op. 24, d. 3587, l. 41, Information on settlement of migrants into Southern *oblasti* of the Ukrainian SSR.

TsDAGOU, f. 1, op. 24, d. 3755, l. 96, Letter of N. Kal'chenko and A. Kirichenko to the USSR CM, 10 April 1954.

TsDAGOU, f. 1, op. 24, d. 3755, l. 119, Extract from the draft of the Resolution of the USSR CM and the CC CPSU 'On measures to further develop agriculture, towns and resorts of the Crimean *oblast'* of the UkSSR'.

TsDAGOU, f. 1, op. 24, d. 4022, ll. 1–2, Letter of A. Kirichenko to G. Malenkov, 2 January 1955.

TsDAGOU, f. 1, op. 24, d. 4022, ll. 4–5, Remarks of the CC CPUk and the CMUk on the USSR CM resolution 'On the transfer of brickworks and lime plants and granite mining and processing enterprises situated in the SSR of Ukraine under the jurisdiction of the Ukrainian Ministry of Construction Materials', submitted to N. Bulganin on 26 February 1955.

TsDAGOU, f. 1, op. 24, d. 4023, ll. 60–2, Letter of A. Kirichenko to N. Khrushchev, 2 February 1955.

TsDAGOU, f. 1, op. 24, d. 4023, l. 225, Letter of A. Kirichenko to N. Khrushchev, 11 April 1955.
TsDAGOU, f. 1, op. 24, d. 4023, ll. 277–8, Letter of the First Secretary of the CC CPUk A. Kirichenko, the Chairman of the CMUk N. Kal'chenko and the USSR Minister of Construction N. Dygai to N. Khrushchev, 22 April 1955.
TsDAGOU, f. 1, op. 24, d. 4024, ll. 260–6, Comments of the CC CPUk on the plan draft of state purchases of agricultural products for 1956 and 1957 compiled by *Gosekonomkomissiya*, 4 October 1955.
TsDAGOU, f. 1, op. 24, d. 4248, ll. 55–64, Remarks of the CC CPUk on the Directives for the Sixth FYP for Ukraine, addressed to the CC CPSU on 6 February 1956.
TsDAGOU, f. 1, op. 24, d. 4248, ll. 111–2, Remarks of A. Kirichenko regarding sending specialists to international exhibitions and fairs, submitted to the CC CPSU Presidium on 22 February 1956.
TsDAGOU, f. 1, op. 24, d. 4248, ll. 130–3, Conclusions of the CC CPUk and the CMUk on suggestions of the USSR *Gosekonomkomissiya*, USSR Ministry of Commerce, USSR Ministry of State Purchases and USSR Ministry of Agriculture on changes in supplying population with meat production.
TsDAGOU, f. 1, op. 24, d. 4248, l. 138, Draft of the Resolution of the CC CPSU Presidium from March 1956.
TsDAGOU, f. 1, op. 24, d. 4248, l. 188, Note of A. Kirichenko attached to the report of G. Sakhnovskii on the XI session of the UN Economic conference for Europe, submitted to the CC CPSU on 8 May 1956.
TsDAGOU, f. 1, op. 24, d. 4248, ll. 189–91, Report of G. Sakhnovskii on the XI session of the UN Economic conference for Europe.
TsDAGOU, f. 1, op. 24, d. 4250, l. 293, Letter of N. Podgornyi to the CC CPSU, 25 September 1956.
TsDAGOU, f. 1, op. 24, d. 4257, ll. 215–8, Remarks of the CMUk on the draft of the resolution 'On the transfer of a number of economic branches under control of the Union republics'.
TsDAGOU, f. 1, op. 24, d. 4294, ll. 1–2, Letter of A. Kirichenko to the CC CPSU Presidium, 2 February 1956.
TsDAGOU, f. 1, op. 24, d. 4294, ll. 52–5, Proposal of the Ukrainian Minister of Finance N. Shchetinin to A. Kirichenko on the transfer of the control–inspection department for Ukraine of the USSR Ministry of Finance to republican jurisdiction, 5 March 1956.
TsDAGOU, f. 1, op. 24, d. 4294, ll. 65–6, Proposition to invite employees of the abolished all-Union ministries to work in the Ukrainian ministries made by N. Podgornyi and O. Ivashchenko to A. Kirichenko, 13 March 1956.
TsDAGOU, f. 1, op. 24, d. 4294, ll. 329–52, Proposals on enhancing the authority of the CMUk, drafted by the CMUk and submitted to the CC CPUk on 3 April 1956.
TsDAGOU, f. 1, op. 24, d. 4295, l. 322, Resolution of the CC CPSU from 25 January 1954 'On considerable shortcomings in the work of the Party and Soviet *apparat*'.
TsDAGOU, f. 1, op. 24, d. 4310, ll. 35–42, The CC CPUk draft of the resolution 'On changes of procedures of supplying meat products', March–April 1956.
TsDAGOU, f. 1, op. 24, d. 4347, ll. 89–91, Extract from the USSR CM resolution from 31 May 1956 'On procedure and deadlines for composing drafts of the USSR production plans and the USSR State budget for 1957'.
TsDAGOU, f. 1, op. 24, d. 4474, l. 9, Extract from the letter of the CC CPUk to the CC CPSU (no date).

186   Bibliography

TsDAGOU, f. 1, op. 24, d. 4475, ll. 2–14, Propositions of the CC CPUk to the CC CPSU on the improvement of the organization of administration of industry and construction of the UkSSR.

TsDAGOU, f. 1, op. 24, d. 4475, ll. 56–66, Draft of Gosplan of Ukraine 'On organization of the material-technical supply system due to the reorganization of administration of industry and construction'.

TsDAGOU, f. 1, op. 24, d. 4489, ll. 139–64, Information to a draft of the USSR CM resolution 'On further transfer of economic and cultural issues into jurisdiction of the CM of Union republics', 12 July 1957.

TsDAGOU, f. 1, op. 24, d. 4518, ll. 24–5, Attachment to the note of Gosplan of Ukraine 'On economic regionalization of the UkSSR', 18 March 1957. Department of perspective planning of Gosplan of Ukraine, February 1957.

TsDAGOU, f. 1, op. 24, d. 4519, ll. 68–71, Letter of the Chairman of the Stalino *Sovnarkhoz* I. Dyadyk to N. Khrushchev and A. Kirichenko, 22 June 1957.

TsDAGOU, f. 1, op. 24, d. 4519, ll. 137–41, Letter of the head of the CC CPUk department of machine-building Savel'ev to A. Kirichenko, December 1957.

TsDAGOU, f. 1, op. 24, d. 4520, ll. 10–31, 'Propositions on the economic administrative regions of the UkSSR' compiled by the CC CPUk and submitted to the CC CPSU between 15 February and 4 March 1957 (Old version).

TsDAGOU, f. 1, op. 24, d. 4520, ll. 230–4, Propositions of the Ukrainian Minister of Construction N. Gorbas' on the improvement of the supply system in Ukraine, submitted to the CC CPUk on 1 February 1957.

TsDAGOU, f. 1, op. 24, d. 4520, l. 235, Information drafted by N. Kal'chenko regarding the transfer of the meat and dairy industry to the *sovnarkhozy*.

TsDAGOU, f. 1, op. 24, d. 4520, ll. 236–8, Letter of the CC CPUk secretaries A. Burmistrov and Kurilenko to A. Kirichenko on the advantages of transferring the meat and dairy industry to the jurisdiction of the *sovnarkhozy*.

TsDAGOU, f. 1, op. 24, d. 4521, ll. 8–12, Groups of the *sovnarkhozy* according to the wages of employees. Attachment 2 to the USSR CM resolution, composed in the period 25 May 1957 – 12 June 1957.

TsDAGOU, f. 1, op. 24, d. 4521, ll. 73–82, Resolution of the CMUk 'On the reorganization of the material-technical supply system in the UkSSR'.

TsDAGOU, f. 1, op. 24, d. 4547, ll. 45–6, List of goods for export produced by the UkSSR in 1957.

TsDAGOU, f. 1, op. 24, d. 4570, Shorthand record report of the meeting of the first *obkom* secretaries and the chairmen of *oblispolkomy* held on 20 February 1957.

TsDAGOU, f. 1, op. 24, d. 4685, l. 324, Extract from a draft of the Statute of Gosplan of Ukraine.

TsDAGOU, f. 1, op. 24, d. 4727, ll. 17–19, Letter of the Vice-Chairman of Gosplan of Ukraine N. Lesechko to the CC CPUk secretaries V. Shcherbitskii and O. Ivashchenko, 25 January 1958.

TsDAGOU, f. 1, op. 24, d. 4727, ll. 55–65, Propositions of the L'vov *obkom* secretary M. Lazurenko and Vice-Chairman of the L'vov *Sovnarkhoz* S. Lokot' on further improvement of economic administration submitted to the CC CPUk on 3 March 1958.

TsDAGOU, f. 1, op. 24, d. 4727, ll. 143–8, Propositions of the Drogobych *obkom* secretary V. Druzhinin on the improvement of work of Gosplan of Ukraine, submitted to the CC CPUk on 1 March 1958.

TsDAGOU, f. 1, op. 24, d. 4727, ll. 231–3, Propositions of the Ukrainian *obkomy* and *sovnarkhozy* on the improvement of administration and work of the *sovnarkhozy* and Gosplan, 1958.

TsDAGOU, f. 1, op. 24, d. 4727, l. 299, Propositions on the improvement of the administration of the defence industry of Ukraine, compiled by the CC CPUk commission, signed by N. Kal'chenko, I. Senin and V. Shcherbitskii, submitted to the CC CPUk Presidium on 11 March 1958.
TsDAGOU, f. 1, op. 24, d. 4727, ll. 314–8, Letter of N. Podgornyi to the CC CPSU on the measures planned to be taken in order to improve the supply system of Ukraine, 14 March 1958.
TsDAGOU, f. 1, op. 24, d. 4727, l. 324, Letter of the CC CPUk to the CC CPSU, mid-March 1958.
TsDAGOU, f. 1, op. 24, d. 4727, ll. 427–8, Propositions of the CC CPUk to the CC CPSU on reorganization of administration of railways, April 1958.
TsDAGOU, f. 1, op. 24, d. 4764, ll. 7–13, Report of the First Vice-Chairman of Gosplan of Ukraine A. Baranovskii on the issues discussed at the meeting of the chairmen of republican Gosplans and chairmen of the *sovnarkhozy* held in USSR Gosplan on 27–28 December 1957, submitted to N. Podgornyi on 3 December 1957.
TsDAGOU, f. 1, op. 24, d. 4794, ll. 89–90, Remarks of the head of the CC CPUk department for commercial, financial and planning organs V. Starunskii 'On the report of Esipenko', submitted to the CC CPUk in October, 1958.
TsDAGOU, f. 1, op. 24, d. 4794, l. 92, Note of G. Esipenko to the CC CPUk and the CMUk, 20 September 1958.
TsDAGOU, f. 1, op. 24, d. 4794, ll. 94–102, Information attached to a draft of the Law on budgetary rights of the USSR and Union republics and draft of the Regulations on Composition and Fulfilment of the State Budget, 13 September 1958.
TsDAGOU, f. 1, op. 24, d. 4910, ll. 164–5, Letter of N. Podgornyi to the CC CPSU containing Ukraine's remarks on a draft of the resolution 'On procedures of using industrial production manufactured and stocked above the plan', 21 July 1959.
TsDAGOU, f. 1, op. 24, d. 4911, ll. 4–5, Letter of N. Podgornyi to the USSR CM, 3 April 1959.
TsDAGOU, f. 1, op. 24, d. 4968, ll. 98–105, 'Propositions on the improvement of the supply system' presented by the Chairman of *Ukrsovnarkhoz* N. Sobol' to the CC CPUk on 16 November 1959.
TsDAGOU, f. 1, op. 24, d. 5109, ll. 97–105, Letter of Podgornyi to the CC CPSU and the USSR CM containing Ukrainian remarks on the project of *Gosekonomsovet* 'On the economic regionalization of the USSR in connection with the elaboration of a general perspective plan of the economic development of the USSR for the period until 1980', 15 August 1960.
TsDAGOU, f. 1, op. 24, d. 5109, l. 152, Letter to the CC CPUk Presidium from secretaries of the CC CPUk O. Ivashchenko and A. Baranovskii with remarks on the project of *Gosekonomsovet* 'On the economic regionalization of the USSR in connection with the elaboration of a general perspective plan of the economic development of the USSR for the period until 1980', August 1960.
TsDAGOU, f. 1, op. 24, d. 5363, ll. 7–89, Speech of Khrushchev at the January 1961 CC CPUk Plenum.
TsDAGOU, f. 1, op. 24, d. 5550, Shorthand record report of the meeting of the Party, Soviet and State functionaries of Ukraine with the CC CPSU Secretary N.S. Khrushchev held on 24 December 1962 in Kiev.
TsDAGOU, f. 1, op. 24, d. 5990, ll. 142–4, Letter of P. Shelest to the CC CPSU regarding the creation of the Ukrainian Ministry of the Local Industry, 2 April 1965.
TsDAGOU, f. 1, op. 24, d. 5990, ll. 168–9, Annex to the letter of P. Shelest to the CC CPSU, 13 April 1965.

188 Bibliography

TsDAGOU, f. 1, op. 24, d. 5990, ll. 270–5, Remarks of the CC CPUk and the CMUk on the FYP (1966–1970), submitted to the CC CPSU and the USSR CM on 9 June 1965.

TsDAGOU, f. 1, op. 31, d. 573, ll. 31–4, Memorandum of the Ukrainian Deputy Minister of Commerce A. Romanov to A. Kirichenko 'To the problem of the improvement of controlling the economic development of the republic', 6 February 1956.

TsDAGOU, f. 1, op. 31, d. 573, ll. 35–8, Letter of the Ukrainian Minister of Commerce G. Sakhnovskii to N. Podgornyi 'To the problem of the improvement of economic work in the UkSSR', 20 February 1956.

TsDAGOU, f. 1, op. 31, d. 573, ll. 40–50, Propositions of Gosplan of Ukraine to A. Kirichenko 'To the problem of the improvement of economic work in the republic', 5 March 1956.

TsDAGOU, f. 1, op. 31, d. 573, ll. 57–85, Information of Gosplan of Ukraine and the TsSU of Ukraine 'On economic development of the Ukrainian SSR in 1951–1955', May–June 1956.

TsDAGOU, f. 1, op. 31, d. 573, ll. 109–19, Critical notes on the work of USSR Gosplan and USSR *Gosekonomkomissiya*, compiled by Gosplan of Ukraine and submitted to A. Kirichenko on 19 December 1956.

TsDAGOU, f. 1, op. 31, d. 762, ll. 1–49, Shorthand record report of the meeting of the Chairmen of the Ukrainian *sovnarkhozy* in the CC CPUk held on 6 December 1957.

TsDAGOU, f. 1, op. 31, d. 762, ll. 50–9, Comments of the Stalino *Sovnarkhoz* on the supply system in Ukraine, 15 November 1957.

TsDAGOU, f. 1, op. 31, d. 762, ll. 65–8, Comments of Gosplan of Ukraine on the resolution of the CMUk 'On organization of the supply system in the UkSSR', 24 July 1957.

TsDAGOU, f. 1, op. 31, d. 867, ll. 52–9, Propositions on the economic regionalization drafted by the Institute of the Economy of the Ukrainian Academy of Science for the CC CPUk, submitted on 11 March 1957.

TsDAGOU, f. 1, op. 31, d. 872, l. 17, Information on the staff for the Ukrainian *sovnarkhozy* available on 18 June 1957.

TsDAGOU, f. 1, op. 31, d. 872, ll. 51–2, Letter of P. Rozenko to A. Kirichenko and N. Kal'chenko, 29 June 1957.

TsDAGOU, f. 1, op. 31, d. 872, l. 79, Information on the staff for the Ukrainian *sovnarkhozy* as of 10 July 1957.

TsDAGOU, f. 1, op. 31, d. 872, l. 95, Information on the staff for the Ukrainian *sovnarkhozy* as of 1 August 1957.

TsDAGOU, f. 1, op. 31, d. 873, l. 18, Note of the head of the CC CPUk department of heavy industry A. Burmistrov to A. Kirichenko, 9 February 1957.

TsDAGOU, f. 1, op. 31, d. 873, l. 234, Information on wages of employees of Gosplan of Ukraine, mid-July.

TsDAGOU, f. 1, op. 31, d. 873, ll. 20–1, Suggestions of the Ukrainian Minister of Construction of Enterprises for the Coal Industry G. Krasnikovskii on the rights that should be granted to the Ukrainian ministers. Submitted to the CC CPUk on 25 January 1957.

TsDAGOU, f. 1, op. 31, d. 873, ll. 22–34, Ideas of the Ukrainian Minister of Coal Industry A. Zasyad'ko on devolving a number of functions of the central ministries to the CMUk and the Ukrainian Ministry of Coal, submitted to the CC CPUk on 29 January 1957.

TsDAGOU, f. 1, op. 31, d. 873, ll. 37–48, Additional information drafted by the office of G. Krasnikovskii for the CC CPUk department of heavy industry on the rights that should be given to the Ukrainian ministers, 8 February 1957.

TsDAGOU, f. 1, op. 31, d. 1117, ll. 64–6, Report of the head of the CC CPUk department of consumer goods and foodstuffs Kurilenko to N. Podgornyi 'On planning consumer goods and foodstuffs', 30 January 1958.

TsDAGOU, f. 1, op. 31, d. 1117, ll. 110–5, Letter of the Vice-Chairman of Gosplan of Ukraine A. Lalayants to N. Podgornyi, 12 March 1958.

TsDAGOU, f. 1, op. 31, d. 1117, l. 136, Annex to the resolution of the CMUk from May 1958 on the measures taken with regard to those who violated State discipline when not fulfilling delivery plans.

TsDAGOU, f. 1, op. 31, d. 1117, ll. 158–64, Request to modify certain indices in the 1959 supply plan for Ukraine, submitted by A. Lalayants on 15 December 1958.

TsDAGOU, f. 1, op. 31, d. 1607, ll. 28–31, Letter of the secretary of the Crimean *obkom* V. Khomyakov and deputy of the Crimean *oblispolkom* N. Moiseev to N. Podgornyi, 30 January 1960.

TsDAGOU, f. 1, op. 31, d. 1607, l. 128, Note of the Chairman of *Ukrsovnarkhoz* N. Sobol' to N. Podgornyi and N. Kal'chenko from 4 August 1960, attached to the proposal on the structure of *Ukrsovnarkhoz*.

TsDAGOU, f. 1, op. 31, d. 1607, ll. 129–35, Proposal of *Ukrsovnarkhoz* on the structure of *Ukrsovnarkhoz*, 4 August 1960.

TsDAGOU, f. 1, op. 31, d. 1880, ll. 101–2, Letter of the Chairman of *Ukrsovnarkhoz* A. Kuz'mich to O. Ivashchenko, 11 April 1961.

TsDAGOU, f. 1, op. 31, d. 1880, ll. 146–220, Shorthand record report of the meeting of the chairmen of *sovnarkhozy* at the office of the CC CPUk secretary I. Kazanets held on 15 May 1961.

TsDAGOU, f. 1, op. 31, d. 1880, ll. 329–30, Letter of the CC CPUk commission to N. Podgornyi regarding transfer of the local industry to the jurisdiction of the *sovnarkhozy*, 6 March 1962.

TsDAGOU, f. 1, op. 31, d. 1880, ll. 335–9, Letter of A. Tsokol' to N. Podgornyi and V. Shcherbitskii on the administration of the local industry, 20 December 1961.

TsDAGOU, f. 1, op. 31, d. 2102, ll. 158–71, Project of Gosplan of Ukraine 'On the improvement of economic administration and planning' submitted to the CC CPUk on 10 April 1962.

TsDAGOU, f. 1, op. 31, d. 2102, ll. 303–6, Propositions of the Ukrainian Ministry of Finance on the improvement of industrial administration.

TsDAGOU, f. 1, op. 31, d. 2103, ll. 187–98, Report of the CMUk 'On the work of *Ukrsovnarkhoz*', submitted to the CC CPUk, 26 July 1962.

TsDAGOU, f. 1, op. 31, d. 2105, ll. 193–205, Propositions on enhancement of the economic rights of the *sovnarkhozy* and of the directors of enterprises and construction sites, October 1962.

TsDAGOU, f. 1, op. 31, d. 2585, ll. 5–33, Propositions of an *Ukrsovnarkhoz* commission on organization of the republican administration of industry and construction, submitted to the CC CPUk on 6 November 1964.

TsDAGOU, f. 1, op. 31, d. 2585, ll. 118–25, Proposals of *Ukrsovnarkhoz* on the extension of the republican rights, End of November–beginning of December 1964.

TsDAVOU, f. 2, op. 8, d. 10234, Materials 'On reorganization of Union-Republic ministries of Ukraine', 20 February 1953–29 November 1954.

TsDAVOU, f. 2, op. 9, d. 329, ll. 97–126, Extract from the report of the Vice-Chairman of the CMUk V. Valuev to the CMUk on the conclusions of the commission headed by A. Kosygin on the republican rights. Submitted in April–first half of May 1955.

190   Bibliography

TsDAVOU, f. 2, op. 9, d. 1744, ll. 65–74, Extract from the protocol of the meeting of V. Valuev commission of 13 March 1956.

TsDAVOU, f. 2, op. 9, d. 2700, ll. 131–4, Report of A. Baranovskii to N. Kal'chenko, 30 July 1957.

TsDAVOU, f. 2, op. 9, d. 2700, ll. 190–1, Letter of the CMUk to the CM of RSFSR 'On organization of material-technical supply', 4 October 1957.

TsDAVOU, f. 2, op. 9, d. 3084, ll. 260–6, Draft of the CMUk 'On organization of the supply system with regard to the reorganization of the administration of industry and construction', July 1957.

TsDAVOU, f. 2, op. 9, d. 3088, ll. 98–136, Proposals of the Ukrainian government on the extension of the rights and responsibilities of the governmental organs at the republican, *oblast'* and *raion* levels, 8 May 1954.

TsDAVOU, f. 2, op. 9, d. 3947, ll. 1–6, Letter from the Chairman of the Voroshilovgrad *Sovnarkhoz* A. Kuz'mich to the Chairman of the CMUk N. Kal'chenko on the problems with supplies, 12 December 1957.

TsDAVOU, f. 2, op. 9, d. 3947, l. 8, Letter of N. Kal'chenko to the Chairman of the Moscow city *Sovnarkhoz* K. Petukhov, January 1958.

TsDAVOU, f. 2, op. 9, d. 3947, ll. 25–31, Propositions of the Vinnitsa *Sovnarkhoz* 'On abolition of existing industrial ministries and the modifications in the structure of Gosplan of Ukraine and the CMUk', 4 February 1958.

TsDAVOU, f. 2, op. 9, d. 4306, ll. 47–8, Extract from the shorthand record report of the meeting at the office of the Vice-Chairman of the CMUk M.S. Grechukha held on 1 August 1958.

TsDAVOU, f. 2, op. 9, d. 4308, Shorthand record report of the meeting held in the CMUk on 7 January 1958.

TsDAVOU, f. 2, op. 9, d. 4313, ll. 197–203, Comments of the CMUk to the USSR CM on the draft of the Law on Budgetary Rights of the USSR and the Union republics and draft of the Regulations on Composition and Fulfilment of the State Budget, 10 June 1958.

TsDAVOU, f. 2, op. 9, d. 5761, ll. 13–25, Report of the Vice-Chairman of Gosplan of Ukraine P. Rozenko to the CMUk on the measures that had been taken to reduce the stocks of unmarketable production, 24 January 1959.

TsDAVOU, f. 2, op. 9, d. 7201, ll. 65–84, Remarks of the Ukrainian government on the 1960 delivery plan for Ukraine, submitted to the USSR CM on 9 February 1960.

TsDAVOU, f. 2, op. 9, d. 7201, ll. 244–6, Extract from the comments of the CMUk on the draft of the USSR CM resolution 'On procedure and deadlines for compiling the draft of the State plan of economic development of the USSR and the State budget of the USSR for 1961', 2 April 1960.

TsDAVOU, f. 2, op. 9, d. 7204, ll. 255–67, Letter of Gosplan of Ukraine to the CMUk 'On prices in 1959 and shortcomings in the pricing policy', 22 June 1960.

TsDAVOU, f. 2, op. 9, d. 7206, ll. 43–5, Request of USSR Gosplan to ensure the fulfilment of deliveries by the Ukrainian metallurgical mills sent to the CMUk on 25 July 1960.

TsDAVOU, f. 2, op. 9, d. 7206, ll. 218–20, Note by P. Ivanov, N. Strokin, V. Dymshits, A. Podugol'nikov and P. Furduev, attached to the Proposal of the commission of USSR Gosplan on organization of economic councils for coordinating and planning work of the *sovnarkhozy* in large regions, 22 July 1960.

TsDAVOU, f. 2, op. 9, d. 8130, l. 15, Note of the Chairman of USSR Gosplan to the USSR CM from 11 November 1960 attached to the draft of the resolution on the economic councils for enlarged regions.

Bibliography 191

TsDAVOU, f. 2, op. 9, d. 8130, ll. 16–22, Final draft of the resolution on the economic councils composed jointly by USSR Gosplan and CM of the republics, 11 November 1960.

TsDAVOU, f. 2, op. 9, d. 8655, ll. 1–2, Letter of the General Manager of the Republican Branch of the USSR State Bank G. Kovalenko to the Chairman of the CMUk V. Shcherbitskii, 31 July 1961.

TsDAVOU, f. 2, op. 9, d. 9497, l. 6, Information on the staff of *Ukrsovnarkhoz*, 25 July 1961.

TsDAVOU, f. 2, op. 9, d. 9497, ll. 27–32, Letter of B. Tsomaya and A. Mikhalyov to V. Shcherbitskii on the functions of *Ukrsovnarkhoz*, 30 October 1961.

TsDAVOU, f. 2, op. 9, d. 9497, l. 33, Information on the letter of B. Tsomaya and A. Mikhalyov (from *Ukrsovnarkhoz*) compiled by O. Gordenyuk to V. Shcherbitskii on 20 November 1961.

TsDAVOU, f. 2, op. 10, d. 2523, ll. 3–4, Letter accompanying a draft of the Regulations on the *Sovnarkhozy* that was compiled by the V. Dymshits commission, sent to the USSR CM on 8 January 1963.

TsDAVOU, f. 2, op. 10, d. 2523, ll. 104–5, Letter of the USSR CM commission that worked on the proposal of the Law on the socialist enterprise submitted to the USSR CM, 23 February 1963.

TsDAVOU, f. 2, op. 10, d. 2523, ll. 164–9, Information attached to the proposal of the Regulations on the *Sovnarkhozy*, compiled by the V. Dymshits commission, 11 February 1963.

TsDAVOU, f. 2, op. 10, d, 2524, ll. 1–3, Letter of the CMUk commission to the First Vice-Chairman of the CMUk I. Senin 'On envisaged structure and personnel for the *sovnarkhozy* of enlarged economic regions', 23 December 1962.

TsDAVOU, f. 2, op. 10, d. 2524, ll. 9–12, Letter of the Chairman of *Ukrsovnarkhoz* A. Kuz'mich to the CMUk on the reorganization of the work of *Ukrsovnarkhoz* after the November 1962 Party Plenum, 29 December 1962.

TsDAVOU, f. 337, op. 2, d. 714, ll. 1–2, Instruction of the Vice-Chairman of Gosplan of Ukraine A. Selivanov to Gosplan of Ukraine, 24 January 1957.

TsDAVOU, f. 337, op. 2, d. 714, ll. 27–9, Resolution of Gosplan of Ukraine from 12 December 1957.

TsDAVOU, f. 337, op. 2, d. 716, ll. 1–8, Extract from the minutes of the meeting of Gosplan of Ukraine held on 28 February 1957 'On economic regionalization of the Ukrainian SSR'.

TsDAVOU, f. 337, op. 2, d. 716, l. 103, Extract from the shorthand record report of the meeting of the board of Gosplan of Ukraine of 6 September 1957 'On the procedures of composing reports on industry and construction for July–September 1957'.

TsDAVOU, f. 337, op. 2, d. 719, ll. 224–62, Extract from the shorthand record report of the meeting of the board of Gosplan of Ukraine held on 26 September 1957. Discussion of the 1958 draft plan of electrification of the UkSSR.

TsDAVOU, f. 337, op. 2, d. 719, ll. 430–5, Extract from the shorthand record report of the meeting of the board of Gosplan of Ukraine held on October 3, 1957. Discussion of the 1958 draft plan of the State agricultural procurements and purchases.

TsDAVOU, f. 337, op. 2, d. 719, ll. 474–87, Extract from the shorthand record report of the meeting of the board of Gosplan of Ukraine, held on 8 October 1957. Discussion of the draft of the 1958 delivery plan.

TsDAVOU, f. 337, op. 2, d. 771, ll. 141–54, Extract from the shorthand record report of the meeting of the board of Gosplan of Ukraine held on 16 April 1958 'On the results

192   Bibliography

of the fulfilment of the production plan and major construction works in the 1st quarter and on measures to be taken to ensure the fulfilment of the plan in the 2nd quarter of 1958'.

TsDAVOU, f. 337, op. 2, d. 771, ll. 162–7, Extract from the shorthand record report of the meeting of the board of Gosplan of Ukraine 'On the fulfilment of contractual deliveries in the 1st quarter of 1958 and measures to be taken to ensure the fulfilment of the deliveries in the 2nd quarter', April 1958.

TsDAVOU, f. 337, op. 2, d. 772, ll. 85–100, Extract from the shorthand record report of the meeting of the board of Gosplan of Ukraine held on 8 July 1958 'On the structure of the departments of Gosplan of Ukraine and their personnel'.

TsDAVOU, f. 337, op. 2, d. 772, l. 319, Extract from the shorthand record report of the meeting of the board of Gosplan of Ukraine held on 25 June 1958 'On specialization and contractual relationships'.

TsDAVOU, f. 337, op. 2, d. 774, ll. 81–4, Extract from the shorthand record report of a meeting of the board of Gosplan of Ukraine held on 18 October 1958 'On the draft of the budget of the UkSSR'.

TsDAVOU, f. 337, op. 2, d. 774, ll. 172–87, Extract from the shorthand record report of the meeting of the board of Gosplan of Ukraine held on 10 December 1958 'On procedure and deadlines for specifying and clarifying 1959 production and supply plans for the products managed by USSR Gosplan and republican Gosplans'.

TsDAVOU, f. 337, op. 2, d. 774, ll. 200–11, Extract from the shorthand record report of a meeting of the board of Gosplan of Ukraine held on 15 December 1958 'On violations of the procedures for establishing prices for industrial production in the *sovnarkhozy* of Kiev and Khar'kov'.

TsDAVOU, f. 337, op. 2, d. 873a, ll. 3–34, Extract from the shorthand record report of the meeting of the board of Gosplan of Ukraine held on 3 January 1959.

TsDAVOU, f. 337, op. 2, d. 874, ll. 111–26, Extract from the shorthand record report of the meeting of the board of Gosplan of Ukraine held on 12 May 1959 'On the fulfilment of the delivery plan in the first quarter of 1959'.

TsDAVOU, f. 337, op. 2, d. 876, ll. 236–57, Extract from the shorthand record report of a meeting of the board of Gosplan of Ukraine held on 22 December 1959 'On improvement of the supply of the economy'.

TsDAVOU, f. 337, op. 2, d. 878, ll. 80–2, Letter of the Vice-Chairman of Gosplan of Ukraine N. Babich to the Vice-Chairman of USSR Gosplan S. Vasilenko, 10 February 1959.

TsDAVOU, f. 337, op. 2, d. 878, ll. 84–5, Letter of the Vice-Chairman of Gosplan of Ukraine A. Lalayants to the Chairman of USSR Gosplan I. Kuz'min, 2 February 1959.

TsDAVOU, f. 337, op. 2, d. 878, ll. 209–11, Letter of the Chairman of Gosplan of Ukraine I. Senin to the Chairman of USSR Gosplan A. Kosygin, 6 April 1959.

TsDAVOU, f. 337, op. 2, d. 878, l. 268, Letter of the Vice-Chairman of Gosplan of Ukraine A. Lalayants to the Chairman of USSR Gosplan A. Kosygin, 27 April 1959.

TsDAVOU, f. 337, op. 2, d. 987, ll. 89–90, Letter of the Vice-Chairman of Gosplan of Ukraine A. Lalayants to the Vice-Chairman of USSR Gosplan S. Vasilenko, 15 January 1960.

TsDAVOU, f. 4820, op. 1, d. 12, ll. 1–7, Resolution of the CMUk from 30 August 1960 on the structure and staff of *Ukrsovnarkhoz*.

TsDAVOU, f. 4820, op. 1, d. 198, ll. 1–14, Extract from the shorthand record report of the meeting of the heads of main branch departments of *Ukrsovnarkhoz* and *glavsnabsbyty* held on 23 September 1961.

TsDAVOU, f. 4820, op. 1, d. 200, ll. 1–13, Statute on *Ukrsovnarkhoz*, 11 March 1961.

Bibliography 193

TsDAVOU, f. 4820, op. 1, d. 736a, ll. 19–39, Extract from the shorthand record report of the meeting of the *Ukrsovnarkhoz* Presidium held on 9 February 1963 'On the fulfilment of the production and construction plan by the *sovnarkhozy* in January 1963 and measures to ensure the fulfilment of the plan in the first quarter of 1963'.

TsDAVOU, f. 4820, op. 1, d. 736b, ll. 15–20, Extract from the shorthand record report of the meeting of the *Ukrsovnarkhoz* Presidium 'On fulfilment of production and supply plans for production of the machine-building industry in the 1st quarter and April 1963', May 1963.

TsDAVOU, f. 4820, op. 1, d. 1629, ll. 63–6, Letter of the Vice-Chairman of *Ukrsovnarkhoz* V. Garbuzov to V. Shcherbitskii, 12 March 1962.

TsDAVOU, f. 4820, op. 1, d. 1629, ll. 193–200, Letter of *Ukrsovnarkhoz* to the USSR CM regarding financial incentives as a means of improving economic performance of enterprises, 14 September 1962.

TsDAVOU, f. 4820, op. 1, d. 1676, ll. 11–15, Remarks of *Ukrsovnarkhoz* on a draft of the resolution 'On improvement of the work of *Ukrglavsnabsbyty*, organization of deliveries and control over spending material resources', submitted to the CMUk on 8 January 1963.

TsDAVOU, f. 4820, op. 1, d. 1676, l. 144, Letter from *Ukrsovnarkhoz* to the CMUk on concealed material resources in the *sovnarkhozy*, 24 June 1963.

TsDAVOU, f. 4820, op. 1, d. 1676, ll. 197–202, Extract from a draft of the resolution 'On fulfilment of the delivery plans of industrial production to other Union republics and in the all-Union funds during the 1st half of 1963 and the measures taken in order to ensure the fulfilment of the annual delivery plan', July 1963.

TsDAVOU, f. 4820, op. 1, d. 1676, ll. 243–9, Letter of the Chairman of the CMUk I. Kazanets to USSR *Sovnarkhoz* and the USSR Ministry of Finance on the modifications in the Ukrainian supply system after the November 1962 CC CPSU Plenum, September 1963.

TsDAVOU, f. 4820, op. 1, d. 1762, l. 105, Letter of the Vice-Chairman of *Ukrsovnarkhoz* D. Polyakov to the permanent mission of Ukraine in Moscow containing remarks of the CMUk on the resolution regarding the norms of accumulated stocks, 29 April 1964.

TsDAVOU, f. 4820, op. 1, d. 1762, ll. 106–8, Information of *Ukrsovnarkhoz* on measures taken by *Ukrsovnarkhoz* in order to reduce above-norm remains of material values in the *sovnarkhozy* of Ukraine, 30 April 1964.

TsDAVOU, f. 4820, op. 1, d. 1762, ll. 281–7, Letter of *Ukrsovnarkhoz* to USSR *Sovnarkhoz* on the reasons for accumulating above-norm material stocks, 15 October 1964.

TsDAVOU, f. 4820, op. 1, d. 1896, Main results of the work of Ukrainian *sovnarkhozy* in the period 1957–1965. *Ukrsovnarkhoz*, Liquidation commission.

TsDAVOU, f. 582, op. 2, d. 1058, Shorthand record report of the meeting of employees of the Statistical Agencies of Ukraine and Moldavia held on 27–28 August 1957.

TsDAVOU, f. 582, op. 2, d. 1187, ll. 25–6, Report of the TsSU of Ukraine 'Growth of Ukrainian gross industrial production by branches', October 1958.

TsDAVOU, f. 582, op. 2, d. 1187, l. 169, Report of the TsSU of Ukraine 'Production growth of most important industrial goods in the USSR and Ukrainian SSR', October 1958.

TsDAVOU, f. 582, op. 3, d. 5002, l. 1, Note of the USSR TsSU to the TsSU of the Union republics accompanying the list of the production forbidden for above-plan production in 1964.

TsDAVOU, f. 582, op. 3, d. 5011, ll. 141–55, Report of the TsSU of Ukraine on the economic development of Ukraine in 1950–1964.

Index

above-plan: accumulations 18; production 19, 27, 53–4, 76–8, 80, 95, 122, 161, 163; revenues 27, 63–6
administrative *apparat* 3, 6, 13, 16, 36, 40, 52, 129–30
Agricultural Bank *see Sel'khozbank*
agriculture 3, 12–13, 15, 18, 24, 27, 71, 78, 107–8, 115, 147; agricultural bureaucracy 15; agricultural machinery 19, 22, 36, 77, 108, 163; production/ products 12, 14, 48, 60, 71, 80–1, 108, 118, 141, 158, 163, 171; problems 12, 15, 108, 141, 146; tax 65
Aksyutin, Yurii 35, 145, 148, 150, 152–3, 171
All-Union Central Council of Trade Unions *see* VTsSPS
all-Union interests xix, 7, 86, 123, 132–3, 135, 139
apparat xvi–xvii, 2, 6, 12–13, 16–21, 26–8, 30, 33, 36, 39–40, 45, 52, 61, 87, 91, 93, 96, 98, 102–5, 108, 111, 114–15, 120–1, 123–5, 129–31, 133–5, 138–9, 145, 150–1, 159, 170; ex-ministerial 5, 8, 41, 46, 48–9, 92, 107, 134; functions 3, 14, 23–4, 145; responsibilities 15, 31, 37, 134; size 3, 15, 109; *see also* bureaucracy
Aristov, A. 38
Armenia 65
Armstrong, John A. 5, 142, 154, 171
army 1, 14–15
associations (of enterprises) 5
autarky 37
aviation industry 14, 162
Azovstal' 12, 70, 145

Bahry, D. 4, 142, 148
Baibakov, N.K. 22, 29–30, 38, 146, 148, 153
banks *see Gosbank*; *Prombank*; *Sel'khozbank*; *Torgbank*
Baranovskii, A. 25, 31, 157, 161, 168
Beria, Lavrentii 1, 11–13, 15, 144
bifurcation of Party organs 107–8, 115, 124, 171
bonuses 2, 53, 76–7, 112, 173
branch committees (state) 40, 104, 107, 109–13, 119, 154, 172
branch development 4, 98, 115, 130
branch principle 4, 35, 38, 51, 58, 68
Brezhnev, L. xvii, 1, 29, 38, 124–5, 127, 141
budget: all-Union 27, 63–6, 132 *see also* USSR state budget law 63–5, 159; budget regulations 63, 65; fulfilment 63–4, 66; local 17, 27, 63–4, 66, 117; republican 18–19, 30, 60, 63–6, 159; Ukraine's 1956 proposal 27; Ukraine's 1958 proposal 78; Ukrainian SSR 32, 163, 165
Bulganin, N. 18, 20–1, 29–31, 39, 146–8, 151
bureaucracy 4, 8, 11, 15, 24, 31, 34, 36, 39, 41, 46, 48, 75, 81, 107, 134, 173; *see also apparat*
Byelorussia 14, 18, 65

capital investment 17, 28, 60, 69, 74–5, 106, 112–13, 136, 150, 169
cash 27, 64–5, 75, 78, 164
CC CPSU xix, 3, 7, 14–16, 23, 27, 31, 35, 38–9, 46, 48–50, 69–70, 73, 81, 94, 97, 100–1, 105, 108, 124, 143, 145, 149, 162; Presidium 1, 3, 5, 11–12, 22, 27–9, 35, 38, 49, 98–9, 103, 105, 124, 126, 145–6, 176 *see also* central leadership
CC CPSU Plenum: 1953 (Jul) 11; 1953 (Sept) 15; 1955 (Jan) 18, 158; 1955 (Jul)

13, 21; 1956 (Dec) 23, 29–35, 150; 1957 (Feb) 39, 57; 1957 (Jun) 144; 1962 (Nov) 4, 8, 93, 105, 107–14, 135, 137, 169, 175; 1965 (Sept) 127
CC CPUk 6, 13–14, 27, 31–2, 46–50, 55–6, 58, 65, 67, 74–5, 80–1, 87, 97–100, 102–5, 115–16, 119, 125–7, 151, 155, 158, 162, 167, 172; Presidium 5, 102, 104–5, 112, 117, 149, 155, 162, 164, 168, 172–3
CC CPUk Plenum, July 1953 13
Central Committee of the Communist Party of the Soviet Union *see* CC CPSU
Central Committee of the Communist Party of Ukraine *see* CC CPUk
central government *see also* Central leadership 6, 18, 26–7, 40, 63–4, 66, 77, 91, 107, 120, 125–6, 164
central leadership 6, 8, 13, 15–16, 18–21, 28, 41, 66, 72, 76, 81, 86, 95, 105, 109, 111, 114, 119, 126, 131–3, 135, 156, 167–8
central planners 3, 7, 17, 29–31, 52, 60–1, 70, 73, 77, 82, 84–5, 91, 93, 95, 105, 110, 112, 119–23, 129, 131–5, 138, 150, 154, 158
central policies xix, 6, 131
centralization xvii, 3, 8, 14–16, 19, 30–1, 36, 56–7, 73, 77, 80–2, 85, 87, 91–3, 98, 106–8, 110–12, 118, 123–4, 127, 130, 134–5
centralized control 7, 33, 38, 69, 71, 92, 95, 104, 110, 123, 139, 170
centrally distributed products 69, 81
chemical industry 14, 17, 50, 60, 72, 74, 79–80, 86, 97, 128, 136, 160
CM: republic 26–7, 53, 55, 64, 113, 138, 161, 163, 167 *see also* republic governments RSFSR 66, 127, 161; Ukraine *see* CMUk USSR *see* USSR CM
CMUk 17, 27, 32, 47, 50, 52, 57, 63–6, 71, 74–5, 98–104, 112, 121–3, 134, 146–7, 150, 152, 156–64, 166, 169–70, 173–7; reserve fund 27, 63–5; *see also* Ukrainian government
coal mining (industry) 14, 16, 19–20, 32–3, 36, 50, 74–5, 79, 102–3, 128, 136, 164
collective farms *see kolkhozy*
commerce 14, 24, 78, 110, 117
Commercial Bank *see Torgbank*

commission: on enhancing republican rights, August 1953 13; joint commission of *Gosekonomkomissiya* and USSR Gosplan 22
Commission of Soviet control 75, 91
complex economic regions 61, 109, 131; idea of 21
construction 19–20, 27, 35–6, 40–1, 50–1, 57, 60, 74–5, 77, 83, 99, 101–2, 106–7, 109, 117, 121, 140, 143, 147, 160, 169–70; administration/ministries 3–4, 7, 12, 14, 17, 20, 28, 31, 33–4, 39, 113, 118, 127, 147–8, 152, 155–6, 175; housing *see* housing (construction) industry 19–20, 75, 166; materials 17, 19, 60, 75, 77, 80, 97, 128, 157, 160, 163; sites/works 51–4, 56, 63, 94, 97, 103–4, 112–13, 117–18, 157, 162, 173
consumer goods 1–2, 14, 18–19, 26–7, 54, 59, 61, 63, 78, 80, 108, 112, 117–18, 126, 136, 146, 160, 163, 173
control figures 29, 62, 133
Conyngham, W. 4–5, 96, 115, 141–2, 167–8, 171, 174
cooperation 31, 37, 46–7, 53, 55, 57, 74, 82, 95, 98–9, 115; inter-branch 3, 5, 126
cooperative industry 25, 27, 63
corruption 20
costs 2, 16, 19, 22, 27, 33, 36, 57, 61, 77, 82, 123
Council of Ministers *see* CM
Council of Ministers of Ukraine *see* CMUk
councils of the national economy xvi, 3, 52; *see also sovnarkhozy*
credit policy 17, 19
Crimea 7, 46, 96–7, 116–17, 147, 168

decentralization xvi–xix, 7, 14–15, 26, 32–4, 38, 40–1, 68, 72–3, 75, 80, 87, 91–3, 95, 105–7, 109, 118–19, 123, 129–36, 138–40, 153, 159–60, 162, 170; of controlling organizations 23–8; of railway 81; of resource management 69
decentralization policy 91, 134, 136
decision-making xviii–xix, 3, 5, 13, 15–16, 18–19, 21, 34, 36–7, 41, 52, 72, 79, 87, 91, 96, 98, 100, 105–7, 111, 129, 133, 139–40, 148; authority 7, 11, 17–18, 21, 28, 31–2, 34, 102, 110, 125–6, 135, 139; operational 3, 39, 71, 129

deliveries 4, 15, 26, 33–4, 53–4, 67–75, 77, 80–1, 86–7, 94, 98–9, 141, 152, 156, 158, 160–2, 164–5, 175; and 1958 plan 59–61, 157; to all-Union funds 67, 73, 120, 164; contractual 53, 68–9, 74, 82–3, 134, 160, 166; direct 73, 160; for export 67, 73–4, 104, 116, 164; inter-republican 8, 67, 72–4, 81–7, 91, 101–4, 120–3, 132, 134, 158, 164; orders for (*naryady*) 69, 73–4, 84–6; payments for 72
departmental interests 36, 134
departmentalism 4, 22, 35–6, 130; *see also* departmental interests
direct contacts/direct relations 33, 37, 52, 69, 72–3, 99, 134
districts *see rayony*
Dnepropetrovsk 12, 16, 46–50, 69, 104, 116, 121, 154–5, 161, 170, 183
Donbas 14, 21, 29, 33, 147
Donetsk 77, 104, 116, 145, 155, 170; *obkom* 48; *Sovnarkhoz* 112, 170, 172
Dyadyk, I. 47, 49, 69–70, 156
Dyker, D. 4, 142–3, 177

economic councils xix, 7, 11, 36, 40, 53, 58, 92, 95, 98, 115, 124, 129, 138, 167
economic regions 4, 6–7, 21, 34, 36–7, 46, 48, 53–6, 58, 61, 68–9, 74, 95–8, 102–3, 105, 108–9, 115, 118, 131, 148, 154, 164, 167; *see also* regionalization
economic relations 53, 55, 82–3, 95, 138; centre-republic 3, 23, 27, 61, 119, 135; inter-republican 7
economic research 23, 25
economy: economic growth 3, 7, 11, 31, 45, 82, 92, 110, 116, 129, 132, 177 *see also* growth rates economic policies 3, 7, 11, 31, 45, 70, 82, 92, 110, 116, 129, 132, 177; GNP 2; regional 3–5, 37, 82, 92, 129–30; republican 3, 7, 23, 31, 33, 41, 55, 57, 61, 86–7, 93, 99, 102–3, 105, 118, 125, 129, 132, 135, 140, 150
economy of scarcity 87, 131
education 2, 37, 53, 60, 144
electricity 17, 53, 158, 160; Ukrainian production 60
Estonia 65, 86
Evseenko, M. 38
export licences 26

ferrous metallurgy (industry) 16–17, 19, 60, 120, 128, 145

Filtzer, D. 4, 141–2, 171, 175
financial control 17, 23
five-year plan *see* FYP
Fomenko, N.M. 12
food industry 19, 58–9, 69, 75, 110, 117–18, 128, 131, 136, 146, 157, 160, 163; *see also* meat and milk production
food supply 2, 14
foreign trade 23, 26–7, 93
Frank, Z. 5, 143
funded materials 54–5, 74, 101, 103, 160
funds 17, 19, 53–4, 65–6, 72, 74–5, 79, 94, 106, 111–12, 120–1, 131, 158; all-Union 59, 67, 73–4, 80, 123, 164, 175; centrally allocated 17, 60, 67–9, 160; non-realized 71
FYP: 2nd 145; 3rd 148; 5th 48; 6th 23, 29, 45, 150

Georgia 18, 86
Glavbumsbyt 17
Glavkhimsbyt 17, 69
glavki 16–17, 36, 52, 138
Glavsbyt(y) 37, 69, 71–3, 82–3
glavsnabsbyty 68, 71–2, 169; *see also* Ukrglavsnabsbyt(y)
GlUMPP 73, 79, 84–7, 91, 94, 103, 106, 119–20, 162
Gorbachev, M. xvi, xviii–xix
Gorbachev's *perestroika* 5
Gorbas, N. 33, 69, 152, 160
Gorbasev 69
gorkom(y) 12
Gosbank 3, 16–17, 32, 54, 75, 83, 112–13, 145–6, 173; Ukrainian office 19, 24–5, 27
Gosekonomkomissiya 22, 29–32, 36–8, 50, 55, 148, 150–1, 157–8
Gosekonomsovet 92, 96, 103, 107, 110, 167–9
Goskontrol' 23–5, 28, 149; *apparat* of 23–4; committee of 124; suggestion to abolish 24
Gosplan of Ukraine 18, 23, 25–6, 31, 45–6, 65–6, 71–2, 74–6, 79–87, 91, 97–105, 117–19, 123, 125, 133, 135, 148–51, 155–66, 168–70, 172, 174–5; and 1958 plan 55–8; access to resources 79; ambitions 71; conflict of interests 58; formal authority 7; intentions 7; Moscow office 68; position on central policies 7; relations with Moscow 7–8, 68; relations with Ukrainian

sovnarkhozy 8, 52, 57–8, 68–9, 71, 79–80; responsibilities 55–6; staff 45, 50, 67, 76, 86, 104, 119, 123, 156, 162; tension between Ukrainian and USSR Gosplans 8, 55, 57–8, 80, 85; *see also* Ukrainian planners
Gosplans *see* Gosplan of Ukraine; republican Gosplan; USSR Gosplan
Gosstroi 30, 107, 113, 118, 171–2
Granick, D. 5, 142
gross output 19, 48, 55, 58, 60–1, 70, 77, 79, 117, 136–8
Grossman, G. 4, 142–3, 168
growth rates 2, 70, 79, 130, 136–7, 177

health care 2, 15
Hough, J. 4–5, 50, 142, 155–6
housing 1–2, 19, 49, 54, 75, 143, 147, 150; campaign 19; construction 15, 19–20, 29, 54, 151
Hungary 1

Industrial Bank *see Prombank*
industry: aviation 14, 162; chemical 14, 17, 50, 60, 72, 74, 79–80, 86, 97, 128, 136, 160; coal mining 14, 16, 19–20, 32–3, 36, 50, 74–5, 79, 102–3, 128, 136, 164; construction 19–20, 75, 166; construction of automobiles and tractors 14, 61, 73, 77, 160; fishing 97; food 19, 58–9, 69, 75, 110, 117–18, 128, 131, 136, 146, 157, 160, 163 *see also* meat and milk production heavy 2, 15, 38, 58–60, 69, 127, 136, 151, 166, 175; instrument-making 14, 78, 128; light 2, 14–15, 60, 75, 110, 117, 136, 146, 160; machine-building 12, 14, 22, 38, 48, 58–61, 78–9, 82, 85–6, 92, 109–10, 128, 134, 136, 175; mechanical engineering 50; metallurgical 12, 14, 19–20, 50, 69–70, 74, 84, 86, 97, 120, 145, 155, 164, 175; military 14, 162, 172
information 6, 8, 13, 26, 33, 45, 49–52, 56–7, 67, 69–71, 74, 79, 81–6, 94, 100, 119–21, 129, 134; *see also* statistics; TsSU
intelligentsia 2
international relations 23, 93, 149
investment 20, 27–9, 31, 36, 48, 78–80, 97, 100, 103, 108, 112, 118, 131, 143, 146, 156; and 1958 plan 55–6, 59–62; capital investment 17, 28, 60, 69, 74–5, 106, 112–13, 136, 150, 169; decisions 2;

plans 4, 94, 163; redistribution of 15, 108, 113, 126; targets 19, 59
Ivanova, G. 2, 141, 144, 164, 171, 176
Ivashchenko, O.I. 47, 49, 149, 162, 168–9

Kaganovich, L.M. 35, 39, 144, 146
Karavaev, K.S. 24
Kaser, M. 4, 142
Kazakhstan 18, 29, 41, 46, 65, 86, 95–6, 98, 101–2, 127, 154
Kemerovo *Sovnarkhoz* 39, 94, 173
Khar'kov 46–9, 51, 57, 69, 72, 75, 96–7, 116, 145, 155, 168
Kherson 14, 46–9, 58, 96–7, 116
Khrushchev, Nikita Sergeevich xvi–xvii, 5, 8, 11, 19, 21, 56, 61, 73, 92–3, 97, 105–6, 123, 128–30, 135, 138–9; CPSU First Secretary 1–3, 15; January 1957 note 3, 7, 35–41; motives for *Sovnarkhoz* reform 2, 4; at the November 1962 CC CPSU Plenum 93, 107–14, 116; position by December 1956 Plenum 23, 29, 31–4; removal from power xvii, 3, 114, 123–6; response to Molotov 40; setting a republican vector 13–15; and Ukraine 6–7, 16, 81, 83, 97–8, 123, 126; visits in August 1956 29; XX CPSU Congress 1, 23–4
Khrushchev, Sergei 33, 92, 169–70, 173
khrushchoby 1; *see also* housing
Kiev *obkom* 39, 173
Kiev *Sovnarkhoz* 48
Kirghizia 65, 115
Kirichenko, A.I. 13, 19, 26–7, 30–1, 47, 49, 144–5, 147–9, 151, 156, 165, 174
kolkhoz(y) 15, 65, 118, 141, 144, 158
Koropeckyj, I. 6, 93, 167, 176
Kostenko, D. 75
Kosygin, Aleksei 1, 18, 38–9, 91–5, 113, 116, 146, 160; *Kosyginskaya* reform 123, 126–7, 137, 139
Kosygin commission (1955) 18, 20, 148, 159
Kovalenko, G. 25, 177
kraikomy 38, 115, 174
krai(-ya) 36, 38, 56
Krasnikovskii, G. 32, 146, 151
Kuz'mich, A. 33, 47, 58, 100, 102–3, 152, 162, 164, 168–9, 174–5
Kuz'min, I. 38, 80, 91–2, 158, 161, 165

198 Index

labour policy 31
labour productivity 2, 20, 60, 138
Latvia 12, 61, 65; Latvian Gosplan 61
Legal Commission (USSR CM) 64
Leningrad 14, 35, 38, 82, 111, 173
Lesechko, M.A. 74, 162
Lewytzkyj, B. 6, 97, 168
Lithuania 12
loans 17, 27, 147
local authorities 3, 14, 16, 31, 49
local industry 21, 27, 55, 63, 66, 68, 81, 128, 150, 157, 174; transfer to *sovnarkhozy* 115–18
local inputs 7, 112
local interests 7–8
localism xvii, 4–6, 70, 86, 97, 130, 170; *see also mestnichestvo*
long-distance cross-hauls 7, 21, 37, 81–2, 131, 165
Lugansk 75, 116, 168
L'vov 46–7, 49, 75, 116–17, 156
Lyashko, Aleksandr 5, 48, 127, 142, 155, 176–7

machine-building industry 12, 14, 22, 38, 48, 58–61, 78–9, 82, 85–6, 92, 109–10, 128, 134, 136, 175
magazines 1, 26, 149
Malenkov, Georgii 2, 11, 13, 15–16, 18, 29, 31, 35, 143–4, 146–7, 153–4
material funds 19, 68
material stocks 16, 74, 76, 121–2, 175
materials *see* resources
meat and milk production 14, 48, 59–60, 106, 108–9, 116, 127–8, 139, 158, 160, 165, 174
Meshik, P.Ya. 13
mestnichestvo 4, 6–8, 70, 78–9, 93, 97, 104, 106, 109, 127, 139; in deliveries 67, 70, 72, 121 *see also* non-deliveries; perception by Moscow 87; perception by Ukrainian authorities 8, 131; political implications of 8; as reason for recentralization 130–5; reasons 4, 122; regional 4, 8, 87, 98, 120, 130–5; *see also* autarky; localism
metallurgical (industry) 12, 14, 19–20, 50, 69–70, 74, 84, 86, 97, 120, 145, 155, 164, 175
Mieczkowski, Z. 4, 142, 167–8, 173
Mikoyan, A.I. 39, 150
military industry 14, 162, 172
Mil'shtein, S. 13

ministerial bureaucracy 31, 34, 39, 41, 46, 48, 107
ministerial system 4, 8, 11, 16, 31, 36, 63, 92–3, 124, 126, 130, 138, 140, 151
ministries: abolished ministries 3, 11, 24, 35, 37–9, 41, 47, 50, 56, 68, 70, 83, 129, 132, 138, 149, 151; all-Union 12–14, 16–17, 21–2, 24, 28, 31–2, 41, 47, 52, 73, 81, 128, 146, 148–9, 157; construction 3–4, 20, 39, 127; functions 3, 23, 25, 28, 37; industrial 3, 12–13, 17, 25, 39, 45, 110, 126, 129; reorganization 3, 7, 11, 15–16, 28–9, 31, 63, 110, 113, 127, 129; republic 18, 28, 32, 52, 110, 125; responsibilities 7, 11, 24; rights 11–12, 15, 23–4, 33–4, 65, 111, 143, 151; staff 15, 24, 149; Ukrainian *see* Ukrainian ministriesUnion-Republic 16–17, 27–8, 41, 52, 125, 127, 147, 155; *see also apparat*; ministerial system; *individual ministries*
Ministry of Agriculture 15, 158
Ministry of Chemical Industry 20, 38, 71, 110
Ministry of Coal Mining Industry 12, 20, 32–3, 39, 152
Ministry of Commerce 25, 28, 65, 158
Ministry of Construction 20, 147–8
Ministry of Construction Materials Industry 12, 20, 28
Ministry of Consumer Goods 20
Ministry of Defence 7
Ministry of Finance 24–5, 27, 38, 54, 63–6, 68, 83, 112–13, 146–7, 159, 173, 175
Ministry of Fishing Industry 21, 28
Ministry of Food Products (Industry) 20, 28
Ministry of Foreign Trade 26–7
Ministry of Internal Affairs *see* MVD
Ministry of Justice 28, 143, 150
Ministry of Light Industry 28
Ministry of Machine-Building and Instrument-Making 20
Ministry of the Metallurgical Industry 12, 144
Moldavia 65, 86, 95–6, 156, 158, 161
Molotov, V. 11, 144; response to Khrushchev's January 1957 note 35, 38, 40, 154; views on decentralization 40
Moscow *oblast'* 49, 156
Moscow *sovnarkhozy* 49, 156
MTS 15, 144
MVD 12–13, 144

Index 199

non-deliveries 70, 72, 74, 120–1, 123; *see also mestnichestvo* (in deliveries)
Nove, Alec xvii, 4, 141–3, 153, 155, 159, 169–70

obkom(y) 5, 12, 38–9, 45–8, 50, 53, 75, 95–7, 108, 115, 124, 144, 154, 164, 166, 168, 173; *nomenklatura* 48
oblasti 12, 16, 19, 33, 36, 38, 45–51, 54, 56–7, 66, 71, 95–7, 107, 115–17, 145, 147, 155–8
oblispolkom(y) 25, 40, 50, 55–7, 66–8, 71, 81, 96–7, 110, 117–18, 154, 157, 168, 172
Oblstatupravlenie 50–2
Odessa 46–9, 51–2, 75, 116, 161, 175
Omarovskii, A. 58, 154, 158
operational decision-making 3, 39, 71, 129; *see also* operational management
operational management 3, 23, 40; *see also* operational decision-making

Party xviii, 2–3, 11–12, 15–16, 21, 29–32, 34, 37, 39–41, 46, 48–9, 53, 70, 76, 95–6, 103–4, 107–9, 126–7; control 5, 12, 46, 124; relations with ministries 13, 36; responsibility for economy 41; rivalry with *apparat* 15, 31, 61, 96, 98, 104, 107–8, 139; role in the reform 5, 45; secretaries xvii, 5, 15, 38, 108, 125, 130; *see also* bifurcation of Party organs
pensions 2, 108, 164, 171
peripheral managers 4, 7, 39, 41, 52, 61, 82, 92–3, 129, 138, 140; *see also* republican managers
personal incentives 77
Pervukhin, M. 29–30, 36, 38–40
plan for 1957 29–30
plan for 1958 55–62, 71, 74, 132, 161; and Gosplan of Ukraine 58–62; and Ukrainian *sovnarkhozy* 55–8
planners 29–31, 36–7, 40, 45–6, 50, 56–8, 62, 67, 70, 73–81, 83–4, 86–7, 93–6, 100, 109, 119–21, 124, 131–5, 140, 157; *see also* central planners
planning: 'from below' 56–8, 62, 70–2, 76, 132; failures in 29–32; perspective planning 26, 28, 30, 37, 55, 92, 96, 98, 107, 118, 129, 155, 167–8, 176; planning procedure 32; unbalanced planning 55, 139
Planovoe khozyaistvo 45, 55, 148–9, 154, 157, 164

plans: delivery 33, 69–70, 80–1, 85–6, 98–9, 103–4, 157, 162, 164–6, 175; investment 4, 94, 163; plan deception 4; plan indices 32, 37, 59, 61, 100; production 15–17, 56–8, 69–70, 72, 80, 86–7, 119, 121, 131, 135, 150, 162, 164, 175; profit 76; realization 33; transportation 33, 81, 133
Podgornyi, N.V. 47–8, 73–5, 81, 91, 96, 98, 117, 147, 149, 159, 161, 163, 165–6, 168–9, 173–4
Poland 1
Poltava 14, 46, 96–7, 100, 116
Pospelov, P.N. 38
Pravda 38
Pribyl'skii, I. 47, 58, 116, 155
prices: on agricultural production 14; control 76; price formation 25; retail 18, 27, 63, 75, 118, 171; temporary 18, 54, 75–6; wholesale 18, 27, 54, 63–4, 76, 118
pricing 17–18, 25–7, 63, 75–8, 163; policy 19, 76, 163
production: capacities 3–4, 17–19, 24, 30–1, 36, 53, 56–7, 60–1, 76, 79–80, 85, 173; commercial 19, 52, 55, 58; concealed capacities 60, 80; costs 16, 19, 22; funded 17, 69, 71, 160–1; hoarding 4, 122; planned 69, 74, 76–7, 119, 123, 160; unmarketable 78, 164
profits 78, 112, 173; of local industry 66, 76; of *sovnarkhozy* 54, 64–5
Prombank 17, 19, 32, 75, 145
provinces *see oblasti*

Raiispolkom(y) 66, 174
railway 1, 14, 146; decentralization of 81; transportation 22, 81
raistatupravlenie 50
rayony 66
recentralization xvii, 3–4, 6, 85, 92–3, 99, 105, 107–9, 112–14, 122–3, 130–1, 134–6; policy 6, 8, 105, 109, 118–19, 170
red tape 3, 15–16, 20, 31, 102
regional managers 3, 6, 67–8, 74, 77–8, 95, 98; *see also* peripheral managers
regionalization 4, 21–2, 45–50, 95–6, 105, 115, 148, 155, 167; *see also* economic regions
Regulations on a *Sovnarkhoz* 53–4, 72, 156, 163–4

republican authorities 6–8, 11, 24, 30, 34, 46, 62, 64, 91, 93, 98–9, 105, 112–13, 121, 131–2, 134, 176; *see also* republican government
republican budgetary rights 63–6
republican economic rights 3, 13, 21, 25, 27, 31, 41, 63, 93, 125–6, 140, 150
republican Gosplans 54–6, 58, 67, 69, 73, 81, 84, 87, 110, 113, 131, 133, 161–2, 170
republican governments 13, 17–19, 21, 25, 27–9, 31, 37, 39, 41, 46, 48, 61, 66, 73, 93, 124–5, 129, 131, 134
republican interest xix, 6, 24, 87, 123
republican legislation 64–5
republican managers 18, 103; *see also* peripheral managers
republican reserve fund 63–5
resource management xix, 4, 67, 69, 73, 79, 106, 119–23
resources 7, 32–3, 46, 53, 55–6, 61, 65, 68, 70, 76, 82, 86, 99–103, 106, 125, 163; accumulation of 5, 78, 80, 121–2; control over xviii–xix, 3, 8, 68, 71, 73–4, 77–9, 91–2, 95, 114, 118, 120, 123, 131, 139; dissipation of 4; financial 4, 21, 75, 103, 129, 134; management *see* resource management; material 33, 75, 101–3, 121, 129, 134, 169, 175
responsibilities 3, 7–8, 11, 15, 17–18, 24, 29–31, 33–4, 37, 55–6, 63, 66–7, 71–3, 77–8, 84–6, 99, 101, 103–5, 113–14, 122–3, 127–9, 133–4, 139, 145–6, 164, 170
retail trade 27, 121
Rigby, T. 5, 142, 154
Romanov, A. 23–5, 149
Rozenko, P. 50, 102–3, 118, 156, 164, 175
RSFSR 18, 21–2, 28, 41, 46–7, 65–6, 69, 95, 98, 101–2, 104, 115, 127, 131, 148, 154, 156, 161, 168; and 1958 draft plan 60–1; Gosplan of RSFSR 38, 50, 84–6, 93–4, 166–7
RSFSR Ministry of Local Industry 26
Rudakov, A. 38

Saburov, M.Z. 22, 29–30, 35, 39, 148, 153
Sakhnovskii, G. 25–7, 75, 149
salaries 2, 17–18, 20, 24, 27, 50, 63, 76–8, 108, 143, 149; *see also* wages
sales 17–18, 67–8, 72, 84–5, 101, 121, 123, 126, 145, 159, 166, 169
sales organizations *see sbyt(y)*

Satyukov, P. 38
sbyt(y) 17, 33–4, 38, 68, 73, 91, 119, 122–3, 160
science 25–6, 28, 30, 37, 56, 60, 98, 108, 110, 112, 124, 126, 128, 162, 172
self-financing offices 68
Sel'khozbank 17, 19, 75
seven-year plan 92, 96, 108–9, 134, 142, 163, 171, 176
Shchetinin, N. 24–5, 149
Shelest, P. 39, 126–8, 153, 155, 163, 173–4, 176
Shepilov, D. 38, 144, 150
shortages 19, 27, 49, 70, 120, 122; of consumer goods 2, 19; of food 2, 19
shturmovshchina 4, 176
Siberia 29
site construction of the metallurgical industry 47, 50, 147
snabsbyt(y) 86–7, 101, 119–20, 134, 161, 164
snab(y) 17, 34, 38, 68
social life 60
social problems 2
social programs 2
social protest 2
Sovnarkhoz reform xvi–xix, 3–4, 6–8, 34–41, 45, 51, 55–6, 60, 63, 70, 76, 82, 91, 102, 108, 117, 121, 124, 136, 138–40, 148, 153–4, 159, 171; *see also Sovnarkhoz* system; territorial administration
Sovnarkhoz system 3–6, 8, 67, 79, 82, 92, 98, 124–7, 129, 135–6, 138–9
specialization 3–4, 36–7, 45–6, 53, 55, 82, 95, 98, 108–9, 112, 115–16, 118, 162, 165
staff cuts 15–16, 20
Stalin, I. xvi, 1–3, 11–13, 33, 92–3, 107, 130, 139–40, 143–4, 158
Stalino 16, 46–50, 53, 69–70, 72, 75, 85, 156, 161; *see also* Donetsk
Stanislav 46–7, 49, 52, 116
Starovskii, V. 38, 121
Starunskii, V. 65, 159
State Bank *see* Gosbank
state branch committees *see* branch committees
State Committee for Construction 30
State Committee for Labour and Wages 30, 54
Statistical Agency of Ukraine 17, 27, 50, 146

statistics 23, 25, 51–2, 94, 136, 138, 146, 152, 154; statistical departments, agencies 17, 27, 38, 50–2, 57, 70–1 *see also Oblstatupravlenie*; *Raistatupravlenie*; *Ukrstatupravlenie*
supply organizations *see snab(y)*
supply system 33, 37, 40, 67–78, 84–5, 91, 94, 119, 121, 126, 131, 152, 156, 159–62, 165–6, 175
supply/ies: channels 4; decentralized 68, 160; food *see* food supply; inter-republican 7, 86; of local industry 68; obligations 7–8; peripheral offices 70–2, 161; problems 4, 12, 68; system *see* supply system; uncertainties 4; *see also* deliveries
Supreme Council of the National Economy *see* VSNKh
Suslov, M. 40, 177
Swearer, Howard 4–5, 97, 142–3, 168

tax(es): agricultural 65; on bachelors 65; forestry 65; income tax 64–5, 126, 159; income tax from *kolkhozy* 65; for peasants 15, 141; on single women 65; on small families 65; tax policy 15; turnover tax 27, 63–4, 66, 78, 118
technological innovations 27–8, 31, 54, 76, 108, 110; *see also* technology (progress in)
technology 36, 125, 133; policy 28, 35, 37, 112; progress in 2, 4–5, 76–7, 110–11, 113 *see also* technological innovations; slowdown of progress 4, 6
territorial administration 5, 35–8, 107, 124
Tevosyan, I.F.(T.) 12, 35, 144
theatres 1, 63
Tikhomirov, S. 38
tolkach 8, 37, 70, 74, 103, 140, 153
Tompson, William xvi, 4, 142, 153–4, 176–7
Torgbank 17, 19, 75
trade 14–15, 26; foreign 23, 26–7, 93; retail 27, 121
trade unions 36–7, 54
transfer of enterprises 21, 28, 31
transportation 22, 24, 33, 37, 46, 54, 57, 81–3, 133, 165
transportation costs 22, 33, 36
tsekhi 74
TsK 75
TsSU: central 38, 50–1, 65, 76, 83, 121, 163; of Ukraine 50, 138, 148, 150, 155, 177 *see also* Statistical Agency of Ukraine

Turkmenistan 65, 115
Twentieth (XX) CPSU Congress 1, 23, 29–34, 45; decentralization 23–9; secret speech 1
Twenty-Second (XXII) CPSU Congress 105, 107, 169, 175

Ukrainian administrative *apparat* 6
Ukrainian authorities 6–8, 25, 27–8, 86, 91, 105, 111–12, 121–3, 133–4, 139, 145; *see also* Ukrainian government; Ukrainian leadership
Ukrainian Gosplan *see* Gosplan of Ukraine
Ukrainian government 17–18, 23–4, 28, 54, 60, 64, 68, 70–1, 84–6, 99, 105, 120, 122, 145, 166; *see also* Ukrainian authorities; Ukrainian leadership
Ukrainian leadership xix, 6–7, 20, 27–8, 30, 55, 59–60, 63, 65, 77, 79–81, 93, 97–8, 102, 106, 111, 133, 135, 147; *see also* Ukrainian authorities; Ukrainian government
Ukrainian ministries 7, 13, 17–20, 23–6, 28, 31–2, 34, 45, 47, 50, 55, 57, 83, 143, 145–6, 149, 151, 172; *see also individual ministries*
Ukrainian Ministry for Material and Technical Supplies 33
Ukrainian Ministry of Agriculture 25
Ukrainian Ministry of Coal Mining 16, 27, 32–3, 47, 58, 102
Ukrainian Ministry of Commerce 18, 23, 25, 75, 149
Ukrainian Ministry of Construction Materials Industry 17, 20, 33, 147–8, 152
Ukrainian Ministry of Consumer Goods 17
Ukrainian Ministry of Ferrous Metallurgy 27, 145
Ukrainian Ministry of Finance 18, 23–5, 100, 103–4, 149, 169–70
Ukrainian Ministry of *Goskontrol' see Goskontrol'*
Ukrainian planners 30–1, 62, 70, 80, 86–7, 121, 132–5, 157
Ukrainian SSR xviii, 7–8, 32, 147–8, 150, 155–61, 174
Ukrglavsnabsbyt(y) 67–8, 71–2, 74, 83, 85–6, 91, 103, 106, 159, 169, 175; and the delivery system 101–5; functions 119; instalment of 99–101; managing resources 119–23; reinstalling 118–19; staff 48–50, 68, 99, 119, 123, 126, 155, 169–70

Ukrsovnarkhoz (Ukrainian Republican Council of the national economy) 6, 98–106, 112, 115, 118–23, 125–6, 135, 150, 157, 160, 162, 164, 166, 168–70, 172–7; purpose of 98–9
Ukrstatupravlenie 50–2
UN Economic Conference (Geneva 1956) 26
Ural 14, 21, 29, 36
USSR CM 16, 18, 22, 24–5, 29–30, 32, 35, 37, 39, 41, 48, 53–4, 56, 63–5, 70, 77–8, 84–5, 92–3, 95, 100–1, 106, 109–10, 112–14, 124–5, 143, 145–8, 150–1, 156, 158–63, 168, 172–3, 176; *see also* central government
USSR Constitution 32, 41
USSR Gosplan 3, 6–8, 19, 22, 29–30, 33, 37–9, 50, 55–61, 64–71, 73–4, 80, 83–7, 91–9, 102–14, 117–19, 122, 131–5, 137, 148, 150–1, 153, 156–8, 160–1, 164–75; architect of the reform 61, 135; tension between Ukrainian and USSR Gosplans 8, 55, 57–8, 80, 85; *see also* central planners; central planning agency; planners
USSR Ministries *see individual ministries (eg, Ministry of Agriculture)*
USSR *Sovnarkhoz* 105, 107–8, 110–11, 113, 119–20, 122–3, 170, 172–5
USSR state budget 63–5, 108, 129, 150, 166
USSR Supreme Soviet 13, 32, 39, 41, 56, 93, 144, 148, 157, 164, 166–7
Uzbekistan 14, 18, 41, 65, 115, 154

Valuev, V. 47, 146, 159; Valuev commission (1955) 27, 33; Valuev commission (1956) 27, 150

Vasil'ev, Valerii 6, 47, 141, 166, 168, 171, 174
Vedeneev, Yu. 5, 142–3, 168, 172
Vinnitsa 46–7, 49, 69, 72, 75, 82, 116, 157
Virgin Land campaign 1; *see also* virgin lands
virgin lands 108
Vivdychenko, I.I. 49
Voronezh 69–70
Voroshilov, K. 11, 38
Voroshilovgrad 46–9, 58, 102–3, 116, 161–2, 164, 168
VSNKh 105, 108, 110, 122–3, 168, 172
VTsSPS 54, 124

Waelbroeck, J. 5, 143
wages 20, 49–50, 53–5, 117, 141, 149, 156; *see also* salaries
wages funds 18, 24, 27, 77, 113, 149, 159, 173
Western Ukraine 12

XX CPSU Congress *see* Twentieth (XX) CPSU Congress
XXII CPSU Congress *see* Twenty-Second (XXII) CPSU Congress

Yudin, P.A. 12
Yugoslavia 1

Zademid'ko, A. 38–9, 94, 152
Zaleski, E. 77, 142, 163, 173
Zaporozh'e 46–9, 69, 116, 161
Zasyad'ko, A. 32–3, 152, 169
Zhdanov 12, 85, 145
Zverev, A. 38–9, 66